2 3 APR 2008

THE ELEMENTAL PASSION FOR PLACE
IN THE ONTOPOIESIS OF LIFE

ANALECTA HUSSERLIANA

THE YEARBOOK OF PHENOMENOLOGICAL RESEARCH

VOLUME XLIV

Editor-in-Chief:

ANNA-TERESA TYMIENIECKA

*The World Institute for Advanced Phenomenological Research and Learning
Belmont, Massachusetts*

THE ELEMENTAL PASSION FOR PLACE IN THE ONTOPOIESIS OF LIFE

Passions of the Soul in the *Imaginatio Creatrix*

Edited by

ANNA-TERESA TYMIENIECKA

The World Phenomenology Institute

Published under the auspices of
The World Institute for Advanced Phenomenological Research and Learning
A-T. Tymieniecka, President

KLUWER ACADEMIC PUBLISHERS
DORDRECHT / BOSTON / LONDON

Library of Congress Cataloging-in-Publication Data

```
The Elemental passion for place in the ontopoiesis of life: passions of
  the soul in the Imaginatio creatrix / edited by Anna-Teresa
  Tymieniecka.
       p.   cm. -- (Analecta Husserliana ; v. 44)
     "Published under the auspices of the World Institute for Advanced
  Phenomenological Research and Learning."
     Includes index.
     ISBN 0-7923-2749-7 (hb : acid free paper)
     1. Setting (Literature)  2. Home in literature.  3. Dwellings in
  literature.   I. Tymieniecka, Anna-Teresa.  II. World Institute for
  Advanced Phenomenological Research and Learning.  III. Series.
  B3279.H94A129   vol. 44
  [PN56.S48]
  142'.7 s--dc20
  [809'.93355]                                                 94-4569
```

ISBN 0-7923-2749-7

Published by Kluwer Academic Publishers,
P.O. Box 17, 3300 AA Dordrecht, The Netherlands.

Kluwer Academic Publishers incorporates the publishing programmes
of D. Reidel, Martinus Nijhoff, Dr W. Junk and MTP Press.

Sold and distributed in the U.S.A. and Canada
by Kluwer Academic Publishers,
101 Philip Drive, Norwell, MA 02061, U.S.A.

In all other countries, sold and distributed
by Kluwer Academic Publishers Group,
P.O. Box 322, 3300 AH Dordrecht, The Netherlands.

Printed on acid-free paper

All Rights Reserved
© 1995 Kluwer Academic Publishers
No part of the material protected by this copyright notice
may be reproduced or utilized in any form or by any means, electronic
or mechanical, including photocopying, recording or by any information
storage and retrieval system, without written permission from
the copyright owner.

Printed in the Netherlands.

TABLE OF CONTENTS

THE THEME ix

ACKNOWLEDGMENTS xi

INAUGURAL STUDY

ANNA-TERESA TYMIENIECKA / *De Patria Mea*: The Passion for Place as the Thread Leading Out of the Labyrinth of Life 3

PART ONE
POETISING PLACE AT THE FRONTIERS OF NOSTALGIA

HANS H. RUDNICK / The *Locus Amoenus*: On the Literary Evolution of the Relationship between the Human Being and Nature 23

WILLIAM D. MELANEY / Spenser's Poetic Phenomenology: Humanism and the Recovery of Place 35

SITANSU RAY / The Asrama-Anthem: Tagore's Passion for Santiniketan 45

MARY F. CATANZARO / The Elemental Space of Passion: The Topos of Purgatory in Beckett's *Play* 49

BRUCE S. WATSON / Apples without Snakes: Proust's Sapphic/Organic Rewritings of Eden 59

PART TWO
THE ELEMENTAL ROOTEDNESS – HOUSE AND HOME

NANCY CAMPI DE CASTRO / The Archetype of the House in *The Great Gatsby* 71

BERNADETTE PROCHASKA / The Elemental Passion of Home and Walker Percy's Lancelot 81

CHRISTOPH EYKMAN / The Imperfect and the All-Too-Perfect Home: The House as Existential Symbol in Franz Kafka's "The Burrow" and Thomas Bernhard's *Correction* 89

DAVID SULLIVAN / Inter-View: Emily Dickinson and the
Displaced Place of Passion   101

PART THREE
INTIMATE PLACES

MARLIES E. KRONEGGER / From Profane Space to the Sacred
Place or Center in *Désert* by Le Clézio   121
LESLIE DUNTON-DOWNER / Languageless Places and Poetic
Language: The Boundless Desire of Cannibal Clément X.   135
SHERLYN ABDOO / "Before Daybreak": The Unfinished Quest
of Washington Irving's Headless Horseman of Sleepy Hollow   145

PART FOUR
ELEMENTAL POETICS OF PLACE IN THE PERSPECTIVE OF $ARCH\bar{E}$, *TELOS, PATHOS*

LAWRENCE KIMMEL / Journeys Home: The Pathos of Place   163
JORGE GARCÍA-GÓMEZ / Poetry as a Worldly Vocation: Home
and Homelessness in Rilke's *Das Stunden-Buch*   173
DAVID SCHUR / A Phenomenal Hiding Place: Homer, Heraclitus, Heidegger   213
CHRISTINE RAFFINI / The Passion for Place: Medieval and
Renaissance Re-Creations of Paradise   221
JADWIGA S. SMITH / The Concept of Space in Medieval
Drama: Toward a Phenomenological Interpretation in
Medieval Studies   231

PART FIVE
PLASTICITY OF PLACE IN CREATIVE IMAGINATION

WILLIAM S. SMITH / Medieval Ruins and Wordsworth's *The
Tuft of Primroses*: "A Universe of Analogies"   243
ELDON N. VAN LIERE / Monet and the Pillars of Nature:
Articulation and Embodiment   251
MICHAEL LOSCH / A Vicarious Victory: Cézanne's Paintings
of Mont Sainte-Victoire and the Dual Nature of Love   271
ALAIN LAFRAMBOISE / Les portraits emblématiques de
Bronzino, aux marges des pratiques symboliques consacrées
dans les arts visuels   297

PART SIX
POETIC ASSOCIATIONS, TRANSPOSITIONS, TRANSFORMATIONS

GEORGE L. SCHEPER / "Where Is Our Home?" The Ambiguity of Biblial and Euro-American Imaging of Wilderness and Garden as Sacred Place — 321

JOAN B. WILLIAMSON / Jerusalem: The Poetics of Space in the Works of Philippe de Mézières — 339

CYNTHIA OSOWIEC RUOFF / Heaven: Val-de-Grâce, Molière's "La gloire du Val-de-Grâce" and Rotrou's *Le Véritable Saint Genest* — 353

RAYMOND J. WILSON III / "Et in Arcadia Ego" in John Fowles's *A Maggot*: Postmodern Utopia — 367

INDEX OF NAMES — 379

Control no.: X5939963

Site	MIDDLESEX UNIVERSITY LIBRARY
TM	
Accession No.	9429487
Class No.	142.7 ANA
Special ✓ Collection	Q.REF

THE THEME

The elemental passion for place marks a further step in our ongoing aesthetic experience of the Human Condition. Following the lead of the passions of the soul at its subliminal circuits, we have been progressively investigating and exfoliating the groundwork of sense characterizing the Human Condition. We have discovered that creative imagination operates a transition from the vital significance of life as it projects itself in its ontopoietic course onward to the specifically Human Condition which, drawing it in, transforms it into myriads of rays, each a source of ever-renewed and differentiating factors devising the richness of the human significant universe. The elements of air, sea, appeared as conveying a passage from the human involvement with Nature into the specifically human orbit of creative expansion. With the elements of light and place we seem to have reached much further – beyond Nature itself – into the relevance of the cosmos for *life as such.*

While light ascertains itself as a proto-generic force working already at the very incipient instance of life's genesis, the passion for place brings the imaginative quest to the other primogenital instance of life's self-individualizing course: its primordial inscription into the pre-ordaining of Nature's establishment – nay, constituting even the principal modus of this pre-ordaining. Self-individualization of life means for the beingness to seek 'its place' within the conundrum of Nature's spacing, and simultaneously to expand this spacing and qualify it. This place among other living beings involved in progress, interchanging forces, measuring and adjusting to others' needs, and introducing proportions, amounts to weaving the fabric of Nature and the unity-of-everything-there-is-alive. Acquiring with the creative imagination a vast field for expansion and means of proliferating in transformative freedom, the passion for place reaches its proper measure as well as its peak.

An outburst of creatively differentiated circuits of the subliminal workings of the soul accounts for the specifically human 'style' of dwelling upon the planet earth. It is qualified by the ever newly projected and yet always repeated effort to be made by the human being who seeks to establish and fortify his/her foothold in existence. This pluridimensional beingness seeks to 'situate itself' by means of the innermost imaginative efforts in its 'very own' place among other beings within the space of the natural, social cultural fabric of existence.

Its very own place becomes the human being's groundwork for assuming 'a position' in life, his/her sphere of personal expansion, a nest for promoting further generations. One's very own place becomes the mirror to reflect personal taste, project a world-view and one's aspirations in life. One's own place provides a means also to incarnate our personality as well as a springboard for launching our yearnings and nostalgia. We attach ourselves to a 'place' in order to long to leave it.... We have to be chained in order to shake ourselves free.

ANNA-TERESA TYMIENIECKA

ACKNOWLEDGMENTS

Now when this volume is going into print I wish to express my warm thanks to Louis Houthakker, who helped with its composition, and to Robert Wise Jr. for his dedicated proofreading.

A-T.T.

In front: Beth van Liere, Raymond Wilson, Michael Losch and Jorge García-Gómez; at the back: Eldon van Liere.

INAUGURAL STUDY

The pond, meadows, forest, mountain, and the horizons beyond . . . at Oak Ledge Farm, North Pomfret, Vermont.

ANNA-TERESA TYMIENIECKA

DE PATRIA MEA
THE PASSION FOR PLACE AS THE THREAD LEADING OUT OF THE LABYRINTH OF LIFE

SECTION ONE
DECLARING FOR A PARADIGM

1. *Philosophical Anthropology, Aesthetics, Metaphysics Reformulated*

How intriguing it sounds, when we think of it: "inhabiting" the earth, "dwelling" upon the earth – as if the living being, the human being too, and earth were two separate spheres, the one of individual life, the other of an indifferent "entity," a planet. It is as if the living being could also inhabit or dwell elsewhere, on some other planet, in an unknown neutral sphere. We ask ourselves, indeed, whether there are other planets favorable to the existence of life, and other intelligent beings there. Does this mean that the human being needs to "occupy space" for his/her existence? Does the human being need to "have a place" in which to establish him/herself? Would then "space" and "place" be a middle term between the earth and the living being? Or, rather, would "spacing" and "placing" as such constitute one of the primogenital modalities of life?

This juxtapostion inherent in the current and old expressions ("inhabit" and "dwell") that put the living being – the human being – in contradistinction to his/her sphere of existence, his/her territory, his/her soil . . . raises, indeed, some basic questions of life. Here is the very question of life's foundation, grounding, elementary conditions, on the one hand, and its most complex manifestation, freedom from them, on the other. We will attempt to enter the subterranean labyrinth of this intricate and enigmatic situation through the investigation of the human passion for place.

It is a labyrinth truly. We could say that the Minotaur that we meet on venturing into its meanders is another human passion, that for philosophizing. As if it were not enough to approach the issue of this most intricate phenomenon of inhabiting, dwelling through the elemental passion for place that the human being exhibits in all his/her dealings with life and which leads to striking manifestations in our own reflection upon it – feelings expressed in science, literature, the fine arts – it appears that we cannot stop in our quest at any one of them; to pursue it, we are drawn into the heart of the labyrinth by our philosophizing reflection, of which the three fields usually called 'philosophical anthropology,' 'aesthetics,' and 'metaphysics' reveal themselves as the proper fields for reflection. In them the entanglements that seem otherwise to be loose ends are tied together and the *elemental passion for place* may be adequately approached, grasped, and clarified.

In saying so, we are obviously indicating that there is a "center" for this inquiry. In current postmodern thinking all centralized organization is denounced; there seems to be no center to anything; it seems that we could venture into any investigation from any place, at random.

Yet the evidence of experience contradicts this lighthearted assumption at every point. In our journey into experience or the world we go astray unless we find a starting-point that is either a center from which the main lines of our inquiry flow or a center into which all otherwise dispersed lines of research gather. We ourselves at the outset of any physical or mental journey are such a center around which the world and universe of questioning is grouped. In the investigation of the human significance of life as well as in the investigation of the universe around us, it becomes obvious that in the human approach to the world of life – and for that matter, in that of all living beings – we envision everything as lying either "within" or "around" us, we, living persons, being the "centers" of these inquiries. It is as if through the wishes, desires, appetites, appreciations that surge from within us, from the center, and by which we bestow significance on the "objects" that lie "without", we establish all that is without as a world "around" us. This is by no means a haphazard throwing out of hooks for a catch; the "within" is establishing itself as a "center" of our lived, experienced, envisioned universe. The hooks thrown send out circles around themselves like those that expand from the points where pebbles hit the surface of a body of water, circles that are always at a certain distance from each other, always in a certain order beginning with those closest to the breaking of the surface and spreading in ever further circles till the vibration of the water diminishes, making them broader, dispersing, and disappearing altogether.

This order of spreading circles upon the surface encountered by our hooks seems to be the real principle of mutual exchange between the two substantial factors of center and periphery, although it varies as the waves are of different thicknesses, widths, depths, and even number according to the differing modes of the two factors and their respective conditions; these modes may differ but the order of the waves that they respectively set in motion and receive enacts the vibrating that encircles them. It is from their center thus projected in exercise that the living beingness that reaches out establishes its existential realm.

There is no point in following a passing fashion or in beating about the bush before repudiating it. Inasmuch as the human being is a center from which his/her individual and personal concerns spread, establishing it within the unity-of-everything-there-is-alive, the human being is also a center into which lines form innumerable other centralizing life-processing agencies gather, maintaining it in existence and allowing it to advance.

In point of fact, the passion for place is to be pursued, investigated through those lines of reflection that flow from what we could consider a "central" philosophical focus, namely, from the Human Condition. This focus corresponds to so-called 'philosophical anthropology'; but this inquiry gathers lines proceeding from the many circuits of what we call the *ontopoiesis of life* – which circuits sustain life, reacting to the circuits of the *cosmic laws* that meet in man, and which manifest too the aesthetics factor, that is crucial to the Human Condition in its lifting of its significance to its specifically human level in the *human creative act* with its *intellectual, aesthetic,* and *moral sense-giving factors*. It is the aesthetic factor that comes to the fore in our inquiry into the elemental passion for place. Our inquiry lies then within these three intertwined philosophical domains: the Human Condition, metaphysics, and aesthetics in the novel formulations they acquire within the phenomenology of life.[1]

2. *The Passion for Place and the Metaphysical Center of Aesthetics*

Just as the center of aesthetics is metaphysics, so the aesthetic center of metaphysics is the elemental passion for place. This remains, however to be shown, and I intend to demonstrate it in a succinct fashion.

First of all, the passion for place – like all subliminal passions – lies at the heart of the Human Condition in the unity-of-everything-there-is-alive from whence this very condition is mapped out in all directions. However, while all the subliminal passions – except that for light –

emerge within a territory – a frontier, so to speak, territory which the Human Condition with its creative forge draws upon and encircles within this unity in which it partakes – the passion for place while leading us has the unique role of traversing this entire territory and not stopping at that, for it mediates all the steps of unfolding bios, of individualizing life, to life's furthest frontiers.

Among the elemental passions for the air, infinity, the sea, light, etc. that spur heroic deeds, elevation of the soul, human communion and expand the spheres of life in all directions into specifically human ones, the passion for place, as we will see, is matched by none (except that for light). It reveals itself upon scrutiny as the basic driving force of the *spacing/timing* function of the logos, in particular of the network of life being projected by the living beingness initiating its course, with specifically human beingness drawing from it its full-fledged inspiration.

This far-reaching role of the passion for place yields a precious thread that allows us to situate in a definitive way our inquiry into the creative source of the specifically human significance of life, an inquiry to which we have devoted two decades of work in the International Society of Phenomenology and Literature. This inquiry has been focused on the elemental passions of the soul proceeding from the creative forge of the Human Condition as it sets out on its specifically human adventure, the passions which are the bearers of the sublimation or "humanization" of the soul promoting the life of the spirit. Thus, our work has, on the one hand, discovered and elaborated the mysterious workings of the creative mind (the study of which belongs to what is usually called anthropology/philosophy of mind), and, on the other (but these are inseparable and intermingled aspects of our quest), it has pursued the sources and the unfolding of the beautiful, the sublime, and the elevated, which would usually be classified as aesthetic/moral inquiry. Thus, our hitherto accomplished digging into the sources, nature, and unfolding of the elemental passions has been a study of the Human Condition with a highly aesthetic bent.

The inquiry into the passion for place will, on the one hand, make a breakthrough: *from the human condition we will be brought into the spheres of the bios and cosmic system*; this will be its situating of the human condition itself within the vast network of life as such and of its cosmic contingencies. But simultaneously, the passion for place – as the driving force of life in all its circuits – effects its most essential impact through and upon the creative, subliminal footholds of specifically human existence on earth (which has its roots in the soil and its hands, head, and spirit raised upwards toward the sky, and the furthest horizons of which are those that only the soul may guess).

It is precisely the aesthetic élan, *the aesthetic/cosmic breath*, the aesthetic/creative sense of the Human Condition, that is at the center of the role played by the passion for place.

As we have shown in our previous writings, the aesthetic significance of life as exemplified in exemplary works of the fine arts, literature, technology, architecture, etc. – as a matter of fact, all exemplary works of human creative genius – cannot be approached at random, nor in any however ingenious perspective; it cannot be adequately understood through its already accomplished and reified products – works of art, poetry, prose literature, theories – or through a focus on its expressive medium, what is fashionably called the 'text,' alone.

Nor may we expect to discover the pervasive role of aesthetics in our grasping of the life-significance of the human universe through an emphasis on man-the-creator alone.

Aesthetic inquiry, that is, inquiry into the emergence and manifestation of *imaginatio creatrix*, has thus far been situated in human works, that is, within the sphere of the human condition, which inquiry falls into the field of philosophy called 'philosophical anthropology.' Although I have challenged the usual conceptions of philosophical anthropology, in which the accent falls upon *anthropos*, the human being singled out from the rest of living beings, in its own 'nature,' and although I have broken with the unwarranted artificial isolation or demarcation of the human being from the web of life and have emphasized the Human Condition as a unique territory in the evolving web of life, as a unique, novel vitally significant station in the evolutive advance of living forms, I have not so far in this aesthetic pursuit of the origin and genesis of the specifically human significance of life accomplished – launched – by the elemental passions of the soul, gone to the end of the road. With all of the passions so far investigated, we have held back at a halfway point.

What has been brought out in the main is that the human condition which springs forth from the unity-of-everything-there-is-alive and constitutes a creative novum does not isolate itself from the web of life. We have seen that through the soul it remains a link in the chain of life's forces, and forms as a transformer the vitally significant energies into specifically human, creative ones; we have shown that this creative human station functions as the final accomplishment of the vastly diversified degrees of an increasing flexibility in the workings of life, having greatly extended the rigor of the entelechial pre-ordering of life's rules and regulations. Here life, in fact, passes into a system of creative freedom; the human being invents his/her own routes of life.

This creative freedom comes, again, from a "center," and so it may be seen as a novel, specifically human "creative entelechy."

Within this framework, the study of the elemental passions of the soul has meant for us the pursuit of the origin and genesis of the specifically human creative endowment, of the new freely unfurled significance of life over and above its vital significance, though continuing it. It is the specifically human course of existence and the human dominion reposing in the human spirit and its origin in the creative forge that we kept in focus.

But with the passion for place – as with that for light – we withdraw from this dominion. We still locate the center in the creative forge of the human condition; but we penetrate much further into the vital territories of the poiesis of life – into metaphysics and ontology in traditional terms. With the passion for place we reach the nest that the human condition finds in the womb of life. This nesting of life leads us further – through the spheres in sequence, through the further and further existential horizons in their referential networks in the system of life, with its cosmic contingencies, and on to the cosmic laws themselves.

The proto-aesthetic element accompanies the passion for place throughout. Hence, through this meandering way we arrive at our initial submission: just as the center of aesthetics lies in metaphysics, so the aesthetic center of metaphysics is the elemental passion for place. The specifically significant factors that imbue the human significance of life with aesthetic sense lead us through their dispersed rays to the center: through the human condition to the metaphysics of life.

SECTION TWO
SPACING/SCANNING AS THE FOUNDATIONAL FUNCTION OF THE INDIVIDUALIZATION OF LIFE WITHIN ITS TERRITORY

1. *The Nesting of Individualization*

We have to begin our inquiry with a clear recognition that we envisage things from a "center" within. By attributing to elementary spacing/

scanning an aesthetic quality, I am by no means giving, as some thinkers do, deliberate priority to the aesthetic function of the human being in establishing its "humanness." The recognition of the inquirer's position as the central position in mapping any territory of mind whatsoever allows us to avoid the one-sidedness of that view. We must disavow also the priority that several contemporary thinkers give to moral experience and ethics, just as much as we would have to do if priority were given to the senses, etc. The starting point of the human condition that we have adopted prevents any such one-sided and limiting arbitrariness and makes it obvious that in the making of specifically human beingness all dominant factors are indispensable and play an equal role; they need to be harmonized at the very surging of their respective faculties in order that the human significance of life as such may surge and unfurl. If with respect to the passion for place we have to bring out the aesthetic function of the human condition as being "first," it is because it is the *poetic* factor in human functioning that accounts for the infusion of psychic acts with a "breath of life," which brings expansion, a "spacing" of the acts such that they may spread their "content" into experience, which then spaces itself as our own intimate domain – our domain within, our innerness, our innermost self.

The "breath of life" is already the expression of experiential acts, introducing a novum into the empirical dynamism of the vital acts and operations of the psyche. It resides in the empirical vital operations and yet it spaces and scans itself in an "intellectual" fashion with the intellectual act of experience. As a matter of fact, the intellectual act, as the specifically human act, is carried by the aesthetic breath of life through which its continuing performances coalesce into "inwardness," the "sphere of the self."

We are here in a borderline territory between the ingrownness of living beingness and the spread of its tentacles through the circuits of "nature-life" – with its system of relevances that stretch to the cosmic laws, on the one hand, and to the specifically human expansion of this living beingness, on the other. The groundwork does not change: it remains always the empiric nature-life; however, with intellectual acts, the specifically human significance of life takes a new turn; it expands through the aesthetic breath and spaces itself, so that "inward space" is expanded through experience, an inner realm that breathes the specifically human significance of life.

Thus, when we pursue the rays of this significance back toward the center from whence they come or into which they are gathered, we find first in every sense – vital, sentient, emotional, affective, intellectual, etc. – a basis for the outer/inner placing of individualizing life within the universal system: a nesting of individualization. A bird builds the station in which it lays its eggs in relative safety, a cozy place in which to nurture its young; in the security of its circumference they may grow, The wolf, the boar, seek out a lair in the wild for comfort and security. For a human being who seeks it out or builds it, the nest is more than a place to be nurtured or to seek retreat from danger, cold, tempest, etc. The human being for his self-individualization in existence unfolds the aesthetic/moral/intellectual senses.

2. *The Human Nest: Home*

What for animals at-large is a "nest" in which the individualizing life grows and from which it inserts itself into the network of nature before it is ready to enter on its own the avenues of its life-world, a place in which, as at a hearth, the animal family keeps mutually "warm" – and which is abandoned until conditions, inclement weather, perhaps, prompts a return or the construction of a new one – is an enduring reality for the human being who unfolds from within a much vaster area of meaning, of existential self-interpretation-in-existence. The human being makes its nest "for keeps," does not abandon it after seasonal use, or use it intermittently. A human being endows objects, materials, events which pertain to his building his "nest" with the entire spectrum of his own unique personal experience. Thus, his nest becomes a hearth into which ever new experiences are thrown, keeping alive the flame that throws a glow all about, for the sake of a continuous flow of existence that ever renews itself. In fact, most friendships we kept and keep, books we read, pictures we like become tightly interwoven with the innermost spacing of our experience which becomes a place where we surround ourselves with all that we enjoy, where we retreat to refuel, to find repose, security, healing – to retrieve our very own selfhood, if it be faltering due to gales without. For the human being this nest within the situation of life and the world's schemas becomes a "home": a place not merely to retreat from the pressures of the outside world, but a place in which we expand our very self, with which we identify in our tastes and tendencies, a place for intimacy, a center of our very own in an alien world, a place for intimacy with ourselves and to relish and share with others.

This atmosphere of intimacy we attempt to carry with us to the workplace, the vacation spot, the hospital by installing pictures, posters, pots of flowers that will recreate some of its atmosphere. In brief, nature's nest aestheticized by the human being becomes his home.

Our nest-home itself does not hang on some tree in an indifferent, neutral space; on the contrary, it is "spaced," that is, situated within a specific circumference spaced by itself, "marked" as a special place by the natural unfolding of the individual's functioning. Animals instinctively mark their vital territories in a forest, on a meadow, in the sky, etc. as their very own areas for hunting, pasture, repose. Human beings who extend their vital/instinctive life-involvement by developing their own means for developing their territories – innumerable means, to begin with tools that transform nature's resources in their vital significance to realities that correspond to newly crystalized life-modalities – also expand their nest-homes. But, what is more, human beings seek to anchor home in nature's groundwork: a "field," a "garden."

While the animal anchors the nest in which the individualizing lives of a new generation are nurtured in the nature-life system with its web of symbiotic ingrownness with everything-there-is-alive, the human being besides expands his spacing by tying together all within his experiential personal and interpersonal reach: affective appreciative taste, will, judgment, all contribute to the establishment of his nest-home as a "relatively stable" station that has to maintain a balance between his nature-life. Our bents and attitudes, our very personality contribute to the "aesthetic atmosphere" of the home; a home breathes and exhales an aesthetic atmosphere; could we not say that in constructing a home it is an atmosphere of our very own self, of our soul in its tastes, habits, convictions, beliefs, allegiances, and traditions that we aim at?

Home is, in short, a "place" that is established by the spacing of the specifically human aestheticizing function of our experience: morals, thoughts, reflections, lyric inspiration, all interwoven with the necessities of vital existence in a unique sort of convergence. All is prompted toward coming together in this convergence, toward the weaving together of a consistent web of personal significance, first of all by the elementary animal instinct to weave a nest as the center from which to confront the crucial moments of existence. Then, however, this elementary instinctive urge is simultaneously blown, like the surface of a soap bubble, into myriad colors by the specifically human "passion for place," a passion for setting a cornerstone for the working out of our very own interpretation of existence, for finding a place to anchor our very own means, talents, desires in the fully creative crystallization of the Human Condition, for having our very own fulcrum with which to probe our environment, get our bearings within life's expanse, and so gain self-confidence.

Yet from his/her home the human being digs deeper, seeking to excavate and rejoin his/her roots. First, he/she moves into the nearest ground, the garden, but then, ever on the move, he/she seeks what is beyond.

3. *The Garden*

It is in what we are used to calling a "garden" (in contradistinction to a "field") that we would establish our nest, our home, as a site upon which we unfurl our inhabiting/dwelling life modality, our springboard as well as retreat, our inner sphere among living beings wherein we encircle ourselves in our very own territory, "on the land," as it were, differentiating it from without – that is, a terrain the spacing of which is measured and apportioned according to our own personal appetite and rhythm of life.

It is not objective, survey-measured space that determines the rhythm of life in our garden; the smallest objective space may manifest a life exuberance, dynamism, and appetite for life that a large city park spread over a large acreage of objective space will lack.

The reason is that our garden is ours insofar as we throw our very own vital as well as spiritual functioning into its life – a garden is alive, is prompted and maintained by our vital functions, and its modality of life basically translates our vitality, the pattern of our experiential system; it carries the stamp of our taste and even of some of our dispositions. In brief, what we call a "garden" is nature-life's dispositions and resources as admitted by the human being into his/her dominion – his/her womb – by specific human means in order to fashion it as his/her very own grounding. Gardeners live with the growth of their plants; their blossoming opens a new space in their vision of the world. The plants' maturation and fruition fills their very being. Theirs is nature's harvest, nature's accomplishment or failure. Thus, the paths radiating from the center to the corners and bounds are sectioned and measured according to the "spacing" of the cultivation project; the garden and the gardener are both spaced; the measure is that of the vital spaces for growing that plants, trees, bushes call for, it is the space of walks to be enjoyed at leisure in the moving light of the sun or of the moon. Concurrently, there is the synchronization of the gardener's life occupations and the organic demands of the plants, trees, bushes, etc. In gardening, the human being enters into the spacing/timing rhythm of organic life; and that life becomes part of the very circulation of the blood in his veins.

4. *Our Cosmic Breath*

Spacing our desires, intentions, projects in relation to our measuring, apportioning space, and the placement of our vegetable and flower beds, sowing and planting them in coexistence according to their vital requirements, we discover in our movements and calculations the scheme of contingencies of nature-life. Apportioning the objective "geographical" plots in size and shape according to the requirements that determine the places in which the various plants will flourish, reaching further, we discover the relevance to nature-life of the cosmic laws. In fact, we situate the members of our body, their positions, their reach, their efficacious maneuvering of the tools that measure surfaces in a neutral "objective" way common to the measurement of everything without distinction within the system of cosmic laws, and we draw from their intersection with nature-life.

Tending the plants, the soil, watering in view of the conditions beneficial to growth, we discover and enter into in our day-to-day preoccupations the contingencies of individualizing life in the schemas of the forces of nature-life first and then those of meteorology, planetary motion, till we arrive at laws of spacing/placing/timing that reveal the ultimate structural condition of life, laws equaled only by those of light.

5. *The Cultivation of Nature-Life*

It is touch, the touch of the living, life-vibrating soil that makes our fingers, our hands, our entire body vibrate with life's pulsations. By planting and weeding with our naked hands, by digging the soil and crushing the clumps of dirt in our fingers, we pulsate with the moves of organic life itself.

Gardeners feel "grounded" in nature's life in their garden. The soil is the soil of gardeners' very existence when they themselves become rooted in its depths. The human being dwells in his/her home but keeps his/her roots in the soil of the earth: in gardens, fields, forest, etc.

Yet, as I have mentioned, in the garden the entire human being is involved, present, manifested. The garden fulfills some practical functions: it produces vegetables and fruit for food; it may – and almost always to some degree does – serve a "disinterested" pleasurable function, offering delight to the eye and nose. A pleasure garden, be it even only a tiny flower bed in front of a house, is an aesthetic creation par excellence. We speak of knowledge of agriculture, on the one side, and of the art of gardening, on the other. Agriculture and gardening intermingle, of course, but the emphasis differs.

The main features of human temperament, character, taste may manifest themselves in the harmony of a garden or its disorderly arrangement, whether it be in an orchard, a patch of corn, or a flowerbed. Artistic taste for either formal perfection (in the arrangement of lines and the choice of flowers, plants, colors) or for a random mix and spread will distinguish the so-called formal garden with its structuring of space and plant selection, and even the determination of timing, from a romantic garden inspired by fantasy, in which the garden spontaneously follows the natural lie of the land and the flowers are mixed, and, with only some intervention from the gardener's hand, are left free to adapt themselves and proliferate, as in a meadow.

In the garden we encounter in an immediate experience the soil within which ultimately the basic roots of our own organic/vegetal place among the play of vital forces in the unity-of-everything-there-is-alive is established, our basic organic/vegetal sphere. From thence one's own core bios sprouts and spreads further into one's psyche in its varied spheres within the Human Condition, and on entering the psychic sphere it brings about creative virtualities that revolutionize the entire ontopoietic design. Our elementary bios and the empirical psyche/soul, which has tentacles that spread in all directions, are together the source and main processors of energies, forces, synergies.

In everyday practice I am not aware of my ties with the universal play of vital forces in which I am "located" through my own energy-processing system; we seem, upon reflection, to lie within the dimension of "civilized," technical modes of societal existence, far away from where the elementary game of life takes place.

Gardeners, however, vicariously enter life's womb. It is not their own existence that is played out in the vegetable beds, but that of tomatoes, parsley, corn, lettuce, etc.: but with their naked hands they enter into life's workings. I prepare the ground for life to sprout from, digging, fertilizing, smoothing the earth. I plant the seeds, and then water until the seedlings throw moisture-seeking roots into the ground and become strong enough to stand on their own against the sun, no longer needing moisture from my hand.

I look anxiously for the sprouting of the seeds and follow, with a breath of solicitude, their first moves on the earth; with fingers that amorously handle the soil, I weed around them as they grow and, taking the tenderest care not to cut their roots, stems, or leaves, I will translate them in an appropriate location, that is, I will prepare with my hands soft, loose soil in a new bed and plant them one by one, preparing cautiously a place for their roots, a place for their delicate adjustment.

6. Aesthetic Creativity

Yes, it is the basic sphere of life's progress that I enter through work with the soil and through putting into it the indispensable participation of my most delicate and tender feelings, expectations – following that up with the thought that is care. Thus, I renew in myself the primogenital and primordial affectivity – the vital/moral affectivity that springs into life with the emergence of the human condition, entering its game. These are the creative virtualities that distance me from my absolute allegiance to my individual interests and spread into affective networks embracing others. The care – the moral involvement – will not break but serve the freedom of expansion within limits.

Personal character, disposition, taste in enjoyment, and beyond that our aspirations for beauty, for free expression, for manifesting in the world those of our inward dispositions that no words can express, and, what is more, our inward inclinations, whims, fantasies, nostalgia, desires, in short, the most intimate pulsations of our subliminal self, are all developed in the garden.

So, while, on the one hand, we work out the growth of our roots in the visceral sphere of nature-life, on the other hand, we find in our garden the proper climate for the unfurling of our innermost subliminal dynamisms. Indeed, from the soil of a garden that we fashion according to our intimate selfhood, we swing with our yearnings toward further subliminal placing.

7. *The Rhythm of Life, the Rites of Life and Death, and the Garden as Sacral Space*

In the garden we are involved in the cycle of life. Plants spring forth and on meeting with favorable rains, warmth, sunshine they flourish. But drought will make them wither away. Thriving life and death are constant inhabitants of a garden; to ever begin and wither away is its usual rhythm. Entering into its rhythms we experience it as a ritual: the ritual of cyclic growth, death, and return to life. Life's law is renewal. We follow the ritual of life from spring to late fall and through a waiting space of seemingly inert but in fact burgeoning life.

Into this rhythm of life which we enter with the vegetation and ants, bees, earthworms, mice, rats, woodchucks, frogs . . . (the innermost rhythm around which spacing/timing/placing revolves, the rhythm that lies at the heart of our vital and subliminal concerns, the rhythm to the measure of which our imagination moves) are swept up the resources and energies of our entire soul, empirical and subliminal.

The human being who catches this rhythm scans his/her specifically human life and transforms it into a life ritual. Then his/her subliminal nostalgia releases life-transcending yearnings. He/she endows the ritual of life with transnatural significance; it is within the precincts of a garden that he/she establishes special places, "sacral space," in which the rituals of life are performed in an elevation from the level of pedestrian vegetal or simply animal significance to that of a fully human sphere, one that answers to soaring human yearnings. Hence, sacred grottos, springs, fountains. The place where a human being is laid to rest, a cemetery, is a type of sacral garden to which generation after generation goes to revive remembrance of forebears and loved ones.

SECTION THREE
THE RELEASE OF SUBLIMINAL YEARNINGS

1. *The "Ideal" Place: Eden, El Dorado, Secret Garden*

It is on the land that humans enter into the works of life itself and share in them. Working the fertile soil serves to expand the innermost resources of the soul, its longing, its striving, its innermost passions.

As we are attempting to show, the search for a place is not only the principle requirement of life as such but is also the most fundamental and forceful passion of the soul.

Indeed, the passion for place in all of its esoteric variations, such as a passion for a sacred mysterious site, for a temple, a spring, the place of a cult, a cemetery, a hidden labyrinth, subterranean caverns, ocean depths, a place where wealth is stored, where the secret of life, eternal youth, genius, etc. would be deposited, answers to an all-pervasive human thirst for the marvelous, the extraordinary, the miraculous. It is no wonder then that the garden has offered humanity fertile soil on which to nourish these yearnings in a full spectrum of deeply felt imaginary significance. It is a springboard from which to take flight and a center on which all can converge.

First, we seek "another place" where life would be redeemed from its shortcomings. East of Eden, there was a garden of life without end in which all vegetation and animalia happily coexisted with humans without the weaknesses inherent to the present material order with its servitude, danger, conflict, and death, a place of undisturbed felicity and innocence of life. This "paradisiac" place we would like now to reach as we navigate our tiny craft over the waves of existence. It remains always on the far-off horizon of our dreams – an "El Dorado," a place where gold, opportunity, and happiness await the adventurous. This dream recurrently haunts humanity. Only its locations changes. We always believe that by going to a new place our life would radically change.

Second, human beings endowed with these yearnings may not, cannot immerse themselves entirely in the ritual of life with its ever turning wheel of renewal. They cannot become absorbed in the cycle or fully identify themselves with its laws. As the ancient myths of every culture testify, human longing to overcome the necessities imposed by the laws of life, the inexorable turn of the wheel from birth to extinction, together with all the other limitations that life implies, has found outlet in innumerable expressions. The longing to overcome their confines are as deeply ingrained in us as are the laws of life themselves and haunts the deepest quietude of our absorption, complacency, enjoyment, fulfillment.

The human being looks to a far-off horizon seeking total transcendence over the servitude that life imposes, over its unbending requirements.

2. Homeland

I look now from the shade of a tree at the pond, at the sprawling meadow beyond the sheep fence, which separates the territory of the grazing sheep from my garden, the plants and flowers of which have to be protected from their voracious appetite. They graze contentedly and yet throw inquisitive glances beyond the fence: "The grass is greener on the other side of the fence." The sheep stand ready to sample that other vegetation the moment the fence would lose its effectiveness. The surface of the pond, into the depths of which my thoughts plunge, reflects serenity, repose. The blue lupine in blossom on a hillock before the fence separates the pond from the field beyond – a closer realm of intimacy, of shared roots and life cycles, one that expands, however, throughout the field, which is for the most part left to itself and to the sheep. but this vision of an intimate place expands still further – trees, another hill, a forest, and a mountain upon the horizon. And beyond that stretch other fields, ponds, creeks, pastures, gardens, and houses for sure. The delicate bluish haze hanging over the forested mountainsides tickles my imagination and spurs reflection.

The horizon opens from my home, my garden, and myself incorporated within it – from the center. It moves with my changing positions in this my very own milieu, the milieu of myself. My musing reflection extends far beyond visible contours, proceeding from the very depths of viscera that are centered in the very soil of life. It runs through the entire span of my existence and comes back to the center from whence it flew.

We humans participate in the rhythm of life, know its cycles, but unlike plants and animals we do not vanish without a trace on our passing. There is another rhythm, that of generations, and in the line of generations we all leave a trace after we are gone, a trace of the work of our spirit on others. This work – the cultivation of the logos of life – is shared by families, communities, nations. We share in the spirit that was deposited as a common trust by past generations; we maintain some of its seeds and cultivate them in our own existence. Thus, those with whom we share these sedimentations of past generations cultivate similar passions for a place of their own: house, garden, meadow. They cultivate the same ideal of a home, of its habits, mode of life, mode of human relations, and of language, which expresses it all. Hence, there is an extended place – around my home and garden – that reaches as far as those sedimentations of culture have been deposited by succeeding generations. This is my homeland.

We are bound viscerally to the "native soil," the field, garden, forest where we have our roots, "native" not only because we, like any animal, first saw the light of day on a particular site, but because our forebears had their roots there and left behind the culture of this "land." No matter where we physically move within that land in order to establish our very own place, to put down roots, we can participate in and cultivate a way of life, the tastes, ideals, and virtues that are those of the land's people.

When my gaze wanders along the horizon past my meadow, my memory wanders too to a faraway homeland that I have left behind to make a new nest in a foreign land. I have found here a new intimate place, but memory takes me back to my ancestors, to their valorous deeds remembered, recorded, and passed into legends that molded my mind, then to the cycles of life of people I knew and cherished, to their fates, their heroic virtue, magnanimous heart, their weaknesses and strengths, who – whether victors through their selfless dedication to others or victims of history's visitations – have passed to others the torch of endurance, of perseverance, of hope against all hope. Some have died, some continue to cultivate their legitimate places in the homeland, rendering full allegiance to its spirit. I cultivate my own spot in far-off parts.

3. De Patria Mea

Where is my Home? So my idly wandering spirit asks. Are my roots in the soil, in my very own place, my garden and my home, not merely my receptive organs – receptive to the forces of Nature-Life as well as to my creative virtualities deriving from the Human Condition? Is not all the outgrowth that begins with my deepest involvement in life-cyclic growth and extends to personal desires, tastes, cultural habits, virtues, and ideas of human destiny not situated at the center where they brew and from whence they spread, at the center of my heart? There I may embrace the past and the present of my innermost experience in one harmonious whole. That is where all converges and bursts forth.

But do I with my deepest longings repose in my heart? The heart might well join all the arteries through which the life-significance processed by the vital organs, the subliminal forge, practical life-enactment, etc.

pass to the center, but it does not retain them. Just as the natural horizons beyond my garden, my meadow, beyond the sea, recede ever further as they are approached, so the webs of significance that emerge from our naturally processed experience, recede on reaching their zenith as new waves of experience come in. The sedimentations gathered by generations are adumbrated by incoming material, and, at best, these may advance with some impetus for a time. But they may also be disrupted and vanish. Social pressures may transform them beyond recognition. The natural existence of humanity for all of its creative inventiveness in surpassing nature has a horizon that ever recedes, that offers no definitive halt.

Carried by my subliminal longings for the final repose of fulfillment, the fulfillment of my life's course in life as such, I muse about a place beyond any place, a place of repose that is not caught up in the repeated rotations of the wheel of life, a place that my soul alone will recognize, for it has been seeking it from the beginning.

The World Phenomenology Institute

NOTE

[1] Cf. Anna-Teresa Tymieniecka, *Logos and Life:* Book 1, *Phenomenology of Creative Experience and the Triple Critique of Reason;* Book 2, *The Three Movements of the Soul;* Book 3, *The Passions of the Soul and the Elements in the Ontopoiesis of Culture* (Dordrecht: Kluwer Academic Publishers, Bk. 1 1988, Bk. 2 1988, Bk. 3 1990).

PART ONE

POETISING PLACE AT THE
FRONTIERS OF NOSTALGIA

Cynthia Osowiec Ruoff, Hendrik Houthakker and Jadwiga Smith.

HANS H. RUDNICK

THE *LOCUS AMOENUS*: ON THE LITERARY EVOLUTION OF THE RELATIONSHIP BETWEEN THE HUMAN BEING AND NATURE

In this article I want to draw attention to an elemental passion that seems to have undergone substantial change over a long time in the history of our Western tradition. As you know very well, we have pursued the subject of elemental passions under the leadership of Professor Tymieniecka for many years; and, I feel, in defining its scope, as if we were at this time descending downward from the Paradiso of Dante's *Divine Comedy* toward the Inferno, we find an increasing measure of cultural shift that has moved from an initial and exclusive concept of serene happiness toward the dark dungeons of depression. Clearly, light is defined on its elemental level by virtue of the existence of darkness and vice versa. But as soon as we are investigating the subject before us, for example, from a perspective of historical development, the apparently assumed balance between light and darkness is upset and strenuous efforts must be exerted to set the balance right again. These rectifying efforts are based necessarily on a value system that must be shared by those who live as a human community under these values representing the ideal that captures the elemental passion.

Elemental passions are creativity-generating. They emerge as expressions of creativity, innovation, and overall movement toward the ideal fulfillment of the human task of meaningful living, not only referring to an individual, but also to the family, group, community, nation, and ultimately, humankind as a whole. The creative passion or spirit is specific to the human being in particular and implies an obligation, I would argue, to adhere to values that further the well-being of humankind and with it the human being itself in the nature-given context, which is, in present-day terms, the environment, be it cultural or personal. Any flagrant violation of this "pact" upsets the balance and provokes reaction – the natural give-and-take defining the vitality of a culture and its powers of creativity, be they, crudely named, "good" or "bad"; i.e. they are frequently narrowly defined on the basis of what is "useful" or "profitable" with respect to a certain, albeit limited, perspective.

It may seem unlikely at first sight that we might consider a place or location the object of one of the elemental passions; but at a second glance we begin to realize that, e.g., the power of feeling home-sick, displaced or exiled indicates that we seem to have lost in those instances a place that has kept us contented and happy. Removal from that "haven," which must have provided protection and peace of mind, suddenly shows us the power of what we have lost. Something that we have been quietly valuing and taking for granted, has been taken from us; or, as some may want to ask, has it even removed itself? Our *feeling* of loss tells us that we are missing something; and that means, I take it, that we have not voluntarily given it up, but rather want it back. The giving-taking-and-attempting-to-restore process is the formative force behind socio-cultural vitality. This is the creative spirit that moves human existence to new horizons. It is a profoundly historical process if it is allowed to move naturally at its own pace without institutional interference; it is a violent process if it is forced, implying the imposition of an agenda or plan that tries to alter the value system and its constituent components. Both phases may occur in sequence or side-by-side, characterizing vitality, movement, and, of course, creativity in the "good" or "bad" sense. Whether the resulting event(s) is (are) beneficial, if such judgment is at all possible given the complexity of the situation, must remain a question which can best be answered within the historical context at a later time, although different times may ask the same question guided by a different context establishing the preferred meaning, implying "cultural value."

Socrates' "Apology" may be an early example for the potential loss of meaning and cultural value. In a broader sense it could also have been a loss of place within the Greek value system. But it was Plato who recorded Socrates' self-defense and made the speech, which was only heard by those within earshot, into a cultural document whose content could now be preserved, read, studied, translated, and lived by all subsequent generations. Through Plato's service to his teacher a saddening speech about the displacement of one of the earliest great minds of the Western tradition turns into a cultural document whose value has surpassed and survived the moment. It has inspired an entire culture and set the principles by which an individual of this tradition would most likely prefer to live. ". . . the unexamined life is not worth living" Socrates says and, driven by the essence of creativity, he assures his accusers "I shall . . . continue my search into true and false knowledge," whatever the consequences.[1]

In spatial terms, Socrates' speech defines a location, socially and intellectually, an ideal place containing the conditions by which many of us would like to abide. The ancients knew to locate such an ideal place *in literature*, the element of language that has the power of surviving the relative shortness of the human life. Ernst Robert Curtius identified such a place in his famous book *Europäische Literatur und lateinisches Mittelalter*[2] as one of his topoi, namely the *locus amoenus*. Place marks our being, our physical existence. It is, therefore, no wonder that we find such places as the *locus amoenus* in the earliest literary documents beginning with Homer, Ovid and Virgil. The *locus amoenus* is consistently used to describe nature in European literature from the time of the Roman emperors to the sixteenth century. This motif shows Nature as being particularly pleasant and beautiful, characterized by shadow-providing trees, a meadow, a cool creek, singing birds, flowers in bloom, a gently blowing breeze. The *locus amoenus* was an integral part of literature for well over 1500 years. It was part of rhetoric, the art of effective speaking, during late antiquity and the Middle Ages; it was, e.g., incorporated into the poetics of the 12th century by Gervasius von Melkley.[3] Such formulaic *descriptio loci* was to represent the ideal landscape which during the late middle ages might even have included a castle reminiscent of the cave in Homer's Kalypso episode where Kalypso and Odysseus always "had their pleasure."[4] Furthermore, there was of course also a *locus amoenus* in a deep forest with a grotto as in Gottfried's *Tristan*. The *locus amoenus* was "à travers les siècles, le signe d'une manière commune de voir et de ressentir la nature."[5] The *locus amoenus* topos describes a pleasant place, a place of pleasure, *einen Lustort* in Nature, which survived in some refined form in the cultured gardens of Europe's baroque era and in a Nature-substituting version in the later so-called "English Garden" that allowed nature to grow with the appearance of the least interference from humans for the enjoyment of humans mostly confined to living in cities. There is no doubt that the *locus amoenus* is a place in Nature which provides pleasure to the human being and propagates harmony with nature; it is the all-embracing haven for humans in nature. Gottfried von Straßburg's *Tristan* describes a famous *locus amoenus* in mediaeval literature as follows:

From their twigs they [the birds] sang their joy-giving airs with many variations. There were innumerable sweet tongues singing their songs and refrains in tenor and descant, to the lovers' rapture. The cool spring received them, leaping to greet their eyes with its beauty, and sounding in their ears with even greater beauty, as it came whispering towards them to receive them with its murmur. How sweetly it whispered its welcome to those lovers! The lime-trees in all their blossom, the lustrous meadow, the flowers, the green, green grass, and everything in bloom – all smiled its welcome! On either hand, the dew, too, gave them a tender greeting, cooling their feet and solacing their hearts.

But when Tristan and Isolde had had their fill, they slipped back into their rock [grotto] and agreed together as to what they should do to their situation. For they were much afraid – and events were to prove them right – . . . .[6]

In this heavenly place, Nature and the human are one; Nature celebrates the lovers who on human terms are not to love each other! Nature, however, sanctions their love, there are no storms or thunderbolts of disapproval as at some other instances in *Tristan*. And yet, Tristan and Isolde's place of pleasure, love, feeling, and happiness is threatened by discovery which, of course, is not far away since soon after this scene a hunter will find his way into this haven and report to King Mark what he has seen. The undisturbed communication of feeling between the lovers is either constantly threatened or interfered with. Tristan is very well aware of danger and applies reason and symbolism to show to any intruder that the etiquette of courtly love has been maintained. Tristan uses location for symbolic demonstration. Tristan and Isolde are observed sleeping next to each other, but spatially separated by a sword indicating propriety within the terms of chivalry. The hunter sees this scene and will report his observation to Mark who finds the nasty rumors and suspicion he had received before unsupported. But only ten pages later will Mark receive a tip from a servant; and this will make him feel "his mortal pain," when he is finally seeing Tristan and Isolde "so closely locked together that, had they been a piece cast in bronze or gold, it could not have been joined more perfectly. Tristan and Isolde were sleeping very peacefully after some exertion or other."[7] At this point the lovers' harmony and pleasure provided by the natural environment of the *locus amoenus* are finally revealed overtly and directly to Mark; the holiness of feeling has not been covered up or camouflaged by reason and the application of symbolism; this now is an open statement and confession. All moral rules of chivalry and propriety have been abolished. This time the feeling is not symbolized or allegorically represented: it has been denuded of the concealing and consentment-signalling cloak of the *locus amoenus*. The message is now clear, Tristan and Isolde are lovers, Gottfried of Straßburg does not need the *locus amoenus* any more, the happy times of this romance are over.

Tristan and Isolde were able to hide their love for some time. Their feelings for each other prevailed with the help of their reason and skill in cover-up and deception, aided by the nature of the locality that seemed to encourage their albeit improper happiness since the love-potion was doing its irresistible work. Love and self-preservation motivated their actions. The application of reason became tantamount to the preservation of their being. Looking ahead historically and finding increasing literary evidence since *Tristan*, reason has turned more and more into a creative force which, like Odysseus' intelligence and cunning, could make things turn out the way the protagonist wanted. Boccaccio's Pampinea (in 1336?), on the first day of the *Decameron*, says

... proper use of one's reason does harm to no one. It is only natural for everyone born on this earth to aid, preserve, and defend his own life to the best of his ability; this is a right so taken for granted that it has, at times, permitted men to kill each other without blame in order to defend their own lives.[8]

Here, already in the early 14th century, Pampinea has outlined the future course for the use of reason. By the 17th century, when the *locus amoenus* disappears from literature, at the time which T. S. Eliot claimed for the emergence of the dissociation of sensibility, when Descartes writes the *Discours de la méthode* (1637), a new literary topos, the *locus terribilis* begins to take the place of the *locus amoenus*. The *locus terribilis* is the place of the lover's lament, reminiscent of Petrarch's "Grieving Rimes" sonnet of the *Canzoniere* with its *dolore amoroso*, of the hermit and of the contemplative observer.[9] This is no longer the unified world of Tristan and Isoldes's *Liebestod*. The active and creative aspect has been replaced by an exclusively suffering individual, feeling sorry about his situation, or lamenting, like Petrarch in his sonnet, the death of Laura and the resultant feeling of abandonment. Nature is dark and somber as at the outset of the Inferno when, in mid-life crisis, Dante is threatened by the Leopard, Lion, and Wolf. A typical *locus terribilis*, fully developed by 1624 – 300 years after Gottfried – sounds like this:

> This place is completely surrounded by trees,
> There is nothing but fear and shadow;
> There is also sadness,
> There is everything lying waste and fallow,
> There is no sun reaching in,

> There is poisonous vermin crawling everywhere;
> There is no water flowing at all
> But the one that flows from my eyes;
> There is no light in sight,
> But the one burning in my heart;
> Although I like to be comfortable,
> There is much sorrow because of my pain,
> Because of my pain, because of my suffering;
> So I will now make my departure.
> But before long-desired death
> Will gladly deliver me from my pain,
> I want to complain about my love.
> And I want, although in vain, merely ask,
> Is there nobody who will console me
> Because I am so very sad? . . .
> (Opitz, "Echo and Reverberation", my translation)

A French precursor in a poem contained in Monteux' Shepherd's romance "Bergeries de Juliette" seems to have provided the pattern for the German poet Hermann Opitz' "Echo and Reverberation" of 1634.[10] Place and nature are characterized as being sad and utterly unpleasant. The speaker tells the listener that there is no water flowing anywhere but from his eyes. Sadness prevails throughout.

In some cases we have poetry that documents the transition from *locus amoenus* to *locus terribilis*,[11] beginning with a typical *locus amoenus* setting that then changes into a *locus terribilis* because the pleasant nature outside does not agree with the inner feeling and sadness of the poetic voice. But in making a special effort to offer a harmonious setting, the speaker reasons that, given the pleasant conditions around him, he finds himself inspired to leave pain and sorrow behind. The pleasure of Nature prevails in this instance over the darkness of despair. Reason, still inspired by Nature, provides for a way out of the inner pain. But there is much evidence of discontent in 17th century literature as, e.g., in Shakespeare's *Hamlet* and John Donne's poetry, complaining about stale life at court, creative stagnation, and even suicidal melancholy. Besides all the wordplay, puns, equivocations, paradoxes, ironies, analogies, conceits, and foolery, besides all the debunking and euphemisms, there was much playing with words and meaning that grew more and more complicated, which means more and more dominated by the order of reason, as we turn to the 18th century of Dryden and Pope. Reason crowds out Nature and the mystery of the sacred.[12] Feeling becomes secondary to rationality. Losing the closeness with Nature, seeking solace in reason and its pre-arranged order, lamenting one's fate, lamenting the loss of love and, by extension, lamenting the loss of creative freedom in the face of the rote of boredom, dullness, ennui, habit, and order results in a typology of the *locus terribilis* which links the secludedness of place with a desert setting, a deep forest, mountains and rocks, or a desolate island. The feeling of loneliness prevails in the remote forest separating the suffering lover from the beloved.

In Book One, Chapter 25 of *Don Quixote*, Cervantes caricaturizes such a feeling when Don Quixote, "disdained" by his lady and penitent, decides to imitate in the roughest and most remote wilderness of the Sierra Morena "the famous Amadis of Gaul, . . . one of the most perfect of all knights-errant," thinking "that the knight-errant who copies him most nearly will come nearest to attaining the perfection of chivalry."[13] Ignoring his own reality since his lady has never communicated with him, but intent on imitating Amadis of Gaul out of empathy by following the conventions of (the novel of) chivalry, having no valid reason of his own, Don Quixote will, quite appropriately, seek out a *locus amoenus* near a mountain ridge and begin his own distraught lover's lament as a demonstration of his faithfulness to Dulcinea, who, of course, knows nothing at all of Don Quixote's feelings for her. Imitating Amadis inspires pseudo (creative) sadness in Don Quixote; imitating Orlando, outright violence

> I mean to *copy* Amadis of Gaul by acting here the part of a despairing, mad, and furious lover; at the same time following the example of Orlando when he found by a spring evidences that Angélica the Fair had dishonored herself with Medoro, and was so grieved that he went *mad*, rooted up trees, troubled the eaters of clean springs, killed shepherds, destroyed flocks, fired their huts, demolished houses, dragged off mares, and committed a hundred thousand extravagant deeds worthy of eternal renown. And although I do not intend to imitate Orlando . . . accurately in all the mad things he did, said, or imagined, I shall outline them as best I can in what appears to me most essential. Perhaps I shall content myself by imitating Amadis alone, as he by his tears and sorrows won as much fame as the best without committing any mischievous follies.[14]

When Sancho Panza responds that he has heard from his master "nothing but wind and lies" and that "a barber's basin is Mambrino's helmet", and that his master has not realized his mistake in four days, Don Quixote replies:

you have the shallowest understanding that any squire has or has ever had in the whole world. Is it possible that in the time you have been with me you have not yet found out that all the adventures of a knight-errant appear to be follies, dreams, and turn out to be the reverse? Not because things are really so, but because in our midst there is a host of enchanters, forever changing, disguising, and transforming our affairs as they please, according to whether they wish to favor or destroy us. So, what you call a barber's basin is to me Mambrino's helmet, and to another person it will appear to be something else.[15]

Shortly after this passage, still torn between copying Amadis or Orlando in his penitence, Don Quixote finds a perfect *locus amoenus*

they arrived at the foot of a lofty mountain that stood like a mighty hewed rock apart from the rest. At the foot flowed a gentle rill that watered a meadow so green and so fertile that it was most pleasing to behold. It was planted with many wild shrubs and flowers that made the whole area very peaceful. This was the place the Knight of the Rueful Figure selected as the spot where he would do his penance, and seeing it, he cried out in a loud voice as if he were out of his mind: "This is the spot, O Heavens, that I select to bewail the misfortune into which you yourselves have plunged me. This is the spot where the moisture from my eyes shall swell the waters of this little stream and my unending sighs shall stir incessantly the leaves of these mountain trees in testimony of the pain that my tortured heart is suffering. And you, rustic gods, whoever you may be, who dwell in this inhospitable place, listen to the plaints of this unlucky lover whom long absence and some fancied jealousy have driven to mourn among these rugged rocks and to complain of the cruel temper of that ungrateful beauty, the sum total of human beauty.[16]

Here a *locus amoenus* is turned into a *locus terribilis* because the mood of the unhappy lover superimposes a different interpretation onto the scenery. *Locus amoenus* and *locus terribilis* are perceived as opposites, although the former is observed as a pleasant literary device set in the most forbidding desert, the latter develops not out of the natural setting, but rather from the projection of the suffering lover's feelings upon the scenery. In this case the figurative setting of the *locus amoenus* appears purely figurative, whereas the projected *locus terribilis*, in effect, seems to correspond more to the actual desert location at which Don Quixote finds himself.

Further characteristics of the *locus terribilis* are the barrenness of the desert and an uncivilized, barbaric environment. A *locus terribilis* is shrouded in silence; there are no bubbling waters or singing birds. The location of unhappiness and lament is populated with wild animals, wolves, snakes and owls, all threatening creatures, combined with disgust – the later nausea of the existentialists. In the 17th century remoteness is always connected with danger and fear. Quite different is the understanding of remoteness in the late 18th century and early 19th century when Nature, still relatively untouched by humankind, is attractive, respected, sought, and inspiring. This is the time when the Romantics began to venture out into Nature to climb mountains (what Petrarch had already done 500 years before when he was climbing Mount Ventoux). The Age of Reason, the Enlightenment, though, shunned Nature, withdrew from it and ignored its power of place and being haven. Reason tried to be the measure, instead of the human being. Darkness and fear, unilluminated by either sun or moon, spread despair because of the loss of natural light. Trees were too dense to let the light through. Since the sun is not shining, and darkness prevails, the lonely lover laments the death of the beloved at a deserted, desolate place, the *locus terribilis*, the exact opposite of the *locus amoenus'* pleasant ambiance.[17] The relative closeness of the *locus terribilis* to the machinery of the horror novel of the 18th century may just be mentioned in passing.

It is quite remarkable that German writers of the 17th century paid so much attention to the *locus terribilis*. The origin seems to go back to antiquity.[18] In Propertius' 18th elegy the lover seeks a remote location for his lament since he would thereby remain *impune* (unpunished) by his *domina* (beloved). Apparently it is fear of punishment by the beloved that drives Propertius' lover into the desert. Petrarch has his lover also seek solitude in deserted locations in order to avoid being seen in his sadness by fellow humans. Wanting to hide one's pain, and one's extreme suffering seem to make the unfortunate one avoid society. The lover wants to suffer his pain alone, in secrecy, unobserved, and undisturbed. Nature does no longer provide consolation: the lover is alone with himself in his despair. Nature remains removed and aloof although the lamenting lover is directly surrounded by it. The modern poet Hermann Hesse says in his poem "Im Nebel": "kein Mensch sieht den andern, jeder ist allein."[19] The *locus terribilis* is the place of refuge from society and from the world. It is the place of retreat of the human being into the loneliness of the suffering self.

By seeking the *locus terribilis* the lover proves his unshaken love however much it may be threatened by dangers and obstacles surrounding him. Love remains steadfast as we have already seen in *Tristan* and *Don Quixote*, the latter even fakes his lament in order to copy the exemplary Amadis. The *locus terribilis* is the place of challenge in this setting of courtly romance, painful love, and perseverance.[20] In a way, the *locus terribilis* is an outgrowth from the medieval concept of adventure since it provides the location of activity for the lamenting lover, the lonely hermit, and the contemplative person, who are all driven by a discomfort, a despair, and a feeling of loss for which they want to compensate by retreating and submitting themselves to solitary suffering. We could speak even of a *locus destructionis* that has already been hinted at in the context of the Sierra Morena episode in which Don Quixote imitates and satirized the lover's lament without having a better reason than imitation.

While Descartes and the encyclopaedists may have believed themselves able to lay the groundwork for the best of all possible worlds sometime in the future, it is Leibniz' propagation of that very idea that will again be satirized, this time by Voltaire in *Candide*. Seeking the best of all possible worlds, and even finding it in the utopia of El Dorado, Candide cannot tolerate the perfect locus of being which reason has dreamed and speculated so much about. Candide tires of the condition of an eternal *locus amoenus* when he has come to El Dorado as much as he would tire of a constant life at a *locus terribilis*. He has to return to the world of opposites, of contrasts, of changes, of seasons, and, above all, to the world of creativity. Only in this context can Candide finally find and build his own El Dorado. On the way to that perfect place, apparently, has to be despair, suffering, and *destructio* as a means of learning and experiencing sensitivity to the world surrounding us. The *locus destructionis* is our own place of self-affirmation, involving rejection and re-acceptance in a creative manner. It is the feeling of *Angst* and despair which Kafka and Auden defined as central to our being in this century. It is the fear of Heidegger's being *unbehaust*, of "being without a home", that in our days drove Heidegger's philosophy, when the *locus amoenus* of the youth of our literary culture began to turn into the *locus terribilis* of modernity. Destruction of the happy past, removal from Nature and from the happy self are now to be taken for granted. preceded already by Cézanne, Picasso's visible de-assembling, the breaking up of form into its elements and the re-constructing of the human image into simultaneous representation of profile and front view in one frame, Heidegger's probing and etymological description of the destruction of metaphysics, and Derrida's de-construction of its intellectual forms with their own meaning and context are all invitations to the creation of new, albeit strainingly-grafted *loci amoeni* of our own making, devoid of Nature's essence, but pretending form of an artificial nature. The invitation to the elemental passion of creativity remains; and hope, reaching far beyond the darkness transcending, finally, the empty space on Mark Rothko's last, solely black canvasses just before his self-destruction, must persist.

The elemental passion of place makes us seek our own *locus amoenus* in which we can feel at home with our own level of creativity. El Dorado, the dream of the best of all possible worlds, remains a utopia if we do not appropriate it and bring it down to reality which is, in effect, our own level. On our own level we find the location of our own potential; at that level our own El Dorado is real and no longer utopia. At that level it is our garden which we can work contentedly ourselves at our own pace: at that level it is the creation of our own *locus amoenus* with all its wonderful characteristics that set the mind free into a state of creativity and the openness of peace. So that creativity as an elemental passion can flourish, feeling and reason must seek the state of balance at all times. The strife for order must be flexible with the full awareness that the locus of human existence is modified and flexibly defined by the proverbial fact that "to err is human" and that errors shall at least be forgiven "sine ira et studio" according to the principle of Roman law that says "in dubio pro reo" (when in doubt, [rule] in favor of the accused). And yet, there is always in a world of duplicity a caveat that Candide also knew about and which is called in modern terminology "special interest" that misleads but pretends to lead. In Edmund Spenser's sixteenth-century *Fairie Queene* it is stated in verse and allegorically by the savage tempter in the coat of rusty iron and gold

> God of the world and worldling I me call,
> Great Mammon, greatest god below the sky.[21]

Southern Illinois University at Carbondale

NOTES

[1] Plato, *The Apology of Socrates*, transl. Benjamin Jowett.
[2] (Berne: Francke, 1948), pp. 201ff.
[3] See Dagmar Thoss, *Studien zum Locus Amoenus im Mittelalter*. Wiener Romantische Arbeiten, Vol. X (Vienna, Stuttgart: Braumüller, 1972), p. 35.
[4] Homer, *Odyssey*, transl. Robert Fitzgerald, Bk. V, 211.
[5] My transl.: throughout the centuries [the *locus amoenus* was] the sign of a shared way of perceiving Nature and feeling in harmony with it. See Roger Dragonetti, *La poétique des trouvères dans la chanson courtoise: contribution á l'étude de la rhétorique médiévale* (Brugge: De Tempel, 1960), p. 163.

[6] Gottfried von Straßburg, *Tristan*, transl. A. T. Hatto (London: Penguin, 1987), p. 270.
[7] Gottfried, p. 280.
[8] Giovanni Boccaccio, *The Decameron* (The First Day), transl. Mark Musa and Peter E. Bondanella.
[9] Francis Petrarch, *Sonnets to Laura*, no. 333 (Ite, rime dolenti, al duro sasso), transl. Morris Bishop.
[10] See Klaus Garber, *Der locus amoenus und der locus terribilis. Literatur und Leben*, Vol. XVI n.F. (Cologne, Vienna: Böhlau, 1974), pp. 226ff.
[11] See Garber, reference to Schirmer's "Echo," p. 228.
[12] As an extreme example see Diderot's *Encyclopédie* in which the entry "Christianity" refers the reader to "Cannibalism."
[13] Miguel de Cervantes Saavedra, *Don Quixote*, transl. Walter Starkie (New York: Signet Classic, 1964), pp. 240–241.
[14] Cervantes, p. 242, underlining mine.
[15] Cervantes, p. 243.
[16] Cervantes, p. 244.
[17] See Garber, p. 261.
[18] See Garber, p. 265.
[19] My transl.: nobody takes notice of the other, everybody is occupied with himself.
[20] See Garber, p. 269.
[21] Edmund Spenser, *The Faerie Queene*, Bk.II, Canto VII (The Cave of Mammon), 8.

WILLIAM D. MELANEY

SPENSER'S POETIC PHENOMENOLOGY: HUMANISM AND THE RECOVERY OF PLACE

The present paper defends the thesis that Spenser's recovery of place, as enacted in *The Faerie Queene*, Book VI, can be linked in a direct way to his use of a poetic phenomenology which informs and clarifies his work as an epic writer. Traditional humanism is sometimes defined as an attempt to appropriate the meaning of classical art and literature in terms of "timeless" philosophical truths. Spenser's originality as a Renaissance poet, however, has much to do with his use of literary procedures that express but also complicate his relationship to traditional humanism. While the heart of Spenser's "Book of Courtesy" enacts a Neo-Platonic movement from the lower levels of temporal existence to an exalted vision of spiritual perfection, this same section can be read along phenomenological lines as a mysterious adventure that embraces self and other, personality and community, aesthetics and ethics, in a sequence of images that opens up a new interpretation of imaginative fulfillment.[1] The burden of this paper, therefore, is largely concerned with demonstrating how this poetic sequence instates the "truth" of place in a way that is inseparable from the meaning of Spenser's humanism.[2]

Spenser's celebration of Courtesy as a virtue involves an appreciation of social values as well as a commitment to transcendent notions of Good. This peculiar combination cannot be understood apart from a dialectical appraisal of Spenser's view of nature. This view embraces two extremes. On the one hand, Spenser identifies nature with the principle of fecundity and abundance. According to this view, which mainly derives from Aristotle, nature is a visible source of human values. In the Garden of Adonis, for instance, nature emerges as a productive force and a spectacular point of origin (III.vi.42). On the other hand, Spenser also maintains that nature can function as the invisible source of moral virtue. This more Platonic conception informs his representation of major characters, and also influences his critical attitude toward pagan mythology.[3]

The difference between these two conceptions of nature can be understood in terms of the tension that governs *The Faerie Queene* as a whole. The Aristotelian conception is more closely related to traditional conceptions of political authority. At the beginning of Book VI, for instance, courtesy as a virtue is associated with the reign of Queen Elizabeth (VI.proem 6, line 4). Thus Spenser seems to associate courtesy as a virtue with the legitimate rule of a contemporary monarch. At the end of Book VI, however, the idea of pastoral as a place of magic and innocence reinforces the Platonic conception of nature, and suggests that Spenser does not wish to derive virtue from either a limited experience of nature or from basically political arrangements.

The idea that virtue can be institutional as well as basic to human communities underlines Spenser's epic narrative as a recovery of place which happens *in* language and ultimately concerns the movement of the soul toward imaginative fulfillment.[4] In the introductory stanzas of his epic, Spenser wishes to establish the connection between courtesy and everyday concerns. While courtesy as a virtue belongs in the hall of princes, it is also said to be "the ground, /And root of ciuill conuersation" (VI.i.1, lines 1–6). Spenser indicates in this way that courtesy goes beyond specific political interests and penetrates the very language of civilized life.

An early allusion to the meaning of courtesy invokes the figure of Calidore, whose "gracious speach, did steale men's hearts away" (VI.i.2, line 6). However, Spenser also refers to "the triall of true curtesie" where an ecclesiastical court must pass sentence on a loveless Mirabella (VI.proem.5, lines 1–2). The illusions of the world are often mistaken for ideal beauty: "But vertues seat is deepe within the mynd, /And not in outward shows, but inward thoughts defynd" (VI.poem.5, lines 8–9). Hence Spenser rejects a narrowly political conception of virtue in order to affirm the importance of subjectivity to moral understanding. Primarily for this reason, I wish to contend that the figure of Calidore takes part in a phenomenological movement toward spiritual insight.[5]

While functioning as a counter to pure nature and its attendant virtue, Calidore must discover the relationship between the wisdom of humanity and the demands of political life. Near the beginning of his adventures, we learn about the "innate gifts" of Calidore: his honesty and love of truth are commended (VI.i.3, line 9). The philosophical basis for this combination of talents can be found in Castiglione's *Book of the Courtier*. Here Gasparo explains to Ottaviano that certain important virtues cannot be learned: "but I think that to those who have them they have been given by nature and by God."[6] Calidore's moral education within the epic context takes the form of a "recollection" of virtue that allows him to partially overcome the difference between nature and politics.

Unlike other heroes in Spenser's epic, Calidore is absent from the center of his own text: Calidore disappears at the end of canto ii and does not re-appear prior to canto ix. It would seem that Calepine in some way substitutes for him during the interim. As a much less skillful Calidore, Calepine tries to perform the function of the traditional hero. However, his presence never ceases to remind us of Calidore's absence. Because he lacks the manifest qualities of the traditional hero, Calidore's virtue is credible and unobtrusive.

Calidore helps us see that "courtesy" is probably the Spenserian form of Aristotle's "near-friendliness": it, too, properly belongs to the man who is neither subservient nor disagreeable.[7] Occupying the mean between two extremes, courtesy thus defined is a kind of goodwill that enables us to relate to everyone in a like manner: "Eunoia or goodwill bears some resemblance to friendship, but is not in fact friendship, for we may feel goodwill towards strangers and persons who are not aware of our feeling – a thing impossible between friends."[8] However, while it draws strangers into its warm embrace, courtesy also might be a precondition for the emergence of more exalted forms of experience. Aristotle clearly understood the possible connection between the experience of beauty and the attainment of spiritual truth: "Nobody falls in love who has not been first delighted by the sight of beauty, although it does not follow that a man who is delighted by the beauty of a person is in love."[9]

At the beginning of Book VI, we retreat from the plains, mountains and rocky coast and enter the wood of Faerie land. The scene of courtesy is a pastoral countryside. Violence and sadness pervade this world of archaic values: "There is an older tradition of 'gentilesse' derived from Provence and France, running through medieval romance literature, which had its rules and casuistry too, but expressed itself chiefly in actual example and a pervading chivalrous tone."[10] The tradition of courtesy, however, can involve the sudden appearance of various truths. Harry Berger contends that the repetition of specific motifs structures Book VI as a whole: "The most frequently repeated motif is, significantly enough, that of a character surprised in a moment of diversion."[11] All such moments must be understood within a moral context. For instance, the motif of the interrupted couple occurs twice (VI.ii.16–17; VI.iii.20–23). Each time, the discovery of love moves us closer to the vision of Mount Acidale. Many scenes of recognition must precede the great unveiling near the end of the Book of Courtesy (VI.x.27–28).

The trial of Mirabella establishes the low point in the history of courtesy. It precedes the slow ascent from a discourteous world. This entire movement takes place in three episodes that are represented by three different women: "Mirabella projects the germinal form of frustration, Serena and her Cannibals the germinal form of desire, Pastorella and her swains the germinal form of poetic recreation, all of which are infolded and transfigured by Colin's vision."[12] The extreme discourtesy of Mirabella results in an ecclesiastical court summons. The glorification of Serena among cannibals is the parody of a religious ceremony. Finally, the capture of Pastorella by Calidore is the prelude to the final vision of love on Mount Acidale. These three episodes have been said to imitate a Plotinian philosophy of love. However, they also might be interpreted as constituting a poetic phenomenology whereby courtesy is defined on the basis of three discontinuous moments.

The first episode dramatizes the pitfalls of immediate experience. Rejecting the moderate claims of courtesy, Mirabella uses her beauty in order to obtain power over men. Mira-bella is literally the "look of beauty" that enamors men and attempts to ruin them. The jury that presides over her trial condemns her to do penance: tomorrow she must walk the earth and love as many men as she formerly ruined (VI.vii.37). Mirabella's suitors are feudal retainers of Cupid and her plea of mercy is a religious petition. Both of these facts seem to indicate that Mirabella takes part in an ecclesiastical, rather than a civil, trial.[13] This interpretation supports the view that love (in the religious sense) is a central issue in Book VI. It also suggests that lovelessness is the supreme discourtesy in Spenser's phenomenology.

In contrast, the abduction of Serena by cannibals leads to a basic conflict in interpretations. On the one hand, we condemn the behavior of the cannibals as completely abhorrent. The abduction of Serena is particularly shocking insofar as it places a brutal practice in an aesthetic perspective. The cannibals who adore Serena eventually raise her "divine" body upon an altar of sacrifice (VI.viii.42–45). We instinctively reject any figurative analogy between a savage practice and civilized modes of worship.

This response, however, could prevent us from coming to terms with the full meaning of the episode as an adventure in Renaissance anthropology. Before the festivities begin, the cannibals must be restrained by a spiritual superior: it seems that "religion held even theiues in measure" (VI.viii.43, line 9). Spenser's humanistic perspective allows him to imagine genuine order in a primitive context. By directing his people to the altar, this figure seems to organize these forms into a social whole. Compared to this event, the love of Mirabella is regressive: her beauty does not "rise" but actually "descends" into a physical world: "Spenser's transition to the cannibal ring logically reduces the sophisticated evil to its confused origin and, in effect, allows him to begin all over again."[14]

It is probable that Spenser knew of Montaigne's famous essay on cannibals: his anthropological imagination seems to owe a great deal to it. After discussing the habits of cannibals at some length, Montaigne integrates relativism into an argument against his would-be detractors: "I am not so anxious that we should note the horrible savagery of these acts as concerned that, whilst judging their faults correctly, we should be so blind to our own."[15] Like Montaigne, Spenser attempts to link anthropological awareness to the potential enhancement of moral sensitivity.

Hence the "raising up" of Calidore's Pastorella both glorifies nature and prefigures its transformation (VI.ix.8). There is an irony in this act that becomes evident in retrospect: "In naming her, the swains reduce her from an aristocrat to a shepherdess; in worshipping her, they exalt her from an aristocrat to a goddess, identifying the symbol with the reality to which it refers."[16] Later on, we will discover that this child of nature is really a high-born daughter (VI.xii.20). If the cannibal ring represents the lowest starting-point of human culture, then the pastoral ring represents the beginning of an aesthetic departure. The poetic qualities of the ring prepare us for the reduced geometry of intellectual beauty and a less ambiguous symbolism.

A further contrast is implied in the encounter between Calidore and Pastorella's protector, old Meliboe. After chasing the Blatant Beast from court to country, Calidore returns at the beginning of canto ix. His absence from the center of the poem has not gone unobserved. It created a moral vacuum that his return promises to fill. In his encounter with Meliboe, however, Calidore merge as the typical heroic protagonist. While visiting Meliboe's peasant lodging, Calidore expresses envy for the life of rural simplicity (VI.ix.19). An "entraunced" Calidore momentarily rejects his political vocation as he speaks to the wise recluse (VI.ix.27–28). But Meliboe will have none of this, and refuses to view political life as an external achievement: "It is the mynd, that maketh good or ill," he tells Calidore (VI.ix.30, line 1). Spenser presents Meliboe as a relative contrast to the more worldly Calidore: "Boethian stoicism was not Spenser's whole card; but neither was there any reason to doubt that he meant Meliboe's 'sensible words' (VI.ix.26) as the expression of one facet of an acceptable attitude."[17]

Prior to the vision on Mount Acidale, Calidore fails to understand the unity of real and ideal worlds.[18] Traditionally, the figure of Calidore is associated with the name of Sir Philip Sidney. This identification lies at the basis of our optimism with respect to Calidore's future. Calidore is a man of the world whose natural gifts lift him above common ambitions. As the exemplar of courtesy, he must mingle with others and advance the cause of virtue. But his idealism derives from an ideal court, rather than from a purely political one: "In Book VI diplomacy is less a technique than a symbol, and Spenser does not show Calidore's exquisite tact simply in order to make him more convincing as a Renaissance courtier."[19] Hence the "fulfillment" of political service requires a poetic vision of the supernatural. Nature is less resourceful than the most truthful poets: "Her world is brazen, the poets deliver a golden."[20]

In Spenser's epic, therefore, the return to pastoral culminates in the overcoming of nature as an external obstacle. Our first glimpse of Venus is significant in this respect: her place appears to exclude nature in its grosser aspects (VI.x.7, lines 1–5). It is here that Calidore has his vision of the hundred dancing maidens (VI.x.11, lines 6–9). Three Graces appear in the center of a ring and circle a solitary figure, who wears a rose garland. Because her beauty surpasses that of all the others, she is "that faire one/ That in the midst was placed parauaunt" (VI.x.15, lines 6–7). We learn from the narrator that this mysterious figure is Colin Clout's lost love: "Thy loue is there aduaunst to be another Grace" (VI.x.16, lines 8–9). In a moment, this whole apparition suddenly vanishes.

The rough shepherd who has played his pipe in a fit of anger then proceeds to offer his intruder an interpretation of the vision as a whole. It is what we learn about the central figure that primarily interests us. At first glance, she is "but a countrey lasse, /Yet she all other countrey lasses farre did pass" (VI.x.25, lines 8–9). Her pre-eminent beauty distinguishes her from all other women. From another standpoint, however, she seems to condense or contain the qualities of her companions (VI.x.27, lines 1–3). No longer a country maiden, she finally becomes "Great *Gloriana*, greatest maiesry" (VI.x.28, line 3). Reconciled in spirit to the virtue of his Queen, Calidore can now return to his beloved

Pastorella. The thrust of what he sees points toward a vast firmament: "For a moment the beloved is poised alone in a visionary splendor; in the next moment she recedes to make room for Gloriana though, with the words, 'Sunne of the world,' the two Ideas make brief contact."[21]

The vision on Mount Acidale reveals Spenser's indebtedness to traditional iconography. Although he may not have actually known of Botticelli's "Primavera," Spenser works with the same principles that govern this composition. For instance, the painting shows Venus standing between two groups of maidens: one group produces an earthly Flora; but the other group contains a lovely Castitas, who turns toward a heavenly Mercury. Taken as a whole, this entire sequence (or action) reproduces the basic structure of Plotinian spirituality.[22] The separate moments of this sequence only become "simultaneous" within the sphere of the canvas.

As a poet, Spenser reproduces the same movement by means of language. In the uncertain identity of the central figure on Mount Acidale, we discern the flickering visage of an earthly maiden or a celestial Queen. The rhythm of the poem intensifies from one stanza to the next: beauty that can only exist in time haunts us as it turns into silence. Calidore patiently listens, but he cannot separate himself from what he hears: his chivalrous mission may have led him to discover an actual Gloriana, but it also suggests that ideal beauty must transcend the limitations of space and time. Unlike the piping shepherd, Colin Clout, with whom the identity of the poet at last ceases to be confused, Calidore must live in the tension between ideals and their fulfillment. This tension commits him, in advance, to a future life of concrete acts and the company of historical persons. As he leaves his pastoral setting, Calidore prepares to perform his remaining duties.

I would like to conclude this discussion by restating my position concerning the relevance of phenomenology to Spenser's work as an epic poet. On the one hand, what I have chosen to call Spenser's "poetic phenomenology" at least suggests that the traditional interpretation of this philosophical sources might be considered from a phenomenological standpoint. At the beginning of this paper, I alluded to the role that both Aristotle and Plato might have had in developing Spenser's concept of virtue. Within the course of the paper, however, I presented the goal of the Book of Courtesy in terms of a poetic phenomenology that helps situate the recovery of place within a narrative context. This goal is inseparable from the mission of Calidore himself as a typical representative of Renaissance conceptions of virtue and political education. At the same time, it cannot be identified too closely with Calidore's personal function in the epic narrative.

The recovery of place involves a slow spiritual awakening that embraces the lowest levels of erotic awareness as well as the highest reaches of "ideal" experience. While this phenomenological progression requires social interaction, it also assumes the form of a subjective adventure that does not completely coincide with the actions of any single character. At the end of Spenser's epic, therefore, the recovery of place becomes a sublime metaphor whose deeper meaning is corroborated by tradition and phenomenology alike: "But what do I bid you love in the soul? – the beauty of the soul. The beauty of bodies is a visible light, the beauty of the soul is an invisible light; the light of the soul is truth."[23]

NOTES

[1] In this paper, I do not limit the meaning of phenomenology to the work of its founder, or to any single phase of its long development. Nevertheless, I derive the concept of "imaginative fulfillment" from Husserl's attempt to describe the experience of truth on a phenomenological basis. I believe that this concept can be related to a broad range of human activities.

[2] While the sense of place that relates to poetry may not coincide with truth, it opens up a world in which truth can occur. In *Being and Time*, Heidegger explores the concept of world as a phenomenological alternative to Cartesian dualism. His late writings on art and language demonstrate how this concept can be linked to place as a poetic concern.

[3] For instance, while *FQ* II.xii abounds in classical references, Spenser inverts a facile naturalism in his use of ancient sources. Guyon resembles Odysseus in his voyage into the Bower of Bliss, but he also shows how the rejection of artifice can parallel the affirmation of natural abundance as an ethically mediated value.

[4] By emphasizing the role of language in the recovery of place, I leave open the issue of whether or not interpretation must be ontologically grounded. On the other hand, I contend that imaginative fulfillment is already a "linguistic" phenomenon on the most primordial level. Hence my use of phenomenology is especially suited for the examination of literature.

[5] The claim that Calidore takes part in a phenomenological movement toward truth should not be confused with the identification of Calidore with an imputed narrative subject. While subjectivity plays a crucial role in Spenser's epic as a whole, Calidore himself is by no means the narrative "center" of Courtesy.

[6] Baldesar Castiglione, *The Book of the Courtier*, Book IV, sec. 11, p. 295.

[7] See Aristotle, *The Ethics of Aristotle*, II. vi, pp. 70–71:

In the other sphere of the agreeable – the general business of life – the person who is agreeable, supposing him to have no ulterior object, is 'obsequious'; if he has no such object, he is a 'flatterer'. The man who is deficient in this quality and takes every opportunity of making himself disagreeable may be called 'peevish' or 'sulky' or 'surly'.

[8] Aristotle, *The Ethics*, IX, p. 269.
[9] Aristotle, *The Ethics*, IX, p. 269.
[10] Graham Hough, *A Preface to the Faerie Queene*, p. 202.
[11] Harry Berger, "A Secret Discipline: *The Faerie Queene*, Book VI," in *Form and Convention in the Poetry of Edmund Spenser*, p. 40.
[12] Berger, "A Secret Discipline" in *Form and Convention*, p. 51.
[13] Cf. Arnold Williams, *Flower On A Lowly Stalk: The Sixth Book Of The Faerie Queene*, p. 108.
[14] Berger, "A Secret Discipline" in *Form and Convention*, p. 58.
[15] Michel de Montaigne, "On Cannibals", *Essays* (I.31), p. 113.
[16] Berger, "A Secret Discipline" in *Form and Convention*, p. 61.
[17] Alastair Fowler, *Spenser and the Numbers of Time*, p. 224.
[18] I contend that Calidore's reconciliation of ideal and real must be understood in terms of the phenomenological difference between *noesis* and *noema* as paired terms. In the political sphere, this means that Calidore's actions as a Renaissance courtier never leave the world of experience entirely behind. In the sphere of art, it means that the difference between the natural Pastorella and the supernatural Gloriana expresses an essential ambiguity that lies at the heart of the noematic correlate.
[19] Donald Cheney, *Spenser's Image of Nature: Wild Man and Shepherd in the Faerie Queene*, p. 185.
[20] Sir Philip Sidney, *The Defense of Poesy* in *Sir Philip Sidney: Selected Prose and Poetry*, p. 108.
[21] Harry Berger, "A Secret Discipline" in *Form and Convention*, p. 72.
[22] Cf. Edgar Wind, *Pagan Mysteries in the Renaissance*, p. 105. Its basic form is: emanatio – conversio – remeatio. The Zephyr's "descent" into Flora leads to the "conversion" in the Dance of the Graces. "Re-ascent" occurs in the turning of Castitas toward Mercury.
[23] Ficino, *Ficino's Commentary on Plato's Symposium*, XVIII: "How The Soul Is To The Beauty Of God", p. 213. Compare to Husserl's citation of Augustine in *Cartesian Meditations*, section 64, p. 157.

BIBLIOGRAPHY

Alpers, Paul J. *The Poetry of the Faerie Queene*. New Jersey: Princeton U.P., 1967.
Aristotle. *The Ethics of Aristotle*. Trans. J. A. K. Thomson. London: Penguin Books, 1971.
Berger, Harry. *Form and Convention in the Poetry of Edmund Spenser*. Ed. by William Nelson, "A Secret Discipline: *The Faerie Queene*, Book VI." New York: Columbia U.P., 1961, pp. 35–75.
Castiglione, Baldesar. *The Book of the Courtier*. New York: Anchor Books, 1959.

Cheney, Donald. *Spenser's Image of Nature: Wild Man and Shepherd in the Faerie Queene*. New Haven: Yale U.P., 1966, pp. 1–17, 176–258.

Ficino, Marsilio. *Marsilio Ficino's Commentary on Plato's Symposium*. Trans. Sears Reynolds Jayne. New York: U. of Missouri, 1944.

Fowler, Alastair. *Spenser and the Numbers of Time*, Chapter VIII: "The Book of Venus". London: Routledge and Kegan Paul, 1964, pp. 222–226.

Gadamer, Hans-Georg. *The Idea of the Good in Platonic-Aristotelian Philosophy*. Trans. P. Christopher Smith. New Haven: Yale U.P., 1986.

Heidegger, Martin. *Being and Time*. Trans. John Macquarrie and Edward Robinson. New York: Harper and Row, 1977.

Heidegger, Martin. "The Origin of the Work of Art," "What are Poets For?", "Language". *Poetry, Language, Thought*. Trans. Albert Hofstadter. New York: Harper and Row, 1977, pp. 15–87. 89–142.

Hough, Graham. *A Preface to the Faerie Queene*. New York: The Norton Library, 1963, pp. 15–137, 201–212.

Husserl, Edmund. *Cartesian Meditations: In Introduction to Phenomenology*. Trans. Dorian Cairns. The Hague: Martinus Nijhoff, 1960.

Husserl, Edmund. *Ideas I: General Introduction to Pure Phenomenology*. Trans. W. R. Boyce Gibson. London: Collier Books, 1969.

Husserl, Edmund. *The Phenomenology of Internal Time-Consciousness*. Ed. Martin Heidegger. Trans. Thomas S. Churchill. Bloomington: Indiana U.P., 1966.

Montaigne, Michel de. *Essays*. Trans. by J. M. Cohen. Book One, Chapter 31: "On Cannibals". New York: Penguin Books, 1976, pp. 105–119.

Parker, M. Pauline. *Allegory of the Faerie Queene*. Oxford: The Clarendon Press, 1962, pp. 1–65, 228–322.

Sidney, Sir Philip. *The Defense of Poesy*, in *Sir Philip Sidney: Selected Prose and Poetry*. Ed. by Robert Kimbrough. Wisconsin: U. of Wisconsin P., 1983, pp. 102–158.

Spenser, Edmund. *Spenser: Poetical Works*. Ed. by J. C. Smith and E. De Selincourt. London: U. of Oxford P., 1969.

Williams, Arnold. *Flower on a Lowly Stalk: The Sixth Book of the* Faerie Queene. Michigan: Michigan State U.P., 1967, pp. 4–128.

Wind, Edgar. *Pagan Mysteries in the Renaissance*, Chapter VII: "Botticelli's Primavera". New York: The Norton Library, 1968, pp. 113–127.

SITANSU RAY

THE ASRAMA-ANTHEM:
TAGORE'S PASSION FOR SANTINIKETAN

> *Amader Santiniketan*: Our Santiniketan, Ah! Our beloved Santiniketan! She is the dearest of all to us.
>
> Our heart swings in her lap of open sky. We perceive her ever anew every now and then.
>
> We have our fair of flora and the recreation of open terrain. Our dawn and dusk are fondled by the affectionate firmament.
>
> Our shady avenue of *sal* trees plays the music of forest to us and the leafy *amlaki* grove is always delighted with the dance of its leaves. O, Our Santiniketan!
>
> Wherever we may have to go away, she is not far from us. The *Sitar* of love within our mind is attuned to her music. She has attuned our minds in unison. She has brought forth our collective mind in the bond of brotherhood. O, Our Santiniketan!

This is just an approximate meaning of our *asrama* anthem "*Amader Santiniketan*", composed by Tagore. It is also our institutional anthem, i.e., the university anthem of Visva-Bharati. It has been sung in chorus by the academic community and campus dwellers at the close of each function and festival, including the annual convocation.

Its tune is in the mixed tonal array of *Bilawal* (a major tone mode) and *Kalyan* (the mode with the augmented fourth). It is set to a jubilant three-beat rhythm. On the whole, the lyrico-tonal entity of the song bears Tagore's love and passion for this place. The word Santiniketan means abode of peace. The original building, built by Tagore's father Maharshi Debendranath, was called Santiniketan. The name of the whole place is derived after it.

The word *asrama* has various phenomenological connotations. It means a hermitage, a residence, a cottage, a refuge, a stage of life, a religious institution etc. The place Santiniketan is called an *asrama* in the sense of an academico-cultural colony, created with a view to reviving the spirituo-academic atmosphere of the ancient Indian forest colonies of sages and preceptors.

Now, let us flash back into the phenomena of Tagore's previous absorption in this place.

When Tagore was just a young boy of ten to eleven years of age, he came to this place with his father Maharshi Debendranath Tagore. Two miles away from Bolpur railway station, it was just a barren land at that time. Maharshi built his abode of peace there. The boy Tagore moved freely here and there, playing and collecting pebbles. He was, as it were, a newer Livingstone exploring the place, as he described himself in the reminiscences of his boyhood days. Maharshi meditated on a mound or under the *Chhatim* tree, a few steps away from his abode. Later on a temple of coloured glass set into iron frames was erected for the congregation.

Tagore's school days in Calcutta were horrible to him. He could not stand the confinement of a class room. Contrarily, the vast open terrain adjacent to Bolpur attracted him most. During Maharshi's days it was just a resort for change and meditation. Later on, when Tagore was forty he started his school, which gradually evolved as a world university or Visva-Bharati (*Yatra visvam bhavatyekanidam*, where the whole world finds its nest), along with Tagore's noble philosophy of education of freedom of self, love for nature and realization of the infinite. Starting with educating infants, all the levels of secondary, higher secondary, under-graduate, post-graduate education and research in science, humanities, fine arts and music are within the scope of Visva-Bharati. One more specialty of the place is that it imparts, not mere bookish lessons, but harmony of nature, culture and creativeness; aesthetics and motivation in all levels of students and teachers; a little meditation every morning followed by chanting of the Vedic hymns and singing of songs; a congregation once a week; seasonal festivals throughout the year including those of the spring season, the rainy season and the autumn with appropriate music and dance etc., surcharge and maintain the spirit of the place.

It is to be noted that most of Tagore's *Gitanjali* (song-offerings) songs and poems, his later plays and lyrical dramas, songs and dance-dramas were composed at Santiniketan. Tagore's passionate nostalgia for this place is still imbibed in most of these works as it were.

Tagore's ancestral palace at Jorasanko in Calcutta may have archival value, but Santiniketan is the ideal creation of his own. It must be admitted that the original atmosphere and span of Santiniketan during Tagore's life-time cannot remain the same since its posthumous growth cannot but accommodate present-day needs. Still, it has retained some of its original characteristics and specialties and ideals by virtue of our co-curricular chores. On the whole, Tagore's belonging to San-tiniketan, his creative nostalgic passion for this place, his spirituo-romantic involvement with this place reverberate again and again with the asrama-anthem:

>*Amader Santiniketan*
>*Se ye sab hote apan* . . . etc.
>O, our Santiniketan, the dearest of all to us . . .

Visva-Bharati University, Santiniketan, India

BIBLIOGRAPHY

Mukhopadhyay, Prabhat Kumar. "Santiniketan", *Rabindra-Jivani* (Rabindranath's biography), Visva-Bharati Publishing Department, 1970 edition, pp. 39–41.

Tagore, Rabindranath. Notation of the asrama anthem, made by Sailaja Ranjan Majumdar, *Swarabitan* (notation books) Vol. 55, Visva-Bharati Publishing Department, 1958, pp. 50–62.

Tagore, Rabindranath. *Asramer Rup O Vikas* (the form and growth of the Asrama). *Rabindra Rachanavali* (Collected works of Tagore, henceforth abbreviated as *R.R.*). Birth Centenary Edition 1961, Government of West Bengal, Vol. 11, pp. 723–744.

Tagore, Rabindranath. *Visva-Bharati*, *R.R.*, Vol. 11, pp. 745–810.

Tagore, Rabindranath. *Santiniketan Brahmacharyasram*, *R.R.* 11, pp. 811–824.

Tagore, Rabindranath. "*Asramer Shiksha*" (the teachings of the asram), *R.R.* 11, pp. 711–714.

Tagore, Rabindranath. "*Himalaya Yatra*" (On the way to the Himalayas), *Jibansmriti* (the reminiscences), *R.R.*, Vol. 10, pp. 40–43.

Tagore, Rabindranath. "*Amader Santiniketan*": the asrama anthem, *Gitabitan* (collection of songs), Visva-Bharati Publishing Department, 1970 edition, p. 562.

Tagore, Rabindranath. "My School", *Personality*, Macmillan (1917), Indian edition 1985, pp. 111–150.

MARY F. CATANZARO

THE ELEMENTAL SPACE OF PASSION: THE TOPOS OF PURGATORY IN BECKETT'S *PLAY*

With *Play*,[1] Beckett dared to write a drama whose language does violent things. In a play where there are no longer any recognizable subjects, speech, repetition, and musical structure depict the elemental passion of the masked figures, forming the discursive frame, or space, of the grotesquely visible. Saint Augustine's famous motto, first used in *Waiting for Godot*: "Do not despair, one of the thieves was saved; do not presume, one of the thieves was damned," is the dialectic upon which *Play* is built. It generates the symmetry of despair and hope that preserves the trio's misshapen passion. After all that the subjects in *Play* suffer as a result of m's "affair" and his troubled marriage, the threesome find themselves still confronted with perils not less but far more formidable than those through which they have so narrowly made their way. Prior to their present purgatory, the subjects now emerge from a scene of ruin and moral havoc the like of which had never darkened their imaginations.

The choric structure of *Play* is the scaffold through which the subjects recount the unimaginable: those terrifying impressions from their former existence. The threesome are drawn together by their shared experience of having everything come to nothing; of finding that even the simplest routines become acts of will, self-created bulwarks against a sense of isolation and futility that engulf them. They have no dreams for the future or a better place; it is all they can do to live in their present purgatory of unremitting torment. To fully appreciate the grotesqueness of their space, it is necessary to explore the aleatory roles of pain and mental anguish that constitute the unimaginable communication among them.

Play probes the recesses of the individual's dark interior, its disturbing netherworld. Secluded, occluded, excluded, the subjects extend the limits of discourse, regardless of whatever anxieties it may produce. This drama discloses how the subjects' space and identity are dependent upon a voice whose nature is ambivalent and where the listener – the spotlight – is problematic; how the structure and habits of the subjects' delirium is the manifestation of social isolation and marginalization, or, possibly, madness. In the fragmented "codes' of their speech patterns, shattered forms of everyday communication are laid bare. *Play* explores the arena of pathological passion in language and how it may be the prime agent of danger in partnerships; how the middle course *in language* adopted from desires for safety may be found to lead directly to the bull's-eye of disaster; it shows how absolute is the need for a broad path of clear communication to maintain partnerships, irrespective of the ebb and flow of personal whims. If two people run away from each other, it is surely not to separate utterly but to flee the watching self.

In a world without past or future, the lack of hope removes urgency from the usual verbal games the voice plays with itself to fill linguistic voids. Here, where nothing is certain, language itself begins to dissolve. Not only does the voice contradict itself, but it also repeats its words. In the physical impediments of their purgatorial urns, and in their emotional and verbal ruptures, the subjects discover a virtual metaphysics of discord. The demonic light and the voice reveals that the subject *speaking* is no more than a succession of subverted, if not invisible, selves.

One of the complications arising from the voice that speaks, however, is that each subject becomes aware of a need for an other whose presence might offer some comfort to the multitude of his changing selves. The impasse, however, is never removed. *Play* addresses alienation in the realm of voiced memory, which calls into question the capacity of language to solve domestic problems. Here, the voice's structure demonstrates finite time within infinity; what it says in effect is that to live is to repeat in succession the fragments of one's past. To speak is to lie, in this case, and as a result the figures all the while realize the insufficiency of memory.

Using the fragmentary form, *Play* challenges the boundaries between how a subject *speaks* words and how words "frame" the other. Gregory Bateson[2] first developed the concept of "framing" to indicate how fleeting understandings and misunderstandings disrupt how we mean what we say and figuring out how others mean what they say. Using the "frame" form, Beckett questions the limits between the literal and the implied. With the obsessive rigor that has always marked his writing, Beckett returns to the themes that have haunted his work since the beginning: writing, death, and the self, but here the figures around which his discussion turns are the chimeric voice and the insular self.

The metaphor with which Beckett employs the frame in *Play* is gaming, or, as the title implies, play. Fragmentary speech is a play of limits, a play of ever-multiplied words in which no one word ever takes precedence. Through the randomness of the fragmentary, Beckett explores the relation of speaking to the spoken, the displacement of the voiced self in partnership and marriage, the temporality of life, and, specifically, sexual transgressions of the self toward others. In a space without past or future, where nothing is certain, language itself begins to dissolve. So it is that the adulterous affair of m and w 2 had all "been . . . just play" (p. 54). That w 2 suffers because her lover pulls back in his wooing stems from her need to be seen; she thus creates companionship for herself through her voice: "Is anyone listening to me? Is anyone looking at me? Is anyone bothering about me at all?" (p. 55). Her strategy is based on an inner, voiced narrative, a means at once of denying intolerable contradictions hidden beneath the surface of her relationship with m – as intolerable as the necessity that gives rise to relations of domination in their interactions – and of constructing on the very ground cleared by such a denial a substitute truth that makes her existence at least partly bearable, as she whines, "They might even feel sorry for me, if they could see me" (p. 56). Herbert Blau expresses the self-consciousness of being seen as an essential part of theater itself:

[T]he economy of the theater seems based upon the conversion of overinflated characters into objects of self-liquidating perception . . . never more intensely than in the liminal figures and corroded heroes of Beckett's antiplays: . . . [who are] eminently conscious . . . of . . . being seen; . . . as the buried memory bottoms out: 'Mere eye. No mind' – the talking heads in the funereal urns, stabbed by light and repeating themselves in *Play*. 'Am I as much as . . . being seen?'[3]

One of the turning points in telling the "story" over and over makes the obsessive need to talk an act of profound ritual importance. It also satisfies the Inquisitor, the light, double-checking to see if their accounts remain the same under interrogation. The light also causes the subjects to echo the doctrine of guilt and suffering. They can't get certain words out of their heads; they speak in clichés – a cartoon language, an excrescence of speech, in short, a jeremiad against married love. Tone of voice, consequently, becomes important for its own sake as well as speaking. The drama's text is grounded in erroneous perceptions of speech to emphasize the problems incurred by couples whenever their language veers towards passionate images and reminiscences of the past. On the one hand, the gap between the present and past is linked by memory, "accounts" of the past, verbal abuse, cynical repetitions. On the other hand, the demonic neutrality of the subjects' speech enables them to project onto each other the *image* of passion. The voice is marked in *Play* by diatribes and gossip to which they cleave relentlessly. As the light bathes each figure locked in a purgatorial urn, it forces them to rehearse a love gone sour. In addition, the hellish light is not consoling; rather, it hardens the features and emphasizes the subjects' isolation. *Play* contains no memorable characters, no great scenes. People, in its view, are puppets engaged in bizarre, unordered scenes, most containing no more than repetitions of jagged dialogue as they chronicle their fanatic destinies. These marginal subjects are secondary to the atmosphere: the silences suddenly descend upon conversations of the waking dead. Only the most primal emotions crack the Novocained facades of these vagabonds, blind to everything but their own sense of self-importance.

Love is the other, contrapuntal, theme about souls who cannot wrest themselves free of pervasive ennui, botched opportunities and the right truth uttered at the wrong time. In a remarkable scene, Beckett translates the uncanny into homely, even physical, terms, as w 1 says: "Judge then of my astoundment when one fine morning, as I was sitting stricken in the morning room, he slunk in, fell on his knees before me, buried his face in my lap and . . . confessed" (p. 48). A passage like this gets down to a kind of bedrock, an irreducible affiliation, between people. It is not the tale of infidelity that matters nearly so much as the *manner* of its telling, and, more precisely, the inability of these anatomized souls to keep from speaking, to express themselves, to account for their passion and torment.

Then too, the spotlight, instrument of publicity, conjuror of presence, coercer of the expressible, holds the three in their rehearsal of what their lives came to, of what life comes to. What is happening in *Play* is a curious phenomenon in which the non-linguistic medium of thought is a mental imagery that differs from the "verbal" sequences in that they are *triggered*. The subjects "picture" their former love-triangle, and then recount the ensuing visual images as they advance into language when provoked by the spotlight. Their accounts indicate that the progression of images are directed not only by the subject matter entertained but also by specific contingent properties of the particular image – the "smell" (p. 48) of w 2 by w 1 for example, or w 2's image of herself "doing [her] nails" (p. 49) just as m's wife comes calling. The shape of the image then initiates the image of another object or event sharing that form or color. One can envision a sequence of the subjects first verbalizing the "affair," then proceeding to ideations of shame, revenge, and even suicide: "Give up that whore ... or I'll cut my throat", quotes m of his suicidal wife (p. 47), recounting that she carried a razor in her vanity-bag" (pp. 49–50). The image of the affair then fades into guilt and self-pity; when the original "thought" returns to the verbal medium, it follows with something quite self-conscious, such as one's appearance, as its next topic.

Similar patterns have been noted in sequences of frames in animated movies, hence this drama's cartoon-like presentation and its text built around clichés. Often such sequences progress not on the basis of a development in the narrative content as in commonalities in the graphic form. Stripped of its content and reinterpreted, they lead to a new, unrelated content. In *Play* it becomes the grotesque. Elisheva Rosen explains elsewhere: "[T]he first episode in the history of the Grotesque, [is] linked to the appearance of the word "grottesca" from the Italian *grotta* – cave."[4] This neologism was used metonymically for the ornamentations on ancient graves. It is befitting that the figures are in semi-caves, or death-urns; and that they in turn are grotesques, since they have emerged as *imitations* of something prior. The question Rosen raises is: "Where and how can the Grotesque be placed? . . . what place *can* be accorded to something concrete, a recognizable phenomenon with no ascribed place of its own? One can guess the answer: the dream or the nightmare, the fantasy or the delirium; the Grotesque can only belong to the shadows of night" (pp. 126–7). In obscurity, a no-place, Grotesques receive a new life and space – a topos of Purgatory. In a darkness inter-spersed with blinks of the terrifying beam, light serves not only as a powerful agent of confusion, but it also exposes dying relationships – scenes of attrition between people. The grotesques embody both a promise of freedom (an eventual way out *through* speech and confession) and a foreshadowing of chaos – since they repeat themselves, since they cannot "settle down," since they interrupt each other. There is also the way in which the very *structure* of the grotesque subjects calls attention to them; as ornaments, they are both too noticeable and too expressive. They upset the organization of a figurative system and the hierarchy on which it is based. This accounts for why their speech is awry, their persons unrecognizable as humans. In employing grotesques, the emphasis is that humans go astray when they talk, so there is a built-in noncommunication.

Play has a violent edge with its theme of sexual encounters that are at odds. The play's technical brilliance captures the formal elements of light and the compositional form of the chorus to create an emotional battle in which the sorting out of guilt, relief, longing and pleasure is a field where the process of grief is visualized. It appears that the figures find no comfort in finding a fellow sufferer, a companion in abandonment. Insinuating charm, capriciousness, and wily femininity characterize w 1 and 2, while m exudes self-loathing. Given the muted palette of the atmosphere, and the flour-white, ghoulishly impassive faces, these "masks" intone stony hymns of suffering and deprivation that elicit no visible reaction. When the light resumes, and the subjects in crypts revert to ugly verbal spasms and twitches, *Play* possesses the magnificent, yet horrifying, grandeur of a Greek frieze. Yet it also seems to have been plucked out of time and place – damnation without end. This double perspective produces a stunning dual effect. The incantations are hopeful rituals summoned up to restore faith in their ability to speak and to visualize their prior lives, while the visions of the past recur not so much for a fondness for details as for the security they now provide in their entombed world. The past offers a view of measurable, wrapped up order, marred though it was. Life had its place, once upon a time, and its own clear rules. That they broke those rules is quite another matter. Now, it is all confusion. Small wonder, then, in this perplexing environment, that they should be drawn to repetitive, verbal battering. For however tenuous or conditioned it may appear, their space is subsumed under the light, which flourishes in cyclically linguistic and visual patterns. Their voices say in effect: to be transitory is what we are. There is *no* new story to tell, nothing new to report. But to *want* it – a story to tell – is to be separate, to be apart. Their voices indicate that they suffer two contrary miseries: to suffer the others' visibility, and to suffer the others' invisibility. They are doubly wretched, but feel compelled to rehearse their pasts through the image that the light provokes in their confinement. The texture of the voices is polyphonic, composed of three voices. The "soul" of the work is in a severe declension of light and dark which gives rhythm and terrifying structure to their space.

  Is there a purpose in this seamless flurry of activity between light and voice? Is one to assign to light and voice a duplicity to their visualizations of passion? In a crucible of grief and mourning, dark and luminous effects are calculated to heighten the suggestion of a fine anguish, of people aloof and enigmatic and set apart. Among the countless factors that contribute to the speakers' negative perceptions of each other are the visual images that they conjure up. All the clandestine emotions of rejection and jealousy imprint themselves on their textual, verbal "faces," until they accuse each other of bad faith. Cliché as truth enables them to withstand their withered present, but the fact is that many couples act out love/hate relationships. When m's first utterance exposes the love triangle – "We were not long together when she smelled the rat" (p. 47),[5] a reverse fairy tale is recited, barbarously at odds with their present entrapment. It is in the cruel remarks, those thrust upon the story by w 1, for instance ("Pudding face, puffy, spots, blubber mouth, jowls, no neck" [p. 50]) – that strike the audience as most urgent.

At its strongest, *Play* clarifies their states of mind; the dreamlike images remain in their imaginations as symbols of their inner struggles. At times, they are overtly melodramatic, and, with melodrama, as in dreams, one always flirts with the disparity between appearance and reality. W 1's statements are replete not only with melodramatic overtones that dramatize that the parts are more important than the sum, but also that the recurring motifs deal very much with the way people submit to each other: "Then I forgave him. To what will love not stoop!" (p. 49); and yet, a few lines later, she states, "When I was satisfied it was all over I went to have a gloat. Just a common tart. What he could have found in her when he had me –" (p. 50). The frightening thing echoed in these lines is that ordinary people do terrible things. Beckett sees that trouble with expressing pain is one of the hallmarks of couples who aren't in tune with each other. Thus, rather than *speak* her anger outright to her spouse, w 1 alternately threatens to kill herself or passively indulges in self-pity – she takes to her bed – "stricken for weeks" (p. 52). Then she resorts to passive-aggressive maneuvers. She drives over to "her place. It was all bolted and barred . . . . I made a bundle of his things and burnt them . . . . All night I smelt them smoldering" (p. 52). Although the repeated images are modified by the different contexts in which they are seen, the subject of this work remains the violence of the spirit.

Shock and blunted feeling suffuse the figures in the urns, as, one might argue, they do in terrorist occupied camps. Strangely, it is in the violent episodes – even the gratuitous ones – that they seem most at home. The cruellest remarks are the most vigorous, as m's comment, "God what vermin women" (p. 51); or in w 2's statement to the provocative light: "Go away and start pecking at someone else"; and, likewise, w 1's remark, loaded with the same sexual innuendo as w 2's: "Get off me! *(Vehement.)* Get off me!" (p. 53). The text does not evade the sexual and it is related to the subjects' need to control their sense of confinement and physical deterioration.

Play can be understood as an abstracted idea of pathological sex refined down to a skeletal framework. The theme of adultery is not presented straight away. Instead, one hears its outline in the form of its bass line (the opening Chorus), first by itself, and then decorated in a three-part texture. At last the theme appears, when m explains his wife's protestations: "Give up that whore, she said, or I'll cut my throat" (p. 47), followed by five or so variations of diverse incidents, the most being melancholy and quite somber. The fugue style of the Chorus is succeeded by two final repetitions of the main theme and a final cadential phrase by m, as he began, "We were not long together – ", closed finally by the *Blackout* (p. 61). The space surrounding the expressionless faces is a drabness, offsetting their sense of futility. The simplest diction is everywhere employed, and this laconic declamation is organized into blocked-out set-speeches and choruses. The play is small in scale, violent in density and intensity of character, and strongly involved in the re-creation of the *act* of speaking. The "ultimate reality" of the piece is to be found in the solution, the *da capo* (no solution of course). The chorus is characterized by its direct engagement of each figure's relationship to speech, stripped of everything but its immediate impact as sound, or, more precisely, "percussive-white-noise." This syncopated speech thrusts viewers to *see* the perturbing space before them: three bodies nine-tenths hidden and immobilized. The notion that one can act on another but not exact anything from him or her is posited through language, which commands the subjects' speech into a dependency with that of their fellow subjects.

When the subjects' moral fiber is shaken by physical deterioration and confinement, they turn their gaze and language in on themselves; they alone inflict suffering on themselves with malice towards what lies ahead – perhaps an endless purgatory more painful, of course, than a cessation of the ability to speak, or see. Like Giacometti's trio of walking figures, they look straight ahead, and though nearly touching, they make no contact with each other.

Play exposes the subjects' complicity between confessional voicing and the tedium of an unending future. It speculates on persons who are appallingly unable to refrain from speaking, who are doomed to rehearse their tales of disappointed passion. The space that their lives have become never allows them to find a solution through language. These grotesques reinforce our attentiveness to the space of elemental, voiced passion to comprehend human existence, for beyond speech are *words* with their traces of truth, whose body lies elsewhere.

NOTES

[1] Samuel Beckett, *Play* in *Cascando and Other Short Dramatic Pieces* (New York: Grove, 1964). All citations will be made in the text from this edition.

[2] Gregory Bateson, *Steps to an Ecology of Mind* (New York: Ballantine, 1972), p. 82.

[3] Herbert Blau, *The Audience* (Baltimore: The Johns Hopkins University Press, 1990), p. 78.

[4] Elisheva Rosen, "Innovation and Its Reception: The Grotesque in Aesthetic Thought," *SubStance* 62/63, Vol. XIX: 2/3 (1990), p. 126.

[5] Note the use of mouse and rat images in both *Happy Days* and *Play*. For an extended comment on the rat as psychic image, see C. G. Jung, "The Function of the Unconscious" in *The Symbolic Life*, in *The Collected Works*: 18, trans. R. F. C. Hull (Princeton: Princeton University Press, 1976), p. 106. I am grateful to Mary Doll for this observation in her essay, "The Demeter Myth in Beckett," *The Journal of Beckett Studies* **11–12** (1989): 109–122. Doll writes in her note 11: "Winnie's story halts at image, which works like a rat of the unconscious gnawing at the psyche" (p. 112). The rat and the scolding are evident also when Milly "began to undress Dolly *(Pause)*. Scolding her . . . the while" (p. 55) just before the "mouse ran up her little thigh," causing her to scream, but it was "too late" (p. 59). See also Mary F. Catanzaro, "The Voice of Absent Love in *Krapp's Last Tape* and *Company*, *Modern Drama*," Vol. XXXII, no. 3, Sept. (1989): 401–12: "Speech serves as a visual incantation, a hopeful ritual to keep up [the narrator's] crippled faith in his ability to enjoy real company, and, ultimately, to engage in reciprocal love . . . . Small wonder, then, in this perplexing environment, that he should so often be drawn to bizarre images for company – . . . flies, rats long dead. . . ."

BRUCE S. WATSON

APPLES WITHOUT SNAKES: PROUST'S SAPPHIC/ORGANIC REWRITINGS OF EDEN

In this paper I propose a close reading of selected passages from Proust's novel-sequence *Remembrance of Things Past* in which the Edenic model surfaces and creates lastingly resonant imagery, especially with reference to fragments of Sappho's lyrical poetry which are woven into the complex thematics of the Proustian text in such a way as to suggest an alternative vision to the Biblical model of 'paradise lost.' Proust's famous edict that 'the true paradises are those which we have lost' will be shown to evince a deeper sense of poignancy upon examination of the 'mixing of memory and desire' active in the creation of the character of Albertine. The young heroine's ambiguous status in current Proust studies[1] will also be considered with reference to the conflicting extant editions of the second-last volume of the novel, variously titled (in translation) *The Sweet Cheat Gone, Lost Albertine, The Fugitive*, etc. The principal focus of these editorial disputes concerns the various 'deaths' of Albertine, real, threatened or imagined; these disappearances also connect with the Sappho model, since as Joan DeJean[2] and Elaine Marks[3] have recently reminded us, Western authors since Ovid have frequently imagined legendary 'deaths' for the poet of Lesbos. I suggest that the Sappho model provides a key to the understanding of the character of Albertine and thus to Proust's evocations of utopian desire. The 'elemental passion of place' evoked in the novel will be explored in relation to Albertine's death 'on the banks of the Vivonne' in the new editions; this new development in Proust interpretation acts as a 'unifying stroke'[4] drawing together the constellations of poetic and thematic associations related to the 'jeune fille en fleurs.' Proust's subtle poetic devices will be further explored with reference to the famous 'hawthorn' passage of *Swann's Way*; which I intend to read as a rewriting of Sappho's wedding celebration lyric, truly a celebration of "apples without snakes."

Proust's "biting of the Edenic apple" is even more subtly hidden in the dark wartime passages of *Time Regained*; the passage describing the descent into the Paris subway following the disturbing scenes in Jupien's hotel proposes a radical resolution of the tragic dichotomy of identity and desire developed by Proust elsewhere in the novel. A brief review of the workings of the Proustian text in relation to the tormented 'love' affairs of the main characters[5] will be followed in my paper by an empathetic reading of the subway passage's organic sense of unity created by the darkness. The French novelist's rewritings of Eden will be shown to invest the terrain of consciousness with a nourishing 'elemental passion of place' which has been too often overlooked by critics focusing predominantly on Proust's status a formalist or postmodernist artist.[6]

Albertine, the ambiguous and enticing young girl who appeared in the Proustian novel around 1914, provides the author with the opportunity for the most exhaustive analysis of love, desire, and jealousy in modern fiction; as George Steiner has reminded us in his perceptive study, "Eros and Idiom":

> The affair between the narrator and Albertine is one – and there are obviously not many in the history of art and literature – that literally enlarges the resources of our sensibility, that actually educates our recognitions to new possibilities of feeling. Proust has widened the repertoire of sexual consciousness. Areas of adolescent sexuality, of imaginary possession, of jealousy, of sexual loss have, through Proust's formulation, become larger or newly accessible. As is the uncanny case with very great art, *Remembrance of Things Past* (*A la recherche du temps perdu*) has acted as a prescriptive mythology, calling into being nuances of emotion, twists of being and pretence, which were, somehow, a *terra incognita* of the self. (pp. 332–333)

The mystery of Albertine survives long after her death in a riding accident, in the volume entitled *Albertine Lost*; the narrator's quest for the truth of her identity leads to exhaustive and self-defeating investigations, none of which establish conclusively the nature of his heroine's desires; this feature of the text has led to Albertine being considered what the French call 'un personnage sans fond', a 'bottomless' character. More recently, however, the mysteries of Albertine have been reawakened by the discovery of a 'new' manuscript which re-locates her death near the narrator's childhood paradise, 'along the banks of the Vivonne.'[7] This discovery has in turn led to a re-reading of the other 'deaths' of Albertine concealed in the text which so far have received little critical attention;[8] these disappearances, real, threatened or imagined, reinforce the ambivalence in Proust's creation of characters and their inscription in the space-time framework of the novel, as Malcolm Bowie has pointed out:

> The 'real' death of Albertine – the only one that matters to the narrator – is her death as a structure of his own thought; the creation, flowering, and extinction of that

structure are subject to their own causal laws, and these are not reducible, or even coherently relatable, to the laws which govern the life and death of Albertine's body. (p. 74)

Of the many such 'deaths' in the novel, the most poetically evocative is surely Albertine's threat to drown herself, in the second volume of *Cities of the Plain*; the narrator's suspicions of his friend's lesbian inclinations leads to this outburst from Albertine:

– I've never known you be so cruel. The sea shall be my tomb. I shall never see you any more. At these words my heart missed a beat, although I was certain that she would come again next day, as she did.
– I shall drown myself, I shall throw myself into the sea. – Like Sappho.
– There you go, insulting me again. You suspect not only what I say but what I do. – But, my lamb, I didn't mean anything, I swear to you. You know Sappho flung herself into the sea. – Yes, yes, you have no confidence in me. . . . She dashed from the room, crying "Goodbye for ever" in a heartbroken voice. (2: pp. 829–830)

As Nathalie Mauriac has underlined, Proust here links (Albertine's) threatened suicide to the homosexual theme, which will later be stressed in her 'actual' death. (p. 51) In addition, Proust refers here to Ovid's *Heroides 15: Letter from Sappho to Phaon*, in which Sappho's legendary drowning is described in an imaginary letter from the poet to her lover, the boatman Phaon.[9] Proust's remark in a letter of 1916, at the time when he was writing the 'Albertine' volumes[10] (that):

even to write one word on some topic, and sometimes in order to say nothing at all (about it), I need to saturate myself in it completely.

is indicative of the author's depth of knowledge concerning the apparently haphazard references throughout his works. The reference to Sappho is particularly provocative since the reader is encouraged to search out not only evidence for Albertine's status as a 'Sappho model' in terms of her lesbian inclinations and behavior but, more richly and imaginatively, for echoes of Sappho's lyrical poetry in Proust's famous nature descriptions;

Like the last red apple, sweet and high, high as the topmost twigs, which the apple-pickers missed -o no, not missed but found beyond their fingertips
   Like the mountain hyacinth which feet of shepherds trample leaving the ground in bloom with blood of purple. (Roche's translation, p. 104)

Critics of Sappho's poetry, especially Ann Burnett, have admired the simplicity and clarity of this evocation of virginity on the eve of marriage;

Burnett notes approvingly the 'keenness of Sappho's visual sense, even when she is using nature for a manifestly figurative purpose.' Jenkins remarks in addition Sappho's introduction into Western literature of 'a sentiment of place – not just a 'feeling for nature' – but a feeling for what it is to be like at a *particular* place at a *particular* time.' (p. 38)[11] On a symbolic level, Proust's poetry of flowers seems disturbing in a similar thematic vein:

> And indeed it was a hawthorn, but one whose blossom was pink, and lovelier even than the white . . . And indeed I had felt at once, as I had felt with the white blossom, but with even greater wonderment, that it was in no artificial manner, by no device of human fabrication, that the festal intention of these flowers was revealed, but that it was Nature herself who had spontaneously expressed it . . . High up on the branches, like so many of those tiny rose-trees, their pots concealed in jackets of paper lace, whose slender shafts rose in a forest from the altar on major feast days, a thousand buds were swelling and opening, but each disclosing, as it burst, as at the bottom of a bowl of pink marble, its blood-red stain, and suggesting even more strongly than the full-blown flowers, the special, irresistible quality of the rose-bush which, wherever it was about to blossom, could do it in pink alone. Embedded in the hedge, but as different from it as a young girl in festal attire among a crowd of dowdy women in everyday clothes who are staying at home, all ready for the 'Month of Mary'', of which it seemed already to form a part, it glowed there, smiling in its fresh pink garments, deliciously demure and Catholic. (l: pp. 152–153)

Randolph Splitter has commented on this passage in a revealing manner which underscores the thematic proximity of these 'flowers' to Sappho's apples and hyacinths:

> The opposition between pink and innocent white, . . . the particular emphasis on blossoming, the opening of buds into mature and beautiful flowers, the glimpse of the girl behind the hedge, through an arch of pink flowers, and the crucial exposure of a blood-red splash of color on the inside of pale buds, all imply an underlying preoccupation with the mysteries of virginity and sex: with the loss of virginity in intercourse (the blood-red stain caused by 'deflowering') . . . with the mysterious metamorphosis of a girl 'blossoming' into a sexually mature woman (marked on the most literal level, by the blood-red stain of menstruation), or simply with mysterious, frightening, barely glimpsed sight of a girl's genitals, which seems to disclose (in the fantasy of a boy familiar with his own anatomy) a blood-red wound. In short, the pink hawthorns, white flowers tinged red, are reassuringly innocent and yet ambiguously seductive at the same time, like the young, pubescent girls *en fleurs* who will be Marcel's special province in love. (p. 64)

Splitter's emphasis on the sensuality of the hawthorn passage also offers a point of contact with antiquity; the 'feast days' described evoke fertility rites such as Sappho's epithemalia far more than orthodox Catholic rituals. Proust's inversion of the sacred and the profane, which is operative throughout his novel,[12] contrasts tellingly with Sappho's simplicity and unaffectedly natural vocabulary; the Proustian nostalgia for 'natural' expression emerges from his comment at the beginning of the quoted passage that, "it was in no artificial manner, by no device of human fabrication, that the festal intention of these flowers was revealed, but that it was Nature herself who had spontaneously expressed it." As Marcel Muller has stressed, in the Proustian universe, "any form of automisation or mechanization introduces a form of inauthenticity"; Anne Henry concludes her thorough study of the philosophical background to Proust's thought by noting that *Remembrance of Things Past* evokes "a nostalgia for the natural that can only be expressed through extreme sophistication." (p. 366) The syncretist, carnival atmosphere conjured up by Proust's tantalising flower-girls can thus be read as a privileged evocation of Eden in the text. The girls, like Sappho's apples, are almost out of reach, 'high up on the branches'/'high as the topmost twigs'; yet they seem to offer an invitation to the mysteries of adolescence and sexuality untainted by guilt or inhibition: apples without snakes.[13]

Albertine's presence in the novel is used by Proust to detail the Lesbian world of salons and casinos; most critics, including the perceptive George Steiner, find evidence of a "moralizing, damning force in (Proust's) mapping of the world of perversion." (p. 333) Bearing the Sappho model in mind (and heart) however, it is possible to interpret several key passages of the text as expressions of utopian desire beyond the framework of guilt and suspicion that does structure so much of the Proustian narrator's pursuit of Albertine; this late passage in particular resonates with the elemental passion of place of our conference's title, orchestrated by a complex constellation of mythological and artistic associations;

At first the laundry girl refused to tell me anything, she assured me that Mlle Albertine had never done anything more than pinch her arm . . . Then she told me that Mlle Albertine often used to meet her on the banks of the Loire, when she went to bathe, that Mlle Albertine, who was in the habit of getting up very early to go and bathe, was in the habit of meeting her by the water's edge, at a spot where the trees are so thick that nobody can see you, and besides there is nobody who can see you at that hour in the morning. Then the laundry girl brought her girl friends and they bathed, and afterwards, as it is already hot down there and the sun beats down on you even through the trees, they used to lie about on the grass drying themselves and playing and stroking and tickling one another. The young laundry-girl confessed to me that she enjoyed playing around with her girl friends and that seeing that Mlle Albertine was always rubbing up against her in her bathing-wrap she made her take it off and used to caress her with her tongue along the throat and arms, even on the soles of the feet which Mlle Albertine held out to her. The laundry-girl undressed too, and they played at pushing each other in the water. (3: p. 535)

This utopian Sapphic paradise is ironized to some degree by Proust through narrative distancing and an element of humor; it evokes in addition several classical allusions, including the bath of Diana and the cave of Venus.[14] Perhaps the most germane comparison for our theme is to the Renoir painting *The Great Bathers*, which Proust knew and admired; this canvas has been beautifully described by Christopher Riopelle:

The Great Bathers is a langourous and seductive evocation of an all-female Eden. Two young women lounge beneath a tree on a verdant river-bank while a third, younger girl teasingly threatens to splash one of them. Further off, two girls frolic in the water, seemingly indifferent to anything but the play of hot sun and cool, fresh water on their bodies. (p. 12)

The Renoir painting also provides a thematic connection with the myth of Diana and Acteon, since research has demonstrated affinities between the Impressionist's *Bathers* and François Girardon's seventeenth century *Fountain of Diana*, in the Versailles gardens, which Renoir used as a model; the classical nymphs frolic freely in the water, free from male intrusion. Proust rewritings of Eden thus reach back to classical antiquity and baroque sculpture for inspiration in the creation of textual utopias of desire[15] which would probably seem out of place for those who persist in considering *Remembrance of Things Past* "the gloomiest book ever written."

Albertine's textual fate, as I indicated earlier, has been problematised due to the discovery of a late emendation of the novel by Proust who apparently intended to replace the investigations into his heroine's sexual adventures with a concise and thematically dense paragraph: Albertine dies 'on the banks of the Vivonne.' Although not directly germane to the Edenic model, this transformation brings powerful confirmation to Proust's passion of place: the young girl dies where the narrator was born, and also what will become the birthplace of art. This passage illustrates the isotopie between the cradle and the tomb explored by Gilbert Durand in his *Anthropological Structures of the Imagination*:

The mummy like the chrysalid is at once tomb and cradle of the promise of survival. Our word 'cemetery' signifies this through its etymology, koimêtêrion meaning nuptial chamber. (p. 271; my translation)

It is however in the war passages at the end of *Time Regained* that Proust performs his most courageous and far-reaching revaluation of Eden; the tragic 'intermittences of the heart' described so poignantly by the novelist in the central volumes[16] are precariously overcome in a neglected passage in which the dialectic of identity and desire so mercilessly demonstrated earlier in the novel is finally resolved:

"Some of these, like the Pompeians upon whom the fire from heaven was already raining, descended into the passages of the Metro, black as catacombs. They knew that they would not be alone there. And darkness, which envelops all things like a new element, has the effect, irresistibly tempting for certain people, of suppressing the first halt on the road to pleasure – it permits us to enter without impediment into a region of caresses to which normally we only gain access after a certain delay. Whether the coveted object be a woman or a man, supposing even that the first approach is easy and that there is no need of the gallant speeches which in a salon might run on forever (at any rate in daylight), on a normal evening, even in the most dimly lit street, there is at least a preamble in which the eyes alone feed on the repast which cannot yet be enjoyed and the fear of passers-by, the fear also of the man or woman before us, prevents us from doing more than look and speak. In the darkness this time-honoured ritual is instantly abolished – hands, lips, bodies may go into action at once. There is always the excuse of darkness, and of the mistakes that darkness engenders, if we are not well received. And if we are, this immediate response of a body which does not withdraw but approaches, gives us of the woman (or the man) whom we have selected the idea that she is without prejudice and full of vice, which adds an extra pleasure to the happiness of having bitten straight into the fruit without first coveting it with our eyes and without asking permission. Meanwhile the darkness persisted; plunged into the new element, imagining that they had travelled to a distant country and were witnessing a natural phenomenon like a tidal wave or an eclipse, that they were enjoying not an artificially prepared, sedentary pleasure but a chance encounter in the unknown, the men who had come away from Jupien's house celebrated, while the bombs mimicked the rumblings of a volcano, deep in the earth as in a Pompeian house of ill fame, their secret rites in the shadows of the catacombs." (3: p. 864)

This astonishing passage draws on a wealth of thematic and literary sources, including classical antiquity, organic unity created by the darkness, and perhaps most significantly, on the Biblical myth of the forbidden fruit, here eroticised by Proust in a mythical construct. In the heart of the earth, 'the still point of the turning world' described by Eliot, the conflict between self and other is harmoniously resolved in an area resonant with nostalgia for unity before separation, childhood innocence before adulthood,[17] apples without snakes.[18] Eden is thus invested with a paradoxical innocence; the heart of the nightmarish wartime labyrinth invites the reader to a confrontation not with 'the torment/Of love unsatisfied', nor to 'the greater torment/Of love satisfied' but to a nourishing elemental passion of place beyond sexuality and individual psychology described by George Steiner as "that fusion of erotic being which we find at particular summits of the Western tradition. Where our imagination moves deepest it strives beyond sexuality, which is, inevitably, division, to an erotic whole." (p. 333)

Baylor University

NOTES

[1] See Reginald McGinnis' article, "L'Inconnaissable Gomorrhe: à propos d'*Albertine disparue*" and chapter 3 of my book, *Les figures du labyrinthe dans À la recherche du temps perdu*, "Le Tombeau d'Albertine."
[2] See her recent study, *Fictions of Sappho*, 1989.
[3] See her article, "Lesbian Intertextuality: the Sappho model."
[4] I owe this term to Nathalie Mauriac. See her article, "The Death of Albertine."
[5] See, among many excellent Proust studies, the works of Samuel Beckett, Roger Shattuck and Gilles Deleuze.
[6] See, for example, Margaret Gray's recent *Postmodern Proust*.
[7] See the article by Nathalie Mauriac.
[8] See my article "La mer sera mon tombeau: remarques sur les morts d'Albertine."
[9] On the question of the letters exchanged between Albertine and the narrator, see Richard Goodkin's perceptive remarks in his recent book, *Around Proust*.
[10] These volumes constitute over a third of the final text: the two visits to Balbec, *The Captive* and *The Fugitive*.
[11] Jenkins develops an interesting comparison in the same section between the spontaneity of Sappho's poetic perceptions and Proust's metaphorical discourse; the French author observes nature, according to Jenkins, 'with an almost scientific precision.' On this topic, see the article(s) by Marcel Muller which argue persuasively that Proust was opposed to the scientific viewpoint on the world. Proust's 'organicism' is stressed in Muller's article, "Charlus dans le métro ou pastiche et cruauté chez Proust." I will develop this argument further below.

[12] See Enid Morantz's article, "Topography of Combray or the Inversion of the Sacred and the Profane."
[13] Compare my reading with Burnett's comments, "With great subtlety Sappho uses her smile to suggest not only the desirability and inaccessibility of the apple but also, simultaneously, that it is about to fall into the hands of whoever may be waiting below when the time is right." See also Jenkins' comments on the apply imagery with reference to mythology and girls' breasts (p. 44); this could be compared profitably with the famous passage describing Albertine naked in *The Captive:* "Her two little uplifted breasts were so round that they seemed not so much to be an integral part of her body as to have ripened there like fruit." (3: p. 74) This passage is followed by a description of lovemaking which relies heavily on Edenic, Biblical imagery.
[14] See Florence Weinburg's excellent study, *The Cave, The Evolution of a Metaphoric Field from Homer to Ariosto* for a thorough and accessible study of these motifs. See also my article, "Daphné: Dédale: Diane: l'intertexte ovidien chez Proust" forthcoming in *Romance Languages Annual*, 1993.
[15] See Charles Segal's study of Ovid's highly volatile landscapes: "The landscape symbolical of virginity may thus suddenly become the landscape of lustful sensuality; images of sanctity may become images of desire. The shaded pool of Diana may symbolize virginity in the stories of Callisto and Acteon; but such a pool may entice to sexual surrender, not restraint, in tales like those of Narcissus, Salmacis, Arethusa." (p. 25)
[16] See Beckett's explanation of the 'intermittences' in his essay, *Proust*.
[17] For the narrator, adult life with its attendant responsibilities and betrayals began on the night his parents indulged his forbidden wish to sleep near his mother. See Muller's article, "Charlus dans le métro."
[18] See Weinburg's description of the *locus amoenus*. "It is very close to a secular Eden in its atmosphere of an absolutely safe haven where all physical wants are attended to, with this limitation, that, in the christian era, it is afflicted with the consequences of man's Fall from Grace, which affects all of Nature. Hence, the joys of love in the grotto are liable to be dampened by an all-pervasive sense of sin."

BIBLIOGRAPHY

Beckett, S. *Proust* London: Chatto and Windus, 1931.
Bowie, M. *Freud, Proust and Lacan*. Cambridge: Cambridge University Press, 1989.
Burnett, A. *Three Archaic poets: Archilochus, Alchaeus, Sappho*. Cambridge: Harvard University Press, 1983.
DeJean, J. *Fictions of Sappho*. Chicago: University of Chicago Press, 1989.
Deleuze, G. *Proust et les signes*. Paris: Presses Universitaires de France, 1976.
Durand, G. *Les structures anthropologiques de l'imaginaire*. Paris: Dunod, 1974.
Goodkin, R. *Around Proust*. Princeton: Princeton University Press, 1992.
Gray, Margaret. *Postmodern Proust*. Philadelphia: University of Pennsylvania Press, 1992.
Jenkins, R. *Three Classical Poets: Sappho, Catullus, Juvenal*. Cambridge: Harvard University Press, 1982.
Marks, E./Stambolian, G. *Homosexualities and French Literature*. Ithaca: Cornell University Press, 1979.

Mauriac, N. "The Death of Albertine." In *The UAB Symposium in Celebration of the 75th Anniversary of Swann's Way*. Birmingham: Summa Publication, 1989: pp. 49–57.

McGinnis, R. "L'Inconnaissable Gomorrhe: À propos d'*Albertine disparue.*" *Romanic Review* **81**.1 (1990): pp. 92–104.

Morantz, E. "Topography of Combray or the Inversion of the Sacred and the Profane." In *Proust et le texte producteur*. Guelph: University of Guelph, 1980.

Muller, M. "Etrangeté, ou, si l'on veut, naturel." In *Recherche de Proust*. Paris: Editions du Seuil, 1980: pp. 55–67.

Muller, M. "Charlus dans le métro ou pastiche et cruauté chez Proust." In *Cahiers Marcel Proust*, 9 (1979): pp. 9–25.

Segal, C. *Landscape in Ovid's Metamorphoses: A Study in the Transformation of a Literary Symbol*. Wiesbaden: F. Steiner, 1969.

Shattuck, R. *Proust*. Boston: Modern Masters Series.

Splitter, R. *Proust's Recherche: A Psychoanalytical Interpretation*. Boston: Routledge Press, 1981.

Steiner, G. "Eros and Idiom". In *George Steiner: A Reader*. London: Oxford University Press, 1984.

Watson, B. *Les figures du labyrinthe dans À la recherche du temps perdu*. New York: Peter Lang Publishing, Reading Plus series, vol. 11, 1992.

Watson, B. "La mer sera mon tombeau: remarques sur les morts d'Albertine." In *Romance Languages Annual*, 1992.

Watson, B. "Daphné: Dédale: Diane: l'intertexte ovidien chez Proust." Forthcoming in *Romance Languages Annual*.

Weinburg, F. *The Cave: The Evolution of a Metaphoric Field from Homer to Ariosto*. New York: Peter Lang Publishing, 1986.

PART TWO

THE ELEMENTAL ROOTEDNESS –
HOUSE AND HOME

NANCY CAMPI DE CASTRO

THE ARCHETYPE OF THE HOUSE IN *THE GREAT GATSBY*

Human imagination is involved in lights and shadows, in presences and absences, in doubt and certainty – man carries on the mystery to be solved: that of imagination in continuous labor, through the ages, exciting, in uninterrupted activity, the curiosity of men, avid in knowing and in revealing themselves. From the great many books addressing the study of imagination, come many doubtful assertions and uncertain negatives; nevertheless, there are some points of consensus. One of them is the impossibility of establishing rigid boundaries between reason and imagination, which does not mean to assert equality between what is rational and what is imaginary. It can be said that integration exists and, sometimes, that there is antecedent evidence of what is imaginary with its archetypal, symbolic and mythic elements.

Archetypes, referring to human imagination, are characterized as primordial images, or prototypes, which assume the idea's primordial phase, the idea's matrix zone; idea is, then, the pragmatic engagement of the imaginary archetype, within a given context, both historical and epistemological.

An archetypal motif fundamentally exists in the idea. Maybe this is an explanation for rationalism: pragmatism can never be completely freed from an imaginary halo.

Archetypes have a special importance: they are the meeting point between imagination and rational proceedings. Archetypes have, too, a great stability: they differ from symbols, essentially polyvalent, because of their lack of ambivalence: they are universal. Different cultures, however, give different images to the archetypes – this is where, *sensu stricto*, symbols appear, characterized by their singularity. This singularity is expressed in material objects, in archetypal concrete illustrations.

Archetypes are linked to the idea and substantiality; symbols are linked to the substantive, to the noun; therefore, because of their concrete engagement, the maintenance and durability of the symbols are fragile. Symbols easily lose their polyvalence, because they are submitted to the recurrent interpretation carried on by human beings. If symbols lose polyvalence, they become simple signs, emigrating from semantics to semiotics.

As an extension of archetypes and symbols, myths can be found as a dynamic system, tending to compose a narrative. Mythical systems guarantee imaginary representations, which can be materialized in works of art. By motivating narratives, with their archetypal and symbolic representations, myths motivate literary creation. Myths announce philosophical doctrines, philosophical systems, or legendary, primitive and historical narratives. A mythical approach to a literary work of art has the aim of specifying relations among a narrative and its archetypal and symbolic elements, trying to enrich critical possibilities, in order to enjoy deeply the work of art – enigma and pleasure.

As an art, literature remains alive, even if many literary critics detect the existence of a pathological situation about literature at the present time, or predict its disappearance. But literature, despite all, remains alive. And more than a permanence, the literary work of art is a presence-enigma, a presence-prevalence. As an enigma, the recognition of a superior position is settled, because the literary work of art is an inexhaustible repository of multiple visions about humans. If we accept the condition of causality between man and the work of art, we shall find the reasons for searching for truth, or truths, about human beings mainly in literary works of art, even if the hope for definitive answers is only weak. By its own nature, literary speech is a codified one, expressed through known words. And it is this quality of being codified that excites the curiosity of the reader, or that of the critic. Where can we find the key to solving or decoding the enigma?

Many choices of approach are offered; but none is incontestable. Among them appears the mythical research into the constitutive elements of literary work. Moreover, another source of controversies is found in the identification of the mythical elements in the literary work of art, because the presence of the myth's elements intensifies the enigmatic aspect of the narrative.

In consequence, many questions may arise: would mythical roots have been intentional and consciously used? Or, on the contrary, had they been infiltrated and then broken forth, as a proof of persistence in the spirit of man?

For Jung, archetypes are "psychic residua of numberless experiences of the same type", experiences which have happened not to the individual, but to his ancestors, and of which the results are inherited in the structures of the brain, "a priori" determinants of individual experience. The work of anthropologists and psychologists who have attempted to study scientifically the reactions of minds is of great value to those who want to explore the imaginative responses of artists to the principal archetypal patterns of humanity.

Below the surface of a literary work represented by fine character studies, a varied story and a full command of the technical instruments of the writer, a strange vibration, as an undercurrent of desires and fears and passions, can be suspected by the literary critic interested in deepening the eternal durability of human magical dreams. An archetypology, based on the inner experience of different individuals, can be traced and applied to the study of literary works of art.

Among the most important archetypes, Bachelard (*La terre et les rêveries du repos*, p. 104) mentions "the house". It is a secondary microcosm, between the cosmos and the human body; the house is a microcosmic double of material and mental "corpus"; it is the materialization of intimacy, of protection, of rest, of tranquility. The human being needs a little house in this big house that is the world, to rediscover the primordial securities of a life without problems.

We would like to focus on some aspects of this archetype, the house, in F. Scott Fitzgerald's well-known work, *The Great Gatsby*.

In *The Great Gatsby*, the house, as an archetypal pattern, can be studied in many shapes and representations. The book, an intense and vivid picture of human nature in a definite context (North America, in the twenties), is an unquestionable work of art. Below its perfect surface, constructed by Fitzgerald's excellent technique, a torrent of basic human feelings and needs may be detected.

We shall consider the following characters of the book: Gatsby, Daisy, Tom, Myrtle, Wilson and Nick. Concerning these characters, the house has various forms, situations, temporality and owners:

GATSBY	Big house (West Egg, actuality)
DAISY	Big house (Louisville, youth)
TOM	Big house (East Egg, actuality)
MYRTLE	Apartment (New York, actuality)
WILSON	Garage (Valley of Ashes, actuality)
NICK	Small house (West Egg, actuality)

Bachelard states, about the house, in *La terre et les rêveries du repos*, p. 103:

Dis-moi la maison que tu imagines, je te dirai qui tu es. Cette maison, elle est lointaine, elle est perdue, nous ne l'habitons plus, elle est alors plus qu'un souvenir, elle est une maison de rêves, notre maison onirique. La maison oniriquement complète est la seule où l'on puisse vivre dans toute leur variété les rêveries d'intimité; on y vit seul, ou deux, ou en famille, mais surtout seul. Et dans nos rêves de la nuit, il y a toujours une maison où l'on vit seul. Ainsi le veulent certaines puissances de l'archétype de la maison où se rejoignent toutes les séductions de la vie repliée. Tout rêveur a besoin de retourner à sa cellule, il est appelé par une vie vraiment cellulaire.

Following Bachelard's words, the significance of the house can be lost in the past: it can be only a remembrance, a "house of dreams"; or it can be a present shelter, a real cell, the sureness of quiet insularity. These statements by Bachelard can enrich the analysis of *The Great Gatsby*'s houses. For instance, Daisy had many houses, but only two were important: that in Louisville, where she lived in her youth, and the other in East Egg, in the actuality. The house in Louisville belonged to the past, to a different space, a space of dream. It is "la maison onirique" of Gatsby, who always intended to go back to the past; and Daisy's house was part of this dream in the past:

He went to her house, at first with other officers from Camp Taylor, then alone. It amazed him – he had never been in such a beautiful house before. But what gave it an air of breathless intensity was that Daisy lived there – it was as casual a thing to her as his tent out at camp was to him. There was a ripe mystery about it, a hint of bedrooms upstairs more beautiful and cool than other bedrooms, of gay and radiant activities taking place through its corridors, and of romances that were not musty and laid away already in lavender, but fresh and breathing and redolent of this year's shining motor-cars and of dances whose flowers were scarcely withered. It excited him, too, that many men had already loved Daisy – it increased her value in his eyes. He felt their presences all about the house, pervading the air with the shades and echoes of still vibrant emotions. But he knew that he was in Daisy's house by a colossal accident. (p. 152)

And it was this dream that Gatsby wanted to be definitive and true, but definitive and true as if they could go back in the past:

He wanted nothing less of Daisy than that she should go to Tom and say: 'I never loved you'. After she had obliterated four years with that sentence they could decide upon the more practical measures to be taken. One of them was that, after she was free, they were to go back to Louisville and be married from her house – just as if it were five years ago. (p. 112)

Gatsby searched for a new house for himself, a house at the present time, as described by Nick:

The one on my right was a colossal affair, by any standard – it was a factual imitation of some Hôtel de Ville in Normandy, with a tower on one side, spanking new under a thin beard of raw ivy, and a marble swimming pool, and more than forty acres of lawn and garden. It was Gatsby's mansion. (p. 5)

This is Gatsby's mansion, a big house, but it still is a house of dreams, where he is alone with his dreams, personified by Daisy, whose presence could transmute reality:

'My house looks well, doesn't it?' he demanded. 'See how the whole front of it catches the light.' (. . .) His eyes went over it, every arched door and square tower. 'That huge place there?' she cried pointing. 'Do you like it?' 'I love it, but I don't see how you live there all alone.' 'I keep it always full of interesting people, night and day. People who do interesting things. Celebrated people.' (. . .) With enchanting murmurs Daisy admired this aspect or that of the feudal silhouette against the sky, admired the gardens, the sparkling odor of jonquils and the frothy odor of hawthorn and plum blossoms and the pale gold odor of kiss-me-at-the-gate. He hadn't once ceased looking at Daisy, and I think he revalued everything in his house according to the measure of response it drew from her well-loved eyes. Sometimes, too, he stared around at his possessions in a dazed way, as though in her actual and astounding presence none of it was any longer real. (p. 93)

All the past, a promise of happiness, is alive in the house, even if it seems a lost happiness:

'You can't repeat the past.' 'Can't repeat the past?' he cried incredulously. 'Why of course you can!' He looked around him wildly, as if the past were lurking here in the shadow of his house, just out of reach of his hands. (p. 113)

Gatsby's house was his own cosmos, a particular surrounding space, big enough and well-lit enough to represent his own feelings – an illuminate love, an ardent desire for height – a search for light and for elevation:

Two o'clock and the whole corner of the peninsula was blazing with light, which fell unreal on the shrubbery and made thin elongating glints upon the roadside wires. Turning a corner, I saw it was Gatsby's house, lit from tower to cellar. (. . .) 'Your place looks like the World's Fair,' I said. 'Does it?' He turned his eyes toward it absently. (p. 83)

The house of Tom and Daisy represents, too, an assumed space, a prolongation of queer personalities. Most of all, it was a feminine house, with feminine attributes, full of air, movement, grace and a touch of unreality:

He walked through a high hallway into a bright rosy-colored space, fragilely bound into the house by French windows at either end. The windows were ajar and gleaming white against the fresh grass outside that seemed to grow a little way into the house. A breeze blew through the room, blew curtains in at one end and out the other like pale flags, twisting them up toward the frosted wedding-cake of the ceiling, and then rippled over the wine-colored rug, making a shadow on it as wind does on the sea. The only completely stationary object in the room was an enormous couch on which two young women were buoyed up as though upon an anchored balloon. They were both in white, and their dresses were rippling and fluttering as if they had just been blown back in after a short flight around the house. I must have stood for a few moments listening to the whip and snap of the curtains and the groan of a picture on the wall. Then there was a boom as Tom Buchanan shut the windows and the caught wind died out about the room, and the curtains and the rugs and the two young women ballooned slowly to the floor. (p. 9)

Tom needs a different space, more real and compact. Such is their apartment in New York, his and Myrtle's:

The apartment was on the top floor – a small living-room, a small dining-room, a small bedroom, and a bath. (p. 29)

Myrtle, unadapted to Wilson's garage, whose "interior was unprosperous and bare", achieved at the apartment another dimension as a woman; but the apartment did not fit her as a space, a sufficient space:

Mrs. Wilson had changed her costume some time before, and was now attired in an elaborate afternoon dress of cream-colored chiffon, which gave out a continual rustle as she swept about the room. With the influence of the dress her personality had also undergone a change. The intense vitality that had been so remarkable in the garage was converted into impressive hauteur. Her laughter, her gestures, her assertions became more violently affected moment by moment, and as she expanded the room grew smaller around her, until she seemed to be revolving on a noisy, creaking pivot through the smoky air. (p. 31)

On the contrary, Nick's house could be said to be exactly his microcosm:

He found the house, a weather-beaten cardboard bungalow at eighty a month. (. . .) And so with the sunshine and the great burts of leaves growing on the trees, just as things grow in fast movies, I had that familiar conviction that life was beginning over again with the summer. There was so much to read, for one thing, and so much fine health to be pulled down out of the young breath-giving air. (. . .) And I had the high intention of reading many other books besides. I was going to bring back all such things into my life and become again that most limited of all specialists, the 'well-rounded-man'. This isn't just an epigram – life is much more successfully looked at from a single window, after all. (p. 5)

The complete archetypal pattern of the house, representing security, protection, but also a kind of nest for love and dreams, was not accomplished in practically any of the houses of *The Great Gatsby*. In a way, Nick's house, in its simplicity, was the accomplishment of his own thrifty necessities; but Myrtle, in Wilson's house, or in Tom's apartment, did not achieve her own space. The same seems to happen with Tom and Daisy: their constant voyages, from one city to another, in different countries, always changing places, were a continual change of houses – where could the house of dreams be situated for them both?

Gatsby believed in a house as a protection, but also as a home for dreams. The dimensions of his house were synonymous with the dimensions of his desires; instead of being lonesome, loneliness was not his purpose – Daisy, as the ideal woman, was his intent. So, the house was trimmed and prepared to attract Daisy: so, "the party has begun". As an attempt to reach a different state, as a rite of passage, the party settles disorder to achieve a permanent order. And the house is the center, the point for all references. Around the house, all norms are abolished, decomposition is installed, as an imitation of a huge dissolution, the original chaos:

> The lights grow brighter as the earth lurches away from the sun, and now the orchestra is playing yellow cocktail music, and the opera of voices pitches a key higher. Laughter is easier minute by minute, spilled with prodigality, tipped out at a cheerful word. The groups change more, swiftly swell with new arrivals, dissolve and form in the same breath; already there are wanderers, confident girls who weave here and there among the stouter and more stable, become for a sharp, joyous moment the center of a group, and then, excited with triumph, glide on through the sea-change of faces and voices and color under the constantly changing light. (p. 42)

From this chaotic and orgiastic atmosphere will grow beauty and permanence – the negativeness of a moment when all norms are annulled is a promise of a revivified order. In fact, once, Daisy came to the party. "Daisy and Gatsby danced." And the magic atmosphere from Gatsby's house involved her, called her back inside the house:

> After all, in the very casualness of Gatsby's party there were romantic possibilities totally absent from her world. What was it up there in the song that seemed to be calling her back inside? What would happen now in the dim, incalculable hours? (p. 111)

A feast is considered a projection of an archetypal drama. That was the last party; after it, some secluded moments of happiness. Then, unexpectedly, it happens: Gatsby's dramatic death – "the party was over". And, in consequence, there remained "that huge incoherent failure of a house".

The failure of a house. The role of the archetype of the house has failed too, regarding Gatsby?

In a search for the answers, it is necessary to explore two more aspects:

the symbolism of water and the temporal dimension, both connected to the house and to Gatsby.

Related to Gatsby and to the house, water, under various forms, is a symbol of great significance: the Sound's waters surround his house; it was raining when he first met Daisy at Nick's house; it was raining when his body reached the cemetery, "blessed are the dead that the rains fall on"; and when he was murdered, the waters of the swimming pool received his blood. Always the water: profound and transparent (the Sound waters) as his desires; calm and persistent (rain, not storm) as his love and its possibilities of renewal; water as a symbol of destiny, the vain destiny of an unrealizable dream, dreamt by a human being as transitory as water, that flows and falls, always coming to a horizontal death.

The archetype of the house, in *The Great Gatsby*, is also surrounded and strengthened by the temporal dimension, an important element of mythical structures. Time is, maybe, the most significant dimension of myth: every myth is a search for a time lost, as a Paradise lost. Myth presents the possibility of repeating time, the hope of vanquishing time. It represents an effort at reconciliation with a euphemistic time, more gentle than real time that flows incessantly. Gatsby's determination is to recover an ideal time: the past must be recovered – "Can't repeat the past? Why of course you can!" And Gatsby anchored his past in his present house, entirely trimmed to accomplish his eternal dream of love. His house, as Gatsby's own microcosm, is in the middle of the events that delineate two main movements, characteristics of mythical narratives: an ascending movement, an ascent to height, to happiness and realization; a descending movement, a descent to tragedy, to unhappiness and death. The two movements can be retraced even in Gatsby's character – a long and suffering ascent is followed by a vertiginous descent: tragedy and death.

Both movements were materialized by the house: Gatsby's house was his intimacy, the enlargement of his own personal limits. Gatsby assumes slowly but firmly his privileged place; James Gatz becomes Jay Gatsby; Jay Gatsby is the Great Gatsby, majestic, solemn, superior. His house is a mansion. Only a mansion could protect the dream of an archetypal hero, a tragic hero. When he achieves the essence of tragedy, climax followed by decline, Gatsby was in his house, and in the water. Wilson's interference represents the mysterious element of atonement – the death of the tragic hero has, in some sense, the character of a purifying or atoning sacrifice. By Wilson's hand his tragic holocaust was accomplished in water, as a diving into an eternal time, forever. Gatsby dies in water, in his house; Gatsby dives in his eternal time, in his paradisiac time, materialized by the house, as a huge intra-uterine space. The house had accomplished its archetypal role. And before the eternal diving, in his last moments, Gatsby "must have looked up at an unfamiliar sky through frightening leaves and shivered as he found what a grotesque thing a rose is and how raw the sunlight was upon the scarcely created grass". (p. 185)

University of Juiz de Fora

BIBLIOGRAPHY

Bachelard, G. *La terre et les rêveries du repos*. Paris: J. Corti, 1974.
Bachelard, G. *La poétique de l'espace*. Paris: P.U.F., 1957.
Bachelard, G. *L'eau et les rêves*. Paris: J. Corti, 1974.
Fitzgerald, F. S. *The Great Gatsby*. New York: C. Scribner's Sons, 1973.
Jung, C. G. *Les types psychologiques*. Genève: Georg, 1950.
Jung, C. G. *El hombre y sus símbolos*. Madrid: Aguilar, 1969.

BERNADETTE PROCHASKA

THE ELEMENTAL PASSION OF HOME AND WALKER PERCY'S LANCELOT

Walker Percy's Lancelot Andrewes Lamar is a man whose life has turned into one of madness, loss and sin. His story is told from a psychiatric ward in a mental hospital. In his cell, from which he can see the Louisiana cemetary and the women who are washing the tombstones to celebrate All Soul's Day he engages the listener, Harry, a priest/psychologist, his Percival, in a journey of a soul lost in some place far from Eden. His view of the world outside of his home is narrow and his own house is a "fallen house". Lancelot is a twentieth-century figure in a society gone mad with its terrible loss of the memory which would provide it with its sense of place and home. Like Adam, outside of that first garden, Lance is a fallen man in a fallen world. Lancelot's first utterance to Percival is that "the past doesn't seem worth remembering" (p. 1). Besides the loss that pervades the story of Lancelot, there is also a quest upon which he embarks to find meaning in his life. This quest for the Holy Grail, or for whatever would be salvation in his journey, is long in coming, for like Adam after the Fall Lance is bewildered by his surroundings and his vision is marred by sin. Loss, quest, and salvation are elemental to the journey of Lance and the post-modern environment in which he lives.

Even before the events of the novel take place, Lancelot Andrewes Lamar has lost the élan in his life. The love of his life, Lucy Cobb, has died. He plays golf badly and drinks too much. He is slovenly and dissipated. Reading a Raymond Chandler novel for the fourth or fifth time is the only way he can "stand" his life (p. 24). Moreover, his second wife, Margot, is maintaining a lifestyle as an actress among self-made actors, who create the illusion of meaning in their depiction of the "happy life". Lance lives a life of disillusion and dissipation. A twentieth-century displaced Adam, Lance says of his life: "The only way I could stand my life in Louisiana, where I had everything, was to read about crummy lonesome Los Angeles in the 1930s" (p. 26). Lance says that "Things were split" (p. 26). What he expresses is a condition in his life and the life of the times and place in which he finds himself, a condition of brokenness, loss of a wholeness that must exist somewhere.

Edmund Husserl associates brokenness to the condition of fragmentation an individual experiences on the way to apprehension or recognition (p. 290). Lance, in a roundabout way, is a twentieth-century dissipated figure trying to diagnose his own problem.

Lancelot represents post-lapsarian Adam, sensing a loss of home. The loss of a home which was the place of Adam's residence, is presented in narrative form in the Book of Genesis which speaks of Adam and Eve being expelled from the Garden of Paradise. For the Christian, the Myth of the Fall is understood in the perspective of the salvation-history which began with Creation and will end at the Parousia, the Second Coming of Jesus the Lord. Salvation-history is the account in human terms (for as Heidegger says, that is all we have) of the intervention of God in our world. The new garden of our world, somewhere East of Eden, is much like the place where biblical individuals lived and sinned, were jealous and ambitious and unfaithful, committed murder, theft and lust and revealed, through the inspired writings, the consequences of original sin. In the first garden, however, a Savior was promised. God became incarnate, was born as a humble human being in our lowly estate, and lived among us, until He died in expiation for all sin. His resurrection is our saving grace, for in Christ we shall rise. If it is so that salvation-history began with creation, particularly in the story of the Fall, and continues until the end of the world, then every age, including our present post-modern age, participates in creating and dramatizing the enduring story of salvation. Lance's home, like Adam's, bears the mark of incompleteness. Indeed, our twentieth-century world represents what Lance could only remark as a place where "Things were split".

In an interview that Malcolm Jones had with Walker Percy, Percy declared that he was not a religious writer. He never intended to write about religion. However, he does like to explore the dislocation of twentieth-century individuals. Jones claims that ultimately Percy sees the problem from a religious perspective. The dislocation is not peculiar to the South or even to this age; it is a part of being human. The "something wrong with people is original sin" says Percy. "The fall of man sure enough took place, no matter what the psychologists say" (p. 46). There is no doubt that Percy's characters, like Lancelot, are dislocated individuals. It is ironic that this particular novel, which is clearly a modern allegory, has as its locale, a madhouse.

The story that a madman, Lance Lamar, tells his friend from his home in a psychiatric ward, is a story about loss. Lance has lost his home, Belle Isle, in a terrible destructive fire which he has caused. He has lost his second wife, Margot, in the once-beautiful home which had become a fiery hell. He has lost touch with the blessed place of his memories and he finds himself an outcast from the community. Lance fits the category Gabriel Marcel describes when he defines the "uneasy quester" in his essay "Human Uneasiness" in *Problematic Man*. He is an individual beset with possibilities which are "obscure and devoid of meaning" (p. iii). Simply put, Lancelot loses his way and the loss is like the loss reverberating throughout our land in the twentieth-century. Percy told Jan Nordby Gretlund that *Lancelot* is "an attack on the 20th century, on the whole culture. It is a rotten century, we are in terrible trouble" (p. 209).

Although Lancelot's place in the present post-modern world is a position of delicate imbalance and precarious loss, it is also a place of spiritual possibility and salvation. Like Adam outside of a marvelous benevolent garden, Lance too embarks on a quest for redemption. Percy admits that he created Lance as a bewildered individual, misguided by his own limitations as a fallen man in a fallen world. The author told William Delaney in 1977: "He's fundamentally a religious man but can't make head or tail of the usual religious terminology, God and all that, so he turns the whole thing upside down, looking for the holy grail of evil. When he gets to the heart of evil, what he thinks is evil, he finds nothing – which is, incidently orthodox Thomist doctrine, you know. Thomas Aquinas defines evil as the absence of essence" (p. 155).

What Percy is implying, when he speaks about Lance as a figure of the lost individual in the twentieth-century, is that the real loss is the marvelous awareness regarding the memory of the human condition in its splendid first home. What was that like? In the Book of Genesis we read about that first place: "Then the man and his wife heard the voice of God, for in the cool of the day He would walk with them" (Genesis, 3:8). What is important about this place is the *communitas* in it. God is an integral member of the human family and the man and his wife hear His voice. Lance Lamar, as an allegorical figure of a lost Adam in the twentieth-century, has forgotten so many things. But the most important thing he has forgotten is the sound of God's voice. He has also lost a sense of the presence of God in his life. The wonderful garden of Adam and Eve has turned into a psychiatric ward where Lance bemoans his situation, telling his tale of woe to his old friend, Harry, now a priest/psychiatrist. His new "Eve" is his neighbor in the next cell, who cannot speak, and with whom he communicates by tapping on the wall. Here is another indication that he lives in a fallen world, where "things are split".

The great impulse is to recover what has been lost. When Lance claims that he does not remember because what he has forgotten is not worth remembering, he is voicing the words of a madman. The past *is* worth remembering and recovering. Memory is important for rebirth and the cycle of loss and recovery is allied to the cycle of death and resurrection. Lance's quest for the Holy Grail is a quest for the spiritual renewal of himself. He tells Harry: "I think I see now what I am doing. I am reliving with you my quest. That's the only way I can bear to think about it. Something went wrong. If you listen I think I can figure out what it was.

"It was a quest all right and a very peculiar one. But peculiar times require peculiar quests.

"We've spoken of the Knights of the Holy Grail, Percival. Do you know what I was? The Knight of the Unholy Grail." (p. 124)

As a twentieth-century dislocated and bewildered post-lapsarian Adam, Lance cannot quite figure out the object of his search. From his psychiatric ward he knows that he was on a quest for evil, but while he was contriving to get proof of the sins of his wife, he was quite alert and determined to discover every detail within his power. His house had been dishonored. In his tale, he shapes his life into two parts, his life before he found out about his wife's adultery and his life after he found out. His discovery is so essential to his quest because he senses that his identity is lost in some way. His daughter does not have any trace of his blood type. He senses he has lost his "house", his family. Others have been in his wife's bed. Belle Isle, his ancestral home has been defiled.

Like many Percian situations, there is an irony in the fact that Lance's house is built over an old bed of oil and natural gas. Percy has this penchant for destruction. He creates a world where some terrible, impending danger is ever lurking. We are forever on the "brink" of some terrible catastrophe. So it is with the house. His beautiful mansion, Belle Isle, rests on the seepage of a deep oil well, and on the night of his confrontation with the evil he has been searching for, Lance allows methane to enter through the air vents, and then lights a lamp, blowing his house and its inhabitants to kingdom come. Miraculously he awakens outside the house, against a tree, a foolish sinner beneath a very old tree, awakened to a greater quest, a quest that involves great suffering as Lance examines the wasteland of his own soul.

Without a doubt, Quest is central to the meaning of this novel, as Lancelot and Percival of old were on the marvelous quest for the Holy Grail. While legend has it that Percival saw the Holy Grail, Lancelot never did, for he was a sinner. Indeed, his affair with Guenevere culminated in the sad death of King Authur. And so it happens that even now, in the twentieth-century, there are people like Lancelot and Percival. It is consoling to hear the modern author, Percy himself, say that Lancelot is basically a religious figure who cannot quite understand his situation and has everything upside down. Like Hawthorne's Goodman Brown and Conrad's Charles Marlow, who go out into the dark woods, trying to discover the meaning of evil, so Percy's Lancelot devises plans to discover sin. His quest is all mixed up, so that a year later, from his madhouse home, he can tell Percival that he was searching for the unholy grail.

Quest involves salvation. Even Lance's quest for the unholy Grail is a search for knowledge, and he hopes the knowledge he seeks, as subversive as it is, will set him free in some way. Lance's unholy quest fails and brings him the destruction of his house and family. Rather than freedom, his quest brings him confinement in a madhouse and loss of his very identity. He cannot even recognize himself when he sees a man (himself) in the mirror. Thus, his movement toward salvation begins when he is in the condition of Adam after the Fall, when he is lost outside of the Garden. However, Lance will build a new world beyond this place where he has been living, this world of lies and fire and beasts and illusion. Necessary for his new world is Anna, the mute girl in the cell next to his. Anna has been gang raped and now cannot talk, she will not eat and has to be force-fed. Communication, by tapping on the wall, has increased over the months, and these two extremely lonely people, Lance and Anna, have grown to love each other. Anna has inherited some land, fifty acres in the Blue Ridge, not far from Lexington, Virginia, which includes a house and barn (p. 203). Salvation will come as these two fallen souls move back into *communitas*, back into the great garden home.

Walker Percy is fascinated with the idea of his character's movement to salvation by building a new world. His finest example is Will Barrett, who at the end of *The Second Coming* undertakes the actual construction of garden homes. Lance and Anna will rebuild their lives out in Virginia. He tells Percival:

> Yes, don't you see? Virginia is where it will begin. And it is where there are men who will do it. Just as it was Virginia where it all began in the beginning, or at least where the men were to conceive it, the Great Revolution, fought it, won it, and saw it on its way. (p. 203)

Although Lance is talking about the historical Revolution of the Civil War, he is also predicting that "Virginia is where it will begin." The new Revolution will be his new life, his and Anna's. The new woman and the new world are important themes for Lance. In his last conversation with Percival he says: "I do not propose to live in Sodom or to raise my son and daughters in Sodom" (p. 239). The old House of Lamar is really quite out of his reach now. Belle Isle has been destroyed by fire, and his children are quite grown, Lucy was only a teenager but quite "on her own". Lance speaks of his son only once and does not name him. He tells Percival that his son is gone, a homosexual. He will look after Siobhan, we know, for he defines his family to Anna when she too is recovering her health. Lance tells her: "I need you and you need me. I will have Siobhan with me." And Anna replies "A new family. A new life" (p. 202). The movement to salvation then, for Lance, will be somewhere away from Sodom, in Virginia, in the Blue Ridge Mountains. More importantly, in his quest for redeeming Grace, he will establish a new House of Lamar. *Communitas*, like that in the first ancient Garden is basically the elemental passion which gives the home its salvation. At the end of the Lance's story he asks his friend:

"One last question – and somehow I know you know the answer. Do you know Anna?

"Yes.

"Do you know her well?

"Yes.

"Will she join me in Virginia and will she and I and Siobhan begin a new life there?

"Yes." (p. 240)

The story that Walker Percy tells is a long, ancient, powerful tale that transcends time and place and even language. *Lancelot* is a tale about loss, about quest and about salvation. Poor Lance is a twentieth-century bewildered Adam, outside a splendid garden, shuffling along through life, groping through a haze of bewilderment for an Edenic happiness that must exist somewhere. The last *yes* in the novel, uttered by the priest, is an indication that Lance will get some help on his awesome journey. Percival has seen the Holy Grail and he knows the way back home. Salvation exists, not only at the end of the journey, but along the way. Time itself is holy. Because of the promise in the Book of Genesis, and the life and redemptive death of the Promised One, the human condition of loss and quest is converted into the blessed condition of hope and salvation. Lance's journey will be one of Participation in a life with Christ, in this novel represented by the Priest, Harry, Percival, the one who knows the way home.

REFERENCES

Delaney, William. "A Southern Novelist Whose CB Crackles with Kierkegaard". *Conversations with Walker Percy*. Eds. Lewis Lawson and Victor Kramer. Jackson: The University Press of Mississippi, 1985.

Gretlund, Jan Norby. "Laying the Ghost of Marcus Aurelius?". *Conversations with Walker Percy*. Eds. Lewis Lawson and Victor A. Kramer. Jackson: University Press of Mississippi, 1985.

Husserl, Edmund. *Experience and Judgment*. Trans. James S. Churchill and Karl Ameriks. Evanston: Northwestern University Press, 1973.

Jones, Malcolm. "Moralist of the South". *The New York Times Magazine*. March 22, 1987.

Marcel, Gabriel. *Being and Having*. Trans. Katharine Farrer. Glasgow: The University Press, 1949.

Percy, Walker. *Lancelot*. New York: The Hearst Corporation, 1977.

CHRISTOPH EYKMAN

THE IMPERFECT AND THE ALL-TOO-PERFECT HOME: THE HOUSE AS EXISTENTIAL SYMBOL IN FRANZ KAFKA'S "THE BURROW" AND THOMAS BERNHARD'S *CORRECTION*

The literary motif of the home, especially in the sense of "house", has a long and semantically diversified history. Living in a home that provides shelter, being attached to it and rooted in it, are vital functions of human life. Yet the literary image of the house often transcends these self-evident basic semantic definitions towards a broader symbolic sense, which is linked only in a rather general and rudimentary way to its original semantic content. House or home are then assigned a special idiosyncratic meaning by an author and thereby become existential symbols. In this fuller and higher sense they embody the most gratifying fulfilment of human life as well as its most painful failings, the plight or predicament of human endeavor.

I

The home as a symbol of man's strife, of his quest for happiness, fulfilment and perfection in life, is the focus of two texts from 20th-century German and Austrian literature: Franz Kafka's story "The Burrow" (1923) and Thomas Bernhard's novel *Correction* (1975).[1] The first person narrator of Kafka's parabolic story is an animal, possibly a badger, who lives in an elaborate network of underground tunnels which he has carefully designed and built. Since the animal is obsessed with his need for security, he constantly repairs, extends and remodels his burrow, seeking in vain to perfect its layout and structural soundness. His frantic and ceaseless attempts to correct perceived (or imagined) defects reveal his fundamental need for protection. The home becomes a fortress which shuts out any unwelcome intruder. In spite of the animal's almost pathological concern for security, there are however also moments in his life when his fear and his lack of trust in his own craftsmanship give way to a feeling of blissful and carefree comfort: "there I sleep the sweet sleep of tranquillity, of satisfied desire, of achieved ambition; for I possess a house." (p. 93)[2] Yet no matter how diligently the animal digs and repairs, the goal of total security remains elusive:

> But it is not so pleasant when, as sometimes happens you suddenly fancy, starting up from your sleep, that the present distribution of your stores is completely and totally wrong, might lead to great dangers, and must be set right at once, no matter how tired or sleepy you may be; then I rush, then I fly, then I have no time for calculation; and although I was about to execute a perfectly new, perfectly exact plan, I now seize whatever my teeth hit upon and drag it or carry it away, sighing, groaning, stumbling, and even the most haphazard change in the present situation, which seems so terribly dangerous, can satisfy me. (p. 95)

The potential intruder, the "enemy" who becomes the object of the animal's paranoia seems to be invisible yet omnipresent. He lurks in the outside or above-ground world in which the animal once lived but into which he hardly ventures any more. But he also poses a constant threat *from within*. Towards the end of the story the animal hears a strange noise and concludes that it must emanate from the invisible enemy. Thus he considers digging a trench towards the noise in order to eradicate (or at least to know) its source. Yet the hissing noise, as Hermann J. Weigand and Walter Sokel[3] have pointed out, is a hallucination. It originates in the animal's psyche and is a symptom of his self-destructive paranoia.

The upper world outside the burrow is a hostile world but, regardless of the dangers it poses, it also represents a fuller, richer, more satisfying life, a life which the animal – for reasons never disclosed by him – seems to have abandoned except for occasional forays into it: "I am no longer confined by narrow passages, but hunt through the open woods, and feel new powers awakening in my body for which there was no room, as it were, in the burrow ... The food too is better up here; though hunting is more difficult, success more rare, the results are more valuable from every point of view." (p. 99 f.)

The centerpiece or inner sanctum of the burrow is the so-called Castle Keep which is both a place of refuge and a central storage area:

> In the Castle Keep I assemble my stores; everything over and above my daily wants that I capture inside the burrow, and everything I bring back with me from my hunting expeditions outside, I pile up here. The place is so spacious that food for half a year scarcely fills it. Consequently I can divide up my stores, walk about among them, play with them, enjoy their plenty and their various smells, and reckon up exactly how much they represent. (p. 94)

Since the Castle Keep represents the highest achievement of the animal, he can truthfully claim that it is "so essentially mine that I can calmly accept in it even my enemy's mortal stroke at the final hour . . ." (p. 107) The animal and his work, i.e. the home he has built, belong indissolubly together, they are truly one. The burrow is in that sense "essentially his".

The burrow as well as the Castle Keep are more than the product of mere physical labor. They are also the fruit of a sustained *intellectual* effort which affords the burrower "the sheer pleasure of the mind in its own keenness." (p. 93) Consequently, the most blissful experiences in the animal's life are those of taking stock, of proudly surveying the network of passages and rooms of which it is the sole creator and master. Yet, at the same time, he constantly corrects not only the burrow itself but also the *theories* about the dangers to which it might be exposed.

In many of his texts Kafka presents the reader with a detailed and concrete yet enigmatic story which calls for an interpretation, for an answer to the question: what does it mean? In traditional parables like those in the New Testament a figurative (abstract) explanation follows the story. Kafka withholds from his readers the figurative part. The task of distilling the meaning from the elements of the story therefore falls to the reader. Usually, this allows for several possible interpretations which must be analogous to one another and which have to fit as many segments of the plot as possible. If indeed, as we have assumed above, the burrow is a symbol for human existence, the animal's passionate, frantic quest for security, coupled with deep-seated anxiety, could, according to scholars like Henel,[4] be understood to mirror the *human* effort to eliminate from life any potential dangers, mishaps, or catastrophes. This reminds us of Heidegger's analysis of "Sorge" and "Angst" in *Sein und Zeit*, which appeared only one year after Kafka's story was written. Kafka's animal knows:

that in reality the burrow does provide a considerable degree of security, but by no means enough, for is one ever free from anxieties inside it? These anxieties are different from ordinary ones, prouder, richer in content, often long repressed, but in their destructive effects they are perhaps much the same as the anxieties that existence in the outer world gives rise to. (p. 106)

While Kafka's burrower displays an inner (emotional) tendency towards self-destruction, the outside world in the story also stands for forces which might interfere destructively and often irrationally with our rational precautionary planning. Yet the upper world is also the world of society from which the animal has all but withdrawn. Having given up a richer, more rewarding (but also more dangerous) life "outside", the animal becomes a thoroughly paranoid lonely creature whose only communicative act is the telling of his story.[5]

If one does not view the burrow as a concrete and tangible representation of a human being's life, one might interpret it as an image of the human *psyche*. The *inner* enemy then is one who poses an emotional threat to the psychic balance and well-being of the person. This threat, which triggers the animal's self-destructive and frantic behavior, finds its ultimate expression in the hissing noise the animal claims to detect everywhere in his burrow and which he interprets as a noise produced by an approaching enemy.[6]

Kafka's burrow (in spite of its underground location the German original uses the word "Haus" several times) is a home, an abode that affords comfort, a storage place, and a fortress which shields its inhabitant against potential enemies from the outside world. On a higher, figurative level, though, the burrow may be viewed as the fruit of the animal's physical and intellectual labor, a "Lebenswerk" through which the animal materializes its true self. Furthermore, the burrow stands for human life in a broad sense and for the human effort to protect it against unforeseen mishaps or catastrophes (possibly and ultimately, death). The burrow is also a place in which a lone individual encapsulates and detaches himself from society (for reasons the story withholds from the reader). Finally, Kafka's burrow may be understood as the embodiment of a human psyche and its pathological, self-destructive features in connection with a perceived external threat from society and/or nature. This polarization of self and society and its attendant emotions and passions constitute a theme, the variations of which one finds in many of Kafka's texts.

II

Like the animal in Kafka's story, Roithamer, the protagonist of Thomas Bernhard's novel *Correction*, is a loner. He is one of the many intellectual outsiders and/or artistically gifted eccentrics and monomaniacs we encounter in the texts of the Austrian writer.[7] Roithamer, an intellectual and a scientist, a restless, rootless, and homeless traveller, shuttles back and forth between the university of Cambridge (England) where he teaches yet keeps mostly to himself, and a small place in the Austrian countryside where he occupies a garret in a friend's house. This hideout in which he lives a life of almost total seclusion and into which he crams all his books and manuscripts is his only and true home, a home he never built and does not own. Only here, in self-imposed solitude, is he able to think and write.

Roithamer's manuscripts reveal that he suffered through a painful childhood and adolescence. His wealthy parents and his brothers fail to recognize his special gifts and constantly try to stifle his intellectual and artistic development. Only his sister, whom Roithamer loves dearly, understands him and shares his interests. Consequently, Roithamer's adult life has to be understood as a lifelong flight from his oppressive and authoritarian parents and their estate Altensam, particularly the old and worm-eaten house that bears that name. Roithamer calls the Altensam home a dungeon, a place where people "vegetate", where they live in a state of stubborn imbecility, where no artistic or intellectual talent can flower. Thus Altensam represents a complete perversion of the traditional idea of the home/house where a human being is rooted, where he or she feels "at home" and from which one draws spiritual strength and nourishment. Consequently, Roithamer devotes most of his emotional and mental energies to extricating and liberating himself from Altensam, the exemplary anti-home.

The Altensam experience makes Roithamer a recluse, an eccentric who transfers his contempt of his family to Austrian society at large: "One has to be able to get up and walk away from every social gathering that's a waste of one's time, so Roithamer, to leave behind the nothing faces and the often boundlessly stupid heads, and to walk out and down and into the open air and leave everything connected with this worthless society behind . . ." (p. 264) Although Roithamer does feel close to members of the lower social classes, the woodcutters, coal miners, farmers (and the taxidermist Höller in whose house he lives), he lives essentially *outside* society, his Cambridge teaching activities notwithstanding. He has almost completely and irreversibly detached himself from social life.

Shunning any contact or communication with other "ordinary" members of society, Roithamer surrounds himself with the written works of fellow intellectuals which "speak" to him and with whom he communes in the solitude of his attic room. Its walls are covered with pages torn out of books (for example from Valéry's *Monsieur Teste*).

As an intellectual, Roithamer is an uncompromising seeker of truth. Whenever his mind takes up a thought, it has to be "thought through to the end." (p. 35) To him thinking must strive for universal validity. Yet he knows that his ideas are at the same time nourished by particular concerns, that they possess a highly *personal* existential quality.

Roithamer's struggle to assert himself as an intellectual and artistic individual against an uncomprehending and hostile society finds its ultimate expression in an architectural project of a truly unique and extraordinary nature, into which the scientist pours all his mental energies and almost all his wealth. He spends six years designing and then supervising the construction of a house for his beloved sister. This house, which has the shape of a cone, is indeed a highly unorthodox structure which defies all architectural traditions. Just as Roithamer is an erratic and unique human being who does not fit into the established molds of his society, his brainchild, the cone, stands alone among other known works of architecture. Like Kafka's animal, Roithamer becomes totally obsessed with his building project.

The cone is erected as an "answer" to Roithamer's parental house at Altensam. It is the counter-design, the spiritual as well as physical negation and conquest of the oppressive anti-home. By means of the cone, which is designed to encase a utopian and ideal life, Roithamer strikes back at his uncaring and authoritarian parents. The *reflective* nature of this utopian life which the cone is designed to being forth is symbolized by its central chamber, a meditation room, Roithamer's "Castle Keep", as it were. The room is unfurnished and has a red dot at the center of its floor.

Not only is the cone *extra-ordinary* in the true sense of the word. It is erected out of sight of society, right in the center of a large forest, accessible only by labyrinthine paths. Its location outside human society reveals, just as the animal's underground burrow does, its creator's desire to flee and withdraw from social constraints.

Most of us adhere to the time-honored belief that the sciences either pursue truth for its own sake or that the scientist works – using technological application as an intermediary – for the benefit of mankind. Yet the cone, the concrete embodiment of Roithamer's scientific endeavors, houses nobody, not even his sister for whom it was built. Just when she seems ready to move into the completed structure she dies of a mysterious illness. The paradoxical nature of Roithamer's mission reveals itself in the fact that the *non plus ultra* of his achievement whose purpose is a "better" life, leads to destruction. The cone stifles life even more perfectly than the old house at Altensam. The scientifically calculated abode of an ideal life outside society turns out to be deathly: "I see now", says the narrator, "that Roithamer's life, his entire existence, had aimed at nothing but this creation of the Cone, everyone has an idea that kills him in the end, an idea that surfaces inside him and haunts him and that sooner or later – always under extreme tension – wipes him out, destroys him." (p. 88)

What then, according to Roithamer/Bernhard, is the meaning of science? Is it only the monomaniacal self-gratification of the scientific or artistic intellect which Kafka's animal also knows so well? Indeed both the burrow and the cone derive their existence and (near) perfection from an almost extreme monomania of their respective creators. Roithamer states in his will that the cone, should it never be occupied, must be left untouched so that it can slowly disintegrate, exposed to nature's eroding forces. Knowing that he cannot prevent others from eventually exploiting its architectural innovations, Roithamer nevertheless builds the cone for only one individual. The scientist thus intentionally withholds his services from society and limits his role to that of a deadly narcissistic self-gratification.[8] His unhappy childhood and adolescence make him a radical sceptic who adopts an utterly pessimistic philosophy of life, according to which nothing in this world is worth working for except the relentless and obsessive pursuit of an idea, regardless of the needs of society. In blatant defiance of scientific reason, his *particular* personal experience assumes the validity of a universal law. "Everything is ultimately the cone" (p. 259) writes Roithamer, which could mean: everything is ultimately useless, absurd. Even if it expresses an individual's idea perfectly, it destroys and will be destroyed. It is the idea that kills Roithamer in the end, not his decision to become a recluse. The paradox of Roithamer's life consists, however, in his single-minded attempt to assert himself as an individual over the pre-established structures and regulations of society, i.e. to shape the world in the image of his own mind, even at the price of self-destruction. The cone is also a symbol of this individualistic self-assertion:

We enter a world which precedes us but is not prepared for us and we have to cope with this world, if we can't cope with this world we're done for, but if we survive, for whatever constitutional reason, then we must take care to turn this world, which was a given world but not made for us or ready for us, a world which is all set in any case, because it was made by our predecessors, to attack us and ruin us and finally destroy us, nothing else, we must turn it into a world to suit our own ideas, acting first behind the scenes, but then with all our might and quite openly, so that we can say after a while that *we're living in our own world, not in some previous world* . . . (pp. 174 f.)

The biographical aspect of Roithamer's cone project is underscored by the somewhat long-winded title he gives his manuscript: "About Altensam and Everything Connected with Altensam, with Special Attention to the Cone." (p. 130) The manuscript reveals two mutually exclusive existential gestures. On the one hand, as the narrator, a friend of Roithamer's, tells us, he keeps *correcting* his manuscripts.[9] To him the truth seems to be for ever elusive. Like Kafka's animal he is obsessed with changing and correcting. Yet his radicalism goes beyond the animal's redesigning and repairing. During the process of "correction", Roithamer's manuscripts grow shorter and shorter until almost nothing is left or the initial thesis is turned into its opposite. Roithamer finally applies this urge to correct to his own life. It too is not "right" and thus has to be crossed out. Shortly after his sister's death, Roithamer commits suicide.

Yet the fact that Roithamer leaves his manuscripts to the narrator who, after some hesitation, decides to show them to a publisher, opens up the possibility of his work being scrutinized by others. Thus it might be put together in an organized fashion, published and ultimately communicated to society. This is, after all, a positive, perhaps even optimistic, gesture. Even though the cone's existence is futile, even though it is, in a sense, like Altensam, an anti-home, its creator at least implicitly allows its "story" to be told, just as the only truly communicable act that Kafka's animal engages in is the telling of his story.

III

Both the burrow and Roithamer's cone are symbols of an individual's highest intellectual and practical achievement.[10] This is why both the animal and Roithamer emphatically identify with their respective creations. In that sense the burrow *is* the animal and the cone *is* Roithamer. As the burrow is a concrete and tangible projection of the animal's self so is Roithamer's cone the fruit of his scientific and artistic genius.

In both cases the individual's achievement is built to suit the personality of one unique individual, not the pre-given norms of society. In Roithamer's words: "The Cone's interior corresponding to my sister's inner being, the Cone's exterior to her outward being, and together her whole being expressed as the *Cone's character* . . ." (p. 158)

As Kafka's animal continuously corrects the burrow, thereby for ever attempting to shore up the life of the unattached individual against a hostile society, Roithamer's corrections are not so much the expression of the polarization of self and society, but of the pessimistic view that the search for truth is endless and fails to find meaning in any human endeavor whatsoever. While Roithamer's scientific pursuits lead to the creation of a seemingly perfect work, the all-too perfect cone which appears to be beyond any correction serves, in the final analysis, no purpose: it never houses anyone. Likewise, the quasi-scientific activities of Kafka's animal – who ceaselessly calculates, observes the entrance to its burrow from the outside, uses abstract reasoning and gathers data – only drive it deeper into its paranoia with regard to the security of its "house".

In both cases, paradoxically, building leads to destruction. The animal is driven into an overwhelming state of anxiety that destroys both the burrow and its creator. Roithamer, on the other hand, is "a man who must force everything he is, in the final analysis, to coalesce in one extreme point, force it all to the utmost limits of his intellectual capacity and his nervous tension until, at the highest degree of such expansion and contraction . . . he must actually be torn apart." (pp. 26 f.) One can only speculate as to whether this *coincidentia oppositorum* in which highest creative fulfilment equals self-destruction might also be interpreted, as Emrich and Sokel do, as a *moral failure* vis-a-vis society (in the case of Kafka's animal), and as an existential flaw in the human species as such (in the case of Bernhard's Roithamer).

The self-destructive quest entails self-doubt. Kafka's animal never quite trusts his work, and Roithamer once calls his cone a "mad aberration." (p. 266) While the animal sinks deeper and deeper into paranoia, Roithamer repeatedly admits to himself that the most strenuous mental effort takes him to the brink of insanity. Again, Kafka's burrow and Roithamer's cone do not protect, they destroy.

Both the burrow and the cone are built with the intention to encapsulate their respective inhabitants. Enjoyment of solitude, withdrawal from society and refusal to adapt to it characterize the protagonists of both texts. Whereas Kafka's burrow shields the animal, though imperfectly, against a hostile society, Roithamer's cone is built as an emphatic "statement" against a despised social order. It is a symbol of a utopian, albeit not realizable, life-style which dares to negate social conventions and regulations.

The individual refuses to be molded by a society it experiences as alien. This is why the upper world in Kafka's story is called "die Fremde" (the alien world). As we mentioned above, Bernhard goes beyond alienation and detachment and calls for the individual to leave his imprint on the pre-given world and to mold its social environment. The cone is an – albeit unsuccessful – attempt on the part of the individual to substitute his own world for that of the "previous", handed-down world.

Achievement and existential self-fulfilment versus self-destruction; refuge, the quest for security, and self-imposed encapsulation versus fear of the "outside" world; pride and intellectual self-gratification versus self-doubt and mental insanity; self-assertion of the individual versus an oppressive society which threatens to stifle his uniqueness and to crush his genius – this is the range of complex and often contradictory meanings associated with the "passion of place" in "The Burrow" and *Correction*, whose authors seek to fathom the human predicament of the dissociation of modern society and the *individuum ineffabile*.

Boston College

NOTES

[1] English quotations from both works are taken from the following translations: *The Basic Kafka*, trans. by Edwin and Willa Muir (New York: Basic Books, 1979); Thomas Bernhard, *Correction*, trans. by Sophie Wilkins (Chicago: University of Chicago Press, 1990).

[2] For a comprehensive look at Kafka's use of the image/symbol of the house see: Hartmut Binder, *Kafka-Kommentar zu sämtilchen Erzählungen* (München: Winkler, 1975), pp. 304 f. For a painstakingly careful and well written analysis of Kafka's story which deliberately limits itself to an elucidation of the story as such see: Hermann J. Weigand, "Franz Kafka's 'The Burrow' ('Der Bau'): An Analytical Essay", *PMLA* 87(2), 1972, pp. 152–166. Weigand's analysis becomes less convincing when he ventures into interpretation (the themes of sex and religion).

[3] Walter H. Sokel, *Franz Kafka – Tragik und Ironie* (München/Wien: Albert Langen/Georg Müller, 1969), pp. 377 ff.

[4] Compare: Heinrich Henel, "Kafka's 'Der Bau', or how to Escape from a Maze" in P. F. Ganz (ed.), *The Discontinuous Tradition* (Festschrift for Ernest L. Stahl) (Oxford: Oxford University Press, 1971), p. 227.

[5] One possible interpretation of Kafka's story is of course the autobiographical one which takes the burrow to mean Kafka's seclusive activities as a writer, while the upper world stand for society, "normal" life. Kafka, in an autobiographical note once used the image of the house, to express the idea that his writing was a total rebuilding of his "house"

out of components of the "old" unsafe (*unsicher*) house; Kafka, "Hochzeits-vorbereitungen auf dem Lande" *und andere Prosa aus dem Nachlaß* (Frankfurt/M.: S. Fischer, 1953), p. 388.

⁶ This emotional behavior on the part of Kafka's animal has tempted some Kafka scholars to understand it as a symptom of a deep-seated guilt complex of which the animal does not seem to be aware. Wilhelm Emrich detects such guilt in the animal's failure to understand in a radical way his moral mission, which is to realize absolute goodness rather than understanding good or evil acts as determined by external circumstances; Wilhelm Emrich, *Franz Kafka* (Frankfurt: Athenäum, 1957), p. 182. In a similar yet different way Walter H. Sokel sees the animal's guilt in his self-glorification, his narcissistic self-gratification and mystical self-love (see Sokel, *loc. cit.*, pp. 371 ff, p. 382). Both interpretations play down the threatening impact of the upper world. They remain somewhat speculative as long as the reader remains in the dark as to the reasons for the animal's permanent withdrawal into his burrow. Heinrich Henel's argument that the unknown threat in the animal's life is God (based on Kafka's use of the word "Sage", i.e. "legend", which he often uses in the sense of "scripture") remains equally speculative (Henel, *loc. cit.*, p. 235).

⁷ For an interpretation of Bernhard's novel which focuses on the role of the intellectual see: Christoph Eykman, *Der Intellektuelle in der westeuropäischen und amerikanischen Romanliteratur ab 1945* (Marburg: Hitzeroth, 1992), pp. 44–48.

⁸ Gudrun B. Mauch, "Thomas Bernhards Roman *Korrektur*. Zum autobiographisch fundierten Pessimismus Thomas Bernhards", *Amsterdamer Beiträge zur neueren Germanistik* 14 (1982) argues (not very convincingly) that the cone is a means to counteract nature's destructive forces (p. 87). The fact that the cone is built for Roithamer's sister does not in itself constitute, as Mauch writes, a link to society (p. 91). Mauch postulates but does not demonstrate the influence of Martin Heidegger's thought upon Bernhard's novel.

⁹ David Roberts, "Korrektur der Korrektur? Zu Thomas Bernhards Lebenskunstwerk *Korrektur*", in Manfred Jürgensen (ed.) *Bernhard: Annäherungen* (Bern/München: Francke, 1981), pp. 199–213 offers a very cogent and fruitful discussion of the notion of "correction" in Bernhard's novel. Ralf Jeutter, "Thomas Bernhards *Korrektur*. Ein Untergang", *Orbis Litterarum* 45 (1990), pp. 363–377 discusses a trend in Bernhard scholarship which claims that Bernhard's novel is non-mimetic, i.e. that it does not describe any "reality" outside the mere act of writing (p. 365). He attempts to synthesize this approach with a psychological interpretation that takes Altensam to stand for "split-off" parts of the protagonist's ego which have been projected into external reality (p. 373). Both approaches, however, conflict with on another and seem unnecessarily far-fetched.

¹⁰ For an excellent comparison of themes and style in the works of Kafka and Bernhard see: Gerald A. Fetz, "Kafka and Bernhard: Reflections on Affinity and Influence" in *Modern Austrian Literature* 21, 3/3 (1988), pp. 217–241. Fetz's contention that the character of Höller in *Correction* is a veiled portrait of Kafka and that Bernhard wrote his novel with Kafka's story "The Burrow" in mind remains rather speculative.

DAVID SULLIVAN

INTER-VIEW: EMILY DICKINSON AND THE DISPLACED PLACE OF PASSION

> Proximity is not a state, a repose, but, a restlessness, null site, outside of the place of rest. . . . No site then, is ever sufficiently a proximity, like an embrace.[1]

Emily Dickinson's writings incessantly posit a time when one would not be writing, when there would be no need for writing because one would be face to face with another person. Yet this ideal of a face to face encounter is itself posited *in* writing, because only in writing can she distance herself from the place of passion and recognize it as passion – understood as both a passive suffering *in* one's self, and as an active desire *for* another. This distancing involves her in a paradox because only in writing can she face facing another.

In writing about a face to face encounter Emily Dickinson becomes a third party describing an event as if she were uninvolved. She examines the image of seeing and being seen in a moment as both a desirable and threatening event. A face to face encounter is desirable because only in time can the place of passion be created, and it is threatening because one must expose one's self to another person without being able to predetermine his or her response. Emily Dickinson frequently displaces the place of this encounter into two written narratives: either an indefi-nitely postponed romantic union, or an unobtainable heaven in the future, but both narratives fail to alleviate the loneliness which remains a more or less discernible trace throughout her writings. These narratives make the place of passion unattainable, but they do not succeed in convincing that such unattainableness is necessary.

A face to face encounter can only exist *in* writing, for one can never be sure of what another person sees, even when one is looking at one's own image in the other's eyes. Reciprocity is always in doubt because one can never know another in the way one knows one's self, although language can suggest a reciprocity that is not possible between persons.[2] The anxiety about that moment produces the paroxysms of displacement that agitate the speaker of the poems I will examine. Emily Dickinson can never have the face to face encounter she desires, because such restful assurance would itself preclude the possibility, so she must settle for the writing which can suggest that event.

The word Emily Dickinson most frequently uses for this face to face encounter is "interview", so I will examine a letter which uses this word before turning to poems which manifest what I have termed the romantic and heavenly narratives. Inasmuch as these two narratives fail to assert the supremacy of the written narrative over one which occurs between persons, they manifest Emily Dickinson's passionate desire for the place of interview.

In a letter to her younger cousins written in 1871, Emily Dickinson articulates this problem of being *for* another person without being corporeally present. She writes about their concurrent efforts to revitalize sick people who seem to be near death: "All this while I was with you all, much of every hour, wishing we were near enough to assist each other."[3] Her phrasing implies that the imaginative act communicated in writing can surmount the physical distance that separates them. Emily Dickinson can extravagantly emphasize their closeness because the distance between them allows her to phrase their situations as similar; differences can be cancelled by distance. But the hyperbole suggests that there is a problem with apostrophe for Dickinson, for even as she turns towards a person through addressing them in writing, she simultaneously turns away from a physical encounter with that person by substituting their written name for such an interview. Only if writing could supply the responses she desires would this substitution be satisfying, but she repeatedly asserts that it cannot.

In this letter Emily Dickinson uses metaphors of size to communicate her relationship to other persons who are corporeally or linguistically present. She writes that "The terror of the winter has made a little creature of me, who thought myself so bold" (L. 360), using the image of her own reduced size and strength to express the fear that her father will not recover from his sickness. But two paragraphs later she writes to the absent Louise Norcross: "Of the 'thorn', dear, give it me, for I am strongest. Never carry what I can carry, for though I think I bend, something straightens me" (L. 360). In these phrases she proclaims her ability to carry burdens others cannot carry; a large person who can endure great pain. The image recalls Christ's wearing the crown of thorns while he carried the cross, and it is his passion, in the sense of a sacrifice for others, that the speaker of the letter rhetorically applied to herself. Before the "lonesome face" of her father Emily Dickinson shrinks, but while reading about the suffering of the Norcross cousins she expands. Because the response to anything written is inherently delayed, Dickinson can portray herself as existing *for* others in a way that exceeds her ability to do so when they are corporeally present.

At the end of the letter Emily Dickinson complains of the hindrances which prevent ideal written communication: "What I would, I cannot say in so small a place. Interview is acres, while the broadest letter feels a bandaged place" (L. 360). In the first sentence Emily Dickinson acts as if the letter were limited by its size, rather than by her inability to have the reader respond immediately, or by the impossibility of including inflection. The spatial metaphor conveys Dickinson's conception that writing compacts meaning into the fewest possible words, and the second sentence makes a more general claim about the difference between an interview and a letter in just such a gnomic way. Emily Dickinson writes about the impoverishment of letter writing when compared with a face to face interview, but she makes this complaint *in* a letter. She denigrates the very activity she is engaged in because letter writing, although less satisfying than a face to face interview, is what she *can* do. She resorts to writing not only because the person she is writing to is distant, but because the expansiveness of an interview presents uncontrollable contingencies, since the responses of the other person can never be predicted. A letter limits such contingencies and makes them bearable.

The sentence: "Interview is acres, while the broadest letter feels a bandaged place" (L. 360), is crucial to my reading of the word "interview" as connoting both a desired and threatening event, so I will examine it at length. The metaphors Emily Dickinson employs are those of cultivating land and binding wounds, both of which uneasily conjoin disparate spatial elements. Dickinson often ascribes human characteristics to landscapes, but here the human interaction is given in terms of the external world. The word "acres" can be used to describe a large open area of land, or as a metaphor for expansiveness. This sense of the word would describe the freedom to gaze without restrictions; an interview would open up vistas to be explored. But it also has connotations of a field of arable or pasture land; the name comes from the unit of measure which was established by the amount of land plowed by a yoke of oxen in one day.[4] Interviews, then, are acres because humans are allowed the freedom to gaze, and yet they must also labor over them. For Emily Dickinson an interview is both an opening up of myriad possible responses, and a difficult cultivation which is uncomfortably contingent on another's response to one's labors.

The comparison of the "broadest letter" to a "bandaged place" suggests an opposing movement. A bandaged place is generally located on a scarred human body. The bandage covers the wound, protecting it from infection even as it draws attention to it. If the "acres" of interview are for cultivation and exploration, an opening up of possible visions, then the bandaged place has been damaged and must heal: all vision of it must be shut down. The plural "acres", which suggests not only spatial extension, but that two parties may be involved, contrasts with the singular "bandaged place", which is spatially limited and suggests one wounded person. "Acres" suggests land furrowed for planting, while the phrase "bandaged place" suggests skin opened by a sharp implement. In both cases visual metaphors are implied: an interview expands the field of vision, while the broadest letter contracts the field of vision.

The word "interview" is derived from *enterview*, to meet face to face or to have a private conversation. It is this act of mutual seeing that Dickinson seems to be invoking in her use of the word, but it also has connotations of a formal meeting with a set agenda and duration, which suggests a hierarchical relationship between the two interlocutors. The word "interview", therefore, maintains the two poles which constitute Dickinson's way of relating to others: in the first there is a strict limitation of contingency and the inequality of the participants is exaggerated, in the second there is a radical openness to contingency and the participants' equality is exaggerated.[5]

In Dickinson's letter to the Norcross cousins she insists that there is mutual reciprocity between them, though the nature of letter writing precludes the physical contact to which Dickinson repeatedly refers. She asserts exactly what she cannot physically do, even as she linguistically does it: "Tell Fanny we hold her tight" (L. 360). Her hyperbole is moving because it continually denies its own limits, which has the effect of reasserting them. By playing on the ability of written words to suggest actions which they cannot make happen Dickinson both articulates their corporeal separation and expresses her wish to surmount it.

The letter ends: "Tell Loo love is oldest and takes care of us, though just now in a piercing place" (L. 360). The love that binds the older Emily Dickinson to her cousins seems to include a certain amount of pain, but the implication is that suffering for them is something she does willingly. This letter is written to Dickinson's female cousins, and its stated relationship between addressor and addressee is one of mutual affection and one-sided care-giving. As Richard Sewall has observed, "In her own way, and at a distance, Emily assumed the role of mother, offering the girls complete, uncritical love."[6] An interview with the Norcross cousins seems to be a possibility for Emily Dickinson; though the letter declares what an interview *is* rather then asking for one.

In the poems which either use the word interview, or invoke it through referring to a face to face encounter, the difficulty of seeing and being seen is explored relentlessly. Inasmuch as these poems insist on the failure of any possible interview they retract before another's supposed presence: either into a position of artificial power, in which the gaze must be maintained through an indefinite postponement of interview; or into a position of unattainable bliss, in which seeing and being seen is an atemporal otherworldly gift. The first postulates a romantic narrative of union endlessly deferred, while the latter postulates a transcendent narrative of spiritual completeness outside of time. But both narratives fail to excise the possibility that an interview can take place between persons who neither dominate nor are dominated but accept the bilateral contingencies of a moment.

Poem 421 addresses the possibility of interview in a coquettish game of romantic hide and seek. The first stanza reads:

> A Charm invests a face
> Imperfectly beheld –
> The Lady dare not lift her Vail
> For fear it be dispelled –[7]

The initial supposition is that the hidden face is not open to be looked at in a mutual exchange, and that it therefore encourages interest in the one who is hidden. This is phrased in terms of a hidden female face which constructs a sexual tête-à-tête with a male who gazes in an unequal contest. She "dare[s] not lift her Vail" to allow the other to see her clearly because staying hidden means that the investment of charm will increase. She is the object of observation throughout the poem, a commodity whose value increases as long as she presents an image and does not become an interacting human being, hence the use of the word "beheld" rather than "seen". Never is the voyeuristic male described, though we seem to observe the lady from his vantage point, and in this coquettish game her veil keeps him at an intriguing distance.

This veil is spelled "Vail" in the poem. The word *veil* designates the cloth that covers a woman's face, the curtain that separates a room, or, as a verb, to conceal or obscure. The word when spelled *vail* has another set of connotations. The root is *avalen*, to fall or to let fall, and means to lower as a sign of respect or submission, and the spelling also suggests the Old French stem for *valoir*, to be of worth. This poem suggests that the veil is a mark of their unequal worth, and that this inequality stimulates the very interest which might be dispelled by a face to face encounter. The banal conclusion would seem to claim that the coquettish interaction is predicated on the inequality between the two people:

> But peers beyond her mesh –
> And wishes – and denies –
> Lest Interview – annul a want
> That Image – satisfies –
>
> (P. 421)

The face to face encounter would eliminate the attraction that the male felt toward the respectfully veiled woman who satisfied him by remaining an image. The word "Image" suggests that the Lady is a statue-like reproduction of a person whose physicality is never tested. The tension of the relationship is predicated on the failure of the male to determine what the image is made of, such that his desire increases in the space between what he sees and what he imagines. The word "Interview" refers to a possible face to face encounter which would undermine the romantic want that stimulated a desire for this encounter.

But the poem does not settle on such a stereotypically familiar observation of flirtation because it is never clear that the face that is hidden is the lady's. If the lady is controlling her view of another's face by not daring to "lift her Vail", then the subject of the poem is her manipulation of her relationship to the other; it is not about coquettish hiding, but the unwillingness to risk facing another. Instead of wishing to expose herself to the mutual looking of an interview, and then denying herself that exposure for fear it will end the other's want, she may be wishing for that exposure, but denying herself that liberty because *her* want would become annulled. An interview would threaten the position of power in which she can control the gazes (both hers and the man's). The power she has is artificial, however, because it is motivated by fear of the man's response. In a romantic narrative distance is necessary for interest, and therefore an interview must be postponed indefinitely. In both readings the participants retract before the other's gaze which each claims to desire.

In poem 398 the speaker does not maintain the distanced speculative tone of "A Charm invests a face", but attempts to characterize a relationship by de-romanticizing it.

> I had not minded – Walls –
> Were Universe – one Rock –
> And far I heard his silver Call
> The other side the Block –
> (P. 398)

The subjunctive already establishes that "Universe" is not "one Rock", and that the analogy that occupies these first two stanzas is built on a fiction which will be undermined. The fiction is that there is a definite barrier between the female speaker of this poem and the male whom she desires to reach. The imagery depicts a romantic prison with rock walls and blocks that separate her from the one who is crying "his silver Call". The second stanza extends the metaphor and implies that each tunnels towards the other in mutual longing.

> I'd tunnel – till my Groove
> Pushed sudden thro' to his –
> Then my face take her recompense –
> The looking in his Eyes –
> (P. 398)

The sexual metaphors of the first lines is underlined by the stress on the gender of the two persons: "his silver Call", is paralleled to "my face take her Recompense." Curiously, the face is given a feminine pronoun only by being disengaged from the speaker of the poem: "*my* face take *her* recompense" (my emphasis). The possessiveness of her disengaged face is at odds with the mutuality that the poem had stressed, for it takes him in without referring to the fact that he looks back. "Recompense" refers to a compensation, a payment for what has been done, and the effort to reach the other is rewarded without his being rewarded in turn. As much as the early lines suggested reciprocity the look itself seems to be the possession of the female alone. He is an object which she consumes specularly.

This romantic narrative of overcoming external obstacles to obtain the other in a climactic moment is not sustained in the second half of the poem. The reversal occurs in the switch to the present declarative:

> But 'tis a single Hair –
> A filament – a law –
> A Cobweb – wove in Adamant –
> A Battlement – of straw –
>
> (P. 398)

The first line refers back to the idea that the "Universe" could be "one Rock", through which the speaker hears the other's call, but now proclaims " 'tis a single Hair". In the first stanza "Universe" designated the external forces that inhibited the desired interview, while in this stanza "Universe" refers to the fragility of their connection which seems to inhibit risking interview. Rather than a definite obstacle that can be overcome, it is a fragile thread which connects them. The next lines divide neatly between elements which are thin connectors, often with physical properties: "Hair", "filament", "Cobweb", "Straw", and elements which are hard, recalcitrant, and abstract: a "Rock", "a law", "Adamant", "A Battlement". The first list consists of strand-like elements which are often unseen or unnoticed, though they cease to oppose the second list, and instead begin to modify it. "A filament – a law", seem to be alternate terms for the same thing, while "A Cobweb – wove in Adamant", marries the two elements in a lethal trap.

These are not opposed elements anymore, but concurrent perceptions of the same thing. The relationship of the speaker to the other can only be communicated through paradoxical images which overlay the initial romantic portrait of surmounting barriers between equally attracted lovers. The romantic myth is predicated on mutual longing which necessitates a certain amount of separation. In the first stanzas the barriers come from outside, but in the last stanzas they are created as much by the lovers as by the external world.

The final stanza returns to knightly metaphors, as if cued by the "Battlement – of Straw", which implies that even the romantic story is created internally.

> A limit like the Vail
> Unto the Lady's face –
> But every Mesh – a Citadel –
> And Dragons – in the Crease –
>
> (P. 398)

The speaker distances herself from this last image by saying this is only a metaphor for her relationship to the other, "A limit *like* the Vail" (my emphasis), yet the rich details make it begin to operate in a way similar to the first stanza's image. Like the paradoxical list that preceded it, this image is of a diaphanous fabric which seems unstable and weak, but contains the opposing forces of "Citadel[s]" and "Dragons". If this last stanza revisits the romantic terrain of the first two, it does so in metaphors that evoke knights, dragons and ladies, rather than a stone prison.

The second half of the poem began by overturning the romantic story, but it now reasserts an equally romantic story. The "Universe" is "A limit like a Vail / Unto the Lady's face", which keeps the "knight" at a distance with promises of future interview, as in "A Charm invests a face". The romantic narrative of external separation now becomes internalized, and it is these narratives themselves which separate them. The man and the woman are complicitous in maintaining the distance which precludes interview.

If the romantic narrative is predicated on indefinitely postponing any possible interview, it fails to convince that such postponement is necessary. The "Vail" that obscures the view of the other is precisely the romantic elements that insist such veiling is necessary. The obstacles do not come from external forces, but from internal resistance. Romance dictates a need for screens to hinder a face to face encounter by insisting that distance equals nearness. These poems argue for such an equation in their rhetoric, but undermine it in their inability to sustain the romantic narrative.

Another strategy for controlling the threatening aspects of interview occurs in Emily Dickinson's poems which postulate an atemporal heavenly union. Poem 625 again focuses on two persons' mutual looking, but it is not a metaphorical exploration of contact in this world, but of imagined contact in a supposed next. It begins ambiguously:

> 'Twas a long Parting – but the time
> For interview – had Come –
> Before the Judgment Seat of God –
> (P. 625)

Does the "long Parting" refer to the slow leave-taking of life experienced by these two lovers? Or does it refer to their lengthy interview while they were fleshly lovers? If the word "interview" refers to the one they will have before God then it is a curious use of the word in which one party judges another. But if it refers to what will take place before the judgment seat, then it may refer to the second interview these lovers had: one in the flesh that was "a long Parting", and the other out of the flesh that is "A Heaven of Heavens".

> The last – and second time
>
> These Fleshless Lovers met –
> A Heaven in a Gaze –
> A Heaven of Heavens – the Privilege
> Of one another's Eyes –
> (P. 625)

The past tense presentation of this event suggests that the speaker of the poem assumes the position of a third party, such as the one described at the end of the poem. The speaker is not "The unobtrusive Guest", however, because he or she seems to see the "Guest" too, and so must be positioned some place above this second meeting. What the speaker sees is "A Heaven in a Gaze". The singular Heaven seems to be shared by both parties, just as the gaze is. The exaggeration in the next line accentuates this mutuality by suggesting that there is "A Heaven of Heavens", in which each receives "the Privilege / Of one another's Eyes", they are not just granted a look at the other, but a look at the other's looking.

Their state is likened to the "new souls" of God:

> No Lifetime – on Them –
> Appareled as the new
> Unborn – except They had beheld –
> Born infiniter – now –
> (P. 625)

The ambiguous last lines suggest that in beholding each other they will be born "infiniter – now –" than others of the "new / Unborn". The two lovers will be superior to them, just as their state will be "A Heaven of Heavens". In the fascicle an alternative word for "infiniter" is "everlasting", which links this stanza to the one that follows by stressing the marriage theme and using a term that often designates God, who is called "the Everlasting". The word "infiniter" is a more subtle reference to God, and hearkens back to the previous stanzas in which the "Fleshless

Lover's" gaze seems to separate them from all others. Using the neologism "infiniter" suggests that language itself must be stretched to describe the unworldliness of their exchange.

The last stanza begins with a rhetorical question:

> Was Bridal – e'er like This?
> A Paradise – the Host –
> And Cherubim – and Seraphim –
> The unobtrusive Guest –
>
> (P. 625)

These last lines could be read as a list, in which case each item would be independent, or as nouns which are then modified by descriptive clauses. But syntactically this list would be problematic, since the last line cannot be describing the third line because it is singular. My reading of the stanza is that the first section is a list which begins with a description of what the place feels like, "A Paradise", which suggests that this privileged look is analogous to that of Adam and Eve, and has been allowed by "the Host" who watches, as well as his attendants, the "Cherubim – and Seraphim". If the host is identified with Christ, he becomes the one who has allowed this visual coupling to take place. The last line does not syntactically add to this list, but adds a categorically different participant, God. The coupling pushes God aside and makes the heavenly wedding one which culminates or recuperates attachments made in life.

This poem revisits a worldly interview and recasts it in a heaven beyond this world. The narrative of transcendence can only be maintained by annulling temporality even while it restates it; "The last – and second time". The metaphorical interview is poignant because it exists outside of time, in an unsustainable moment. The interview is made precious by being designated as the last, but this can only occur to one who is not in time, and the speaker's remove from the situation, further removed even than God, allows for this distanced perspective. The two lovers are watched as they exchange looks, and it is this characterization that allows us to think of it as a reciprocated interview. Yet if we read the poem as a metaphor the extreme pressure which makes this last interview "A Heaven of Heavens" cannot be so easily relegated to external forces. The idea of a final interview in an atemporal heaven seems to be a strategy to avoid confronting the inability to do so in the temporal flesh. Heaven is a story that postpones taking action in this life.

A similar strategy of elevation from a particular situation occurs in a letter of consolation Emily Dickinson sent to her Aunt Katie, who had recently lost her eldest son. As in the letter to the Norcross cousins the difference between the corporeal vies with the linguistic: "I thought by today, perhaps you would like to see me, if I came quite soft and brought no noisy words. But when I am most sorry, I can say nothing so I will only kiss you and go far away" (L. 338). The writer is referred to as visible, the words themselves are referred to as audible, but what they both insist on is that they deliver only a tactile kiss. Dickinson not only plays at being present, but claims to erase all words that will speak too noisily to their receiver.

The quatrain near the end clashes with the reassuring tone of the rest of the letter:

> Were it to be the last
> How infinite would be
> What we did not suspect was marked –
> Our final interview.
>
> (L. 338)

This is a paradox since the final interview becomes infinite only *because* it is bounded. Both "infinite" and "final" are derived from the same Latin root *finitus*, which means limit, boundary, or end, so the infinite interview is only felt as such when it has become the final interview.

But if this contraction of time makes this last interview infinite, then the consolation that preceded the poem is untenable in its banal reassurances. Dickinson writes: "I know we shall certainly see what we loved the most. It is sweet to think they are safe by Death and that is all we have to pass to obtain their face" (L. 338). The metaphors she uses are again visual, we shall "see what we loved the most", and we will "obtain their faces", though the possessiveness of these actions suggests that they will be objects someone will return, not persons with whom we can engage. It is indeed "sweet to think they are safe by Death", but in a sentimental way which denies the force of the "final interview".

The reflexive act of recognizing that an interview has taken place can only happen after the fact, when one of the participants distances herself or himself from the time of the face to face encounter. This quatrain asserts that the heavenly eternity of an interview occurs only after the death of the other participant; the memory of the one who survives makes that final interview "a Heaven of Heavens". When Emily

Dickinson attempts to imagine a heavenly consummation she can only do so in time; it is a consummation which seems to annul time, but only because it will be bracketed by a time before it happens, and a time after it has happened. One is always late for one's interview.

The heavenly narrative is a curious denial of temporality within the temporal. If the romantic narrative indefinitely postpones any actual interview, the heavenly narrative asserts that each interview must be felt as the last to be valued. Death does not cancel the face to face interview, it is the motivating factor that makes the time of the interview expand. Emily Dickinson asserts that one appreciates the face to face interview because one must necessarily lose it. What is precious is not, therefore, the moment of interview, but the limitless remembering of that moment after it has passed. She once wrote to Samuel Bowles: "I went to the Room as soon as you left, to confirm your presence" (L. 515). It is only in the other's absence that Emily Dickinson claims to be able to appreciate their presence; she desires the memory more than the event.

Another poem which seems to suggest that one renounce the possibility of interview for something greater ends by suggesting that the trap of such reasoning is mere avoidance. The implied argument of the heavenly narrative is the subject of poem 745. This poem is about the denial of the sense of sight, here presented as a "piercing Virtue" when one puts out one's eyes, for a faith in something beyond the senses. The speaker is not comfortable with the supposition, however, and the convoluted grammar allows words to oscillate between multiple phrases which complicate our reading. The initial claim is:

> Renunciation – is a piercing Virtue –
> The letting go
> A Presence – for an Expectation –
> (P. 745)

The word "Renunciation" indicates a sacrifice, some type of ascetic self-denial, a virtue; though the word can also have connotations of rejection or repudiation, which implies a painful disengagement. The phrase that follows already indicates that both meanings are applicable because it is "a piercing Virtue". These first lines call up biblical associations, for not only does Christ renounce his life ("Father, into thy hands I commit my spirit!" (Luke 23:46)), but he is pierced in the side with a spear, and there was much debate in the Christian Church of Dickinson's time about the "Presence" of Christ in the Eucharist. In addition, Christ has to let go of his presence in exchange for an expectation, his bodily presence is renounced in the hope of resurrection. These associations link the poem specifically to the crucifixion of Christ, but the next line withdraws from affirming this "piercing Virtue" for the speaker.

"Not now – The putting out of Eyes –". The first phrase of this line is suspended ambiguously. It could comment on the preceding lines by echoing them, in which case "Not now" would refer to the way one renounces what one has for what one expects, denies oneself the present; but it could also contradict the first lines, in which case "Not now" would be the speaker's response to the proposition outlined above, a negation of its supposed "Virtue". The second reading becomes more plausible when we read the phrase that follows: "The putting out of Eyes." For if the speaker says "Not now –" will there be a "putting out of Eyes", then the "Piercing Virtue" has been postponed or renounced; the eyes will not be pierced for a supposedly virtuous renunciation.

The question arises, *whose* eyes are being discussed here? Perhaps there are two people being referred to in the poem, the person whose presence the speaker is loath to renounce, and the speaker herself. "The putting out of Eyes" would be the parting of their looks, here forcibly being parted by some unknown third party, as well as the separation of their "I's". Poem 474, "They put Us far apart –", would then be a corollary to this poem, one which exclusively examines that resentment of two people's shared sight. But whereas "They put Us far apart –" portrays the two individuals as victims, "Renunciation – is a piercing Virtue –" admits complicity in the separation that is being contemplated.

If the "putting out of Eyes" has been delayed, it may be because the speaker cannot renounce the presence of the other just yet. If the sunrise is a figure for the other's face, then the speaker is asserting that she will keep her eyes open for just this one instant, and then close them before seeing the day.

>Just Sunrise –
>Lest Day –
>Day's Great Progenitor –
>Outvie
>
>(P. 745)

In this reading the speaker renounces the "Day" itself, though she cannot bring herself to renounce the "Sunrise". It becomes imperative to determine if that sunrise is a brief span of time or a lifetime; for the first would suggest the speaker is willing to accept loss, the second postpones it until it is inevitable. Does this poem accept the loss of the other as an ascetic sacrifice? Or does she reject it as an inevitable separation?

If we follow the biblical allusions then the "Sunrise" would represent the Son's rise in his resurrection, and "Day" would be Christ's heavenly state which annuls time. To keep her eyes open and see past the human presence of Christ would be to see the miracle of his resurrection. He could then be said to "outvie" "Day's Great Progenitor", he would supplant his Father. The word "Progenitor" designates an ancestor, one who came before the genesis of a species; from *pro* before, and *gignere* beget. In this poem the danger is that the one who came later would become more revered than the one from whom he came. The word "Outvie", means to surpass in a rivalry or competition, and in this situation the jealous God would refuse to grant his son such license. The options for "Outvie" that Dickinson indicated in the margin of the manuscript are "Outshow", and "Outglow", and though both more firmly establish the visual renunciation being discussed, neither has the competitive suggestiveness of the original word.

What does this subtext tell us about the attitude of the speaker to the other whose presence she hesitates to renounce? In this case the speaker asserts that she will not hold her eyes open too long, lest the full glory of the other's face "Outvie" the God who made this person. But is this supposed renunciation tenable? The following lines analyze the impulse:

> Renunciation – is the Choosing
> Against itself –
> Itself to justify
> Unto itself –
>
> (P. 745)

The speaker claims that the one who renounces something denies itself something; it chooses "Against itself". This action is not *for* another, however, but to justify itself "Unto itself"; it is self-reflexive and narcissistic. There is a closed circle being perpetuated here, in which the one choosing believes its action is a renunciation of something external, a letting go through self-denial. But the very action of letting go allows it to more thoroughly assert itself as supreme. Once the speaker recognizes this trap she can argue that renunciation is not a giving up, but a taking on, not a self-denial, but a self-affirmation. God's renunciation of sovereignty in creating Christ ends up being an affirmation of his sovereignty; in that act of creation God justified himself by asserting his largess. This action was not magnanimous, as it first appeared, because only by proclaiming that Christ is not threatening can God reassert his superiority.

If the speaker never renounces the face of the other, never willfully gives it up just to show she can, then the face of the other becomes what breaks her sovereignty, makes her less than God. The face of the other is torn from her by the contingencies of mortal existence, not by a self-serving renunciation. The speaker will *not* give up the momentary interview, nor tell herself stories that giving up is necessary. She will desire the face to face encounter even in its painful transitoriness.

The same idea is rephrased in terms of a sign in the last lines of the poem:

> When larger function –
> Make that appear –
> Smaller – that Covered Vision – Here –
> (P. 745)

In the religious reading God's largess needs its counterpoint to be appreciated. Christ's advent becomes the human-sized revelation that can be comprehended, which accentuates the God-sized revelation which cannot. The presence of Christ in the Eucharist becomes "that Covered Vision – Here" on earth, by which the uncovered vision of God can be guessed. The two manuscript options for "Covered" are "flooded" and "sated". The first is an intrusive foreign metaphor which could conceivably be contrasted with the dryness of renunciation, while the second makes the subject too satisfied with what they have attained. Both options, however, stress the contrast between this final vision and the one that was denied.

The second reading is that the "Covered Vision" is allowed because there is a fuller vision of the other that is being denied. The speaker closes her eyes to receive "that Covered Vision – Here –", one which exists in the memory of the other's face glimpsed, like a sunrise, before it passes. The speaker is "flooded" and "sated" by the lesser vision that she and the other have obtained when they refused to put out their eyes. "That Covered Vision", obtained in the past, is "Here", now, in memory. The implication is that her image may also exist for the other; that they may share an interview in memory after they have shared an interview corporeally.

The previous poems I have examined were all predicated on the failure to maintain a mutual looking in a fleshly encounter, but in poem 745 that failure is assumed to be necessary. The speaker's agitation comes less from the inability to know the other person's response and more from the internal debate over how she can respond. The last line of the poem may refer to recovering the vision of the other, both in the sense of covering it again, and in the sense of finding it again. "That Covered Vision" would be the one that the speaker keeps when she closes her eyelids. She re-covers the vision of the other, "Here," *in* writing.

An interview always occurs in a moment which seems to suspend time, but that moment can only be comprehended reflexively, at another time. Temporal distance is necessary so that one can become a third party and examine what took place as if one were not involved. It is *this* distance that writing, by its nature, necessitates and produces. But if an interview can only exist in writing, then Emily Dickinson's protestations against writing become mere hyperbole, and her reiterated desire to see another person face to face becomes a farce. An interview may only be recovered in writing, but writing never recovers enough. Even if an interview can only be known reflexively, it is still Dickinson's desired place of passion. What Emily Dickinson wants is to be wanted by someone whom she can't control, with whom she can share an interview, and she can't control *this* want.

University of California

NOTES

[1] Emmanuel Levinas, *Otherwise Than Being or Beyond Essence* (The Hague: Martinus Nijhoff Publishers, 1981), p. 82. I am indebted to Levinas's writings for much of my thinking and phrasing throughout this essay.

[2] This is one of the central tenets of Emmanuel Levinas's thought. For example, in "Language and Proximity" he describes speech as touch because the physical contact precludes the illusion of reciprocity; touching is categorically different from being touched. "The hypothesis that the relationship with an interlocutor would still be a knowing reduces speech to the solitary or impersonal exercise of a thought, whereas already the kerygma which bears its ideality is, in addition, a *proximity* between me and the interlocutor, and not our participation in a transparent universality. Whatever be the message transmitted by speech, the speaking is contact." *Collected Philosophical Papers*, trans. Alphonso Lingus (The Hague: Martinus Nijhoff Publishers, 1987), p. 115.

³ *The Letters of Emily Dickinson*, ed. Thomas H. Johnson (Cambridge: Harvard University Press, 1986), 3 Volumes, Letter 360. All subsequent references to the letters will be given parenthetically within the text by the letter's assigned number. Extracts reprinted by permission of the publishers from *The Letters of Emily Dickinson* edited by Thomas H. Johnson (Cambridge, Mass.: The Belknap Press of Harvard University Press, Copyright © 1958, 1986 by the President and Fellows of Harvard College).

⁴ All etymologies discussed in this paper have been derived from *Webster's Third New International Dictionary of the English Language* (Springfield: Merriam-Webster Inc., 1986).

⁵ The word "interview" also maintains this duality in its prefix "inter-". The prefix can mean to deposit a dead body in the earth (terra), a process which Dickinson will examine relentlessly, sometimes referring to it as precluding further interview. For example, in poem 509 the speaker laments the loss of one who is "Past Interview". This is the unequal relationship *par excellence*, since one can gaze on a corpse without risking a response. But "inter-" can also be used as a prefix meaning between or among, which indicates that there is mutual reciprocity between two similar entities, or at least some type of shared commerce.

⁶ Richard B. Sewall, *The Life of Emily Dickinson* (New York: Farrar, Straus and Giroux, 1974), 2 Volumes, p. 628.

⁷ *The Poems of Emily Dickinson*, ed. Thomas H. Johnson (Cambridge: Harvard University Press, 1958), 3 Volumes, Poem 421. All subsequent references to the poems will be given parenthetically within the text by the poem's assigned number. Any discrepancies with Johnson's *Poems* are due to my checking his versions with those in *The Manuscript Book of Emily Dickinson*, ed. R. W. Franklin (Cambridge: Harvard University Press, 1981), 2 Volumes. Extracts reprinted by permission of the publishers and the Trustees of Amherst College from *The Poems of Emily Dickinson*, Thomas H. Johnson, ed., Cambridge, Mass.: The Belknap Press of Harvard University Press, Copyright © 1951, 1955, 1979, 1983 by the President and Fellows of Harvard College. Permission also received for *The Complete Poems of Emily Dickinson* edited by Thomas H. Johnson. Copyright 1929, 1935 by Martha Dickinson Bianchi. Copyright © renewed 1957, 1963 by Mary L. Hampson. By permission of Little, Brown and Company.

REFERENCES

Dickinson, Emily, *The Letters of Emily Dickinson*. Ed. Thomas H. Johnson. 3 vols. Cambridge: Harvard University Press, 1958.

Dickinson, Emily. *The Manuscript Books of Emily Dickinson*. Ed. R.W. Franklin. Cambridge: Harvard University Press, 1981.

Dickinson, Emily. *The Poems of Emily Dickinson*. Ed. Thomas H. Johnson. 3 vols. Cambridge: Harvard University Press, 1958.

Gove, Philip Babcock, ed. in chief. *Webster's Third New International Dictionary of the English Language*. Springfield: Merriam-Webster Inc., 1986.

Levinas, Emmanuel. *Otherwise Than Being or Beyond Essence*. Trans. Alphonso Lingis. The Hague: Martinus Nijhoff Publishers, 1981.

Sewall, Richard. *The Life of Emily Dickinson*. 2 vols. New York: Farrar, Straus and Giroux, 1974.

PART THREE

INTIMATE PLACES

MARLIES KRONEGGER

FROM PROFANE SPACE TO THE SACRED PLACE OR CENTER IN *DÉSERT* BY LE CLÉZIO:
The Experience of Seeing, Hearing, Perceiving, Breathing rather than Thinking Space and Place

> Non, non, ce qui comble, ce qui culmine sur la joie et peut-être même sur une matière d'extase incompréhensible, c'est le REGARD, non pas le regard du contemplateur, qui n'est qu'un miroir. Mais le regard actif, qui va vers la matière, et s'y unit. *Le regard de tous les sens*, aigu, énigmatique, qui ne conquiert pas pour ramener dans la prison des mots et des systèmes, mais qui dirige l'être vers les régions extérieures qui sont déjà en lui, le recompose, le recrée dans la joie du mystère devenue demeure (J. M. G. Le Clézio, *L'Extase matérielle*, p. 176. Quotations from this source are © Éditions Gallimard 1967).
>
> Mais Lalla n'a pas peur de lui, parce qu'elle sait que quelque part, entre les rochers, ou bien dans le ciel, il y a le regard de l'Homme Bleu, celui qu'elle appelle Es Ser, le Secret, parce qu'il se cache. C'est lui qui va venir certainement, son regard va aller droit au fond d'elle et lui donnera la force de combattre l'homme au complet veston, et la mort qui est près de Naman; la transformera en oiseau, la lancera au milieu de l'espace; alors peut-être qu'elle pourra enfin rejoindre la grande mouette blanche qui est un prince, et qui vole infatigablement au-dessus de la mer (Désert, p. 202).
>
> Deux oiseaux, compagnons inséparablement unis, résident sur un même arbre; l'un mange le fruit doux de l'arbre, l'autre le regarde et ne mange point (*Mundaka Upanishad*, 3e Mundaka, ler Khanda, Shruti 1; *Rig-Veda*, I, 164, 20; *Shwêtâshwatara Upanishad*, 4e Adhyâya, Shruti 6) (J. M. G. Le Clézio, *L'Extase matérielle*, frontispiece).

In *Désert*,[1] Le Clézio distingue between a geographical space, measurable expansion, and place, a center or nombril of life and existence. The distinction of space and place is the basis of relations between the world and man; space can be defined in rational terms for greater intellectual security; place expresses the union or fusion of man and world. Space can be conceived by man-made laws and by a rational demonstration of structures and principles, governed by rigorous definitions. Man's place in *Désert*, however, expresses the rhythmic vitality of man and nature, appearing and disappearing in the immense, nameless ocean of infinity, the desert:

Ils étaient les hommes et les femmes du sable, du vent, de la lumière, de la nuit. Ils étaient apparus, comme dans un rêve, en haut d'une dune, comme s'ils étaient nés du ciel sans nuages, et qu'ils avaient dans leurs membres la dureté de l'espace (p. 9) . . . Tournés vers le désert, ils faisaient leur prière sans paroles. Ils s'en allaient, comme dans un rêve, ils disparaissaient (p. 439).

With the inhabitants of *Désert*, Le Clézio achieves a symbiosis of man's place in the sacred universe. Fluid life and endless rhythm, the emanation of immutable, eternal laws from a sacred center,[2] a sacred place,[3] are the foundation of life and existence, the foremost principles of all creation. Space and place appear to be opposites, and their relation to each other enables man to overcome the chaotic and divergent tensions in the world, to reconcile centripetal and centrifugal forces. In *Désert*, Le Clézio contrasts cities with a sacred center and polluted modern cities, where the center cannot hold. The spiritual significance of space and place is a key issue of the world man shares with everything-there-is-alive.[4]

Le Clézio, as we shall see, opposes the world of political expansion of territory to the world of inner fulfillment; the world of man-made laws to the eternal cosmic rhythm of the universe. His protagonists in *Désert*, in the holy city of Smara, relate to both the cosmos and the sacred, in love and worship, as they fill the physical reality of their place with metaphysical essence. The materiality of the elements, of sand, sea, wind and fire, is timeless and their existence is forever their unfolding in being "born with" the desert.[5] In the following pages we shall focus on the "path" or "way" of the major protagonist Lalla Hawa, and meet with her Ma el Aïnine in the sacred city of Smara, listen to Es Ser in the desert, and observe the lessons of Hartani, a shepherd and Lalla's betrothed, who cannot speak.[6]

All these protagonists are reflections of Le Clézio himself. Le Clézio has passed beyond nationalism, and has embraced the entire world as his home, and in all his works knows how to relate the numberless threads extending from this earth to the stars. All his protagonists follow their "path" to gain harmony with Nature.

The book evolves around five orientation points, the four cardinal directions, and the center. The original center of Smara is the mediator of heaven and earth. The center is a breaking point of time and space, with an orientation to and away from the center, in a centripetal and centrifugal movement.

1. THE GEOGRAPHICAL SPACE, THE LOCALE OF FORCES, ENERGY AND INTENSITY

Le Clézio describes the geographical space of the desert as a vast tableau of sand and gravel, surrounded by a terrain of rugged mountains. Wind-blown sands are shaped by weathering into dunes. The vast tracts of shifting sands are compared to waves which cross the ocean, and the desert appears to be a mineralized sea, where earth and sky meet. The desert, located in the North African Sahara, resembles any other uniform, undifferentiated, exterior surface: burning in the heat of the sun and expanding under the fireworks of the starlit sky. Experienced objectively, the desert seems to be an unbreakable continuity and unity of natural relations of the physical world: there are wide temperature fluctuations of heat and cold, and the opposite forces of light and darkness reconcile in the rhythm of risings and fallings, of undulations and vibrations, transforming the eternal world of sand, stone, sky, sun, and silence into a harmony of light and tone variations. Nature is the conductor of infinite harmonies, with the *danse* of wind, dunes, sunrays, and the worshippers of the unseen reality, God.[7]

2. THE HUMAN CONDITION IN THE CENTER OF THE DESERT: INFINITE SPACE AND THE SACREDNESS OF PLACE

At the center of the desert, everything has been possible, and here, all had started *in illo tempore*, in primordial time, when, for the first time, scattered clusters of inhabitants were born here and emerged, similar to the dunes, shaped by weathering under the open sky.[8] They were born here, "nés du désert", where the sun radiates, and where the light of their gaze illuminates the silence of the desert. Here, for the first time, people created their own life-world in open space, and united in centers of sacredness.[9] Immersed in space, their world is extension, and immersed in their innermost being or soul, their world is intension. Their breath of life is the way of truth, composed of expiration, the breath which unites man and space; of respiration, the breath or wind which unites them with the center of sky and earth; and the breath of aspiration which abolishes spaces without hope. Their rituals are a praise of God who existed before all life, as Ma el Aïnine solemnly chants:

> Gloire à Dieu qui est le roi, le saint, le puissant, le victorieux, le glorieux, celui qui existe avant toute vie, le divin, l'immense, le seul, le victorieux de tous tes ennemis, celui qui sait, qui voit, qui entend, le divin, le savant, l'immense, le témoin, le créateur, seul, immense, voyant, entendant, le beau, le généreux, le fort, le parfait, le haut, l'immense . . . (p. 63).

Their *cultus* is the primary source of freedom, and their independence from wider society. In their center of peace and reconciliation, time and space are ritually created. Song and words, silence and dance, conjure the sacred, transcendent, spiritual reality of the community. Their ritually defined center is for them the actual center of the world, their place. For them, the real is the infinite, is the eternal on the very spot they live, at this very moment of their appearance. Their gaze expresses and incarnates the freedom of place. In touch with a fundamental unity at every step they take, they follow the eternal rhythmical dance of water, earth, air and fire, the rhythmical dance of the cosmos. Here, suffering, desire or vengeance don't exist. Man is immune to the effects of the elements, untouched by heat and cold. In solidarity and interaction with nature, the human being assumes his place in the desert. His relationship to the world, to a single integrated organism, is sacred.

Man's acts of worship at a particular Beginning Place within a center of four great directions, recreate the cosmos itself. In music and dance, the sacred is manifested in two dimensions: the vertical (divine-human) as well as the horizontal (man-world), while the experience of a mystery envelopes and surpasses them all. The association of the sacred site with the natural elements (earth, sky, tree, water) constitutes a sacred whole, a sacred landscape: a cosmic harmony and rhythm reverberates through every aspect of man's relationship to the earth, to nature and place:

> C'était comme cela, directement avec un centre du ciel et de la terre, uni par le vent violent des respirations des hommes, comme si en s'accélérant le rythme du souffle abolissait les jours et les nuits, les mois, les saisons, abolissait même l'espace sans espoir, et faisait approcher la fin de tous les voyages, la fin de tous les temps (p. 70).

Life moves in the cadence of constant adjustment of opposites, and the spirit of man adapts to the inner music of existence. Personal relationships with the infinite create the true center of gravity of men's lives.

3. CROSSROADS: THE CENTER, THE ROOT OF EXISTENCE, AND ITS RADIATION: THE HOLY CITY OF SMARA THREATENED BY INVADERS FROM THE NORTH

In silence, the people of Smara are following an invisible path. In the center of silence, in the holy city of Smara, its founder Ma el Aïnine (Water or Joy of the Eyes) and his people, united in prayer and in ritual dance, worship a Being who, in His essence, is the light and life of all – Es Ser (Secret). For the community of Smara, Ma el Aïnine, whose eyes are closed, is the principle of life, the center of breath. Their reality is permeated by the sacred. The community is gathered at the center of the square, the heart of primordial life, with an opening space from the center to the four cardinal points. The emphasis is on the geometrical figures, the square, center, circle and cross. With these geometrical expressions of space we may see vividly the way in which space and history interact to create the sacredness of place. Here, space links all events based on historical facts, when foreign nations attempted to expand political and economic power in North Africa (1905–1906, 1911). The historical invasion from the North becomes the meeting point of conflicting interests, reflecting opposed world views. In distinction to powerful invaders, the people of Smara have a very strong and pervasive sense of place, and do not look at space as a possession. Their land belongs to the past, their ancestors, and to the future, the new generations. However, the roads of foreign invaders coming from the North are traced out by the passion for the conquest of land, the greed to possess gold and precious metals, the desire to enhance both their political and religious power. The invaders' notion of freedom has followed the rational objective of conquest, a finite goal according to the internal necessity of greed, power, and commercial or political expansion. In contrast, the epic grandeur of African natives emerges in their eternal march across the desert under the threat of war, death and evil. The directions taken by the invaders in movements from the North (evil) to the South (the sacred world), and by African natives, away from the sacred center toward the vast horizons from the East to the West, are significantly movements in the form of a cross. The latter's vision always contains a horizon that is not seen, resulting from an encounter with the world of the elements. Earth and people live in a vertiginous turmoil threatened by a mysterious gaze:

> Une force étrange, inconnue, jaillissait de la terre poussiéreuse, enveloppait les hommes dans son tourbillon. C'était la lumière du couchant, peut-être, ou bien le pouvoir du regard qui s'est fixé sur ce lieu, qui cherchait à s'échapper comme une eau prisonnière (p. 370).

Simultaneously, their march from East to West, from sunrise to sunset, points to the horizons. These horizons, now and always, appear to fade away from those in search of place and silence.

The wave-like movement of the visible which appears and disappears suggests that the lives of these people and the rhythm of the cosmos must be considered together. The present moment of their birth in the desert becomes the eternal moment of their creation of sacred values. "Now" for them is always linked with to "appear", and "every day" with to "disappear".

The theme is that of a gradual ascension of the major protagonist, Lalla, and her community, in a forward, onward movement which makes its way against an adverse current of darkness and cold, the threat of foreign invaders. Each day, the native community's sacred way of life is reborn with sunrise, opening another door to exert their freedom: "Il n'y avait pas de fin à la liberté, elle était vaste comme l'étendue de la terre, belle et cruelle comme la lumière, douce comme les yeux de l'eau" (p. 439). In sum, as we have seen before, Le Clézio distinguishes sacred place, with a sacred center, from profane space. Profane space is the space of military conquerors, religious fanatics and commercial intruders. With them, the sky is empty, and the vacuousness of the sky has become unbearable. Their physical presence threatens the equilibrium of man and desert. Freedom, for the invaders, means the conquest of objects. Their roads of triumph cross the sacred place and sacred freedom of the natives.

Now, let us turn to the North, to the profane city of Marseille.

4. PATHS OF SELF-REALIZATION WHICH LEAD NOWHERE: THE CONFINEMENT OF SPACE IN MARSEILLE

The counterpoint to the holy city of Smara and the sacred cities of the desert (pp. 251–254) is Marseille, the city of confinement, the world of slaves. Here, life is confined to the standards of acquisition, divided according to analytical and statistical values; people seem to be enslaved by lust, greed, and pleasure. They are born together with pollution, and pollution fills their inner void, and this kind of corruption has become their second nature. Here, while the artificial light pours down, and brightness whirls and vibrates unwearyingly in offices, darkness and sadness seems to engulf Lalla as she looks for employment. In the polluted world of the city of cement, each confrontation with "the other" is a confrontation with the spirit of cruelty and aggression to subject, to exploit, to degrade and to annihilate Lalla. Utility, want and desires blind the modern world of Marseille. Here, Lalla experiences the organized methods of exploiting people at their market value and for their use in a way one uses machines. The intoxication with power of certain authorities involves the abuse of children, who are bought and trained to become thieves, and of women bought for sexual pleasures. They all experience a spiritual suicide which deadens their consciousness. They have become instruments of someone else's power imposed upon them.

After a period of subservient work, Lalla becomes the model of a photographer. Again, her natural conditions are replaced by the will of others. The photographer takes pictures of Lalla for publicity. Her photos, reproduced, appear on many publications. She looks beautiful for the public, but like a facsimile of life, and without an organic, inner self. In the mechanical world of the city, her picture fills many spaces, but falsifies her inner world and alienates her from the cosmic order of which she was a part. The multiplicity of reproductions show that her natural condition is replaced by the will of the public, her own volition and realization of desires by manipulation. The coercive control over the means of communication restricts her freedom to choose for herself or act on her own initiative, in a society where the sources of life seem to have dried up.

Marseille, for Lalla, is a turbulent and violent city, where she feels sadness and loss of her native, sacred world, and where she experiences the tragic sense of the human condition. Here, insanity, distorted perspectives, brutal violence, eroticism, ceaseless desiring, abandonment, destructiveness, are in contrast with all her inner voices of sea, sky, and nature, as experienced in her native land. In sum, repulsion at the bureaucratic flavor of Marseille, where people are swallowed up by their machines, their coolly designed and trivial ways of human relationships, is a keynote of the void in Lalla's life there.

Her only friend, victim of this polluted world, is Radicz, used and abused by his tyrant boss Lin. Radicz, a little boy and master thief, works for his boss whose blind path he follows to perfection. He is the accomplished thief of cars, his ability to steal keeps him alive, and this finite goal of mere survival dictates a life of actions which are compulsive and spurred by want and necessity. With him, a slave of his boss, human values reach the lowest levels of self-deception. His road of license ends in a vertiginous, frenzied pursuit by the police. When he is accidentally killed by a bus, he shares the destiny of other young people, victims of the modern world; as so often dramatically depicted in Le Clézio's work: in the misuse of freedom, they become prey to self-deception.

Lalla rejects the materialistic civilization of Marseille, the world of ambitious commercial manufacturers and bureaucrats, whose common goal is to classify, possess and control everything and everybody for both moneymaking and warfare, in short, for useful production. Lalla encounters agglomerations of names, lists and catalogs which enumerate things detached from their original frames. They are a reflection of a confusing and chaotic civilization, idealized in the world of things, in department stores, in a world of cement, tar, asphalt and man-made synthetics. These endless enumerations of things in the profane city of Marseille show Lalla the anaphoric, confusing reproductions of man who has lost sight of things eternal. Enumerations are a characteristic of our times, in which distances are annihilated, and human values are as perishable as their artifacts.

5. FROM CONFINEMENT TO FREEDOM: THE BREATH OF LIFE MADE VISIBLE IN DANCE

As we are going to see, dance for Le Clézio not only illustrates the aesthetic significance of life which enters into the existential self-interpretation of the human being, but offers freedom to transcend the conditions of Lalla's life-world in Marseille, in the city of slavery. With the prototype of her creative act she achieves the full potential and spectrum of her vibrant, unique individuality. We arrive at the climax of the book with the ecstasy of her dance. It expresses Lalla's lyrical moment, which lifts her life to a high and authentically human level of the existential experience, conveying to her performance as a dancer a specific life significance, universal and uniquely personal at the same time. Caught between the social mold and the cosmic self, she toils to break out and away in order to retrieve her cosmic heritage. Her creative act, the summation of her existence of ebbs and flows in the ocean of being escapes all entrapments and intrusions and is the highest expression of self-determination. Invited to dance with electronic music, the experience enhances her sensibilities (pp. 354–357). Implicit in her rhythmical movements is the mystic fusion of reality. She becomes the image she is seeing: a bird lifting off, in contact with the ineffable fundamental life forces. The exuberance of enjoyment of this dance releases Lalla and revives the organic relationship between the imaginary space of the desert and the sacredness of that place in her heart.

Elle danse sur le rythme lent de la musique électrique . . . L'ivresse de la danse s'étend autour d'elle . . . Dans la grande salle il n'y a plus tous ces murs, ces miroirs, ces lueurs . . . le regard îvre des danseurs a effacé tous les obstacles . . . Maintenant, autour de Lalla Hawa, il y a une étendue sans fin de poussière et de pierres blanches, une étendue vivante de sable et de sel, et les vagues des dunes . . . Au centre de l'aire immense et nue, loin des hommes qui dansent, loin des villes brumeuses, le regard du Secret entre en elle, touche son coeur (pp. 355–357).

With Lalla, body, mind and nature are a single integrated organism, unity and wholeness. Her dance is performed in harmony with her innermost convictions and feelings, in the solitude of the modern desert of Marseille, a desert without any sacred, positive relationships. Her dance has reached out to touch the people around her in a web or texture of infinite harmonious relations, correlated to a harmoniously understood cosmos; elevated by Es Ser, her Secret, this sublime moment opens up to the infinite. From now on, Lalla will authentically live the values of her desert with every step she takes. Not only does her dance breathe music, it expresses its own innate form and sense of her soul. She finds fulfillment. Within her, external space and time cease to rule, and the links of evolution from her native desert and the artificial world of Marseille are merged in unity, as the immediate and nameless presence of the desert is everywhere in her innermost being. Even in Marseille Lalla discloses the continuous presence of Es Ser. Enveloped by Es Ser, her breath of life, she is conscious of the infinite and filled with the impetus of infinite energy. Spiritual energy has become part of her inner life. For her it was Es Ser, the Eye of Es Ser, who permeated with his presence both the starry heavens of the desert and the heart of its inhabitants, and it was Es Ser who had given wings to her dance. All of a sudden, she seems to soar like a bird into the infinite. Within her, external space and time have ceased to rule. She seems to integrate an eternal music, which makes her gestures spontaneous and beautiful. The desert is a presence in her inner self, the real, the center of love and joy. The rhythm of her dance is the wings to personal freedom and fulfillment. It is through the heightening of her consciousness in love, and in extending throughout her environment, that she attains communion with all those present. Her spiritual climate, her aura, her personal emanation, reaches out into ever-widening circles, and moves and inspires all. Her joy pervades the living space around her and everybody joins her to translate the inner song of her being into circular movement. What we are seeing here is the rules of social conventions and rational expectations overwhelmed by vision,[10] and by music itself, by sound and gestures as an emanation of nature. Her dance movements expand beyond their own limits in a dialogue with the infinite, as she had originally lived it in her native desert. The inner light that radiates in her comes to life in her dance, as if she were in a trance.

With Lalla, dance goes beyond the confining limits of space and time, and beyond the individual, ephemeral aspects of the human condition. It reveals Lalla's innermost essence. A new world is emerging in her, testing its strength, and trying to push back the walls surrounding it. Dance seems to be struggling against stifling pressure from the outside world. Her performance secures the victory of life no longer subjected to the confinement of space. Every one of her gestures is spontaneous, as she feels the presence of Es Ser in her innermost being. Here is in her the everlasting presence, which is not distant, and not anywhere else.

With her dance Lalla makes a universal, permanent statement of what she has experienced. It is her way of escaping from the conditions of life in Marseille and of returning to her desert. Her dance is taken out of mechanical time; it occupies a firmly circumscribed place, for all to see and experience. She emerges from chaotic nothingness and creates a second order of reality, a rebirth of ritual dance which liberates her from a closed order of reality, from a closed and fixed space. Space is bursting open, and intoxicated by the prospect of a space to be traversed, she returns to her origins. The absolute evoked by her dance is the infinite, which absorbs and abolishes space. For Lalla, dance is an emanation of nature. Her aesthetic experience permits her to see anew the human condition, and to liberate herself from the bonds of slavery.

The scene here presents the embattled value systems that cleave the world of reason and the world of vital synergies. Lalla is opposing the dehumanizing, devitalizing values of a modern society to those values of individuals who follow their authentic stream of life, their path or way.

6. THE CLOSING OF THE CIRCLE: CO-BIRTH WITH THE ELEMENTS. HARTANI, LALLA AND NATURE

Lalla, before having left for Marseille, had found a friend, Hartani, who will be the father of her child, to be born under a tree near a spring after her return to the desert. She had loved Hartani, because he did not know how to speak with words, and all his gestures had expressed his sense perceptions of nature. While he could not tell stories with words, he knew how to evoke images with gestures (lips, hands, body) and the light of his eyes, hearing, touching and seeing the truth in the substance of matter. He was concerned with what makes an ant an ant and how to perceive the eternal in trees, birds and beasts, in dust and sand. For Hartani, trees are a cosmos alive, in perpetual and spontaneous regeneration according to the seasons, and depending on a specific climate. A tree's freedom to grow is limited to a specific place and climate, and always irrespective of political, economic, social, national or religious frontiers. For Hartani, the tree, in itself, has a center of being, with a sap of life unfolding in the sacred rhythm of the cosmos. Having its roots in the soil, its passion for its place remains unaltered and always true to itself, as it unfolds its beauty in the appropriate climate. The exterior necessity is to integrate the four elements into its living space: its roots are implanted in the earth, its trunk, linking roots and branches, relate to the air in which the branches vibrate, and nourished by water, its sap correlates water, earth and air in harmony. It needs the sun, and when ignited, resembles the fire of the sun.

This knowledge of Hartani pleases Lalla, being herself born under a tree near a spring. Therefore, following the path of her mother, the source of life and the fire of passion will find expression when Lalla gives birth to her own child near a spring. For her, the tree is the axis of life, a nombril of earth and sky. It shelters a sacred place for her who is now a mother giving birth to a girl, and allows a sacred stream to flow into existence.

7. CONCLUSION

We must ask ourselves, what is the message of the author? In this essay, I have only dealt with the major protagonist, Lalla. She is bound to the cosmos, as strings are bound to the harp. A string must be strung, and the strength of its bond creates music. She is bound to her native desert. Lalla, like any organic being, is bound to a center from which she unfolds. She is bound by rules that enable her to find her range of freedom in music and dance. Lalla's life unfolds like music. She is absorbed by the rhythm of nature whose harmony is spatial. Life, like music, in this book, solidifies in a sound, in a note, a chord, a melody, a harmony, and, like music, is continuously assembling and dissolving.

We have concentrated on two centers, the sacred city of Smara, radiating light, illumination, and freedom, and on Marseille, a center of pollution, darkness and slavery. Finally, we have tried to show that joy and love are at the root of all creation. Being a microcosm, the human being reflects the macrocosm, the musicality of the universe. Le Clézio's *Désert* invities a rebirth of the world and the return to an eternal source for a new birth of Being.

Michigan State University

NOTES

[1] J.M.G. Le Clézio, *Désert* (Paris: Gallimard, 1980). All pages are quoted from this edition. All quotations from this source are © Éditions Gallimard 1980.

[2] Georges Poulet, *The Metamorphosis of the Circle* (Baltimore: The Johns Hopkins Press, 1966), pp. 321–350 on Claudel, Rilke, T.S. Eliot and Jorge Guillén examines the circle and the center as the model of all forms, but Le Clézio, and his major protagonist Lalla, finds the highest purpose of life not merely in living it and making use of it, but in realizing her own self in an expansion of sympathy from man to nature.

[3] Jean Chevalier and Alain Gheerbrant, *Dictionnaire des symboles, mythes, rêves, coutumes, gestes, formes, figures, couleurs, nombres* (Paris: Robert Laffont/Jupiter, 1969).

[4] Anna-Teresa Tymieniecka, *Logos and Life*, Vols. I, II, III (Dordrecht: Kluwer Academic Publishers, 1988, 1989 and 1990).

[5] Claudel, Tymieniecka and Le Clézio understand the relationship of man to the universe as a co-birth not only with the whole, but with every one of the entities composing it. Every object, every human being appears as a center encircled by its radiation.

[6] Teresa di Scanno *La vision du monde de Le Clézio* (Paris: Nizet et Napoli: Liguori, 1983), p. 120: "Dans *Désert* Le Clézio reprend un de ses grands thèmes . . . : la critique de la civilisation matérialiste en contraste avec la spiritualité de la solitude ou du nomadisme".

⁷ Thomas E. Mails, *Sundancing at Rosebud and Pine Ridge* (Sioux Falls: The Center for Western Studies, 1978). The book is dedicated "to all those people who dance each year that the people might live", a dedication which would be appropriate for *Désert*. Indians and nomads seem to consecrate a mysterious circle in sacred dances.

⁸ M. Merleau-Ponty, *Phenomenology of Perception* (London: Routledge, 1962), p. 251: "Everything throws us back to the organic relations between subject and space, to that gearing of the subject onto the world which is the origin of space".

⁹ Mircea Eliade, *The Sacred and the Profane, the nature of religion*. The significance of religious myth, symbolism, and ritual within life and culture (New York: Harcourt, Brace & World, 1959), p. 80: "*In illo tempore* the gods had displayed their greatest powers. The *cosmogony* is *the supreme divine manifestation*, the paradigmatic act of strength, superabundance, and creativity. Religious man thirsts for the real. By every means at his disposal, he seeks to reside at the very source of primordial reality, when the world was *in statu nascendi*".

¹⁰ Mikel Dufrenne, *In the Presence of the Sensuous* (Atlantic Highlands: Humanities Press International, 1986), p. 73: "The eye, putting us into the world by opening a world to us, precedes the mind". Also, Rabindranath Tagore's emphasis on sight and sound, on the close relationship between seeing and hearing, rather than on thinking, seems to be shared by Le Clézio's protagonists.

LESLIE DUNTON-DOWNER

LANGUAGELESS PLACES AND POETIC LANGUAGE: THE BOUNDLESS DESIRE OF CANNIBAL CLÉMENT X.

Free from borders and limits, languageless places are imagined in the Western tradition either as sub-human, nightmarish spaces of chaos or divine points of origin and destination. A good example of this phenomenon appears in the works of Hesiod, who will allow me to set up the relationship between cannibalism and poetic language. Recall that, in Hesiod's *Theogony*, poetic language is itself presented as the medium through which the languageless past and future may be represented and ordered. Before they grant the gift of making poetry to shepherds, the muses call them "mere bellies".[1] But Hesiod tells what happened when the muses "breathed into me a divine voice to celebrate things that shall be and things that were aforetime."[2] It is through his transformation from a mere belly to a mortal with a divine voice that Hesiod captures the essence of the relationship between poetic language and the languageless place, whether it be the nearly divine Golden Age of the *Works and Days* or the hollow caves of the *Theogony* in which monstrous, hyper-animal creatures eat raw flesh. My paper explores the elemental passion for the languageless place in two distinct ways: 1) In the realm of representation, as an inherent feature of poetic language; and 2) Beyond the realm of representation, as an attribute of the psychopathological cannibal. By looking at the differences between represented and enacted desires for languagelessness, I hope to show how the figurative word, or what we might call poetic language, becomes the fragile marker of humanness. Poetic language in this sense comes to condense and reflect upon the central role that language in general plays in the psychical and intellectual fulfillment, as well as the social concord, of human beings.

While it marks our distance from the barbaric or utopian spaces of languagelessness, language also brings with it an irresolvable problem. The distance between the figurative word and the things it may mean becomes, itself, figured as a conflictual here which other, imagined, places are seen to transcend. The Christian tradition idealizes this place as a future space beyond the here and now of our earthly existence and its problematic language. We read in Augustine, for example, that communication occurs in heaven without recourse to language as we know it. Heavenly speech is, in particular, not vexed by the problematic differences between *signa* (signs) and *res* (things).³ Both Hellenic and Judeo-Christian models of the languageless place, whether past or future, feared or desired, suggest that the humanizing charge of language has to do with the indeterminacy of figurative language.

Representations of the constructed ideal place, or man-made utopia, almost inevitably attempt to picture a human transcendence of those conflicts inherent in and identified with language. There are often problems, however, since this transcendence appears to remove the very aspects of language that define humanness. The Brazilian Modernist Oswald de Andrade, for instance, sketches out a post-colonial utopian vision in his *Anthropophagic Manifesto* (1924). Drawing most notably on Montaigne, Hegel, and the cultural practices of Brazilian Indians, de Andrade proposes returning to a cannibalistic world where enemies devour one another, leaving finally a utopian matriarchal society in which language, unable to differentiate between literal and figurative meanings, no longer signifies conflict.⁴

Consider, too, how the Russian writer Zamyatin pictures, in his novel *We* (1920–21), a utopia in which communication is meant to occur seamlessly in the universal language of mathematics. The narrator discovers, however, that the act of writing is antithetical to this social project and its restrictively referential rather than poetic language.⁵ In writing, the protagonist of *We*, D-503, comes to reflect on his individuated self and on the ways in which he differs from the collective of the One State just at the moment when he comes to see that the fertile imperfections of language lie in its poetic nature:

I, D-503, Builder of the *Integral*, am only one of the mathematicians of the One State. My pen, accustomed to figures, does not know how to create the music of assonances and rhymes. I shall merely attempt to record what I see and think, or, to be more exact, what we think (precisely so – we, and let this *We* be the title of my record). But since this record will be a derivative of our life, of the mathematically perfect life of the One State, will it not be, of itself, and regardless of my will or skill, a poem? It will. I believe, I know it.

I write this, and my cheeks are burning. This must be similar to what a woman feels when she first senses within herself the pulse of a new, still tiny, still blind little human being. It is I, and at the same time, not I. And for many long months it will be necessary to nourish it with my own life, my own blood, then tear it painfully from myself and lay it at the feet of the One State.⁶

D-503 sets out to write in a "mathematically perfect" manner a poem of the collective life of his society, its *we*. But writing, in language rather than the figures of mathematics, changes him, draws out the sensation of being pregnant, of containing within himself an "I" and a "not I". This discovery of the intimate relationship between writing and the acknowledgment of a reflective self is here associated with life-giving, pain, the awakening of emotions, and the uncertainties introduced by language.

From the vantage point of this anti-utopian novel, the ambiguities and imperfections of language define it as an irresolvable, problematic, and decidedly human medium. Poetic language in particular, with its highly condensed concern for the indeterminacy of words, celebrates the necessity and humanity of the imperfect relationship between signifiers and signifieds. "I" is not "I", says D-503 of himself and, at the same time, of the non-referential, poetic words he finds himself writing.[7] In the context of our collective work here on "The Elemental Passion for Place" from the vantage point of Phenomenology and Literature, one could make a twofold observation: 1) The utopian place appears to exclude the poetic function of language; and 2) The poetic function of language appears to capture our distance from some desired place, reminding us of our being here in a realm of differentiation and conflict rather than there, in a place that transcends indeterminacy.

Of course, the very nature of figurative language, and most notably in the lyrical genres, involves a desire to transcend the boundaries separating words (the space of language) from the things they signify or desire (a space of languagelessness); to collapse, in effect, the distance between here and there. Richard Sieburth observes the complexity of this phenomenon in the poems of Friedrich Hölderlin when he notes: "To be truly *here* is to be everywhere; any locus is potentially an *omphalos*",[8] a cosmic center of mythological charge. This merging of here and there may take place to a certain degree in poetry, but is necessarily figured or represented, so that the ideal space that is there may only be gleaned through the mediating hereness of the written.

At this point I turn to Heidegger's 1951 lecture on Hölderlin entitled ". . . dichterisch wohnet der Mensch . . .". Heidegger notes that: "Language beckons us, at first and then again at the end, toward a thing's nature. But that is not to say, ever, that in any word-meaning picked up at will language supplies us, straight away and definitively, with the transparent nature of the matter as if it were an object ready for use. But the responding in which man authentically listens to the appeal of language is that which speaks in the element of poetry."[9] Heidegger is here addressing Hölderlin's "In lieblicher Bläue", and poetry in the most literal sense, but his comments bear on language more generally as he continues to reflect on the poem's message:

> For the "poetic", when it is taken as poetry, is supposed to belong to the realm of fantasy. Poetic dwelling flies fantastically above reality. The poet counters this misgiving by saying expressly that poetic dwelling is a dwelling "on this earth". Hölderlin thus not only protects the "poetic" from a likely misinterpretation, but by adding the words "on this earth" expressly points to the nature of poetry. Poetry does not fly above and surmount the earth in order to escape it and hover over it. Poetry is what first brings man onto the earth, making him belong to it, and this brings him into dwelling.[10]

The concept of dwelling is eventually developed in this essay as an aspect of being human; to dwell on this earth is to dwell humanly on this earth. Heidegger makes an important point in this reading of Hölderlin. He is saying that the "poetic" or human aspect of language guarantees that language will not supply us with transparent access to meanings. Instead, poetic language, with its preference for the figurative over and above the literal, celebrates the necessity and humanity of the imperfect word, its splitting of signifier and signified.

While we may trace in Western letters a thematic preoccupation with returning to or proceeding to a pre- or post-linguistic place, poetic language inherently expresses a desire to be somewhere else, to mean something other than what is said on the most literal, referential level. This tension between what language says and what it may mean is captured by the problem of the metaphor, as it has been recently studied by philosophers and theorists.[11] The problems surrounding the metaphor suggest precisely the inherent lack of transparency in language which we have come to think of as its imperfection; and since this lack of transparency generates misinterpretation and conflict, language as we know it appears to be fundamentally at odds with what comes to be represented as a perfect place.

Nevertheless, I would like to argue that poetic language merely foregrounds indeterminacies characterizing what we call ordinary language. That is, the reflectiveness we attribute to linguistic subjectivity involves the very poetic concept of being at once an "I" and a "not I". This phenomenon is clarified when we see how desire for the languageless place is acted upon rather than represented. This is precisely what is involved in cases of psychopathological cannibalism where the subject, failing to process desires linguistically, takes the figurative for the literal. I think you will see that, while representations of a desire for languagelessness prompt self-consciousness and an awareness of the poetic nature of language, actions taken to achieve a state of languagelessness destroy boundaries between Self and Other, as well as between literal and figurative meaning.

My recent research on the relationship between cannibalism and poetic language led me to the library of the Faculty of Medicine in Paris, France. Theoretical and clinical evidence suggests that cannibals act on unrepressed desires to return to a prelinguistic, oral phase of childhood. Unable to process psychically the differences between literal and figurative levels of meaning, cannibals operate according to a principle known as *demetaphorization*.[12] The very process that makes figurative language (the metaphor) psychically functional is never fully developed in the cannibal subject.

Cannibalism resulting from a psychic disorder appears to involve an extreme form of this process of demetaphorization, or literalization. What is initially most striking, for example, in case reports of cannibalism and vampirism, is the subject's connecting the consumed object with the "unobtainable Mother".[13] What the cannibal eats in the flesh of his Other/Mother is, in some form, the metaphorical process triggering his formation of identity, his awareness of differences between himself as subject and his mother as the initial discursive sign of the other.[14] The cannibal's victim is, essentially, language incarnated, metaphor literalized. One might think again of D-503 in Zamyatin's *We*. Although a male "Number" of the "One State", he experiences the act of writing poetically as a stirring of life within himself, a sensation of being at once an "I" and a "not I". In the cannibal subject, however, the "I" and the "not I" are never psychically differentiated; the poetic experience of containing an Other within one's self is instead literalized. In this sense, the cannibal subject comes to represent the antithesis of what Heidegger takes to be the human activity of dwelling poetically.

Consider the case of Clément X.[15] In the Mayenne region of France in September of 1979, Clément goes on a rampage: he rapes a young girl and begins to devour her neck before she is saved by a neighbor; he goes on to injure one person and kill three – one of these victims is an old man whose left thigh Clément eats.

The dossiers on Clément are thick; he has a well-documented history of serious psychic disorder, as do other members of his immediate family. The reports include extensively-detailed background material relating to the events of September 1979. I will address only a few of the details in order to show what happens when, in this instance, the figurative is psychically literalized.

On one occasion around a year before his cannibal attacks, Clément left his house at night, naked, and headed by bicycle for the town of Mamers, where he was later found asleep in a barn.[16] His background as a religious fanatic (hearing God speak to him, traveling to Rome with the intention of visiting the Pope, making a journey to Guadeloupe to look for the Tree of Life, etc.) suggests that Clément's night of nudity in Mamers involves an identification with the infant Christ. But Mamers is also homonymous with *ma mère*, 'my mother'. Naked and asleep in Mamers, Clément is already thinking cannibalistically, objectifying and literalizing psychic lacunae. During the same year, 1978, there is further evidence of *demetaphorization*: Clément believes he is the Holy Spirit and reports having impregnated his own mother because God told him to sleep with her.[17]

Following his cannibal outbreak, Clément explains his motivation to doctors:

Si je suis Jésus et qu'on me mange, je finirai par disparaître; alors, pour reconstituer mon corps, pour exister à nouveau, il faut que je mange quelqu'un et que je boive son sang; ceci est ma chair, ceci est mon sang, mangez-en, buvez-en tous, il faut manger pour exister.[18]

[If I am Jesus and people eat me, I'll end up disappearing; so, to make my body whole, to exist again, I have to eat someone and drink his blood; this is my body, this is my blood, eat and drink of it, each of you; you must eat to exist.]

After consuming the thigh of his victim, the subject explains that he was overcome with a sensation of well-being and satiation, even 'mystical fulfillment' (*satisfaction mystique*).[19] Clément is essentially literalizing the language of the Eucharistic rite.[20] Identified with Christ as food, he imagines others ingesting him; in turn, he ingests them in order to reconstitute his self, which is in danger of dispersal and annihilation. Clément's cannibal literalizing and literal cannibalism involve his rejection of subjectivity, or his linguistically differentiated being, and his regression to an oral phase in which satisfaction is found in the union, at once alimentary and prelinguistic, between mother and self-as-child.

One could say that Clément is enacting an impulse (rather than figuring a desire) to return to an idealized, necessarily languageless place. He performs literally, then, what the poetic function in language figures as a perfect union between signifier and signified.

The case of Clément X., like those of other cannibals, tells us something of the frightening proximity of the figurative to the literal or, perhaps, of love to violence. And this brings me back to the question of the relationship between the elemental passion for place and poetic language. I noted earlier that the desire to occupy a place of languagelessness is a sign of our human desire to transcend the limitations we attribute to language. While the metaphor captures on one level the desire of language to transcend the differences that systematize it, the metaphor also represents the indeterminacy that offers us a means by which to reflect on our imperfect yet poetic humanness.

I would like to close with a comment about the phrase "boundless desire" in my title, which I derived from a passage in Shakespeare's *Troilus and Cressida*. I believe that Shakespeare's play is fundamentally concerned with the dangerous proximity of the idealized, utopian space to the nihilistic, chaotic world of cannibalism. Shakespeare explores in this drama the mystical selflessness of ideal love as a place very close to the cannibal world of languagelessness. Both places are predicated on an absence of borders and limits or, to speak in shorthand, of writing. One of the important messages conveyed by *Troilus and Cressida* is that language, while necessarily a constructed and constricting system, while itself a sign of our distance from an ideal place, is ultimately the medium through which we are able to reflect on and delight in our existence as imperfect, poetic creatures and, above all, to communicate our equally human and necessary desire to occupy a limitless, languageless place. It is, after all, this desire for some kind of transcendence, some unattainable place, that produces our unceasing exploration in language of the indeterminate place that is here. I will leave you with the voice of Troilus as he speaks to Cressida about love or, if you like, about writing:

This is the monstruosity in love, lady, that the will is infinite and the execution confin'd, that the desire is boundless and the act a slave to limit.
(*Troilus and Cressida* III.ii.81–83)

Harvard University

NOTES

[1] Hesiod, *The Homeric Hymns and Homerica* (Cambridge: Harvard University Press; London: William Heinemann, 1914), p. 81.
[2] *Ibid.*
[3] These are Augustine's terms. See *De Doctrina Christiana*, I.2.
[4] See Oswald de Andrade, "Manifesto Antropófago", in *A Utopia Antropofágica*, ed. Benedito Nunes (San Paulo: Globo, 1990), pp. 47–52.
[5] My reading of Zamyatin's *We* owes a great deal to the compelling essay by Jurij Striedter: "Journeys Through Utopia: Introductory Remarks to the Post-Revolutionary Russian Utopian Novel", *Poetics Today* **3** (1982): 33–60.
[6] Yevgeny Zamyatin, *We*, trans. Mirra Ginsburg (New York: Avon Books, 1972), p. 2.
[7] Jakobson describes in similar terms the poetic function or *poeticity* of language: "[B]esides the direct awareness of the identity between sign and object (A is A1), there is a necessity for the direct awareness of the inadequacy of that identity (A is not A1)" (Roman Jakobson, *Language in Literature* [Cambridge, Mass.; London: Belknap Press, 1987], p. 378). Combining direct awareness with an awareness of indirection, the poetic function of language appears to be fundamentally associated with self-consciousness, wherein the observing "I" detects at once an "I" and a "not I".
[8] Friedrich Hölderlin, *Hymns and Fragments*, trans. Richard Sieburth (Princeton: Princeton University Press, 1984), p. 39.
[9] Martin Heidegger, ". . . *Poetically Man Dwells* . . ." in *Poetry, Language, Thought*, trans. Albert Hofstadter (New York: Harper & Row, 1971), p. 216.
[10] *Ibid.*, p. 218.
[11] See, for example, Jacques Derrida, "White Mythology", *New Literary History* **6** (1974): 5–74; and the essays in *On Metaphor*, ed. Sheldon Sacks (Chicago, London: University of Chicago Press, 1978).
[12] Nicolas Abraham & Maria Torok, "Introjecter-incorporer: Deuil ou mélancolie", *Nouvelle revue de psychanalyse* **6** (1972): p. 112.
[13] Richard L. Vanden Burgh & John F. Kelly, "Vampirism", *Archives of General Psychiatry* **11** (1964): p. 546. Cf. Robert S. McCully, "Vampirism: Historical Perspective and Underlying Process in Relation to a Case of Auto-Vampirism", *Journal of Nervous and Mental Disease* **139** (1964): 440–452; A. Bourguignon, "Situation du vampirisme et de l'autovampirisme", *Annales Médico-Psychologiques* **1** (1977): 181–196.
[14] See the discussion of subjectivity and language by Jacques Lacan, *Le Séminaire, livre XI: Les quatre concepts fondamentaux de la psychanalyse* (Paris: Seuil, 1973), p. 199.
[15] One report on this case was published by the medical-legal team treating the patient: M. Bénézech, M. Bourgeois, J. Villeger & B. Etchegaray, "Cannibalisme et vampirisme chez un schizophrène multimeurtrier", *Bourdeaux Médical*, 1980, XIII, pp. 1261–1265. A more complete report was prepared by a larger group of experts: G. Fellion *et al.*, "Du fantasme à l'acte criminel et cannibalique", *Annales Médico-Psychologiques* **138** (1980): 596–608.
[16] Fellion, *op. cit.*, p. 598.
[17] Bénézech, *op. cit.*, p. 1263.
[18] Fellion, *op. cit.*, p. 599.
[19] *Ibid.*

[20] Compare the case of a Papua New Guinea man who similarly takes in the biblical story of Abraham and Isaac, sacrificing his son and eating his heart. "He misinterpreted the intent of those teachings but correctly assessed their content and literal meaning" (B. G. Burton-Bradley, "Cannibalism for Cargo", *Journal of Nervous and Mental Disease* **143** [1976]: p. 430).

SHERLYN ABDOO

"BEFORE DAYBREAK": THE UNFINISHED
QUEST OF WASHINGTON IRVING'S
HEADLESS HORSEMAN OF SLEEPY HOLLOW

> "But whate'er smack'd of Noyance, or Unrest,
> Was far far off expell'd from this delicious Nest."
> James Thomson, "The Castle of Indolence" (I: 54–55)

Washington Irving's tale, "The Legend of Sleepy Hollow", was the last story in his collection of literary sketches published as *The Sketch Book of Geoffrey Crayon, Gent.* in 1819–20. As his most enduring and popular work, *The Sketch Book* followed a ten year hiatus after his spoofing *A History of New York* (1809), written pseudonymously under the name of Diedrich Knickerbocker, like Geoffrey Crayon, another of Irving's alter egos. Knickerbocker's importance is that he is a fictive persona whose writings reappear as twice-told tales throughout Irving's corpus, and allow Irving a way to distance authorial voice.[1] In *The Sketch Book*, "Rip Van Winkle" and "The Legend of Sleepy Hollow" are the only two sketches recounted as "found among the papers of the late Diedrich Knickerbocker" (LSH, p. 329).[2]

The authorial voice in "The Legend" is questionable from the beginning, as Irving's becomes subsumed first behind Geoffrey Crayon – his pseudonymous author of *The Sketch Book* – who, in turn, is retelling old tales written down by Diedrich Knickerbocker. Irving complicates the telling even further by adding yet another narrative layer when, in a "handwritten" "Postscript" to the tale, Knickerbocker passes "The Legend" off as one "given, almost in the precise words in which I heard it related at a Corporation meeting of the ancient city of Manhattoes" (LSH, p. 359). Who, therefore, is the narrator, and which of the stories related in the text is the *authentic* "Legend" – or, does it matter?

One feature that unites "Rip" and "The Legend" is their common origins in supernatural themes of old Germanic myths and folklore. John Clendenning credits Irving as the "innovator" of a sub-genre he calls "sportive gothic" (p. 92), a form which combines the "mystery and terror common to most gothic tales" with an "ironic sense ... to promote humor and satire" (p. 92). But these pseudo-gothic tales served another purpose, too: to debunk the problem of defining the writer's role in an America seemingly bereft of that ostensibly necessary deep past, a history or traditions of its own, from which to draw, or on which to anchor its literary efforts. What America still had that Europe had lost so many millennia earlier was a more recent memory of nature in its unsettled, unpopulated state.

Washington Irving had to travel back to the past before he could progress into the future. It is this paradoxical and often puzzling situation that aspiring American writers and critics found themselves in that provides the serious subtext in "The Legend of Sleepy Hollow": the irreconcilable tensions created between the contrasting mythic states of nature's harmonic rhythms and abundant prelapsarian bounty and the rapid speed which propelled America Westward in "the great torrent of migration and improvement" (p. 331). The search for a past is expressed partly as the need for a mythic golden age. In Irving's imagination it was the magical time before Dutch sailors staked out their first gardens in the New World. It was to an illusionary dream world of purity unblemished, the New World as first seen by Hendrick Hudson when he glimpsed the edge of the new land from the river that now carries his name, that Irving evokes in the opening of "The Legend of Sleepy Hollow":

> In the bosom of one of those spacious coves which indent the eastern shore of the Hudson, at that broad expansion of the river denominated by the ancient Dutch navigators the Tappan Zee, and where they always prudently shortened sail, and implored the protection of St. Nicholas when they crossed, there lies a small modest town or rural port, which by some is called Greensburg, but which is more generally and properly known by the name of Tarry Town. (LSH, p. 329)

Inland from the green expanse is the "little valley," whose "inhabitants . . . are descendants from the original Dutch settlers" and live "sequestered" in a "glen . . . long . . . known by the name of Sleepy Hollow" (LSH, p. 330). One hundred years after Irving wrote his tale, the yearning so deeply imbedded in the American psyche for a "sequestered" *green* place of peace and home was even more poignantly present in F. Scot Fitzgerald's elegy to that far-off mythic age in Nick Carraway's rumination on the forces that had propelled Gatsby toward his own self-betrayal and murder. From Gatsby's lawn overlooking Long Island Sound, Nick

> gradually . . . became aware of the old island here that flowered once for Dutch sailors' eyes – a fresh, green breast of the new world. Its vanished trees, the trees that had made way for Gatsby's house, had once pandered in whispers to the last and greatest of all

human dreams; for a transistory enchanted moment man must have held his breath in the presence of this continent, compelled into an aesthetic contemplation he neither understood nor desired, face to face for the last time in history with something commensurate to his capacity for wonder.

(Fitzgerald, p. 182)

Just as Nick's adventures East ended in disillusion and led him to return to his home in the Western heartland, Irving, too, returned home from his adventures abroad. It is no surprise that, while the majority of the tales in *The Sketchbook* explores the old customs and cultures of England and Germany, he, fittingly I think, ends the collection with a tale about America.

I

Washington Irving's and Ichabod Crane's world was one in which accumulation of material wealth and possessions became the new basis of education and cultural concern, replacing the terror-driven searches for personal spiritual salvation that had occupied the previous generations. Ichabod Crane is the new man in a new country whose independence is so recent that the so-called legendary "Hessian trooper" "whose head had been carried away by a cannon ball, in some nameless battle during the Revolutionary War" still rides his steed by night searching for his lost identity (LSH, p. 330). The Headless Horseman is an unsettled spectre of a warrior whose loss prevents him from peacefully resting in his grave in a foreign land, having been killed fighting an insignificant battle in a war that was not his own. In losing his head, he has lost his identity forever.

Rip Van Winkle, Irving's other protagonist who inhabits a New York village "up the Hudson" in the "Kaatskill Mountains" (RVW, p. 38), has previously confronted his own sense of lost identity when he reappears after his twenty year sleep: "The poor fellow was . . . completely confounded. He doubted his own identity, and whether he was himself or another man" (RVW, p. 50). Seeing the exact double of himself in the image of his adult son, also named Rip, Rip, Sr. becomes frightened:

"God knows," exclaimed he, at his wit's end. "I'm not myself – I'm somebody else – that's me yonder – no – that's somebody else got into my shoes – . . . and I'm changed, and I can't tell what's my name, or who I am!" (RVW, p. 50)

The nightmare is that once a person has departed his place, someone (another you) will fill it.

In "The Legend of Sleepy Hollow", Irving demonstrates how the ways of an old world Dutch settlement transplanted into New York conflicts with the values of the New England Connecticut Yankee, Ichabod Crane, and how an American writer's quest for locating a national identity discovered that America, herself, was and is, his own best subject.[3]

II

Peeling back the many layers of mask Irving uses in "The Legend of Sleepy Hollow", we can finally arrive at the central puzzle that he was concerned with presenting. The aim of this paper is to examine the notion that loss of identity, betrayal and revenge, are primary themes underlying the comic-gothic genre Irving adopted to deflect or displace his angry, subversive message, within the many-layered text. One way he accomplished his task was to contaminate the truthfulness of the tale by giving his story so many voices that after the reader has become accustomed to one voice, he is offhandedly informed that the narrative voice he's been listening to is not the *real* tale-teller. Here the problem of identity as one theme of the story is subtle and sly; Irving plays with the reader by teasingly withholding the storyteller's identity, which ultimately, is never revealed. This destructiveness of authority is self-aimed, as much to reduce narrative responsibility for the tale's meaning, as his playing the trickster undermines the establishment of a legitimate American literature, wholly separate from European tradition. In addition to withholding the identity of the tale-teller, the other issue Irving deftly sidestepped is the question posed by one of the story's Corporate auditor's who demanded to know: "what was the moral of the story, and what it went to prove?" (LSH, p. 359). The answer, requiring that readers "take a joke as we find it" (LSH, p. 359), is put in the form of a two-part riddle; first,

That, . . . he that runs races with goblin troopers is likely to have rough riding of it. (LSH, p. 359)

And, second,

for a country schoolmaster to be refused the hand of a Dutch heiress is a certain step to high preferment in the state. (LSH, p. 360)

The obvious joke is a toss-off: that no one can race with goblins, real or imagined, and hope to win; but the second part, that a refusal of marriage into an established family of means is a guarantee of political success, is one that requires a more serious consideration, and its implications are both personal and national in their misogynistic and misogamistic undertones.[4] Is it ironic that the only times Irving reveals himself in the text are to make pointed commentaries against women and marriage. First, Ichabod's attraction to Katrina Van Tassel is compared to an evil fate, and she to a witch:

he would have passed a pleasant life of it, . . . if his path had not been crossed by a being that causes more perplexity to mortal man than ghosts, goblins, and the whole race of witches put together, and that was – a woman. (LSH, p. 337)

And, later, after Ichabod's suit has been rejected, Irving glibly blames Katrina for opportunistically using Ichabod's suit to gain herself a husband of choice:

Oh these women! These women! Could that girl have been playing off any of her coquettish tricks? Was her encouragement of the poor pedagogue all a mere sham to secure her conquest of his rival? (LSH, p. 352)

But, Washington Irving, himself, was not above a little disingenuous sleight of hand, and was accused of plagiarizing the central plot of "Rip Van Winkle". The accusation apparently rankled, for even after the furor had settled and he had written disclaimers against any intent of plagiarizing, he included in his next book, *Bracebridge Hall* (1822), a piece called "The Historian", also attributed to the pseudonymous Knickerbocker, whose sole purpose seems to be to provide a place for a footnote which refers to "the foul instance of plagiarism marvelously brought to light" regarding "Rip Van Winkle" (H, pp. 298–99). In the note, Irving excuses himself, stating his belief that he

considered popular traditions of the kind as fair foundations for authors of fiction to build upon, and had made use of the one in question accordingly. (H, p. 299)

He continues by claiming "no contest" in refuting the truth of the borrowing, and self-deprecatingly takes the sting out of the reader's judgment when he says:

I . . . consider myself so completely overpaid by the public for my trivial performances, that I am content to submit to any deduction which, in their after-thoughts, they may think proper to make. (H, p. 229)

The plagiarism embroglio is indicative, too, of one central feature characterizing Ichabod Crane's seemingly natural ability to consume and transform with his enormous appetite both food and frightening, supernatural tales of witchcraft. His two main occupations, besides whipping recalcitrant schoolboys under his supervision, is consuming endlessly bountiful meals, and in retelling stories borrowed from his great sourcebook, Cotton Mather's *History of New England Witchcraft*. This encapsulation of his two orally-centered energies reflects the description Irving gives him. He was "a huge feeder, and though lank, had the dilating powers of an anaconda" (LSH, p. 333), that species of boa which first suffocates its prey, then swallows it whole. For as large and as matchless as was Crane's "appetite" for the "marvelous", just as matchless were "his powers of digesting it, . . . No tale was too gross or monstrous for his capacious swallow" (LSH, p. 335). The act of swallowing food is analagous to the act of "swallowing", i.e., believing a "tale". Another way he possesses is through the imaginative feeding of his mouth through his "great green eyes" (LSH, p. 338). In Ichabod's sight "rows of pigeons" become transformed into "a comfortable pie . . . with a coverlet of crust"; "sleek unwieldy porkers" become a "carved . . . sleek side of bacon, and juicy relishing ham"; "sucking pigs", he sees "roasting . . . [each] with a pudding in [its] belly, and an apple in [its] mouth"; he sees a "stately squadron of snowy geese", "swimming in their own gravy", and "fleets of ducks", "pairing cozily in dishes, like snug married couples, with a decent competency of onion sauce" (LSH, p. 338). All for a "luxurious winter fare" (LSH, p. 338). Katrina Van Tassel, likewise, embodies her patrimony by appearing as sumptuous as the farmer's edibles: she is "as plump as a partridge, ripe and melting . . . as one of her father's peaches", and as valuable as "the ornaments of pure yellow gold" which symbolize "her vast expectations" (LSH, p. 337).

Reading is another act of consumption for Ichabod Crane, and devouring tales of witchcraft ripens his imagination and makes him, in the end, a vulnerable target for his adversary, Brom Bones, and his spoofing. Telling old tales is Ichabod's one valuable currency and the way by which he is tolerated in the society of Sleep Hollow. He not only provides entertainment, but by story's end has himself become perpetually absorbed into the local entertainment as the story of Ichabod's disappearance becomes a self-fulfilling prophecy, and enters the mythic subtext of legends circulating in the neighborhood. For, long after he had disappeared, the explanation most favored by "old country wives" was that "Ichabod was spirited away by supernatural means", and as his old schoolhouse "fell to decay", it "was reported to be haunted by the ghost of the unfortunate pedagogue" (LSH, pp. 358–59). In this way, although Ichabod is never accepted into the community of Sleepy Hollow, he is likewise never permitted to leave. His story is devoured as one would a good meal into the fine substance of a winter's tale.

III

The derivation and significance of Ichabod Crane's name is of some interest. In Hebrew, Ichabod means "no glory" or "dishonour", and refers back to the time the biblical Ichabod was born, when the Israelites were defeated by the Philistines. Ichabod's obscurity is that his name does not appear again in biblical reference, except in the lineage of Ahijah – an indirect descendant.[5]

Ichabod Crane is a combination of a crane and a grasshopper. In his choice of "Crane" for Ichabod's surname, Irving drew on ancient folk wisdom in tales and myth, regarding the crane's reputation for slyness and for revealing the identity of murderers, as in the legend of the "cranes of Ibycus".[6] On his way to the Van Tassel's quilting partly where he is rejected as a suitor, Irving describes Ichabod as a grasshopper (also a perennial devourer): "He rode with short stirrups, which brought his knees nearly up to the pommel of the saddle; his sharp elbows stuck out like grasshoppers'; . . . and, as his horse jogged on, the motion of his arms was not unlike the flapping of a pair of wings" (LSH, p. 345). Ichabod is crane-like when he imitates the crane's mating dance at the party with his partner, the heiress Katrina; he behaves like a grasshopper when he descends locust-like upon the food-laden tables as "one might have mistaken him for the genius of famine descending upon the earth" (LSH, p. 332). His enormous appetite, however, is never appeased. He is a parasite, forever seeking greener pastures, and hopes to marry Van Tassel's daughter so the farmlands "might be readily turned into cash; and the money invested in immense tracts of wild land" out West in "Kentucky, Tennessee, or the Lord knows where" (LSH, p. 339).

Ichabod Crane is an anomalous character representing many, often conflicting, interests. Crane-like he is a migrator, an intruder, a passer-by, the mythic bringer of newborn infants; his "long snipe nose" is like a "weathercock, perched upon his spindle neck, to tell which way the wind blew". He resembles a "scarecrow eloped from a cornfield" (LSH,

p. 332). As the perennial boy-man, Ichabod is too thin to have developed a manly body; he is a comic character to be laughed at, but not taken seriously. Fear is what drives Crane's continual motion. He is the gossip mill, moving from house to house, because he has no home; his contribution to the domestic scene is in tending sleeping babies, dandling infants and providing housewives with entertaining stories. Ichabod's fear is the fear of not knowing who he is or where he is headed, and his destiny is determined by the circumstances that drive him to flee the spectre of his own mortality. His midnight ride, facing Brom Bones disguised as the Headless Horseman is an initiation of sorts. What Ichabod sees in Bones's funning is a spectre of himself – headless, identityless, empty – and what frightens him most and keeps him running is the fear of self-knowledge. When Brom Bones, whose name is a shortened form of Abraham, scares Ichabod away, he is parodying Abraham's rejection of his illegitimate son, Ishmael, when he sends him into the desert wilderness: rootless, friendless, and possessionless.

Though he envies the material abundance of Van Tassel's farm and speculates on his chances as a prospective groom, settling down is not on Ichabod Crane's agenda. The new American man is heading West, but Ichabod Crane's intention, whether it be alone "with all his worldly effects tied up in a cotton handkerchief" (LSH, p. 333), or with a fast-made fortune in his pocket, accompanied by

the blooming Katrina, with a whole family of children, mounted on the top of a wagon loaded with household trumpery, with pots and kettles dangling beneath; and he . . . himself bestriding a pacing mare, with a colt at her heels (LSH, p. 339)

is an illusion. I would suggest, however, that the image of himself, suddenly a man of abundance, in possession of a wife, children, and household goods, is the telling image. For, in his ability to successfully turn nothing into something, Ichabod could fulfill his vision of himself ("bestride a pacing mare with a colt at her heels") and be the potent male he is not.

IV

Ichabod is not the only interloper in the community. First, the Headless Horseman, who roams the byways searching for his lost head, is his precursor and haunting spectre, a hired Hessian mercenary to counter the colonists' revolutionary fervor for self-determination. It is Crane's encounter with the Hessian, albeit disguised as his romantic rival, Brom Bones, that is the crucial turning point of the story, for the encounter takes place at the very site of the capture of yet another foreign agent – the British Major John André, another Revolutionary War figure, who had been caught in the no-man's-land that existed between the warring armies. It was widely believed that André was duped, then scapegoated by Benedict Arnold, for while André was tried and hanged for treason for defying a flag of truce and disguising himself in the act of smuggling the plans of West Point's defenses to the British Army, he had only been following Arnold's orders, and Arnold, himself, managed to successfully escape.

On the surface, Ichabod Crane is a comic parody of André, the more convincingly dashing romantic lover. While the story of André's capture and hanging were well-known and protested, perhaps less known was the story of his romantic disappointment at losing Honoria Sneyd who was prevented by her parents from marrying him because of his lack of fortune. André was, thus, twice disappointed: first, by losing his beloved Honoria in marriage to another man, and secondly, when he was betrayed by his countryman, Benedict Arnold, and, symbolically lost his head in hanging.

Ichabod Crane, too, is rejected as a suitor without prospects, in favor of Brom Bones, the local roisterer-trickster, a "burly, roaring . . . blade", with a "Herculean frame and great powers of limb" (LSH, p. 340), who uses Crane's weaknesses to drive him from the neighborhood. Though Crane does not die, he did lose his head through fear and disbelief, was unseated from his horse, brained by a pumpkin, and disappeared altogether from sight, never again to be seen by Sleepy Hollow residents. Like the Headless Horseman, both André and Crane took falls that affected the state of their heads, and both, because of their alien status in Sleepy Hollow, found their destinies *on the road*, and ultimately became incorporated into the mythology of the place as their individual, tragic, stories are kept alive, with relish, by generation after generation of female storytellers. Likewise, as strangers in a strange land, each loses sight of his identity or suffers from displacement of self. Both André and Crane, spurned by their lovers, remain unwed and without progeny. In a landscape of worshipful bounty, where Balthus Van Tassel's barn "might have served for a church . . . bursting forth with the treasures of the farm" (LSH, pp. 337–38), neither is able to emulate the fertility of the fruitful land.

V

All themes come together in the single episode of Ichabod Crane's frightening midnight ride through the forest and his encounter with the spectre of his haunted imagination – the Headless Horseman. Brom Bones's horse of choice is, of course, a black stallion, "a Dare-devil creature, like himself, full of mettle and mischief" (LSH, p. 347). Bones and his cronies frequently rode in packs "like a troop of Don Cossacks", playing tricks, devising pranks, and in the environs were colloquially referred to as "Brom Bones and his gang" (LSH, p. 341). Ritual horse racing has long been recognized as a primitive fertility rite, engaged in for the purpose of insuring crop growth and fertility among newly married couples, alike. Horse racing is regarded as a sign of sexual potency, and "keeping a good seat", or "remaining in the saddle", have off-color connotations in bawdy jokes, even to this day. Brom Bones, though a trickster-boy, playing boy-games, nonetheless gets the girl, and shortly after Ichabod's disappearance, be "conducted the blooming Katrina in triumph to the altar" (LSH, p. 358).

Ichabod's mount for his death-ride through the forest is a borrowed old nag named Gunpowder; he is a "broken-down plow horse" that "was gaunt and shagged, . . . his rusty mane and tail were tangled and knotted with burrs" (LSH, pp. 344–45), and one of its eyes "had lost its pupil" (LSH, p. 344). Gunpowder and Crane, setting out together for Van Tassel's quilting party, parody Don Quixote on his faithful Rosinante – a true knight in quest of his damsel.[7] As a parodic "knight-errant of yore, who seldom had anything but giants, enchanters, fiery dragons and such like easily conquered adversaries" (LSH, p. 340), Ichabod's progress in capturing Katrina Van Tassel's heart is closely monitored by her father, Baltus, by way of the close perusal of his weathervane: that "little wooden warrior, who, armed with a sword in each hand, was most valiantly fighting the wind on the pinacle of the barn" (LSH, p. 343). While Ichabod's head is likened to "a weathercock, perched upon his long spindle neck", in order to "tell which way the wind blew", comparing him to the Don, tilting madly at windmills, or to a toy soldier battling the wind with a wooden sword, speaks to the state of Ichabod's mind, as the site of his most terrible battles.

The night race is life quickened. Being in the dark where the path is rocky and the steed old and unpredictable, pretty much sums up Ichabod's direction on the path of life. Ichabod's lot has been to manage with used clothing, second-hand possessions, riding a borrowed horse, retelling borrowed tales; he is a self-made man, constructed out of self-used borrowings of all kinds.

The "Legend of Sleepy Hollow" is about childhood memory. The first, youngest voice in the story, is of a boy, whether it be Diedrich Knickerbocker (little Dieter in Knickers), or the unknown narrator in a New York corporate boardroom, remembering in a moment of reverie his "first exploit in squirrel shooting . . . in a grove of tall walnut trees" (LSH, p. 329), filtered through Knickerbocker's written reminiscences; it was a memory trace significant enough to have been saved, to have been recounted, and to have been written down finally by Washington Irving.

The memory is of the private moments in a boy's life stolen from a Sunday's worship, when he roamed the forests unfettered by adult constraints, until the discordant "roar" of his own gunshot "broke the . . . stillness around, and was prolonged and reverberated by the angry echoes" (LSH, p. 330), a frightening portent that conflict and even death resides in the land of Sleepy Hollow. The sound of the gunshot, echoes not only in the landscape, but in Irving's text as the beatings "inflicted" upon the bodies of the sturdiest boys by Ichabod's " 'birch of justice' (LSH, p. 343), in farmer Van Tassel's threshing "flail" which was busily resounding . . . from morning to night" (LSH, p. 338), beating the harvested sheaves to yield up its treasure; the sound echoes again in the thundering hoofs of racing horses, driving through the pathways at breakneck speed, and, finally, in the name of Ichabod's old broken-down steed, Gunpowder.

Ichabod's real motives are revealed when, at the Van Tassel quilting party, he allows himself a too prideful reflection that "he might one day be lord of all this scene of almost unimaginable luxury and splendor" (LSH, p. 348). It is then that this "flogger of urchins" (LSH, p. 349) ruminates on the pleasures of possessing a rich wife:

he'd turn his back upon the old schoolhouse; snap his fingers in the face of Hans Van Ripper, and every other niggardly patron, and kick any itinerant pedagogue out of doors that should dare to call him comrade! (LSH, p. 348)

Ichabod's hatred and loathing of his profession determines his disciplinary actions against the hardiest boys, while he clearly identifies with the helpless and the "weak":

he administered justice with discrimination rather than severity, taking the burthen off the backs of the weak, and laying it on those of the strong . . . by inflicting a double portion on some little, tough, wrong-headed, broad-skirted Dutch urchin, who sulked and swelled and grew dogged and sullen beneath the birch. (LSH, p. 333)

It is no coincidence, then, that in the end, Ichabod managed to secure himself a place where justice is served – albeit in the "Ten Pound Court" – as an arbiter of small claims and petty crimes, a place where he can inflict no permanent or serious damage.

VI

Washington Irving begins his tale with an epigraph from James Thomson's "Castle of Indolence", and in the spirit of "repose" (LSH, p. 329), continues to lull the reader with suggestions that Sleepy Hollow is an Edenic, if "bewitched", landscape, a place of "drowsy, dream influence . . . that holds a spell over the minds of the good people, causing them to walk in a continual reverie" (LSH, p. 330). It is a place of refuge, moreover, where one might "dream quietly away the remnant of a troubled life" (LSH, p. 330). Death, indeed, resides in the Arcadia of Sleepy Hollow as a "contagion in the very air" that "breathed forth an atmosphere of dreams and fancies infecting all the land" (LSH, p. 350). It pervades the countryside in childish "terrors of the night, phantoms of the mind", in "dismal tales . . . told about funeral trains, and mourning cries and wailings heard and seen" (LSH, p. 350). But the spectre that frightens Ichabod most is the one conjured up by "old Brouwer, a most heretical disbeliever in ghosts", who relates

how he met the [headless] horseman returning from his foray into Sleepy Hollow, and was obliged to get up behind him; how they galloped over bush and brake, over hill and swamp, until they reached the bridge, when the horseman suddenly turned into a skeleton, threw old Brouwer into the brook, and sprang sway over the treetops with a clap of thunder (LSH, p. 351).

It is this first-hand account of the Headless Horseman, turned skeleton – into the image of Death itself – that primes Ichabod for Brom Bones's appearance as the Headless Horseman. However, Ichabod's experience fleeing the counterfeit Horseman differs from Brouwer's in one important way. In his efforts to escape, Ichabod successfully crossed the "church bridge" (LSH, p. 356), beyond which ghosts, goblins and witches were prevented from pursuing because of the bridge's nearness to water. But, rather than "vanish, according to rule, in a flash of fire and brimstone", his "pursuer" knocked him out of his seat and "passed by like a whirlwind" (LSH, pp. 356–57). Having heard about Death, when confronted by its spectre, Ichabod runs for his life an is granted a reprieve.

The bridge crossing represents passage from one state of consciousness to another and symbolized Ichabod's initiation into a new life, but first he had to confront the nightmares and death fears that bedevilled him. However precarious his ride, Ichabod passed the test. He survived the seduction of the dream land to start over in a "distant part of the country", and bettered his situation according to the American dream. After his exploits in Sleepy Hollow,

he kept school and studied law at the same time, had been admitted to the bar, turned politician, electioneered, written for the newspapers, and finally had been made justice of the Ten Pound Court. (LSH, p. 358)

If Sleepy Hollow represents a dreaming, fanciful state of mind, of childhood revisited, or Eden before the Fall, or the myth of a Golden Age, it is an unattainable illusion, or it is death itself. Ichabod Crane's good fortune was in his fall and expulsion from the land of dreams.

VII

The myth of America as an untouched landscape invaded and overrun by foreigners and spoilers is repeated in various forms, and is encapsulated in the sound of the boy's single gunshot breaking the stillness of the opening of "The Legend of Sleepy Hollow". It signifies, not only the death of childhood innocence, but the death of the innocence of America, that pure "green breast" of land that, imaginatively, was lost after the first Dutch sailor saw it. That idea of lost innocence is revealed in Nick Carraway's elegiac tribute to Gatsby after his betrayal and murder; he talks of the lost spent youth, of self-deceit and crime, always in pursuit of a phantom dream, that economic prosperity would win him back his lost beloved Daisy. Like Ichabod, Gatsby is a self-fashioned man; his name is not his own, nor his life story which he has fabricated; he lives alone, unmarried, childless, and except for Nick Carraway, friendless.

Just as Ichabod Crane's flight and quest become Jay Gatsby's and through his story, Nick Carraway's, the lesson to be learned in the search for the lost innocence of self, is that we can never escape our past, for the secret to our future is already behind us:

Gatsby believed in the green light, the orgiastic future that year by year recedes before us. It eluded us then, but that's no matter – tomorrow we will run faster, stretch out our arms farther . . . And one fine morning –
So we beat on, boats against the current, borne back ceaselessly into the past. (Fitzgerald, p. 182)

NOTES

[1] For a discussion of the fictional sketch as a literary form particularly suited to Irving, and why his use of pseudonyms was necessary to preserving his emotional withdrawal and grieving after the death of his fiancée, Matilda Hoffman, see, in particular, Jeffrey Rubin-Dorsky, "Washington Irving and the Genesis of the Fictional Sketch", *Early American Literature* 21.3 (1986/87): pp. 226–47.

[2] All references to passages from "The Legend of Sleepy Hollow" will be noted parenthetically by the abbreviation "LSH", followed by the page number of the citation; references to "The Historian" will, likewise, be referred by the abbreviation "H", followed by the page number; and "Rip Van Winkle", by the abbreviation "RVW", and the page number of the citation.

[3] For a discussion about the "mutual hostility between New York and New England", see Donald A. Ringe's "New York and New England: Irving's Criticism of American Society", *American Literature* 38.4 (1967): pp. 455–67.

[4] Ironically, Irving himself remained unmarried. He lost his beloved Matilda Hoffman to consumption, and his later marriage proposal (when he was 40 years of age) to Emily Foster was rejected. Nevertheless, he became Minister to Spain in 1842 under President John Tyler.

[5] Both Robert A. Bone ("Irving's Headless Hessian") and Lloyd M. Daigrepont ("Ichabod Crane: Inglorious Man of Letters") mention the significance of the Hebrew derivation of Ichabod's name. For an interesting note about the word derivation, see John L. McKenzie, *Dictionary of the Bible* (New York: Macmillan. 1965) where mention is made of Otto Eissfeldt's belief that Ichabod's Hebrew name "i-kabod" is but a shortened version of "ahikabod", meaning "the brother of glory" (p. 382).

[6] See *Funk & Wagnalls Standard Dictionary of Folklore, Mythology, and Legend*, ed. Maria Leach (San Francisco: Harper & Row, 1972) for the derivation of the legend of the cranes of Ibycus (p. 259).

[7] See Carroll B. Johnson, *Madness and Lust: A Psychoanalytic Approach to Don Quixote* (Berkeley: U. of California P., 1983) for a discussion of the importance of Don Quixote's helmet and the fact that "'his head and not his arm, is the source of his power'" (p. 66).

BIBLIOGRAPHY

André, John. *Major André's Journal: Operations of the British Army Under Lieutenant General Sir William Howe and Sir Henry Clinton, June 1777 to November 1778; to which is added The Ethics of Major André's Mission* by C. De W. Willcox. [Tarrytown]: Arno, 1968.

Benson, Egbert. *Vindication of the Captors of Major André*. Introd. and Preface George Athan Billias. Boston: Gregg Press, 1972.
Bone, Robert A. "Irving's Headless Hessian: Prosperity and the Inner Life". *American Quarterly* **15.2** (1963): 167–75.
Bowden, Mary Weatherspoon. *Washington Irving*. Boston: Twayne, 1981.
Christensen, Peter. "Washington Irving and the Denial of the Fantastic". *The Old and New World Romanticism of Washington Irving*. Ed. Stanley Brodwin. Introd. William L. Hedges. New York: Greenwood, 1986. pp. 51–60.
Clendenning, John. "Irving and the Gothic Tradition". *Bucknell Review* **12.2** (1964): 90–98.
Coad, Oral Summer. "The Gothic Element in American Literature Before 1835". *JEGP* **24** (1925): 72–93.
Daigrepont, Lloyd M. "Ichabod Crane: Inglorious Man of Letters". *Early American Literature* **19.1** (1984): 68–81.
Fitzgerald, F. Scott. *The Great Gatsby*. New York: Scribner's, 1953.
Greene, Donald. "From Accidie to Neurosis: The "Castle of Indolence' Revisited". *English Literature in the Age of Disguise*. Ed. Maximillian E. Novak. Berkeley: U. of California P., 1977, pp. 131–56.
Guttmann, Allen. "Images of Value and the Sense of the Past". *The New England Quarterly* **35.1** (1962): 3–26.
Guttmann, Allen. "Washington Irving and the Conservative Imagination". *American Literature* **36.2** (1964): 165–73.
Hedges, William L. *Washington Irving: An American Study, 1802–1832*. Baltimore: John Hopkins, 1965.
Irving, Washington. "The Adventure of the German Student". *Tales of a Traveller by Geoffrey Crayon, Gent.* New York: G. K. Hall, 1983. Rpt. The Library of America, 1991. pp. 418–24.
Irving, Washington. "The Historian". *Bracebridge Hall; or The Humourists: a Medley by Geoffrey Crayon, Gent.* New York: G. K. Hall, 1977. Rpt. The Library of America, 1990, pp. 297–99.
Irving, Washington. "The Legend of Sleep Hollow". *The Sketch Book of Geoffrey Crayon, Gent.* Afterword Perry Miller. New York: Signet, 1981, pp. 329–60.
Irving, Washington. "Rip Van Winkle". *The Sketch Book of Geoffrey Crayon, Gent.* Afterword Perry Miller. New York: Signet, 1981, pp. 37–55.
Johnson, Carroll B. *Madness and Lust: A Psychoanalytic Approach to Don Quixote*. Berkeley: U. of California P., 1983.
Jones, Ernest. *On the Nightmare*. New York: Liveright, 1971.
Male, Roy R. "The Story of the Mysterious Stranger in American Fiction". *Criticism* **3.4** (1961): 281–94.
Martin, Terrence. "Rip, Ichabod, and the American Imagination". *American Literature* **31.2** (1959): 137–49.
Moore, Cecil A. "The English Malady". *Background of English Literature 1700–1760*. Minneapolis: U. of Minnesota P., 1953, pp. 179–235.
Panofsky, Erwin. " 'Et in Arcadia Ego': Poussin and the Elegiac Tradition". *Meaning in the Visual Arts*. Garden City: Doubleday, 1955, pp. 295–320.
Pochmann, Henry A. "Irving's German Sources in *The Sketch Book*". *Studies in Philology* **27** (1930): 477–507.

Ringe, Donald A. "New York and New England: Irving's Criticism of American Society". *American Literature* **38.4** (1967): 455–67.

Rodes, Sara Purycar. "Washington Irving's Use of Traditional Folklore". *New York Folklore Quarterly* **13.1** (1957): 3–15.

Roth, Martin. *Comedy and America: The Lost World of Washington Irving.* Port Washington: Kennikat, 1976.

Roth, Martin. "Tom Paine and American Loneliness". *Early American Literature* **22.2** (1987): 175–82.

Rubin-Dorsky, Jeffrey. *Adrift in the Old World: The Psychological Pilgrimage of Washington Irving.* Chicago: U. of Chicago P., 1988.

Rubin-Dorsky, Jeffrey. "Washington Irving and the Genesis of the Fictional Sketch". *Early American Literature* **21.3** (1986/87): 226–47.

Samuels, Shirley. "Infidelity and Contagion: The Rhetoric of Revolution". *Early American Literature* **22.2** (1987): 183–91.

Seward, Anna. "Monody of Major André". *The Poetical Works of Anna Seward; with Extracts from her Literary Correspondence.* 3 vols. Ed. Walter Scott. Edinburgh: Ballantyne, 1810. New York: AMS Press, 1974. II: pp. 68–104.

Thomson, James. "The Castle of Indolence". *Liberty, The Castle of Indolence and Other Poems.* Ed. with an Introd. James Sambrook. Oxford: Clarendon, 1986, pp. 161–223.

Von Frank, Albert J. "The Man That Corrupted Sleepy Hollow". *Studies in American Fiction* **15.2** (1987): 129–43.

PART FOUR

ELEMENTAL POETICS OF PLACE IN THE
PERSPECTIVE OF *ARCHĒ, TELOS, PATHOS*

LAWRENCE KIMMEL

JOURNEYS HOME: THE PATHOS OF PLACE

I

The *pathos* of *place* is elemental in grounding the risk of life, the source of confidence requisite to the human quest whether it is conceived as *arche* or *telos*, whether it is where one begins, or the end toward which one's journey is directed. The project of living is such that one's journey is always toward a homeland, however it be conceived: dreams of homecoming the recovery of innocence, the joyful receiving of the retrieved prodigal, the triumphal march of the heroic legions, the quiet return of the native – all hopeful to appear once again in the light of recognition, of acceptance, of victory, to the acknowledged communion of belonging. The perceived cycle of life, a full and human life, is such that one always returns home, whatever its name. If one cannot go home again, one always looks homeward. With luck, effort, intelligence and imagination – features without which Greek philosophy found no life human – one finds a way home, to the arche and *telos* of place, and discovers those boundaries within which the passion of human achievement is realized.

I do not offer these remarks in place of, or as backed by, statistical summary or empirical claim. There are those, of course, who never look back (or for that matter ahead), those who have neither memory and longing, nor dreams, and more tragically, those for whom the very idea of place is a recurring or permanent nightmare or anathema. There is, further, a danger in the philosophical employment of a ubiquitous and vague concept like "home" that one may be drawn into the sentimental sludge of popular misuse, where "home" is a greeting card catalogue of homilies for feelings that never were – improbably Sunday school slogans for sainthood. One can be sensitive to this danger without conceding that a grounding place is, for that reason, beyond philosophical reach, or beneath philosophical interest and inquiry. The categories of "home" and "homeland", in the variations of their meaningful use, are such fundamental references to place, and so crucial to cultural community and individual identity, that we ought not to abandon the topic, despite its popular dispersion and hyperbolic abuse.

In this paper, I will give a short account of the tension between *time* and *place* as defining structures of human life. The fundamental intuition, familiar in Greek philosophy, is that human life is achievement of *place*, not merely birthing in *time*.

There are problems with any attempt to put conditions on human life beyond "born of woman", with seeking to define human life in terms of quality and character, in terms of moral excellence rather than biological commonality. For example, if an individual fails to achieve some level of life deemed to be human, is it permissible to regard her as not due the rights, privileges, considerations of that station? Is such a creature to be treated then as . . . what – an animal, an object, subject only to the efficiency of use? May we inflict experimentation procedures on her body, mind control trials on her spirit? The answer is, of course not. But this, in fact, is still a matter of negotiating guaranteed rights; it can hardly depend on natural disposition, as we well know from 20th century episodes in uncivilized history.

I will hold such concerns as *prima facie* legitimate, but set them in the background for the present paper. The worry is, of course, that any definition of the human not bound by the imperative of natural boundaries is an offense not easily corrected by laws of ascribed rights, is pre-judicial against the sympathy of species kinship and not recoverable through reasoned judgment. But that is part of the ordeal of human civility itself. Even so, in the present essay I will proceed to set out conditions of *place* resonant with *time*, requisite to an understanding of the human. It may be that ours is a time well served by a moral redescription and reaffirmation of human life as an achievement requiring effort. Human life, the Greeks well understood (and in this understanding began the history of moral philosophy), requires a human world. HuMan is not merely a creature and plaything of *time*, but an agent and creator of *place*.

II

Martin Heidegger and Hannah Arendt come to mind immediately as contemporary philosophers who consider the category of *place* elemental in the constitution of both the human condition and the human project. This may at first seem odd in the case of Heidegger, for his own major interest in Being centers in the category and phenomenon of time. But the point to be understood is just here. The essential way in which we are human is being-*in-the-world*; human-being defines *place* in the world in a way uniquely different from other kinds of beings. The human being is *in* the world in the manifold senses of being in Europe, – *en route*, in prison, in mind, in memory, in ill repute, in love, in doubt, in error, in want of, indicted under, involved with, incapacitated by. . . . These are all ways of being in the world, place markings different in kind, but framed within language, which itself houses human sensibility and keeps open, through metaphor and imagination, a place for possibility. So conceived, philosophical inquiry brings into focus once again the concept and context of Being, an account founded in the self-presencing of human-being as reflective inquiry into its place in the complex order of things.

Heidegger's now familiar key words for this human way of being are "dwelling" and "concern". HuMan discovers and creates a defining place through the labor of her body and the work of her hands – labor which sustains life, work which builds worlds. The kinds of works which frame the human place are manifold: houses, gardens, gaols, courts, temples, but also books, plays, war, law, dreams, recollection, and hope; projects of making and doing, of practice and theory. Arendt, following the work of her teacher, Heidegger, performs an analytic of "place" in *The Human Condition*, locating her analysis in the conceptual *polis* of Periclean Athens. Her work, directed at the *arche* of western intellectual history, provides a fundamental politics of place compatible with and in the spirit of Heidegger's ontology of place. Heidegger's *Being and Time* gathers the categories of *time* and *place* into correlative features of human existence. If *life* (*bios*) in its most primitive character is *being in time* (movement), certainly the history of culture, following the Greeks, has defined *human* life (as *bios politikos*) in the additional terms of *being in place*.

III

In the United States there currently exists a social category at crisis point: "the homeless", a designation which seemingly describes alien creatures dispossessed of place; a deprivation which not only functionally erodes their participation in public life as citizens, but excludes them from the simple amenities of human community. In a land of plenty this is typically presented as a social misfortune or political outrage, but for our purposes this estrangement marks a loss of something more essential, an estrangement from fundamental elements of human identity as well as community. Whatever the reasons, which are manifold and complex – economic and personal, biological and social, elective and enforced – it is philosophically significant that we use "without home" as an entitlement of alienation and exclusion, a category below or beyond that of mere poverty, signifying persons cut off from human community, who lack the basic conditions under which "human" is defined and defended.

The dispossession of *place* is an ontological as well as a social problem. This idea is as old as Greek philosophy, where Aristotle defined "Man" as a political animal, a creature in need for his very being of the *polis* or human community. The shared language and form of life of the human is bounded by the walls of this place, which provides for disclosure of unique individual identity in a space of appearance, the public realm of one's community. The broader concept of one's homeland (Greek: "*kome*", village; "*homoios*", same; Latin: "*Homo*", Man) appears in a definitive way in the familiar long journey home of Odysseus. Similarly, in the Hebraic tribal conception of home, the homeless exile, Ishmael, is the "unwanted of God", destined to wander apart from the spiritual community of God and Man.

It is difficult to imagine a category more fundamental than "home" to house the biologically nurtured, socially emergent sense of the human. The collateral analogues of home are inclusive of the phenomenology of place: of body, womb; of world, mother earth; of action and event, encompassing horizons and embracing sky; of hope and transcendence, the domain of the possible, of night and stars and gods, shoring up in space the sustaining sea which gives forth its primal issue – all carry the primal force and spiritual weight of "home". The myriad fictive and real, metaphorical and factual locations, in time and place, of home, are found in cloister and hearth, in the heart or the mind. Home may be lost in childhood, in settlements east of Eden, constituted in kinship, restored in friendship, decided in marriage, discovered in children, temporarily secured in family, invested in community, realized in the sovereignty of a people. "Home" is a primary category of an essential place in time, isolated or integrated, whether remembered in tears amid alien fields of corn, in the shattered ruins of a city laid waste by war, in memory ravaged by age, in fantasy invited by desire, in faith restored by love.

As we have pictured it here, the human is a convergence of *time* and *place*. The former is defined by and constitutes the root of the natural; the latter signals the emergence of culture, the convening of civilization. The long ordeal of civility is made possible only on condition of an escape from cycles of life under the weight of natural necessity, an escape from the immanent imperative of survival. The first-order activity of animal life in response to the conditions under which life is given is the *labor* of survival. The primal life cycle, still under the yoke of necessity was, according to the forming thought of Greek philosophy, not yet human. Where *Homo* is subject to the fundamental condition of contingency, the cycle of life in nature is that one must labor/to get food/to eat/to gain strength/to labor/to get food/to eat . . . *ad infinitum*. Under the most primitive conditions of the natural life cycle, the total energy and activity of being must be committed to sheer survival, to sustaining life in time, life not yet at rest, secure, or empowered with freedom in place.

Only when the natural cycle of necessity has been broken to create leisure, at least for a few, when labor is sufficiently coordinated to meet and overcome the ubiquitous burden of survival through development of surplus, and so allows for some privileged members to escape the binding cycle of "labor to live/live to labor", is there a possibility of moving from process to product, of creating through work the identity and permanence of place. *Work* is thus a second category of fundamental activity in response to the human condition, a movement from the natural metabolism of the *bios* of labor, "the labor of our bodies", to the productive activity of the *poiesis* and *techne* of work, "the work of our hands". The activity and result of work, issuing in works, creates world, the place in which human action becomes possible in its disclosure.

Arendt, following Aristotle, frames the form of fully human life as requiring the place of human community, the *polis*. Not in the boundless time of labor, but in the place of work, can there be a production of world, and with it security, permanence and freedom – the boundaries of meaning within which civilization develops. Arendt's third category of definitive activity in response to the human conditions of natality, plurality, contingency and scarcity is *action*. Only when individuals are free from the necessity of labor and the utility of work is virtue or excellence possible. The *telos* of action (*praxis*) is self-disclosure through great words and deeds among a community of equals, who in their freedom enshrine such action in the remembrance of history. The identity of individual and community are transformed in a moment or a life. Such deeds and words remembered become history, achieve immortality. Thus public place, through the endurance of works and the remembrance of acts, shapes the identity of a people, and forms the substance of civilized existence that we call human life: Ilium and Athens.

IV

There remained, in the complete Greek description of human life, a further transcendent concept of place which was unchanging, and a way of human life and activity of mind which gave access to this place of the timeless, of eternity. This way of life – not open to everyone – the life of the mind, was philosophy: *noesis* for Plato, *theoria* for Aristotle. Aristotle's contemplative life, critically mirroring Plato's notion of transcendence without the notion of the *Eides* or Forms, develops the notion of "home" in transcendence to eternity. If *praxis* (action) can achieve immortality through words and deeds of lasting memory, the discourse of philosophy is one of eternity. Plato and Aristotle share the idea of transcendence, but with a very different sense of the continuing importance of place. Plato is clearly committed to the idea of a transcendent place, an ideal realm of enlightenment, a place in the sun where the *Eides* appear intelligibly visible to the mind which has made the dialectical journey. Aristotle seems to hold to the idea of the public realm as definitive of place. The *vita contemplativa*, the life of the mind, while no longer in an essential or necessary way dependent on shared place, requires no separate place or realm of the Forms. For Aristotle, presumably, the mind is its own place, although not in the sense of Milton's Satan. The latter would introduce an entirely different realm of meta-phorical place which we have no time to pursue in this paper. In the classical Greek life of the mind, one discourses with the gods themselves, or at least joins the eternal conversation pitched in the language of the gods. The transcendental difference is that the idealist Plato speaks of the timeless in the idiom and metaphors of place, and Aristotle, paradoxically perhaps, of the timeless in the idiom of time. Differently stated, for the realism of Aristotle there is but one world, one grounding place, and no reflection removes one from it.

V

Even before the formal grounding of philosophy in the *logos* of place, the *mythos* of Greek culture had formed the ground of place in the primal emergence of meaningful life. Prior to its philosophical appropriation, one can read the text of Greek mythology (e.g., Hesiod) in such a dually interpretive way that its "task" portrays the struggle of both the cultural and cosmogonic overcoming of *chaos*. The lesson is not merely the ontic ordering of the cosmos, but a modelling constitution for human community. In the primal stuff, gathering forces move ponderously toward the intelligibility of place. In the mythic development of language (of place, things, permanence, of the works of mind and hand), the domain of the human strives to overcome the devouring primal conditions of change (time). So seen, human civilization is the overcoming of *time* with *place*, the securing of a realm free of the destructive first conditions of life.

In the mythic story of time beginning, there emerges from the primal conditions of *Chaos* and *Moira* (Destiny), the grounding possibility of the privileged First Ones of *Place* (and so of meaningful life); the feminine *Gaia* (Mother Earth), from whom, in yearning (*Eros*, desire and need of completion, space between), is born the masculine embracing boundary of *Uranos* (Father Sky). We can, herein, tell only the first few words of this long story: His-story and Her-story – the tense yearning of conflict and completion, of human time and place, of world and life – the fabric of immortality which shrouds the mortal animal HuMan. As the *mythos* develops, the ensuing union of *Gaia* and *Uranos* produces *Kronos* (Time) who – with the fertile urging of Earth, caught in the passion of her nature to birth life – wields the Scythe, weapon of his calling, and prevails against the rule of the father. Time thus ascends to hold male dominion, but in betrayal of Earth, swallows the offspring of the resourceful Mother. A final battle definitively frames the constituting values of Greek and Western civilization. The new generation, Zeus and the Olympians, Earthborn of Time, through an exercise of political rationality faithful to the Earth, join forces to subdue and diminish devouring Time, thus establishing for themselves an Olympian community above time and change, one removed from the cyclical destruction of the natural and temporal. It is from this life form of the gods that the race of men descends.

These are mere beginning words in the continuing conversation of literature and culture, stories through which we try to come to an understanding of ourselves, in which Being articulates its own meaning, becomes conscious through *poiesis*, the genius of poetry and language.

This story – both *mythos* and *logos* – can be read in many ways, of course. I am suggesting that it presents and represents a primal expression of the *pathos* of place. It is through the overcoming of *time* – primal enemy of the God in Man – and the creation of *place*, that the shape and space of human community, immortality, and eternity are opened into civilized life. Thus wrought, the City of Men and the City of Gods, the highest form of human life and community in action (*praxis*) and also the highest form of human life and transcendence in thought (*theoria*), find expression in philosophy, mythology, history, and literature.

VI

Once upon a place in time: the journey home.

The modern temper is arguably one of radical dislocation – not time "out of joint", but time out of place. So being it is not difficult to accept the poetic vision of the human situation as tragic. The burden of intelligent, reflective life is the consciousness of time, grains of sand flowing away, fragmented dreams blowing in the wind. HuMan is thus a creature caught between the boundaries of natality/fatality; the brief journey of her life is womb to grave, the prospect only of earth to earth. We rise up and fall, strive to mark our brief passing in the flickering space of life. Though heavens open up to imagination and aspiration, mandarins only brush the fading portrait of genius upon a failing wind.

From the epic journey of Odysseus to the ironic journey of Bloom, the voices of the blind poets merge, the heroic and pathetic meet and endure in a human space wrought by memory and language. Two images of place, of hope and dread, press upon contemporary consciousness. The first, an image of hope, the open beckoning of place: E.T., left behind, pointing a long crooking finger toward a cold if promising infinity of space, speaking plaintively to strangling earth children who, nevertheless, understand very well the word "Home!" The second, an image of dread, the closed beckoning of place: two hapless creatures waiting for Godot, who sum up the dislocation of their lives in a throw away line "They give birth astride a grave".

Hope and dread mark the space of human time between the two

definite and defining structures of place. The deep ambivalence of the journey home – aspiring to freedom, fraught with anxiety, remembering the familiar securing foundations of structure, forgetting the complaining constraints of place – is always with us. The civilizing ordeal continues. To what end? Only to the beginning. If human life has meaning, it is in the reconciliation of time and place, the convergence of *arche* and *telos*. If wisdom is that which we properly seek, the *ergon* or characteristic activity of HuMan, then it consists in closing the circle of the journey home. On the matter of wandering and recognition, the many otherwise divergent texts which inform our lives agree: philosophy and mythology, politics and art, history and psychology, religion and science.

> We shall not cease from exploration
> And the end of all our exploring
> Will be to arrive where we started
> And know the place for the first time.
> – T. S. Eliot, *Four Quartets*

Trinity University, Texas

JORGE GARCÍA-GÓMEZ

POETRY AS A WORLDLY VOCATION: HOME AND HOMELESSNESS IN RILKE'S *DAS STUNDEN-BUCH*

> The authentic *Dichter* is of the rarest . . . For the *Dichter* is "one who knows ethically, who object-knows . . ."[1]

Hölderlin put the question boldly: "Full of acquirements . . . [yet] poetically, man dwells on this earth."[2] And I say "question" advisedly, for it is far from clear what it means to "dwell on this earth", let alone to do so "poetically".[3] It is easy to fall back – let us not consider the motivations – and try to lead our lives by interpreting this dwelling, to express it in Solovyev's words, as a call or "invitation to become finally *naturalized* in earthly exile, to enter without delay into full and hereditary possession of our minute portion, with all its thistles and briars".[4] It is as if we somehow had an inkling of some other dimension, a sort of "lost paradise", or as though we kept from love past a taste of an " 'other-world' mystical basis"[5] and the "tidings of the possibility of [its] recovery",[6] and yet succeeded in forgetting all that, by transforming ourselves into citizens of this world and devoting our lives to the management of its affairs.[7] This is certainly *resignation*, but to give it its due, on the problematic assumption that it is our fundamental modality of dwelling on earth, it would be necessary for us not only to clarify the notions of "vale of tears" and "paradise" so nicely intertangled therein, but also never to lose sight of the struggle and tension between them – which is experienced already in their manner of immediate givenness, namely, in our becoming *"naturalized . . .* in our minute portion" – for this means to be confronted, time and again, with something that always exceeds itself and keeps us alive in discontent (and thus open to the imminence of possible upsurge).

To begin with, then, it is a question of who man is. As a first approximation, I would say – negatively – that he is *no one*, not only meaning thereby that he is as yet to be fashioned (perhaps by his own hand, assuredly with the help of other hands), but as well in the sense that he is constitutively never alone. He is with things and, as he deals with them, and for their sake, he is engaged in conflict and collaboration with others. Or as Heidegger chose to formulate man's essential condition:

> Man is *he* who he *is*, precisely in the affirmation of his own existence . . . But what must man affirm [or bear witness to]? That he belongs to the earth. This relation of belonging to consists in the fact that man is heir and learner in all things. But all these things are in conflict. [That which keeps things apart in opposition and thus at the same time binds them together . . . is called by Hölderlin "intimacy" [*Innigkeit*].] The affirmation of belonging to this intimacy occurs through the creation of a world and its ascent, and likewise through the destruction of a world and its decline. The affirmation of human existence and hence its essential consummation occurs through freedom of decision. This freedom lays hold of the necessary and places itself in the bonds of a supreme obligation. This bearing witness of belonging to all that is existent . . . becomes actual as history.[8]

In short: to be a man means, first and foremost, to belong to the earth. As a man, I do not abandon the earth for the sake of the otherworldly, even if I must, as I do at times, constitute other worlds – for instance, the worlds of poetry, mathematics, or religion. But even then, and not just when I live in terms of everyday familiarity with the things of this world, I abide on earth by going *into* the things of this world. For what could it mean, for example, to say with Rilke, "And if I cried, who'd listen to me in those angelic/ orders?",[9] or to advance with Pythagoras the theorem bearing his name, or to burst into song in the words of the psalmist, "My soul thirsts for God,/ the God of life;/ when shall I go to see/ the face of God?",[10] if such utterances did not *at least* signify my attempt to make sense of the obscurities and vexations of living where I find myself, now and always? Hence, one can appreciate both the tension and the liberty within which we lead our lives by belonging to [the *Innigkeit* of things, especially when such belongingness is at once a surrender to and a soaring above things – or more exactly, a surrender to things that consists in soaring above them for their sake.] Or using Heidegger's words: the creation or destruction of a *world* of things is the outcome of the exercise of our intrinsic freedom, which consists in "[laying] hold of the necessary" and "[placing] itself in the bonds of a supreme obligation", namely, in "bearing witness of belonging to all that is existent".[11]

Let me turn to poetry specifically and attempt to conceive of it as a manner of dwelling, of abiding with things. This is not so far-fetched as it may sound at first, for, as Heidegger has pointed our elsewhere, "we think of what is usually called the existence of man in terms of dwelling".[12] If one takes hold of this thesis in light of Hölderlin's verse, "poetically, man dwells on this earth", it would appear to mean, according to Heidegger, that

> ... poetry first causes dwelling to be dwelling. Poetry is what really lets us dwell. But through what do we attain a dwelling place? Through building. Poetic creation, which lets us dwell, is a kind of building.[13]

Surely, this cannot be the case, if it is intended to signify that poetry is the path to dwelling with things, for in everydayness we are already, indeed originarily, making our way into things and abiding with them. But then I may have been too hasty in judging matters, since my rejection of Heidegger's position could legitimately follow only if one took "poetry" in a restricted sense, that is, in the context of the formal construction of poems. Poetry shows us, to be sure, a special manner of gaining access to "intimacy", since by constructing positive or negative worlds the expanse of things is somehow re-discovered *and* re-fashioned, but in the present nexus one is not speaking of some men and their special accomplishments, but rather of the nature of man and his essential powers insofar as they pre-suppose our belonging to earth. If this is so, Heidegger must then have been pointing to something which is more fundamental and consequential to us, namely, to a dimension that is constitutive of every man, to a part of us by means of which – even in everydayness – we are all installed *poetically* with things. In other words, "poetry" should signify – basically, as opposed to formally – an essential power informing our very make-up, a layer of our being to which poets would have to appeal if we are to be engaged with them and from which they themselves would have to arise. This is, it seems to me, what Heidegger had in mind when he proceeded to comment that we are confronted with

> ... a double demand: for one thing, we are to think of what is called man's existence by way of the nature of dwelling; for another, we are to think of the nature of poetry as a letting-dwell, as a – perhaps even *the* – distinctive kind of building.[14]

Hence, poetry is, in this sense, an *a priori* and *sui generis* openness to things which is fundamentally constitutive of ourselves, and by virtue of which we are rendered capable of dwelling with things in principle. Accordingly, it is not as if one could identify man's power of letting-dwell side by side with the things to be dwelled-with, in the sense that, on such grounds, the event of man's dwelling with things would ensue or originate. The basic phenomenon in question is rather in the nature of a totality of reciprocity, for man does not step out of his would-be interiority – whatever its sort, if any – as if he were fore-armed with a power to which things – perhaps beneficently – would submit. On the contrary, man's way of being is itself the establishment of things which his dwelling with them consists in, and in which his capacity of letting-dwell is matched by a world in which the expanse of things finds a haven and is worked out.

What is then the *eidos* of poetry, if one regards it as the letting-dwell with things in which, in a sense, man fundamentally consists? To be able to answer this question, Heidegger directed our attention to a place just a few lines above, that in which we heard Hölderlin say, "poetically, man dwells on this earth". There the German poet, referring man to the "heavenly ones", asserted:

May, when life is all hardship, may a man look up and say: I too would like to resemble these? Yes. As long as kindliness, which is pure, remains in his heart not unhappily a man may compare himself with the divinity.[15]

The key conception at work here is not so much kindliness, as the special manner thereof which consists in abiding.[16] Kindliness, however, can easily be misunderstood, perhaps as something purely empirical or merely incidental; yet it is meant presently as nothing of the sort, for it is no mere psychological or moral determination or disposition, or even a faculty of the mind, but rather something having to do with man's essential attitude toward himself as someone necessarily placed in the midst of all there is, an attitude which is both totalizing and constitutive. As Heidegger explained it, a comparison between man and the "heavenly ones" is possible, according to Hölderlin, if kindliness is found present in man as a constancy of the *heart* or "dwelling being of man".[17] Kindliness is therefore "the claim and appeal of the measure to the heart in such a way that the heart turns to give heed to the measure".[18] In short: man is fundamentally constituted as *heart*, or in his dwelling being, insofar as he is called upon and measured by that to which he would freely respond, adequately or not, as his own measure.

THE AFFAIRS OF THE HEART

In order to elaborate this notion, which has just been presented only in principle, let me avail myself of another text where Heidegger has also dealt with it. I have in mind a passage from his important piece, "Vom Wesen des Grundes".[19] It is true that the matter of poetry and poetic creation does not come to focus in it, and yet the lines I am about to refer to are crucial, for therein the concept of heart is examined by placing it in the same fundamental context as in his essay on Hölderlin's dictum, that is to say, in view of its relatedness to the world as the expanse of thinghood. It is interesting in itself that, among the various sources in light of which Heidegger chose to examine the latter, the relevant one is taken from St. Augustine's commentary on *The Gospel according to St. John*, in the part specifically devoted to the verse reading, "the world was made by him; yet the world did not recognize him".[20] As is clear from the words just quoted, and as Heidegger hastened to add, the term "world" is used twice, each time with a different sense. In the first mention thereof, St. Augustine indicated that *mundus* was employed with the cosmological connotation of creaturely being (*ens creatum*), and in the second one to designate a manner of dwelling, that of the *habitatores mundi*, namely, those whose manner of "inhabiting the world" is that of being *dilectores mundi* or "lovers of the world", for it is precisely by "loving the world" (*amare mundum*) that they abide therewith (*qui inhabitant amando mundum*).[21] This is indeed remarkable: the world is not so much a place, or even a system of places spatial and temporal in kind,[22] as it is my own manner of being, in the sense of my intrinsic way of dwelling with things. That which I love is then what I am, namely, my world, whether this is the flesh (the world *qua* perishable) or the heavenly (the world *qua* imperishable), even as I remain *hic et nunc*. Accordingly, one is to say that the *heart* is the totality of my being, insofar as it essentially embraces my being in the world in the sense of *loving* it.[23] Following St. Augustine, then, I will say that I am my heart, and that my heart is what I love, and that what I love is my world, "for . . . in [my] heart [I] dwell in the world".[24]

It seems, however, that a certain condition is to be met by my heart, if it is true that it consists in being the self-commission of the totality of my being to the world, or my manner of dwelling therein lovingly. To be exact, it is not a condition properly so called, which would allow for its being satisfied before the fact or even concomitantly; rather it is a *co*-requisite of the openness and self-delivery that the human heart as such is. According to Heidegger, this constitutive co-principle is no other than language itself, for language is likewise not to be approached in this connection restrictedly or formally, i.e., as a tool or system of tools deployable for the purpose of conveying information.[25] On the contrary, it is a nexus to be regarded fundamentally, for, whatever its eventual empirical manifestations and patterns of organization may be, it is something ultimately characterizable by a twofold *telos*. On the one hand, it "has the task of making manifest in its work the existent",[26] and thus of being the medium for rendering available the world or expanse of thinghood to which my heart delivers itself. On the other hand, if what is at play is an essential or non-passing openness and self-commission, then language must be the context for abiding or dwelling with the world and its sense; hence language is also assigned the task of "preserving . . . [the existent] as such".[27] As Heidegger put it, "it is only language", in the sense of the medium for permanent availability, "that affords the very possibility of *standing* [*stehen*] in the openness of the existent",[28] for, as Heidegger hastened to clarify, "[only] where there is language . . . is there world".[29]

It is on the basis of this conception of language as the essential medium for permanent availability that one may effect the transition from the sense that poetry has when it is taken fundamentally, to that which it is assigned in the restricted or formal nexus constituted by the works of poets properly so called. In his poem "Andenken" (Remembrance), Hölderlin had said: "*Was bleibet aber, stiften die Dichter*",[30] which can be translated in two ways, depending on the meaning bestowed on *stiften*, to wit: either "establish" or "provide". And yet there is no contradiction or even an ambiguity involved here, for that which the poets establish is precisely a gift or provision, unreachable in their absence, namely, the naming, by means of their essential word, of the existent as what it is.[31] Hence, Hölderlin's verse could be rendered as: "But what is lasting the poets providentially establish".[32] No wonder Heidegger interpreted it as follows: "Poetry is the act of establishing by the word and in the word. What is established in this manner? The permanent [or lasting]".[33] This, Heidegger contended, "throws light on our question about the essence of poetry",[34] so that, if such were not the formula thereof, it would at least express an essential determination and function of poetry, namely, that of providentially establishing the lasting or "permanent" about things in the medium of words. But this task would prove impossible if poetry and language could not be said – when regarded fundamentally – to be, respectively, man's *a priori* openness to things (an openness which is altogether *sui generis*) and the medium for rendering available and preserving the existent in the world *qua* expanse of thinghood.

We are thus confronted with a peculiar dialectic which may be given expression in two complementary and reciprocally qualifying ways. On the one hand, one is reminded of the fact that poetry, taken fundamentally, is the openness which allows us to dwell with things by soaring above them.[35] In other words, poetry is active, in the sense that, for the sake of things, it does not abandon them, for it allows them to be by dis-playing what they are or could be. Hence, the providential establishment of things which poetry — now in the restricted sense — may come to effect is such that, as Heidegger chose to put it: "that which remains [or lasts] is never taken from the transitory".[36] On the other hand, man is not merely moving in the realm of necessity. What is at stake is the dis-covery of the ground of the apparent, that is to say, of Being as the foundation of things, and not the network of relationships — practical or cognitive — existing between them. But, as Heidegger poignantly remarked, "Being is never an existent".[37] Hence, what is involved is man's radical act of endowing the apparent or existent with a foundation by his free or responsible answer to the call or invitation to dis-close Being. And this "free act of giving is [a providential] establishment".[38] In this act, however, man gains access not only to things as grounded, but as well to himself as essentially gathered thereby, for in poetry "man is re-united on the foundation of his existence".[39]

What then is moving in man that makes him subject to this dialectic between the apparent and its ground ? Why is he called to subvert the hold that necessity and contingency have on him by means of his free and providential establishment of the ground of things? His reason for this seems to be far from disinterested. On the contrary, his very being, that is to say, not only his performance as a man but also the sense by which he leads his life, is at stake, for, as we know, the "way in which you are and I am, the manner in which we humans *are*" is to be "on earth", and this is dwelling;[40] but dwelling, as Heidegger has repeatedly insisted, "is the manner in which *mortals* are on earth".[41] In other words, if I am to be faithful at once to myself and to the world as the expanse of thinghood, I must learn, since my being is such that I am called to dwell on earth, to do it in such a fashion that I remain alive to the transcendence of things as a poverty of foundation.[42] But "mortality" is precisely the name for the awareness and virtue by which we continue to be instigated to dwell on earth, however paradoxical this may sound on a first hearing. Hence, man's calling to dwell with things on earth, if heeded genuinely, is seen to signify neither the concealment of our finitude (whether by obliviousness or consolation) nor the denial of the groundlessness of things as apparent (whether it be in terms of lawfulness or predictability), but rather the mutuality of mortality and Being by which what Solovyev characterized as our "[*naturalization*] in earthly exile" would be foreclosed. But even when genuineness is betrayed, the resulting obfuscation is still rendered possible by reason of the same essential calling, for "what we signify when we say 'on the earth' exists only insofar as man dwells on the earth and in his dwelling lets earth be as earth".[43]

THE HEART AS A MEDIUM

How is it then that poetry, in the restricted and formal sense of the word, lets the earth as our dwelling place "be as earth"? The beginning of an answer can be found, I believe, in a comment made by Heidegger on the two alternative endings to Hölderlin's poem, "Stimme des Volks".[44] This is what the German philosopher had to say in that connection:

> The poet himself stands between the former – the gods, and the latter – the people. He is one who has been cast out – out into that *Between* [*Zwischen*], between gods and men. But only and for the first time in this Between is it decided . . . who man is and where he is settling [*ansiedelt*] his existence. "Poetically . . . dwells man on this earth".[45]

Everything seems to depend on the establishment of this "Between". What is it then? It is not so much a place[46] as something founded upon a constitutive and essential attitude of man. As Heidegger remarked, the poets, though they belong to the sphere of the mortals and thereby to the earth, are nonetheless "cast out . . . into that *Between* . . . gods and men". They have not done this by "choice" (*liberum arbitrium*), and yet they have chosen to be cast out – not by anything (earth or heaven) or anyone (gods or mortals) – but by themselves, from themselves, in the exercise of their originary freedom, for poetic thought and creation are their destiny. Therefore, they dwell on earth in the special modality which consists in living in-between.

To understand this point, one must put together two distinct aspects of the one reciprocal totality. One has, first of all, the poet's self-projection, that is to say, the non-necessitated and responsible act by which he, *as a man*, flings himself[47] between the realm of the heavenly ones and that of the mortals, precisely to be able, in a manner *sui generis*,[48] to build the earth as the dwelling place of humankind. But one finds too the "between" which is thus being-projected, and without which the self-projection would come to naught. Hence it is of the essence to determine the nature of the intermediary sphere.

Accordingly, let me raise the pertinent question once more: what is the nature of that which lies "between" the "gods" themselves and our arduous yet possibly joyful dwelling on earth?[49] Hölderlin took it to be, as Heidegger explained, that which "man spans . . . by measuring himself against the heavenly".[50] Without this, man would be – not only in himself but to himself – boundless and thus unintelligible. To say this, however, does not mean that one automatically understands how man accomplishes his self-measurement against the heavenly standard; and yet one must strive to do this, since, as interpreted by Heidegger, Hölderlin's radical contention is that "man is man at all [only] in this spanning".[51] It is thus no privilege or responsibility assignable only to certain men, the poets, although it is true that they cultivate the said spanning and self-measurement intently by the creation of poems (and the transcendent worlds *in via* of which such poems are the *virtual* parts). In fact, man is able to be himself by dwelling on earth and abiding with things to the extent that he is engaged in transcending the earth on the grounds of the earthly, for, as Heidegger formulated it, this "between is measured out for the dwelling of man".[52]

This notwithstanding, Heidegger refused to name the dimension in question,[53] thus failing to disclose its essence. Are we then to rest our case here? Hardly, no matter how inordinate the endeavor and meager the results may be. The negative and dynamic character of the "between" and the spanning's positive issue[54] (i.e., the transcendent worlds that man or poet creates, and by which he measures himself in his ongoing task of making his abode on earth) seem to suggest that what is involved amounts to man's *providential establishment* of a new "intimacy" into which he grows, namely, that which holds between the things in heaven and those on earth.[55] But for what purpose? Let us not forget that ultimately what one is seeking in living on earth is to dwell with things, that is to say, to abide with them or constitute a *home* in their midst, and yet to do so genuinely and with virtue. Or differently put, using Heidegger's own words:

Taking the measure of the dimension [or area lying between the mortals and the heavenly ones] is the element within which human dwelling has its security, by which it securely endures.[56]

But in order to *secure* our dwelling on earth, we must do so in such a fashion that it does not become an *illusory battlement against death*. What is at stake is our essential condition as mortals, which is the correlative of dwelling and achieves itself in our dis-closure and preservation of the foundation of things. Paradoxically, the way in which we would secure our dwelling on earth is the self-aware practice of our mortality. This is, it seems to me, the sense of Heidegger's addendum to the words quoted above, when he said: "The taking of measure is what is poetic in dwelling".[57] "Poetic" is here taken in the fundamental, not in the formal sense of the term, and it points to our striving after *enduring security on earth*. Our poetic stance is, then, coextensive with our nature, since it is by our openness to the things of this world, when radicalized, that it is possible to secure them on their ground. But to "secure" things does not mean – again, paradoxically – to achieve mastery or control over them; rather it signifies to "release" things from their fetters by "letting them be". The securing is discharged in measuring. But who and what is being measured? They are, respectively, man as the one who seeks to make his dwelling on earth, and the things of his world with which we construct such an abode. Where is the measurement taking place? In that which lies between the heavenly ones and us mortals. But by which limit (*peras*) and standard (*metron*) is the measurement of the mortals in their dwelling on earth accomplished? By the limit and standard of the heavenly ones, ultimately by the limit and standard as such, God or the *ens a se*. Yet here lies not only the solution but the most problematic of origins as well, for, as Hölderlin put it: "Is God unknown? Is He manifest as the sky? This rather I believe. It is the measure of man".[58] But what is truly the measure of man? Certainly not God, for God is unknown.[59] Something can be the measure of something else if it is available to effect the measuring, and this means that it is to become manifest in the measuring. Is God the unknown manifest? If one is to trust Hölderlin, one would have to say that God is manifest precisely as unknown. But this is just the problem, for, as Heidegger remarked,

> . . . [t]his is also why Hölderlin is perplexed by the exciting question: how can that which by its very nature remains unknown ever become a measure? For something that man measures himself by must after all impart itself, must appear. But if it appears, it is known. The god, however, is unknown, and he is the measure nonetheless.[60]

Let us heed Hölderlin's precise formulation. He did not say: "He is the measure of man", but rather: "It is the measure of man". The measure of man, if we are to believe him, is not God proper, but His manifestness, for He is unknown as He is in Himself. But what is manifest of Him? Precisely His being unknown. Accordingly, God's splendor or *doxa* is recognizable by man as his *metron* only insofar as He is active and open to us as unknown. Indeed, He is abidingly accessible to us by His *Shekinah*, which is, to begin with, His dwelling with us as inaccessible.[61] Or in Heidegger's interpretation:

God's appearance through the sky consists in a disclosing that lets us see what conceals itself, but lets us see it not by seeking to wrest what is concealed out of its concealedness, but only by guarding the concealed in its self-concealment.[62]

We are called, in order to be human beings, to make our dwelling on earth as mortals, and yet we are, for the sake of succeeding in this essential venture, to measure ourselves by a limit that primordially shows itself as *Deus absconditus*. Is there any hope for us, then? Yes, indeed, if, as Heidegger said in interpreting Hölderlin's "In lieblicher Bläue", this,

... is done by a taking which at no time clutches at the standard but rather takes it in a concentrated perception, a gathered taking-in, that remains a listening.[63]

It is therefore important to determine whether the instrument to carry out a perception of this sort exists at all and what its nature could be, for it has to be suited to a "grasping" of God that lets Him appear precisely as inaccessible. The instrument in question must result, we are told, in a *concentrated* perception, and yet be no sheer *taking-in* by which we would clutch at the standard. Hence it can be no mere *concept*, which is a tool of mastery or possession;[64] it must, then, above and beyond producing a distance from the grasped as any concept would, bring us near to what or whom is being received. In brief: it cannot be a device that simply allows us to see; it has as well to dispose us to *listen*. Accordingly, what is needed for the task of establishing a realm between the "gods" and men is an *allegory* or *symbol*, for we require something that would place in the light of day that which is radically other (*allo agoreuei*) as it is preserved in itself in its distance from and inaccessibility to us, and yet that would permit it to be near at hand and come to synthesis with us (*sumballein*), precisely where we already find ourselves, and in the way in which we intrinsically are – namely, in our dwelling with things on earth as mortals.[65] In view of this, allegories and symbols are not, in this connection, to be understood as implements that would be employed in the usual manner,[66] as if we could somehow keep our lives as dwellers on earth immune from the Other who is our essential limit and measure. On the contrary, at this outermost boundary, our lives are called to be transformed into an intent hearing or listening, insofar as we can do so by already being poets fundamentally or *lato sensu* – a metamorphosis by which we would be capable of receiving and bearing up under the inaccessible that appears as such. But that means that the radically Other, insofar as He is the radically Other, has to be given as *part of our very lives*. To use Heidegger's own words, the radically Other cannot then be said to be "some representational content in our consciousness",[67] or for that matter a sign or expression thereof, but rather something more fundamental, namely, a *modality of being-human* by which, without yet being where we intend to "go", we would nonetheless find ourselves already "there", for, strangely, it would at once be a means to and the necessary condition for our getting there.[68]

As mortals, therefore, we would be required to project ourselves from the earth (as the domain where we dwell with things) toward the invisible God (as our limit and measure), in order to be who we are. And we do so, *even if we never formally engage in poetic creation*, by *pervading*[69] – and, in this sense, by abiding in – that realm that comes into being between "gods" and mortals for as long as we bring the divine limit to be our measure in our dwelling with things. But we certainly may go, if that is our calling or destiny, beyond living as *mere* mortals (or poets in the fundamental sense), by *choosing* to work out our lives as those who engage in *formal* poetic creation. If we do so, however, the projective realm lying between "gods" and mortals would become articulated by means of poems (and the poetic worlds *in via* of which such poems are the *virtual* parts).[70] But, be that as it may, the fact remains that our dwelling with things, or our condition as mortals, is no static determination of what we are. It is as if we had ongoingly to rehearse, so to speak, our dwelling with things, by trying, time and again, to live up to the inaccessible by way of an ever-renewed constitution and development of the realm lying between "gods" and mortals (be it in a poetic fashion or otherwise, given the possible manifoldness connected with the notion of "between"). As Heidegger chose to make this point: the "real dwelling plight lies in this, that mortals ever search anew for the nature of dwelling, that they *must ever learn to dwell*".[71] If it is true, as is here and elsewhere asserted, that men, "as heirs and learners in all things",[72] can never come to a resting place on earth where they would have formally found their abode, then the prospect of our becoming naturalized in earthly exile which Solovyev pointed to can never come to be fulfilled, insofar as we remain alive to our condition as mortals. For, as the Russian thinker also indicated, our loving commitment to others and the Other contains, as an essential component (however blunted and dormant it may become), the sense of a "lost paradise" and the *unsettling* feeling of an " 'other-world' mystical basis".[73] Accordingly, if to be a man means the renewed endeavor to dwell with things, the earth can never achieve the status of *patria*. A transformation of this sort is in principle impossible, since man is established for what he is on earth by means of his constitutive reference to the inaccessible as his essential measure. Consistent with this, the distortion of being-human that is articulated by some (in terms of a project in which man seeks to become a being-in-and-for-himself in appropriating the totality of the world *qua* being-in-itself), is assuredly the veritable formulation of a "useless passion".[74] In fact, it is a contradiction, unless one understands Being in a classical Parmenidean fashion. But man is no such thing, for to dwell with things on earth is man's way of being at home on earth; yet being at home therein paradoxically never comes to signify quietude and restfulness. On the contrary, as Heidegger suggested, "man's homelessness consists in this, that man still does not think of the *real* plight of dwelling as *the* plight . . . Yet as soon as man *gives thought* to his homelessness, it is a misery no longer".[75] For not only is homelessness, when "[r]ightly considered and kept well in mind, . . . the sole summons that *calls* mortals into their dwelling",[76] that is to say, into self-coincidence,[77] but is as well the condition that would render possible in principle the happiness of which Plato spoke in his *Symposium* as the complete and everlasting possession of the good and beautiful,[78] a state achievable only in the transcendent or heavenly *patria*.

THE POET BEFORE GOD

In this connection, one could say, a I have argued elsewhere,[79] that the poet, in the restricted or formal sense of the word, maximally arises in self-sacrifice, or the delivery of his entire being to the Godhead. One could also assert that the poet now consists, above all, in the effecting of this surrender, for his self-sacrifice is not an occasional event or even an act performed once and for all. On the contrary, it arises from the very roots out of which he emerges a poet. As soon as he has thus been freely established in being, he is ready to exercise humility, for he now can and does acknowledge himself as debtor to the Divinity. There is no longer any room for hubris, or the substitution of a deified self for the darkness of God. In gratitude, he must now turn to God Himself and re-turn to Him his entire lot and origin, which have only been handed over to him in trust. For the poet, this is tantamount to overflowing his own boundaries by transforming his energy into an offering to the Divinity. At this point in his essential history, the poet has become pure listening and lives as "der dienende . . . Levite", the Levite placed in God's service, of which Rilke spoke.[80]

This notwithstanding, the poet's sole accomplishment is that of having come to the practice of a *certain kind of poetry*. Accordingly, one is to say that man becomes a poet by choosing to follow the impulses that God placed in his innermost heart as He fashioned it. There is however no compulsion about this; all that is involved is a call, nay, an urgent invitation, but one which the poet is free to heed or turn a deaf ear to (though, to be sure, only at his peril). If the poet opts for obedience, his path nevertheless does not appear to him pre-charted and luminous. At best, he may begin to have a glimpse of it, as he engages the totality of what he is in working out the intimations at play in the special way he has of relating his being to things. The resulting reciprocal mapping of self and world is therefore a growing structure in his soul.

No doubt there is a mutuality involved here, for the poet constitutes himself as what he is if he heeds the call inscribed in his being, which would come to naught were the darkness of God not given to him as the perfect match thereof. In his self-offering, God is manifest as the One apart from whom no poetry is possible, and yet that hardly suffices for the eventuation of poetry. To be sure, the condition of man as a poet becomes available through self-sacrifice, but it remains only as a condition unless God breaks the seals of His darkness.[81] Therefore, as a modality of being-human, self-sacrifice is activated by God in *vocatio*, and the poet's hope against hope is fulfilled by God in His free self-disclosure.[82]

In short: to the poet God is both darkness and light. Self-sacrifice opens the poet up to the Divinity and preserves him in openness; yet the poet as such is not actual until he has brought the *new* into being by means of his own voice. Such an event cannot come to pass, however, if God, while remaining manifest in his self-concealment or darkness, does not allow His light to come through. This is certainly *kairos*,[83] or the decisive moment in which, if the poet chooses, he may gain access to his poem: for it is then that non-being is constituted for him in the midst of being. But this moment, whatever else it may prove to be, is precisely that – a moment. Whenever its terrible energy vanishes or is consumed, the poet returns to his abode in darkness. It is at this point, after having had a fore-taste of the Divine, that the poet *clearly* experiences the genuine sense of the self-sacrifice and humility that have constituted him as such. He has thus far lived, insofar as he has become a poet *stricto sensu*, in perpetual renunciation of his being (self-sacrifice), for he has proceeded on the basis of the knowledge that alone he is capable of nothing (humility). Yet now his humility is shaken to its roots by a twofold reason: on the one hand, the poet, in a sense, becomes in-finite when God dis-closes Himself as He is, thus running the risk, through ecstasy, of taking himself as the absolute maker of his poems; on the other hand, by being cast from the domain of the bedazzling Light down into the sphere of night (as if proceeding from being into non-being),[84] he may be shattered by the withdrawal or absence of God and tempted to lose his belief in God's existence and diffusive goodness. It is evident then that the poet's mission is *essentially dangerous*,[85] for Infinity is a light threatening the poet with annihilation by virtue of his very creatureliness. Yet the eternal God, in His goodness beyond measure, is sufficient to reduce the poet's temptation and lead him back to the fullness of being. Nonetheless, God's victory is again, by His own choice, subject to the poet's freedom, for the latter may certainly opt for the security of his own self-affirmation. This notwithstanding, he would still remain open as self-sacrifice, and therefore as possible hope, a situation in which he would still be able to express his self-confidence in one way, put by Rilke as follows:

> And so, my God, is every night;
> There are always those who in wakefulness
> go and go and find you not.
> Do you hear them, taking steps like blind men
> in the dark?[86]

The poet is back from infinity and sees, with merciless clarity, that there are men who "go and go and find . . . [Him] not". The paradox lies in the fact that to find God is to be found by Him, and the stumbling block in the fact that men, or poets *lato sensu*, rely on their "everyday life already lived" as "a remote legend overcome".[87] The moment, then, in which a man is confronted with the "arsenal of things yet unlived",[88] that is to say, with the unsuspected and subitaneous light by which God offers Himself to constitute man as a poet properly so called, is the moment he finds himself before

> . . . iron-clasp gates
> resisting those who press for entry,
> but the bars are the handiwork of men.[89]

How is man then to achieve "redemption" precisely as a poet? What is the path he must follow if he is to utter the saving word thus far denied him by his own refusal? He undoubtedly lives in the hope of a unique moment, and yet no expectation of it can find a haven in his heart, for, as Rilke put it,

> . . . sometimes a grave messenger comes
> and passes as radiance through our hundred spirits
> and shows us, trembling, a new way to hold in hand.[90]

Here the lesson to be learnt by the poet is manifold. The one who comes arrives from elsewhere. Indeed, he does so as a "messenger" of a special sort, for he passes so swiftly as to be perceived just as "radiance", that is to say, as someone who, of a sudden, dazzles us only to abandon us thereafter. But this happens only "sometimes", a circumstance that underscores the messenger's alien nature and the treasure-like character of what he leaves behind, so unfamiliar to us until then as to constitute a new way to hold in hand. Now then, all of this serves to make it clear that the messenger does not belong to the expanse of thinghood and, accordingly, that he is in principle beyond our mastery and control. Man, and that by which he becomes a poet – that is to say, his inspiration, if one chooses to give it expression in Platonic terms –[91] not only belong to two different spheres (i.e., the realm of the heavenly ones and that of the mortals), but are severed by a *chasm* as well. It is as if a poet were a man held in abeyance, fact to face with non-being, and in total ignorance of what to abide by. Now, in general, if I wish to learn the "ways" of anything, it stands to reason that, however novel and different the matter in question may be, it must not be altogether alien to me. In the case under scrutiny, it is God's mind as the boundless wealth of power and being *at the root of* possibility that the poet seeks to gain access to. But a possibility is, in this sense, that which is radically outside my field of experience and knowledge, until such time as it makes its appearance or comes into being. In other words, what is possible *a radice* does not exist as the other of God, remaining as it does in God's bosom and in His hands. Therefore, if God's offering to the poet is that which does not yet exist in the realm of creaturely being, but could, and if the poet, like any other man, has his existence in that realm, God's offering and the poet would then be separated by an abyss analogous to the one sundering being from nothingness. Nonetheless, there is only a likeness between the two, for, while nothingness inexorably is *not at all*, a possibility properly so called is somehow endowed with *real being*, although it is denied subsistence outside God for as long as it is just what it is, i.e., a possibility. The existence of a possibility *stricto sensu* is none other than God's, whereby a possibility remains beyond any man's reach. The poet is thus in principle unable to gain access to that which he is meant to bring into being. Yet the poet as such lives by virtue of possibility and would be reduced to naught apart from it. Hence, if the poet is to be at all, he must nonetheless gain entry into the treasury of possibility, but only God can open His mind to him, if only for an instant. Accordingly, an essential constituent of the *eidos* of poetic creation is the passivity of reception on the part of man, however active his life may prove to be otherwise. This passivity is no other than the humility of which I spoke above, and which Rilke gave expression as follows:

> But if you [God] wish me to be before your face
> wherefrom, in darkness, your eyes do rise,
> regard not as pride for me
> to say: no one lives his own life.[92]

Yet this is just the acknowledgment of a *fact*, namely, that the poet himself senses a concealed force acting as the foundation of his creative life. This is a feeling, however, that inevitably leads him to ask:

> Who lives it, then? Is it things,
> which, like a melody unplayed,
> in the evening remain as in a harp?[93]

The question articulates a basic awareness on the poet's part, to wit: that behind his life there lurks no free-floating "personage", but rather someone who is bound up with those things which, in darkness, are first given to him like a "melody unplayed". This melody seems to be of the same kind as that which we have already heard Rilke characterize, in opposition to our "remote legend overcome", as the "arsenal of things yet unlived".[94] Paradoxically, the subject of the poet's creative act is placed at once within and beyond his life, for it is the transcendent offer made to him in darkness. No wonder he comes to discover still another question behind the question: "Who lives it, then? Is it you, God, who lives life?"[95] The answer need not be given in so many words; the poet's very sense of living conveys it to him as a resounding "yes". The Godhead is the one who lives the life of a poet *qua* poet by lifting him to the plane of possibilities, and thereby allowing him somehow to partake of them while in the flesh, in an act of sovereign mercy and fulfillment.

The poet's passivity is thus ascribable to him insofar as he lies in the hands of God and is responsive to His voice. The Divinity bestows a *natural revelation* on him, a revelation which, if accepted, is to guide him in his life as a poet. In that case, one would say that the poet's soul or heart is docility itself, and as such it is the companion of the Godhead. Or as Rilke chose to put it:

> As the watchman in the wine region
> has a cabin and keeps guard,
> so am I, Lord, a cabin in your hands,
> and night, oh Lord, of your night.[96]

The poet's lot could not have been rendered more precisely: he is in God's hands as the cabin for His dwelling. To make a dwelling with things poetically, a man must become himself the dwelling place of the Divinity on earth. By thus placing himself in His service, the poet allows the Godhead to be Lord, that is to say, to watch over what originarily is His own, and to do so through the ministry of the poet's eyes. But what is truly God's own? Not just some wealth unspecified, but the wine-rich earth. And that is the poet's reward for his service: his eyes are newly begotten as the eyes of the watchman of the vineyard of the Lord. He is now fruit-ful *in persona Dei*.

Self-sacrifice, humility, fruitfulness – is this a possible sequence pure and simple? Or is it perchance an actual totality endowed with a deep-seated unity? Rilke, it seems to me, daringly answered this question when he said: "But my soul is as a woman before you".[97] The poet's soul or heart is and must be so, not only during the day, but through day and night, for he ultimately consists in being a free self-offering to the Godhead. However correct this understanding of Rilke's position may be, it nonetheless fails to measure up to it, for he went much further than that when he said:

> And my soul sleeps then till dawn
> by your feet, warm with your blood.
> And she is a woman before you. And she is like Ruth.[98]

Here the nexus constituted by night (or sleep), light (or dawn), and fruitfulness (or blood) stands out quite clearly, especially in terms of the ambiguity characteristic of the expression, *"warm von deinem Blut"* concerning its referent, for one may ask: is the latter God's feet or the sleeping soul? It is both, for the connection is established during the night, as the soul sleeps, that is to say, as she enters – and constitutes thereby – the realm which lies between God and man, a dimension in which, as we have already seen, she comes to meet the manifestness of the Divinity *qua* inaccessible, and this is *God's night*. In my opinion, all this is brought to synthesis in the transfiguration that the soul undergoes thereby, since, as Rilke put it, now she is a woman before God, and yet not woman in general, but the unique one known as Ruth. In other words, the soul, by means of her responsiveness, has attained Ruth's radical and energetic manner of passivity. There is no mistaking the sense of Rilke's utterance, for he provided us with the Old Testament character of Ruth as its necessary background. As you may remember, Naomi dismissed her daughters-in-law and bade them return to their respective mothers' houses, as she was about to go back to the land of Judah after the death of her sons. Of the two, Orpah and Ruth, only the latter clung to her, despite Naomi's entreaty that she should follow in her sister-in-law's footsteps. This was Ruth's reply: "Do not press me to leave you and to turn back from your company, for

> wherever you go, I will go,
> wherever you live, I will live.
> Your people shall be my people,
> and your God, my God.
> Wherever you die, I will die
> and there I will be buried.
> May Yahweh do this thing to me
> and more also,
> if even death should come between us!"[99]

The loyalty shown by Ruth to Naomi (and thereby to her God and people) is so firm and complete that it well served Rilke to signify that the poet's fruitfulness would be non-existent were God's blood not to touch him. If it was true to say that the poet *is-not* at all apart from God, now it is clear that he would be a *mere nothing* were he to refuse to abide in the house of the Lord, if he ceased to be the dwelling place of God that he became through his humility.[100] Accordingly, if a man is to remain a poet after this stage in the process of his self-transformation has elapsed, then his soul must endure by poetically dwelling on earth, as a wife abides by her husband in faithfulness.

Long ago the poet started on his journey toward the foundation. He moved from the discovery of the world of things as a context of familiarity and intimacy to the nearness of God, who refused him the sight and touch of His face and thus became manifest to him as an ever-present offer of transcendence. The voice still resounded in the poet's ear by which he could take delight in the forest and the river banks, and by which he was enabled to transform the fury of the existent into song, and thus to overflow with its energy. Yet he had also gained a new voice, one born by nightly contemplation and hope. The two voices were now to merge in the inner unity of the totality of his life. This achievement was given expression by Rilke as follows:

> Because my voice has grown in two directions
> and become a fragrance and a cry:
> one is to make ready the one that lies afar,
> the other must be the visage and bliss
> and angel of my solitude.[101]

The first direction of his voice is the world's call for a foundation, which is heard by "the one that lies afar" (i.e., the poet insofar as he is immersed in the world for its own sake) and prepares the way for self-sacrifice. The second one is the night's, which lets God be heard after the poet's self-sacrifice has turned him towards the ground of his being and allowed the "cry" of God to be "the visage and bliss/and angel of . . . [his] solitude". Yet he is just *one* voice, in which each direction is constituted for the sake of the other. But, having come to this realization, Rilke is prompted to address God in a new way, which is at once the affirmation of the newly achieved unity and a *formal* act of self-sacrifice:

> And grant that both these voices keep me company,
> if you make me scatter in city and dread.
> Would that I be with them in the ire of the times
> to make a berth ready for you in my song,
> wherever you would so demand.[102]

This is undoubtedly a prayer in which Rilke acknowledges that whatever he had received from God he had not and could not have earned *as a man*, but as well that he could not dispense with it unless he were ready now for his death *as a poet*. In my opinion, it is not possible to convey the paradox at the root of the poet's life in a clearer fashion, for the poet is constituted as an all-consuming desire to bring the new into being, a desire which, to all appearances, cannot be satisfied, since man belongs irrevocably to this world and the radically new does not. Accordingly, if in fact a man becomes a poet (or equivalently: if a genuine poem comes into existence), then it must be that the voice of the unknown God has indeed resounded with the poet's. But this could not have taken place if the poet had not *at least* gained cognitive access to the qualitatively other where he is not. This would indeed mark the poet (who, as a man, essentially seeks to dwell with things on earth) as an uncanny being and a stranger in his house. We are thus confronted, once again, with the conflict identified by Solovyev between our striving after naturalization in earthly exile, and the aftertaste of an " 'other-world' mystical basis"[103] by which we continue to live. And yet there is a difference, for this conflict is now seen as a formal constituent of the poet as such. No wonder Rilke had dared to ask for that which still remains ungiven:

> Send me into your uninhabited lands
> run through by great winds,
> where large convents like vestments make a stand
> about life yet unlived.[104]

Therefore, the poet *qua* poet is not only dependent on God, but he is dependent on Him in a manner entirely *sui generis*, for the poet is not just a *stranger* among men, but also a *voyager* moving towards the alien *stricto sensu*. Indeed, this is so much so that it is as if he were

> . . . to follow a blind old man
> into a path unknown to all.[105]

Nonetheless, the world of the senses does not pass away; the poet continues to be attached to his surrounding world, which is now seen under the dazzling light of night. The poet follows the blind old man into the uninhabited lands and is as perspicacious as his guide. What is left behind, the world gone by, undoubtedly remains, but it does so only as the poet's past, the reason for that special permanence being the unqualified permanence of God, for, as Rilke put it, "It is past because you are".[106] The world, abandoned to its own devices, is the road back to non-being; the way of the senses is ultimately the offering of nothingness; only God is forever present, for only He *is*. This notwithstanding, the world of things cannot pass away altogether, inasmuch as man is the one who essentially seeks to learn how to dwell on earth. As long as the poet remains, he must then vanquish the world *in order to* return it to God whence it came, a paradoxical discipline indeed, yet its practitioner must fall victim to it. As Rilke remarked:

> The great death which is in every one
> is the fruit about which everything revolves.[107]

It is to be underscored that self-annihilation is, as we are told here, at once central and fruitful. But how could that be? We are faced with a conundrum, and one apparently beyond resolution. The poet is seemingly torn between two callings, both leading to his passing, for the way of the senses would ultimately end in the dissipation of his being, and the path to God would have its culmination in the poet's absorption into Being. Yet neither outcome is necessary for the poet, and time and again, in faithfulness, he continues to create. What would then render all of this possible? Only if the poet abides in measuring himself and his life against the Divine standard can he persevere in dwelling with things, for, as Hölderlin said, "Full of acquirements, . . . [yet] poetically, man dwells on this earth".[108] Now, I think, we can appreciate the full import of his "yet", which is constituted by the weight of the senses and the allure of the Godhead. Both are forms of loving or taking delight, of *amor sive dilectio*, which, as St. Augustine taught, is the moving power of the heart.[109] But the heart is the kernel of man, and it cannot be overcome without the removal of man. Accordingly, if the poet is to remain between two impossible extremes, man must endure as well, and if man, so must his heart and love too, for, as St. Augustine said, "*pondus meum amor meus; eo feror quoqumque feror*", "My weight is my love; by it I am borne whithersoever I am borne".[110] And yet man or poet, "heir and learner [as he is] in all things",[111] is to practice love and acquire *discretion* therein, for as St. Augustine also asserted elsewhere: "Are you told not to love anything? Not at all! If you are to love nothing, you will be lifeless, dead, detestable, miserable. Love, but be careful what you love".[112] We are thus to love even as poets, so as to become like God (and not like gods).[113] Only then would man's death be truly poetical or fruitful, and therefore irreducible to both dissipation and absorption. This is why, in my opinion, Rilke's judgment on the great death had been preceded by this prayer:

> Oh, Lord, give every one his own death,
> the dying that arises from each one's life,
> and in which are found his love, instinct, and need.[114]

It is then by virtue of a genuine death that "what was once regarded abides/ as if eternal, even though it is long past . . .",[115] to put it in Rilke's own words, for all that was, is, or will be, if experienced in this spirit, is fore-cast and pre-interpreted therein.

Surprisingly, this manner of becoming *estranged* in the world amounts to the discovery of a new bond between what is past and what is future, namely, their being *sub specie aeternitatis*. Again, it is worth repeating that this does not entail the abandoning of this world; rather it signifies our entering into it more deeply for its own sake, a process by which we would learn a new way of dwelling with things in which we would no longer be sheer prisoners of the transitoriness of the things of the earth. By directing his glance towards the creative light of the Divinity, the poet seeks not to nullify the world, but to complete it by the remedy of its own implicit excess. In this perspective, a profound nexus of this world and the light of the inaccessible God is discovered, for:

> You are the future, great dawn,
> upon the plains of eternity.[116]

The world now appears as it has always been, namely, as that which is in a state of imminence, so that, if a suitable deliverer were to arrive, we would experience something which Rilke presented in these words:

> A wind is felt from a great page
> that was written by God and you and me
> and was turned, above, by an alien hand.[117]

We should not neglect the fact that here Rilke mentions God twice – both as such and as an "alien hand". But this ought not to surprise us, for, after all, we are now *formally* moving in the sphere lying between the pure light of God (the realm of the heavenly ones) and the world as the expanse of thinghood where the mortals strive to make their dwelling, a "middle earth" in which the poet comes to meet the manifestness of God *qua* inaccessible and to *construct it* in his poems. Hence, the poet would have thereby touched the essence and foundation of poetry, which is no other than God as eternal.

POETIC CREATION

What is then the poet's life? Conflict and contradiction, for he is *rooted in* the world (or the domain of the passing and contingent) as he emerges from the *other* of the world, inasmuch as God is for him not just darkness but also the wellspring of immutability and abidingness. Let me say it again: the poet lives in peril of self-annihilation, which he can only forestall by learning to dwell poetically with things on this earth in the construction of a *mediating in-between*. While in the flesh, he is to transform the earth into his *dwelling*, whereby his life is *seeded* in time. To say this is correct enough but hardly a faithful portrait of his life as a poet, for within his sense of fleetingness another is harbored, by which he perseveres on this earth in a *formally* poetic way that especially demands, in Rilke's words, his loving the "dark hours of . . . [his] being in which . . . [his] senses grow absorbed".[118] As the German *Dichter* put it, such indeed are the grounds

> . . . [o]ut of which . . . [he] come[s] to know . . . [he has] room for another life, time-free and wide.[119]

The poet thus abides in the world in the "knowledge" that he is called to constitute – or project himself into – that which lies between the narrow and the wide, the bounded and the boundless, the temporal and the time-free. It is precisely this clear awareness of the essential predicament of the poet that was given expression by Rilke when he said:

> If you [God] are the dreamer, I am your dream.
> But if it is your will to awaken, then I am your will
> and achieve might in full splendor
> and completion as a starry stillness
> over the strange city of time.[120]

It is to be noted that here one finds the odd conjunction of the poet's accomplishment ("completion as a starry stillness") and his dwelling place ("the strange city of time"). It would appear that Rilke was exerting himself to the point of unintelligibility in order to present the poet's *dual citizenship* to us, for, without abandoning this world, he is nonetheless called to transcend it. As a result, the earth becomes "strange", as indeed it must seem when one looks at it from the "completion" and "stillness" above. "Completion" and "stillness" are thus *symbols* of immutable life and, as such, the way and content thereof as experienced *on the face of* the passing and contingent.[121] The threefoldness at play in this connection – the realm of the heavenly ones, the world of the mortals, and the area projected between them – is clearly secured and preserved by Rilke's minimal word "as" (*wie*), for the poet *qua* man is denied in principle direct or unmediated access to completion and stillness proper, being able to reach only the *measured* substitutes thereof.

At this point, the poet is ready to endure his life in the clear awareness that, as a man, he is *irrevocably seeded in time*, and yet that he must, as a poet, approach heaven precisely on that basis. Or as Rilke put it when he addressed God:

> I know that time
> is other
> than you.[122]

Accordingly, the poetic *symbols* he constructs would be the inhabitants of the "middle earth", and therein he cannot effect the total completion and stillness of the living God after which he thirsts, but just a close and ever-growing likeness of the One who is, in the words of St. Thomas Aquinas, "sheerly actual and unalloyed with potentiality".[123] Yet it is the face of God Himself *qua* inaccessible that is given in the very symbols that the poet fashions in the context of time, as he endeavors to dwell with things in this world. To the extent that he poetically succeeds in dwelling on earth, man may be said progressively to ransom the things with which he lives for eternity, a feat that is not – let me say it again – tantamount to abandoning or even annihilating the world, but, on the contrary, to *concentrating it from within* into all that it may be in the eye of God. Or as Rilke gave expression to this insight:

> And painters make their paintings
> only for you to recover imperishable
> the Nature you created perishable:
> everything becomes eternal. See, woman,
> like a wine, long ago ripened in Mona Lisa;
> no other women should ever be,
> for no new woman brings forth anything new.
> Those who fashion are like you.
> They want eternity. They say, stone,
> be eternal. And it means: be yours![124]

This would have been perversity on Rilke's part had he meant thereby that the existence of any woman would be pointless after Leonardo's accomplishment, as if individual womanhood were somehow prescribable by a rule. Mona Lisa is no perfect or absolutely beautiful *existent*, but something quite different. She is the formula of the possibility of perfection for womanhood and, as such, that which would allow any woman, after Leonardo, to measure and reform herself after the standard set in his work, to the extent that it provides her with the point of her existence so far as beauty is concerned. Mona Lisa, therefore, is possibility, not actuality, and yet she is not pure possibility. The pure and real possibility of anything is the manner of being and subsistence it possesses in God as determinately participable, and it is thus inaccessible as such except to God Himself. Mona Lisa is Nature *created* perishable once she has been *recovered* as imperishable or rendered eternal by the agency of the poet, and thus returned to God as the *measure* of what the individual beauty of a woman can be. Her logical status is therefore irreducible to that of a *pure* and *real* possibility, insofar as she has been brought about by the perfecting of perishable Nature, or by her being rescued from her temporal manifestness, a *modus operandi* that presupposes both the manifestness in question and the ontological process of creation and participation at its basis. It is to be emphasized that Rilke said "*es musste nie ein Weib mehr sein*", that is to say, that "no other women should ever be" once the ripening of womanhood in Mona Lisa has been achieved. As the translation already suggests, *manifoldness*, though real and ever-productive, is not the decisive factor at work; rather it is the *unity* sought after by the artist in Mona Lisa, a unity by which to effect the gathering of all women, even those who are yet to arise, in the place called beauty. The artist's hope is then the establishment of a realm lying between heaven and earth, a domain that would consist of the *concretions of perfection*[125] that his works (and the creative worlds *in via* of which they are the *virtual* parts) would embody.

Up to this point, I have insisted on the progressive constitution of the subjective essence of the poet. We have seen, as a result, the unfolding of a structural sequence consisting of self-sacrifice, humility, obedience, faithfulness, and hope, and culminating in service. All these dimensions are unified for the sake of service and therefore in their nexus to God, for poetry may ultimately be defined as service rendered unto God. But how could anyone, let alone the poet, render any service to the Divinity? To answer this question, it might be useful to return to the part of *Das Stunden-Buch* in which Rilke likened the poet's soul to Ruth.[126] His soul is destined to perform "*die tiefe Dienste*"[127] or "the profound service", certainly by day, but above all by night, when "everything about you is at rest",[128] as Rilke put it. What is then the service rendered by the poet unto God at that highest of moments? As Ruth expressed it in the words of Rilke:

> Extend your wings over your maiden.
> You are the heir.[129]

There is no way to mistake her intent – she seeks to beget the world for God, or to ransom it in unity and perfection, but she can only do that by God's own power ("Extend your wings . . ."). As we saw, this is confirmed later by the verse "*warm von deinem Blut*".[130] There is then a meaningful, not a vicious circularity at play in poetic creation, for the poet is to return the things of this world (which, to begin with, are God's creation, or perishable Nature) to God Himself (as inaccessible and immutable light), though only if His creation has been suitably transformed into imperishable Nature. This is the poet's service to the Divinity, both by God's will and His enabling power, for only if God joins with the poet's soul or heart can such a metamorphosis eventuate, inasmuch as the poet's moment of giving is his moment of receiving. The relation of the poet's soul to Ruth can then be approximated to that of Ruth to Job, who also achieved his dwelling with the things of earth in terms of the same equation. As Job said:

> Naked I came from my mother's womb,
> naked I shall return.
> Yahweh gave, Yahweh has taken back.
> Blessed be the name of Yahweh![131]

Both Ruth and Job are, in this sense, identical, despite their opposite attitudes and the difference in tone of their respective utterances. A man's soul (*anima*) is to be no less if she is to achieve fulfillment as the soul of a poet in the formal sense of the word, but even meeting such a condition would hardly prove sufficient, for a man's soul must also follow a path that is distinctly her own insofar as she is the heart of a poet. The equation in question (and the circularity of procedure based thereupon) must be bodied forth in a way which is appropriate to the transformation of Nature from perishable into imperishable. In this connection, Rilke's testimony is, in my opinion, most instructive. According to him, the process of poetic transmutation involved is threefold:

First of all, the poet's word must be such as to be able to return to God even what common sense would declare in principle unavailable. As Rilke gave it expression:

> And you [God] inherit the green
> of gardens gone and the quiet blue
> of skies in ruin.[132]

Therefore, God's power, as imparted to the poet, must bestow on the poet's voice the capacity of restoring to Him the *absolute past of the world* of which the given poet has not even had any experience. This is a transformation of non-being into being by means of the poetic word, an achievement bearing a resemblance to that most radical of transmutations that is ascribed to the *Logos*, through whom "the world . . . had its being".[133]

Secondly, the poet's word must be such as to give expression to that which, though non-existent too, still has a measure of being. In Rilke's words:

> You inherit those autumns which, like opulent vestments,
> lie in the memory of poets,
> and every winter which, like an orphaned land,
> seems to cling to you imperceptibly.[134]

In other words, the poet is to return to God that which no longer exists and yet is endowed with being of a sort, namely, that which autumns and winters past have acquired by taking residence in the poet's memory. This is the transformation of being into *doxa* or glory that is effected by way of *exaltation* and *acceptance*. It is then as unified and rescued from temporality that autumns and winters are given back to God by the ministry of the poet. But what about those that are yet to pass? Despite the fact that they have never existed they are not to be lost to God at all, for the transformation undergone by autumns and winters past in the poet's memory is, as we just saw, one that turns them into concretions of perfection,[135] and this transmutation is sufficient too for those still lying in the future. The concretions of perfection are states of affairs or experiential patterns of organization that are being constituted by the poet in his memory, and by which he can actively rescue for eternity that which is endowed not only with past (or present) reality, but also with that which is merely a future possibility. This may only come to pass if, on the one hand, it is, to begin with, an actual determination of a past (or present) reality and if, on the other hand, it is made to move from the status of being perishable to that of being imperishable by the agency of the poet.

Thirdly, the poet is also to rescue and give back to God the presentness of this world. In my judgment, this is what Rilke meant when he said:

> . . . and sounds will be yours: violins, horns, tongues,
> and every song that has resounded deeply
> shall sparkle next to you like a jewel.[136]

Accordingly, even such things as are affected by the fleetingness of actuality, namely, the sense-perceptual events and items of the world existing *hic et nunc* (and which are here signified by "sounds"), are to reach – again, by the poet's agency – the status of the beautiful (here represented by the jewel's sparkle) in which they are rendered suitable to being returned to God.[137] This of course may come to pass if what is involved are not mere sounds (which are experienced just insofar as they are fleeting), but those which have resounded deeply and have therefore been readied by their being incorporated in concretions of perfection, that is to say, in those determinate, sensuous unities into which anything is to be transformed if it is to have a rightful place in the poetic realm between God and man, for nothing short of that will allow a poet in the formal or restricted sense of the word to make an offering properly so called and thus to be of service to the Godhead.

It is important to keep in mind that the poet's style of performance does not strictly belong to the intellective order, even if concepts and judgments and even arguments do play a part in what he does. Rather, poetry is an activity and a virtue of the practical understanding[138] mediated by cognitions achieved by affective connaturality.[139] Accordingly, the path on which the poet moves as prompted by the excessiveness of the real is characteristically "dark" or "divinatory". The poet intuitively discovers that being is diffusive; indeed, reality becomes accessible to him as a *multiple sign*. A thing forming part of this world is, to be sure, limited by what it is (i.e., its essence) and the conditions of its being (i.e., the order to which it belongs and the existence that it is endowed with), and yet it progressively *appears* as intimately connected with other beings in manners which transcend the sphere of causality. In his own special way, the poet – in the formal sense of the word – works *with* the things of this world in terms of their superabundance at the sense-perceptual level, on which level the contents of Nature are given as perishable to any man. In other words, the poet lives in the *contemplation* of Nature as that which "cannot reach expression univocally, precisely by virtue of the fact that it is full of virtualities".[140] Yet he does not remain content with the form of transcendence rooted therein, for, were he to do so, he would eventually become a prisoner of the perishability of created being, as many a mortal does; instead, he seeks to overcome such transcendence in the direction of the unity proper to Beauty as the ground of Being. This is the sense of what he does by projecting the real into the domain of what lies between God and mortals, a realm that abides only as long as the projection is being effected by him or *can* be effected *once more* by someone else. But, again, this would hardly suffice for his intended task, unless the resulting unities (i.e., the poems he fashions and the poetic worlds *in via* of which they are the *virtual* parts) are themselves seen as arising from God insofar as He is divined to be the wellspring of *natural* superabundance. This aspect of the poet's "work" is just the affirmative counterpart and complement of the givenness, in poetry, of God as *Deus absconditus*. Accordingly, whether reached affirmatively or negatively, God should eventually appear to the poet as the altogether Other that founds poetic experience and performance. Therefore, the poet's style of making consists, formally speaking, in effecting the symbolic return of things to their source. This point was made by Rilke with the greatest exactitude when he said: *"So fliesst der Dinge Überfluss dir zu"*,[141] "So does the superabundance of things flow toward thee". Nonetheless, this could not possibly be or ever come to pass if it were not part and parcel of the Divine Creator's will, which is what Rilke meant by his conception of God as both maker and heir of the poet's accomplishments.[142]

Art[143] could be characterized, as Aristotle for one did, as that by means of which man imitates Nature.[144] But this view may be adopted in a more radical fashion than perhaps he did, namely, according to the sense suggested by St. Thomas Aquinas when he asserted that *"ars imitatur naturam, inquantum potest"*.[145] I wish to insist on the active connotation of the word *potest*, and approach the standard of Nature or *phusis* not statically (i.e., as the totality of material entities extant at any given time),[146] but rather dynamically, or as the power of "begetting" which is present, operative, and secured in the "begotten". To put it in the words of Heidegger: *"physis* is . . . [B]eing itself, by virtue of which . . . [beings] become and remain observable",[147] or the "process of a-rising [*Entstehen*], of emerging from the hidden, whereby the hidden is first made to stand".[148] Therefore, being as *phusis* is that which still lies and pulsates in the manifest, and that by which the things of this world can therefore be gathered or unified and thus returned to the source, as the poet for one does by means of the symbols he constructs as he establishes a realm between God and man at the instigation of the things of this world. But, as we have seen, this is precisely the poet's way [149] of dwelling on this earth. Accordingly, Nature, in the originary sense of *phusis*, is the "spirit" of poetry itself. As such, then, poetry is based upon the very superabundance of Nature and thus tends toward and seeks after it, for it is the practice that consists in *concentrating* the world *in unity* from within, and thereby of rendering it *imperishable*. The products thereof – i.e., the poems and the poetic worlds *in via* of which they are the *virtual* parts – establish or secure the in-between, but can only do so to the extent that they share in the diffusive character of Nature and its originative power, which ultimately is in and derives from God. To dwell poetically with things, in the strict sense of the word, is tantamount to sharing symbolically in the superabundance of things and to transcending it in the direction of its eternal origin, for the presence of God is actual in the world not only progressively (as it is by way of God's creation), but also retrogressively and complementarily (as it is by the agency of the poet).

Now, if this understanding is correct, one may assert that a poetic world (and the poems contained therein) are profoundly similar to Nature as a totality in the making, inasmuch as both a poetic world and Nature proceed on the basis of superabundance under the "guidance" of the ever-beckoning unity of God. Yet the difference is clear, for no mediator is needed in the case of Nature, whereas the poet's attitude and activity are essential for the constituting and "populating" of the in-between. By the same token, one may affirm that the similarity in question and the ground common to both perishable and imperishable Nature allow the poet, by virtue of his creative activity – implicitly, to begin with, and by design, eventually – to perfect the world. But this is precisely what I meant when I said that the subjective essence of the poet is brought to synthesis as God's service.[150]

In my opinion, the essential-descriptive presentation of the poet's "method" that has been attempted in this study makes it apparent that he is advancing – first, *in actu exercito* and, then, deliberately but nonetheless *ad infinitum* – towards God Himself. Furthermore, that he does so by establishing a dimension which would lie between the Godhead and the mortals. But this is equivalent to saying that the poet's "project" is both necessary and unrealizable. Rilke has given clear expression to this when he said:

> With trembling hands we build in you,
> and we pile atom upon atom.
> Yet who can bring you to completion,
> oh Cathedral?[151]

The poet *qua* poet thus leads a life that consists in *building God in God*, on the grounds of instigations pre-contained in the world of things in which he seeks to dwell. Indeed, such a response is his manner of dwelling on this earth. The poetic world or symbolic system in the making that he is engaged in fashioning is the Cathedral that he wishes to erect. Yet, while the building of the Cathedral must go on and does go on for as long as man engages in poetic self-projection, the resulting Cathedral can never come to completion, for essentially or in itself it is an open-ended and centuries-old design that seeks to span the chasm separating us from the Infinite, whence everything comes and to which everything returns. In other words, the poet is a constitutive impossibility inasmuch as he seeks, on the basis of endless but finite resources, to bring the totality of all there is to perfection, for the Cathedral he is raising, by piling atom upon atom, is meant to be the correlate of God *qua* actual infinity. The poet's consciousness, therefore, is marked by the sense of irresoluble conflict and unbearable tension, since his creative activity can only issue in the most paradoxical of results, for the poems he makes (and the poetic worlds *in via* of which they are the *virtual* parts) stand ultimately beyond completion, and yet they are necessary *ab alio* and *ex hypothesi*. But this is the same as saying that the poet's is a *Lebensform* that cannot but come to grief, for it can never attain to its intended perfection, and, if *per impossibile* it did, it would *eo ipso* be absorbed into the transcendent God. Rilke himself came to no other conclusion, as one can see from his characterization of the poet's creations as

> ... vestments which all by themselves
> cannot stand and, foundering, cling
> to the sturdy walls of vaulting stones.[152]

The essential relationship between poem and God – signified here by the poet's coming from, moving towards, and clinging to the "sturdy walls of vaulting stones" – is not an incidental but an intrinsic and fundamental nexus which, though in the last analysis unfulfillable by the poet's sole strength and, to that extent, impossible and devoid of meaning, cannot however be shaken without bringing about the annihilation of the poet and his creations. Therefore, it is in this sense, and only in this sense, that the poet is paradoxically at home in this world, for, in endeavoring to ransom it for the sake of Another (from whom his dwelling with the things of this earth ultimately issues), he learns to abide with them in the way of homelessness and exile. Or at least it so appears *quoad nos* and so far as the guiles of poetic *eros* are concerned.

Long Island University

NOTES

[1] George Steiner, "A Reading against Shakespeare" (W.P. Ker Lecture), *apud* Iris Murdoch, *Metaphysics as a Guide to Morals* (New York: Allen Lane/The Penguin Press, 1993), p. 113.
[2] Friedrich Hölderlin, "In lieblicher Bläue . . .", *Sämtliche Werke*, ed. Norbert von Hellingrath *et al.* (Berlin: Propyläen, 1914–), VI, p. 25, *apud* Martin Heidegger, "Hölderlin und das Wesen der Dichtung", *Erläuterungen zu Hölderlins Dichtung* in *Gesamtausgabe*, Part I, Vol. IV (Frankfurt: Vittorio Klostermann, 1981), p. 33 [31], No. 5. Tr.: *Poems and Fragments*, German/English ed., trans. M. Hamburger (Cambridge: Cambridge University Press, 1980), pp. 600 and 601.
[3] Cf. Martin Heidegger, ". . . Poetically Man Dwells . . .", *Poetry, Language, Thought*, trans. A. Hofstadter (New York: Harper & Row, 1971), p. 213: "If need be, we can imagine that poets do on occasion dwell poetically. But how is 'man' – and this means every

man and all the time – supposed to dwell poetically? Does not dwelling remain incompatible with the poetic?"

[4] Vladimir Solovyev, *The Meaning of Love*, trans. J. Marshall (New York: International Universities Press, 1947), p. 66.

[5] *Ibid.*

[6] *Ibid.*

[7] Cf. Plato, *Republic*, vii, 516 c–e.

[8] M. Heidegger, "Hölderlin und das Wesen der Dichtung", §2, p. 36 [34]. *Tr.*: "Hölderlin and the Essence of Poetry" in *Existence and Being*, trans. W. Brock (Chicago: Henry Regnery Co., 1949), pp. 274–75.

[9] Rainer Maria Rilke, *Duineser Elegien*, i in *Gesammelte Werke* (Leipzig: Insel Verlag, 1927), III, p. 259. *Tr.*: *Duino Elegies and the Sonnets to Orpheus*, trans. A. Poulin, Jr. (Boston: Houghton Mifflin Co., 1977), p. 4.

[10] *The Psalms*, 42–43:2 in *The Jerusalem Bible* (Garden City, N. Y.: Doubleday & Co., 1966), p. 824.

[11] M. Heidegger, "Hölderlin and the Essence of Poetry", p. 298.

[12] M. Heidegger, ". . . Poetically Man Dwells . . .", p. 214.

[13] *Ibid.*, p. 215.

[14] *Ibid.*

[15] F. Hölderlin, "In lieblicher Bläue . . .", *op. cit.*

[16] Hölderlin said "endures" (*dauert*).

[17] M. Heidegger, ". . . Poetically Man Dwells . . .", p. 229.

[18] *Ibid.*

[19] M. Heidegger, "Vom Wesen des Grundes", ii, *Wegmarken* in *Gesamtausgabe*, Part I, Vol. IX (1976), pp. 144–45. *Tr.*: *The Essence of Reasons*, German/English ed., trans. T. Malick (Evanston: Northwestern University Press, 1969), pp. 55 ff.

[20] *John* 1:10. *Tr.*: *The Gospel according to John*, i–xii, intro., trans. and notes by R. E. Brown in *Anchor Bible* (Garden City, N.Y.: Doubleday & Co., 1966), Vol. XXIX, p. 3. Cf. *Biblia sacra iuxta vulgatam Clementinam*, ed. A. Colunga *et al.* (Madrid: Biblioteca de Autores Cristianos, 1965), p. 1042: "Et mundus per ipsum factus est,/ Et mundus enim non cognovit".

[21] *Vide* St. Augustine, *In Joannis Evangelium tractatus*, ii, §11 in *Obras de San Agustín*, Latin/Spanish ed. (Madrid: Biblioteca de Autores Cristianos, 1955), XIII (trans. T. Prieto), p. 106. Cf. M. Heidegger, "Vom Wesen des Grundes", p. 145. *Tr.*: pp. 53 and 55.

[22] Cf. my paper, "Moral Responsibility and Practice in the Life-World", *Analecta Husserliana*, ed. A.-T. Tymieniecka, XXII (1987), pp. 187 ff.

[23] St. Augustine, *op. cit.*

[24] *Ibid.*: "Qui sunt? Qui diligunt mundum: ipsi enim corde habitant in mundo". *Vide* M. Heidegger, "Vom Wesen des Grundes", *op. cit. Tr.*: p. 47. Cf. M. Heidegger, "Building Dwelling Thinking", *Poetry, Language, Thought*, p. 145: "The truck driver is *at home* on the highway, but he does not have his shelter there; the working woman is *at home* in the spinning mill, but does not have her dwelling place there; the chief engineer is *at home* in the power station, but he does not dwell there. The buildings house man. He inhabits them and yet does not dwell in them, when to dwell means merely that we take shelter in them". (The emphasis added is my responsibility.) In light of this, the radical sense of dwelling in the world is to love it and thereby to be at home in it.

[25] M. Heidegger, "Hölderlin und das Wesen der Dichtung", §2, p. 37 [35]. *Tr.*: p. 299.
[26] *Ibid.*, p. 37 [34]. *Tr.*: p. 298.
[27] *Ibid.*
[28] *Ibid.*, p. 38 [35]. *Tr.*: p. 299. (The emphasis added is my responsibility.)
[29] *Ibid.*, p. 300.
[30] F. Hölderlin, *Poems and Fragments*, p. 490.
[31] Cf. M. Heidegger, "Hölderlin und das Wesen der Dichtung", §4, p. 41 [38]. *Tr.*: p. 304.
[32] Cf. F. Hölderlin, *op. cit.*, p. 491.
[33] M. Heidegger, *loc. cit.*
[34] *Ibid.*
[35] Cf. M. Heidegger, ". . . Poetically Man Dwells . . .", p. 218: "Poetry does not fly above and surmount the earth in order to escape it and hover over it".
[36] M. Heidegger, "Hölderlin und das Wesen der Dichtung", p. 41 [38]. *Tr.*: p. 305.
[37] *Ibid.*
[38] *Ibid.* Cf. M. Heidegger, "Building Dwelling Thinking", i, p. 149. This brings things to their freedom (*Friede*), i.e., they are brought to the peace (*Friede*) of their ground from which they arose and continue to arise. "To free really means to spare. The sparing itself consists not only in the fact that we do not harm the one whom we spare. Real sparing is something *positive* when we leave something beforehand in its own nature, when we return it specifically to its being, when we 'free' it in the real sense of the word into a preserve of peace. To dwell, to be set at peace within the free, the preserve, the free sphere that safeguards each thing in its nature. *The fundamental character of dwelling is this sparing and preserving*". (*Ibid.*)
[39] M. Heidegger, "Hölderlin und das Wesen der Dichtung", §5, p. 45 [42]. *Tr.*: p. 310.
[40] M. Heidegger, "Building Dwelling Thinking", p. 147.
[41] *Ibid.*, p. 148.
[42] Cf. my paper, "The Problematicity of Life: Towards the Orteguian Notion of the Universal Spectator" in *José Ortega y Gasset*, Proceedings of the *Espectador Universal* International Interdisciplinary Conference at Hofstra University, ed. Nora de Marval-McNair (New York: Greenwood Press, 1987), p. 34.
[43] M. Heidegger, ". . . Poetically Man Dwells . . .", p. 227.
[44] *Vide* F. Hölderlin, *Sämtliche Werke*, ed. N. von Hellingrath *et al.*, VI, pp. 141 and 144. Cf. M. Heidegger, "Hölderlin und das Wesen der Dichtung", §5, p. 47 [43]. *Tr.*: p. 312.
[45] M. Heidegger, *ibid.* Unlike Heidegger, I am not going to dwell so much on the poet's mediating role between the gods and the people as on that which renders it possible. This choice means that, in what follows, I will endeavor to concentrate on the mutuality of poet and creative work, which is the correlation within which the poet *projects himself* between the heavenly ones and the mortals by bringing about, sustaining, and developing an other-worldly *in-between* for the sake of our life as a dwelling on this earth, namely, that intermediary domain which consists of poems in the making and the poetic worlds of which they are the *virtual* parts.
[46] M. Heidegger, ". . . Poetically Man Dwells . . .", p. 220.
[47] Cf. *ibid.*: ". . . man is allowed to look up, out of it [the realm of hardship], through it, *toward* the divinities". (The emphasis added is my responsibility.)

[48] Cf. M. Heidegger, "Building Dwelling Thinking", p. 146: "For building" – whether poetically or otherwise – "is not merely a means and a way toward dwelling – to build is in itself already to dwell". Or again: "Building and thinking" – including poetic creation as thinking and building – "are, each in its own way, inescapable for dwelling". (*Ibid.*, pp. 160–61.)
[49] Vide F. Hölderlin, "In lieblicher Bläue . . .", *op. cit.*; cf. *Poems and Fragments*, p. 601.
[50] M. Heidegger, ". . . Poetically Man Dwells . . .", pp. 220–21.
[51] *Ibid.*, p. 221.
[52] *Ibid.*, p. 220.
[53] *Ibid.*
[54] *Ibid.*
[55] *Ibid.*, p. 225.
[56] *Ibid.*, p. 221.
[57] *Ibid.*
[58] F. Hölderlin, "In lieblicher Bläue . . .", *Poems and Fragments*, p. 601.
[59] Cf. F. Hölderlin, *Sämtliche Werke*, Grosse Stuttgarter Ausgabe (Stuttgart, 1943–61), 2, 1, p. 210 *apud* M. Heidegger, ". . . Poetically Man Dwells . . .", p. 225:

> What is God? Unknown, yet
> Full of his qualities is the
> Face of the sky. For the lightnings
> Are the wrath of a god. The more something
> Is invisible, the more it yields to what's alien.

[60] M. Heidegger, *loc. cit.*, p. 222.
[61] For the concept of *Shekinah*, cf. Max Kadushin, *The Rabbinic Mind*, 2nd. ed. (New York: Blaisdell Publishing Co., 1965), pp. 222 ff.; for the notion of *kabod, doxa*, or glory, *vide "doxa"* in *Theological Dictionary of the New Testament*, ed. G. Kittel, trans. G. W. Bromiley (Grand Rapids, Michigan: Wm. B. Eerdmans Publishing Co., 1964), II, pp. 246–48. Cf. St. Anselm of Canterbury's concept of God as "quo maius cogitari non possit" or "that than which nothing greater can be conceived" in his *Proslogium, passim* and, particularly, in his "In Reply to Gaunilon's Answer in behalf of the Fool", ix, where he dealt with the conceivability of the inconceivable (St. Anselm, *Basic Writings*, ed. S. N. Deane, 2nd ed. [La Salle, Illinois: Open Court Publishing Co., 1968], p. 168). *Vide* M. Heidegger, ". . . Poetically Man Dwells . . .", p. 222.
[62] M. Heidegger, *loc. cit.*, p. 223.
[63] *Ibid.*
[64] Cf. Juan David Garcia Bacca, "Prólogo", i in Cicero, *Cuestiones académicas*, trans. A. Millares Carlo (Mexico: El Colegio de México/Fondo de Cultura Económica, 1944), pp. 10–11.
[65] For the concepts of allegory and symbol as used here, cf. M. Heidegger, "Der Ursprung des Kunstwerkes", *Holzwege* in *Gesamtausgabe*, Part I, Vol. V (1977), p. 4 [9]. *Tr.*: "The Origin of the Work of Art", *Poetry, Language, Thought*, pp. 19–20.
[66] Cf. M. Heidegger, "Building Dwelling Thinking", p. 153.
[67] *Ibid.*, p. 157.

⁶⁸ *Ibid.*
⁶⁹ *Ibid.*
⁷⁰ I have attempted to elaborate this point elsewhere by means of the phenomenological concept of "vacancy" or *Leerstelle* as understood by Schutz. (Cf. e.g., Alfred Schutz, *Reflections on the Problem of Relevance*, ed. R. M. Zaner [New Haven: Yale University Press, 1970], pp. 159 ff.) As formulated by him, this notion seems in principle adequate to account for continuing the constitution of any world of objects or events which, for whatever reason, remains incomplete (whether it be the earthly world, or "home base" as Schutz called it, or any of the derivative worlds, e.g., the worlds of mathematics or poetry), but it needs to be suitably transformed into the idea of *symbol* (in the sense assigned to the term here and by Schutz too: cf. *ibid.*, p. 107) so as to be applicable to a mediation between worlds. For the employment of this concept in an inter-worldly context, *vide* my study, "Dreaming and Wakefulness: On the Possibility of Crossing between Worlds", *Journal of Phenomenological Psychology*, XXI (1990), pp. 68 ff.; for its use primarily as an intra-worldly element of constitution of the other-worldly, see, my papers, "The Passion of Finitude and Poetic Creation: On Pedro Salinas's *El Contemplado*", *Analecta Husserliana*, XXVIII (1990), pp. 233 ff. and "The Swan and Erotic Love: Light, Color, and Myth in Ruben Darío's Poetics", *Analecta Husserliana*, XXXVIII (1992), pp. 207 ff.
⁷¹ M. Heidegger, "Building Dwelling Thinking", p. 161.
⁷² Cf. *supra*, p. 174 and n. 8.
⁷³ Cf. *supra*, p. 173 and n. 5.
⁷⁴ Cf. Jean-Paul Sartre, *L'Être et le néant* (Paris: Gallimard, 1943), Part IV, c. 2, p. 708.
⁷⁵ M. Heidegger, "Building Dwelling Thinking", p. 161.
⁷⁶ *Ibid.*
⁷⁷ Self-coincidence means here the awareness of one's lack of self-coincidence. As such, it is an *a priori* condition of happiness. Cf. e.g., José Ortega y Gasset, "Sobre la leyenda de Goya", §3, *Goya* in *Obras Completas* (Madrid: Revista de Occidente/Alianza Editorial, 1983), VII, p. 552 and "Goethe sin Weimar", iii, *Vives-Goethe* in *Obras Completas*, IX, p. 584.
⁷⁸ Cf. Plato, *Symposium*, 204 d–206 d.
⁷⁹ Cf. my paper, "Reflexiones para una antropología metafísica. En torno a la creación poética en *El Libro de Horas* de R. M. Rilke" in *Saints, Sovereigns, and Scholars*, Studies in Honor of Frederick D. Wilhelmsen, ed. R. A. Herrera *et al.* (Frankfurt: Peter Lang, 1993), pp. 281 ff.
⁸⁰ R. M. Rilke, *Das Stunden-Buch*, "Zweites Buch: Das Buch von der Pilgerschaft" in *Gesammelte Werke*, II, p. 232. (Henceforth all translations of Rilke's poems are my own.)
⁸¹ Cf. Heraclitus, fr. 18 in *Ancilla to the Pre-Socratic Philosophers*, trans. K. Freeman (Cambridge, Massachusetts: Harvard University Press, 1962), p. 26: "If one does not hope, one will not find the unhoped-for, since there is no trail leading to it and no path".
⁸² Cf. Plato, *Ion*, 534 c–d, trans. L. Cooper in *The Collected Dialogues of Plato*, ed. E. and H. Cairns (New York: Pantheon Books, 1961), p. 220: "Herein lies the reason why the deity has bereft . . . [the poets] of their senses, and uses them as ministers . . . ; it is in order that we listeners may know that it is not they who utter these precious

revelations while their mind is not within them, but it is the god himself who speaks, and through them becomes articulate to us".

[83] Cf. *"Kairos"* in *The Theological Dictionary of the New Testament*, III, pp. 456 ff.

[84] Cf. Plato, *Republic* VII, 518 a. Cf. M. Heidegger, "Hölderlin und das Wesen der Dichtung", §5, p. 44 [43]. *Tr.*: p. 309.

[85] Cf. M. Heidegger, *ibid.*, §2, pp. 35–36 [33–34] and §5, p. 43 [40]. *Tr.*: pp. 297–98 and 308.

[86] R. M. Rilke, *op. cit.*, p. 234.

[87] *Ibid.*, "Erstes Buch: Das Buch von mönchischen Leben", p. 177. In other words, by imprisoning himself in his own sense-perceptual, fruitive experience, he acts as if he were the absolute creator of his poems. When he does so, however, "even though each one from himself strives to part, / as from a dungeon which hates him and holds him in", he fails to gain his freedom (to create), unless and until he "perceives . . . a most wondrous thing in the world . . . [that] *every life is being lived* [by an-other]". (*Ibid.*, ii, p. 242.)

[88] *Ibid.*

[89] *Ibid.*

[90] *Ibid.*, i, p. 191.

[91] Cf. Plato, *Ion*, 553 e.

[92] R. M. Rilke, *op. cit.*, ii, p. 241.

[93] *Ibid.*, p. 242.

[94] Cf. *supra*, p. 188 and nn. 87 and 88.

[95] R. M. Rilke, *op. cit.*, ii, p. 242.

[96] *Ibid.*, i, p. 217.

[97] *Ibid.*, p. 238.

[98] *Ibid.*

[99] *Ruth* 1:16–17 in *The Jerusalem Bible*, pp. 339–40.

[100] Rilke's relevant verse, as quoted above (cf. p. 190 and n. 97), reads: *"Und ist ein Weib vor dir"*, which can be translated as it was in the text, or as "But she is a wife before you", given the two possible meanings of *Weib*. This outcome is not only the result of the free acceptance of God's free offer on the poet's part, but it continues to be contingent on it. The ambiguity of *Weib* is thus significant and productive.

[101] R. M. Rilke, *op. cit.*, "Drittes Buch: Das Buch von der Armut und vom Tode", p. 278. *Vide* my paper, "Reflexiones para una antropología metafísica", pp. 284 ff., for the grounds of the process leading to the unification of these two voices by means of the dialéctical love-relationship of ego and world that is worked out as self- and other-appropriation in reciprocity. Of special relevance for this purpose is the contrast between the notions of *ratio presentiae* and *ratio entis* which I refer to there. (Cf. *supra*, n. 79)

[102] R. M. Rilke, *op. cit.*

[103] Cf. *supra*, p. 173 and n. 5.

[104] R. M. Rilke, *op. cit.*, pp. 270–71.

[105] *Ibid.*, p. 271.

[106] *Ibid.*, ii, p. 253.

[107] *Ibid.*, iii, p. 273.

[108] Cf. *supra*, p. 173 and n. 2.

[109] Cf. *supra*, p. 177 and nn. 21, 23 and 24.

[110] St. Augustine, *Confessions*, xiii, 9, 10; trans. J. G. Pilkington (New York: Liveright Publishing Corp., 1949), p. 347.
[111] Cf. *supra*, p. 174 and n. 8.
[112] St. Augustine, *Enarrationes in Psalmos*, 31, ii, 5 *apud* Étienne Gilson, *The Christian Philosophy of Saint Augustine*, trans. L. E. M. Lynch (New York: Random House, 1960), pp. 135 and 310 (n. 32). Cf. St. Augustine, *Enarraciones sobre los Salmos*, I, Latin/Spanish ed., trans. B. Martínez Pérez in *Obras de San Agustin* (Madrid: Biblioteca de Autores Cristianos, 1964), XIX, p. 391.
[113] Cf. *Genesis* 3:5.
[114] R. M. Rilke, *op. cit.*, iii, p. 273.
[115] *Ibid.*, p. 274.
[116] *Ibid.*, ii, p. 252.
[117] *Ibid.*, i, p. 178.
[118] *Ibid.*, p. 176.
[119] *Ibid.*, i, p. 177.
[120] *Ibid.*, p. 186.
[121] Cf. *supra*, pp. 183 ff.
[122] R. M. Rilke, *op. cit.*, ii, p. 245. Cf. Charles Bigg, *The Christian Platonists of Alexandria* (Oxford: The Clarendon Press, 1968), p. 33: ". . . God is . . . above time, for time is but the register of the fluctuations of the world, and God when he made the world made time also".
[123] St. Thomas Aquinas, *Summa Theologica*, I, q. 9, a. 1, "Responsio", Blackfriars ed. (London: Eyre & Spottiswoode), II (trans. T. McDermott; 1964), p. 126: ". . . esse purum actum absque permixtione alicujus potentiae . . ." *Tr.*: p. 127.
[124] R. M. Rilke, *op. cit.*, ii, pp. 239–40.
[125] Cf. *supra*, pp. 183 ff.
[126] Cf. *supra*, p. 191 and n. 98.
[127] R. M. Rilke, *op. cit.*, p. 238.
[128] *Ibid.*
[129] *Ibid.*
[130] Cf. *supra*, p. 191 and n. 98.
[131] *Job* 1:21 in *The Jerusalem Bible*, p. 730.
[132] R. M. Rilke, *op. cit.*, p. 239.
[133] *John* 1:10 in *The New Testament* of *The Jerusalem Bible*, p. 146.
[134] R. M. Rilke, *op. cit.*
[135] Cf. *supra*, p. 199.
[136] R. M. Rilke, *op. cit.*
[137] It is interesting that Rilke did not include the sounds of mere Nature in his exemplification of the actuality thereof. All the instances mentioned by him are human, whether natural (tongues) or man-made (as produced by violins or horns) or in-between (songs). This may well signify that the sounds of mere Nature, on their way to being ransomed and constituted by the poet into offerings, are to be mediated by human sounds. Moreover, Rilke gave expression to the condition that would tender them suitable to being offerings by means of the word *Edelstein*, here translated as "jewel" and literally meaning "noble or precious stone". Yet the choice of "jewel" is neither purely arbitrary nor just determined by custom; rather, it is deliberate, for, in my opinion, it allows, in a

different but connected sense, the release of Rilke's poetic-linguistic purpose in a clearer fashion. Since the locution "jewel" is etymologically related to the Latin words *iocus* (play) and *gaudium* (joy), one could then say that the transformation in question amounts to the symbolic freeing of the things and events of this world from the fetters of necessity and the incidence of contingency, so as to allow them to enter the "middle earth", wherein they would abide in the pure and active dis-play of what they are for their own sake and for the sake of one another (perfection and unity), and as the fitting match for our re-joicing in them.

[138] Cf. Aristotle, *Nicomachean Ethics*, VI, 3, 1140 a 1–5 and 11–20.

[139] Cf. Jacques Maritain, *L'intuition créatrice dans l'art et la poésie*, c. 4, §6 in Jacques et Raïssa Maritain, *Oeuvres Complètes*, ed. J.-M. Allion *et al.* (Fribourg: Éditions Universitaires; Paris: Éditions St. Paul), X (1985), pp. 246 ff.

[140] José Ferrater Mora, "Obra literaria", *Diccionario de Filosofía* (Buenos Aires: Editorial Sudamericana, 1965), II, p. 315, col. 3.

[141] R. M. Rilke, *op. cit.*, ii, p. 240.

[142] Cf. *supra*, p. 199. and n. 129.

[143] I am taking this term to signify the virtue of the practical intellect when it is geared to the transformation of the outer world. Hence it denotes not only the crafts, but poetry and the fine arts too. Cf. Aristotle, *Metaphysics* I, 1, 981 a 6 and a 25–b 26; *Nichomachean Ethics*, II, 4, 1105 a 26–b 25.

[144] Cf. Aristotle, *Physics*, II, 2, 194 a 21–22.

[145] St. Thomas Aquinas, *In I et II libros Posteriorum Analyticorum*, Leonine ed. (Rome, 1882), 1, 1a.

[146] Cf. M. Heidegger, "Vom Wesen des Grundes", p. 142 [38]. *Tr.*: p. 49.

[147] M. Heidegger, *Einführung in die Metaphysik*, c. 1, §3 in *Gesamtausgabe*, Part II, Vol. XL (1983), p. 17 [11]. *Tr.: An Introduction to Metaphysics*, trans. R. Manheim (New Haven: Yale University Press, 1959), p. 14.

[148] *Ibid.*, [12]. *Tr.*: pp. 14–15. Cf. p. 68 [48]. *Tr.*: pp. 63–64.

[149] Naturally, "poet" is here taken in the formal or restricted sense of the word.

[150] Cf. *supra*, p. 199.

[151] R. M. Rilke, *op. cit.*, i, p. 184.

[152] *Ibid.*, ii, p. 241.

DAVID SCHUR

A PHENOMENAL HIDING PLACE:
HOMER, HERACLITUS, HEIDEGGER

As the fifth book of Homer's *Odyssey* comes to a close, Odysseus is stranded on the island of the Phaiakians, and he seeks shelter before nightfall. Near the shore there is a wood where Odysseus hides under some trees. The description of this hiding place merits careful examination. The wood is said to be "in [the] periphenomenal", but what that means is not immediately clear. In this paper, I shall attempt to confront the strange circumstances of Odysseus' hiding place, showing that it is paradoxically also a place of manifestation. Reference to Martin Heidegger's interpretation of the Greek thinker Heraclitus will aid in the understanding of such a paradox.

Odysseus' hiding place is described in the context of survival. Book 5 of the *Odyssey* begins with Athena renewing her efforts on the hero's behalf. He has been stuck on Kalypso's island for seven years, and Athena complains to Zeus that Odysseus' own people have forgotten him. Indeed, the *Odyssey* can be read as the ordeal of a hero seeking to remember his homeland and to be remembered by it. In other words, oblivion is a powerful threat to Odysseus' survival. Early in the epic, Athena makes this point explicitly. She tells Zeus that Kalypso holds and charms Odysseus "so that he will forget Ithaka" (1.57). The problem of oblivion runs in both directions – if Odysseus forgets, remaining with Kalypso, he will be forgotten, eclipsed. Kalypso's name itself, from the verb *kaluptô* (to conceal), raises this concern.[1]

The risk of oblivion continues after Odysseus has left Kalypso's island, however. Poseidon, who sees Odysseus sailing toward the Phaiakians, creates a dangerous storm by stirring up winds and waves. During this storm, the threat of drowning is described in terms of concealment and submergence. Two main verbs occur repeatedly in this episode: *kaluptô* and *duô*. Concealment is conveyed by the verb *kaluptô*. With various prefixes, the verb *duô* describes either submergence or emergence.

When the storm begins, Poseidon conceals (verb = *kaluptô*) the land and water in clouds (5.293–294). And when Odysseus first comes near to drowning, the verb *duô* is used to describe his emergence out of the water (5.322). Even after Odysseus has been helped by the goddesses Ino

213

and Athena, the danger of eclipse, which was so great on Calypso's island, is still very real. We read about how "a great wave concealed [verb = *kaluptô*]" Odysseus (5.435). But at this point, Athena saves Odysseus from destruction, and he is seen "emerging up out of [verb = *ex-ana-duô*] the wave: (5.438). So we observe that the physical dangers of being eclipsed by the storm and submerged in the water strengthen the general threat of oblivion which Odysseus faces.

Once Odysseus has arrived on land, his stature is at its lowest point. Alone and naked, he hides from wild animals and the elements, not from military enemies or monsters. And this is when Odysseus hides in a wood which is "in the periphenomal". Following Richmond Lattimore's translation, the wood is "in a conspicuous place". I already suggested that this is a strange place, and I did so for the following two reasons. First, it is noteworthy that Odysseus should have to hide himself when he has just barely escaped being hidden. Second, a hiding place is usually the opposite of a conspicuous place. Now I shall consider these two points in more detail.

If we are right in linking submergence and concealment to oblivion, then it is striking that Odysseus must go into concealment after arriving unharmed on land. The fact that the same two verbs which characterized Odysseus' ordeal at sea occur again in the depiction of his hiding on land reinforces this impression. Odysseus hides between a pair of trees which are so closely intertwined that not even the sun's rays can penetrate them. We are told that he "submerged under [verb = *hupo-duô*]" the trees (5.481–482). In a simile, Odysseus is at this point compared to an ember hidden (*kruptô*) in ashes: "so Odysseus hid himself [verb = *kaluptô*] in the leaves" (5.491). Although we may tend to imagine that Odysseus is like a spark waiting to be reborn, his ash-like bed of concealment is also strongly evocative of a grave.

This is clearly a point of crisis in the hero's struggle to overcome oblivion and to survive. It is a moment of intense concealment. Yet, knowing that Odysseus does survive, we may wonder whether this is also a moment of intense manifestation. One fact which supports such a strange conclusion is found in the next book of the *Odyssey*, book six, where Odysseus emerges from his hiding place. The text which tells us that "divine Odysseus emerged from [*hupoduô*] the trees" (6.127) contains a combination of verb and prefix, *hupo + duô*, which is fundamentally the same as that used of his submergence. So, depending on the grammatical case of the word used for trees, the verb *hupoduô* indicates that Odysseus either "plunges beneath" or "rises out from under" them. In a context where the direction of movement has repeatedly meant the difference between life and death, Odysseus' hiding place, composed as it is of two intertwined trees, is remarkably bipolar or ambivalent.

Is this ambivalence present in Homer's use of the word "periphenomenal"? I believe so. Ordinarily, the word periphenomenal would seem to mean either "very conspicuous" or "seen from all around". Accordingly, a wood located "in the periphenomenal" would be, to quote from the Homeric lexicons, in a "clearing" or in a "conspicuous place".[2] When today we try to reconstruct the Homeric geography, however, the notion of a wood in a clearing is a bit odd. In fact, one of the lexicons suggests "bordering on a clearing" as an alternative. Other comparably hidden places in the *Odyssey*, such as Kirke's house or that of the swineherd, constitute clearings in woods rather than woods in clearings. But the only other occurrence in Homer of the specific adjective "periphenomenal" is in the *Iliad*, where a wounded warrior is compared to a tree falling on the top of a periphenomenal mountain (Il.13.179). The difference is great between such a mighty and glorious tree, visible from all around, and the wood where Odysseus sleeps.

But even if we were to grow comfortable with the idea of a wood in a clearing, it is important to observe that the "periphenomenal" is, in this case, a place in itself. Odysseus does not find a periphenomenal wood, nor a wood in a periphenomenal place. Instead, the wood is "*in* [the] periphenomenal". At first glance, the wood is in a place wholly characterized by manifestation. But because the wood is not periphenomenal but rather *in* the periphenomenal, we should recognize that the periphenomenal is not simply the outward aspect of a place which is inwardly concealing. Instead, this one place both manifests and conceals. Having already observed the concurrence here of opposites such as oblivion and survival or submergence and emergence, we are now in a position to come to terms with the dual nature of this place.

Well, perhaps it is not such a strange place after all. At a critical turning point in Odysseus' wanderings, a single place might easily combine contradictory aspects of his transformation. And while submersion in the sea could have obliterated our hero, his bed of leaves is all the more secure by way of contrast. It is at this point, however, that I would like to look at the passage from a different direction, turning to Heidegger's interpretation of an early Greek thinker for a fresh perspective.

Heidegger's approach to the Greeks is instructive. In general, he looks to Greek thinkers (especially Anaximander, Heraclitus and Parmenides, but also Homer) for glimpses of the earliest and purest manifestations of Western thought. Heidegger sometimes uses the terms "pre-phenomenological" and "pre-ontological" to describe such early accounts of humankind's relation with Being, in which fundamental phenomena are revealingly but not thematically discussed.[3] Examples from the earliest Greeks are, in this sense, of special interest for Heidegger; they have not been stamped by the subsequently unavoidable tradition of Western metaphysics.

More specifically, Heidegger's interpretation of Heraclitus raises points of great relevance to our current investigation. In the fragments of Heraclitus, Heidegger discerns a paradoxical version of oblivion which is akin to that seen in the *Odyssey*. Heidegger's analysis of the words *kaluptô* and *duô*, as they occur in Heraclitus' fragments, will add strength to our focus on submergence and concealment in the Homeric passage. And in the light of this strengthened focus, Homer's account of the periphenomenal may allow us to peek into a very early phenomenology.

Given the scope of this paper, my discussion of Heidegger will be limited to a particular aspect of his interpretation. In his analysis of three important fragments of Heraclitus, Heidegger finds a paradoxical concurrence of upward and downward movements. These movements up and down characterize Heidegger's interpretation of the Greek word *alêtheia*. *Alêtheia* is usually translated as "truth", but Heidegger adopts the translation *Unverborgenheit* or "unconcealment", claiming that this translation better conveys a fundamental relation between *alêtheia* and *lêthê* or "oblivion".[4]

My review of these three analyses will be very abbreviated, the point being to expose Heidegger's emphasis on upward and downward movement. In lectures dating from 1943, Heidegger claims that the fragment ordinarily translated "Nature loves to hide itself" describes a pair of simultaneous movements. The fragment falls into two parts. Heidegger identifies "ascent" (*das Aufgehen*) in the nature part and "descent" (*das Untergehen* [GA 55.111]) in the hiding part.[5] And so the fragment comes to say that these two opposites are "the same" (*das Selbe*); "Accordingly", says Heidegger, "ascent is, and indeed precisely insofar as it is ascent, descent."[6]

Especially relevant for us is the way that Heidegger interprets the Greek notion of "hiding" as a downward movement of concealment. The verb *kruptô*, seen earlier in the simile comparing Odysseus to an ember, in this sense describes submergence. Moreover, this downward movement of hiding is inseparable from an upward manifestation. Nature (if we can call it that) is an up-and-down-going, a revealing concealment. To use terms already applied to Homer, submergence and upward emergence are said by Heidegger's Heraclitus to be the same.

Heidegger treats two other key fragments similarly. One of these refers obliquely to Apollo, saying: "The lord whose oracle is in Delphi neither speaks, nor hides [*kruptô*] but indicates" (frg. 93). The verb "to hide" (*kruptô*) in this sentence is a form of the same verb found in the nature fragment. While nature loves to hide itself, Apollo does not simply hide. Etymological considerations lead Heidegger to give the verb "to speak" the meaning "to reveal and to make manifest" (*entbergen und offenbarmachen*), since, he says, "gathering stands here in opposition to concealing".[7] So just as the nature fragment unites contrasting movements upward and downward, this one contrasts manifestation with concealment. That this contrast is another paradoxical concurrence of opposites is seen in Heidegger's essay "On the Essence and Concept of *Phusis*". There Heidegger writes that "the oracle does not precisely reveal nor simply conceal, rather it indicates, which means: it reveals in concealing and conceals in revealing".[8] For Heidegger, the nature fragment and the oracle fragment say much the same thing.

Heidegger gives another fragment a primary position, not only in his interpretive scheme but also in Western thought. The fragment asks the question: "How could someone escape the notice of that which never descends?" The "descent" here is conveyed by the verb *duô*. The verb "escape the notice of" involves the notion of oblivion or *lêthê*, and it is this etymological connection which allows Heidegger to discern in the fragment a radical version of *alêtheia*. Heidegger makes this connection as early as *Being and Time*, but it is in lectures of the early 1940's that the paradoxical up-and-down-going of *alêtheia* comes to the fore.[9]

Heidegger stresses that the verb "escape the notice of" (*lanthanô*) concerns concealment and gives us insight into *alêtheia*. At the same time, "The Greek manner of thinking 'descent'", claims Heidegger, "has its essence from *going into a concealment*".[10] By balancing "that which never descends [*duô*]" against the impossibility of concealment (implied by the question), Heidegger finds a dynamic comparable to the way in which nature (up-going) shares in concealment (down-going). Indeed, one half of the question recalls the up/down contrast of the nature fragment; and the other half corresponds to the unconcealment/concealment contrast of the oracle fragment.

There is yet another Heraclitus fragment which simplifies this complex of interpretations. It says that "the way up and down is one and the same" (frg. 60). Although Heidegger does not, to my knowledge, ever refer explicitly to this fragment, it is implicitly crucial to his general view of Heraclitus and of *alêtheia*. And with this view of *alêtheia*, we may now return to Homer.

In the Homeric *Odyssey*, there is an observable tension between oblivion and survival (survival in terms not only of physical endurance but also of heroic or epic renown). In book 5 of the *Odyssey*, repeated submersions threaten to obliterate Odysseus. The last of these is not at sea, however. Odysseus submerges himself under some trees which are in a wood which is in the periphenomenal.

Heidegger's version of *alêtheia* is a phenomenology which sheds light on Odysseus' periphenomenal hiding place. When I say "a phenomenology", I have in mind Heidegger's explanation of "phenomenon" and "logos" given in the introduction to *Being and Time*. There Heidegger says that phenomenology has as its object what is hidden.[11] The upward movement of *alêtheia* corresponds to the process of unconcealment which in this sense characterizes phenomenology.

The hiding place into which Odysseus descends and out of which he emerges is indeed an exceptionally phenomenal place. Hence the same verb (*hupo-duô*) aptly describes both movements, reminding us of an intrinsic relation between oblivion and truth. However unconscious, unthematic, or pre-ontological Homer's description of that hiding place might be, it shows us a place where the way up and down is one and the same.

Harvard University

APPENDIX

EXAMPLE SHEET

kaluptô = "to conceal"
kruptô = "to hide"
duô = "to enter, submerge"
hupo + duô = "to submerge under; to emerge from under"
alêtheia = "truth" or "unconcealment"

"Now the great sea covered [*kaluptô*] him over, and Odysseus would have perished . . . , had not grey-eyed Athena given him forethought. Emerging out of [*ex-ana-duô*] the wave . . . , he swam on along" (Od.5.435-439).

"He submerged under [*hupo-duô*] these [trees]" (Od.5.481-482).

"Just as someone hides (*en-kruptô*) an ember in black ash . . . so Odysseus hid himself [*kaluptô*] in the leaves" (Od.5.491).

"So speaking, diving Odysseus emerged from under [*hupo-duô*] the trees" (Od.6.127).

Heraclitus: "Nature loves to hide [*kruptô*] itself" (frg. 123).

Heraclitus: "The lord whose oracle is in Delphi neither speaks, nor hides [*kruptô*] but indicates" (frg. 93).

Heraclitus: "How could someone escape the notice of [*lanthanô*] that which never descends [*duô*]?" (frg. 16).

Heraclitus: "The way up and down is one and the same" (frg. 60).

NOTES

[1] "A specific act of divine memory saves Odysseus from the concealment and deathlike forgetfulness in which he lies in Kalypso's (= the Concealer's) house"; "By Athena's act of *mnêmê* [memory], Odysseus comes to life as a *literary* character" (Pucci, p. 20, 21n).

[2] Cunliffe and Autenrieth respectively.

[3] Heidegger refers to Homer as our "oldest realm of evidence" ("im altesten Zeugnisbereich, bei Homer" [GA 55.363]) in questions of fundamental Greek words.

[4] Heidegger's most extensive interpretations of Heraclitus are found in three lecture courses given in 1942-1944 (GA 54 and 55); in a section of a course on Hölderlin (GA 39); in the essays called "Aletheia" and "Logos" (VA); and in the seminar published under the title *Heraklit*.

[5] Speaking of Heraclitus Fragment 16 in the same course, Heidegger says "Descent is a becoming concealed and a hiding; in Greek: *lanthanô, lathô*" (*Das "Untergehen" ist ein Verborgenwerden und Verbergung, griechisch* λανθάνω, λάθω [GA 55.50]).

[6] "Danach ist das Aufgehen, und zwar gerade, insofern es ein Aufgehen ist, ein Untergehen" (GA 55.116-118).

[7] "Sammeln steht hier im Gegensatz zum Verbergen" (EM 179).

[8] ". . . das Orakel *ent*birgt nicht geradezu, noch verbirgt es einfachhin, sondern zeigt an, das will sagen: es entbirgt indem es verbirgt, und verbirgt, indem es entbirgt" (Wgm 277).

[9] Cf. SZ §44.

[10] "Das griechisch gedachte 'Untergehen' hat sein Wesen aus dem *Eingehen in eine Verbergung*" (GA 55.49).

[11] SZ §7.

REFERENCES

Autenrieth, Georg. *A Homeric Dictionary*. Trans. and ed. Robert P. Keep. New York: Harper & Brothers, 1883.

Cunliffe, John Richard. *A Lexicon of the Homeric Dialect*. 2nd ed. Norman: U. of Oklahoma P., 1963.
Diels, Hermann and Walther Kranz, eds. *Die Fragmente der Vorsokratiker*, 6th ed. Berlin: Weidmann, 1952.
Heidegger, Martin. *Gesamtausgabe*. Frankfurt am Main: Vittorio Klostermann, 1976– .
Heidegger, Martin. *Sein und Zeit*. 15th ed. Tübingen: Max Niemeyer, 1986.
Heidegger, Martin. *Vorträge und Aufsätze*. Pfullingen: Neske, 1954.
Heidegger, Martin. *Wegmarken*. 2nd ed. Frankfurt am Main: Vittorio Klostermann, 1978.
Homer. *Opera*. Eds. David Monro and Thomas Allen. 5 vols. Oxford: Oxford U.P., 1912–1920.
Lattimore, Richmond, trans. *The Odyssey of Homer*. New York: Harper & Row, 1965.
Liddell, H. G., R. Scott, and H. Stuart Jones, eds. *Greek-English Lexicon*. 9th ed. Oxford: Oxford U.P., 1940.
Pucci, P. *Odysseus Polytropos: Intertextual Readings in the Odyssey and the Iliad*. Ithaca: Cornell U.P., 1987.

CHRISTINE RAFFINI

THE PASSION FOR PLACE: MEDIEVAL AND RENAISSANCE RE-CREATIONS OF PARADISE

Rabelais's utopia, the Abbey of Thélème, is a model of restrictiveness and exclusivity, off-limits to the greater part of mankind. Even before it is built, Frère Jan excludes the poor, the sick, the old, the homeless, the illiterate, and even the irascible. Women are permitted but, he explains, they must be "belles, bien formées, bien naturées" and the men likewise, "beaux, bien formés et bien naturés – beautiful, well-formed and good-natured.[1] All the inhabitants, we learn,

> had been so well educated that there wasn't one among them who could not read, write, sing, play on harmonious instruments, speak five or six languages, and write easy poetry and clear prose in any and all of them.[2]

An army of artisans, hairdressers, perfumers, tailors, jewelers, weavers, upholsterers serve these gifted *érudits* in their opulent surroundings – grander even than Chambord or Chantilly with:

> ... nine thousand three hundred and thirty-two suites, each furnished with an antichamber, a private reading room, a dressing room, and a small personal chapel, and ... its own huge hall. Between each tower, in the middle of the main building, was a spiral staircase, its stairs made of crystal porphyry and red numidian marble and green marble struck through with red and white, all exactly twenty-two feet wide and three fingers thick, there being twelve stairs between each landing. Further: each landing had a beautiful double arch, in Greek style, thus allowing light to flood through, and also framing an entry way into overhanging private rooms, each of them just as broad as the stairway itself.[3]

The private rooms and suites are equally impressive:

> ... hung with a wide variety of tapestries, which were regularly changed to suit the changing seasons. The floors were covered with green cloth, the beds with embroidery. Every dressing room had a mirror of Venetian crystal, framed in fine gold, decorated around with pears, and so exceedingly large that one could in truth see one's self in it.[4]

Thélème, represented as the property of an exclusive (and non-existent) élite, negates at the outset the possibility of happiness for most of the human race, and, with its emphasis on worldly magnificence, seems to deny as well the existence of heaven.

Concurrently, and in a far less literary context, dreams of real and possible happiness continued to thrive. Safeguarded by untraveled distances, compounded of desire, legends of Cathay, the land of Cocaigne, the voyages of Saint Brendan and Sir John Maundeville and the kingdom of Prester John, inspired belief. During the Middle Ages and the Renaissance, people not only believed, they repeatedly tried to reach these fabled places, and, that failing, they directed their efforts to the recreation of paradise – to bringing it to life in the strictest sense. Medieval legends, the medieval theater, the voyages of discovery and even the great botanical gardens of the Renaissance are at once the evidence and the result of the passion for place, the longing for inaccessibly remote kingdoms and dreams of gardens that never were.

Not passion, but hunger, plain and simple, seems to have been the inspiration of early medieval legends. As Gurevich notes, the author of *The Voyage of Saint Brendan* is preoccupied on every page with the idea of an abundant supply of food and drink. In this early sixth-century narrative:

The Promised Land abounds with every blessing and there is a land of eternal flowering and fruiting; neither hunger nor fatigue is experienced in it. Sheep there are the size of bulls and grapes the size of apples, and the fish are such that the monks thought one of them was an island. On one island they found a monastery whose inhabitants did not age, suffer from illness or cold, or at any time lack for good water and bread, which was supplied to them mysteriously from an unknown source. On another island, food, drink, and rest awaited the sailors, and their table was laid miraculously for three days.[5]

Saint Brendan's Promised Land, part of a vision of the next world, lies, however, perilously close to hell. The monks wandering there are constantly tempted by devils and run the risk of perishing in flames.

The kingdom of Prester John is not only perfectly safe, it is accessible in the waking state. The legend of John's kingdom spread in the twelfth century in the form of a letter which had been translated from Latin into a number of vernacular tongues. A letter from John, "the sovereign Christian, king of kings", greeted Manuel Komnenos, emperor of the East. In 1177, Pope Alexander III composed a bull addressed "to his very dear son, John, the illustrious and magnificent king of the Indes".[6] Almost a century later, the French king Louis IX and his chronicler, Joinville, following the example of Marco Polo, went directly in search of the marvelous kingdom. In the fifteenth century, the Portuguese prince Henry the Navigator made every effort to reach Prester

John, "with whom he hoped to plan a crusade that would clear the Moslems from North Africa and the holy land once and for all."[7]

Century after century, popes, kings and commoners dreamed of discovering the lands of Prester John, located, they supposed, somewhere in Africa – or perhaps in the Middle East. According to legend, John is the richest, most powerful, and most generous monarch on earth. In his kingdom, no one is ever cold or hungry or poor. Thanks to a celestial fountain, whose water has the flavor of "all the spices of the world, but successively",[8] no one ever gets sick or old. Should travelers require, the water will cure all diseases and restore youth as well. Not only the water, but the stones have marvelous properties: some will make you invisible while others will cause everyone to love you.

In the fiery regions of the kingdom, only salamanders can survive, but when removed from the flames they die, and from their skin people make a fireproof cloth, very beautiful and delicate to the touch, which can be easily washed in flames. There are other extraordinary creatures, but none of them is poisonous or harmful. The citizens, likewise, are as virtuous and kind as they are happy. No one is a thief, a flatterer, an adulterer or a traitor.

The king's splendid palace is made entirely of precious stones, illuminated by carbuncles which shine day and night. On a column just outside the palace, there is an enormous mirror which shows everything that is happening in every part of the world. Simply by looking in this mirror, you can learn everything, and because of it, the kingdom has no need of spies. Every day King John invites thirty thousand commoners inside his palace to dine at his gold and ivory tables.

Prester John's kingdom is open to all who are able to find it. In its inclusiveness, it reflects people's shared fears and hopes, showing, on the one hand, their dread of duplicity, greed, inequality, old age, disease, poisonous creatures, while, on the other, revealing the desire for inexhaustible abundance, health, youth, friendship, security, as well as beautiful and durable clothing and knowledge of the world. Allusions to the kingdom's abundant food supply recall St Brendan's voyage, while the sumptuous displays of luxury are reminiscent of Thélème; yet, in this hedonistic heaven on earth, travel, work, and even study are superfluous.

Gossouin's *Image du monde* (1256) insists upon the necessity of study. Happiness is found in erudition. The ancient wise men, he explains, were astronomers: their life was more frugal and healthier than ours, and for two thousand years they labored patiently to perfect the seven liberal arts. Many died, martyrs of wisdom, and thanks to them, we have our knowledge. And if in our day we expect to surpass them, we must equal them in selflessness – difficult, the author warns, for in our times people think only of money.[9]

Like other *images du monde* of the period, Gossuin's book is a kind of encyclopedia of science, medecine, divination, ethics, theology, cosmology and geology. The earth is round, he explains, and, like an egg, it is composed of four layers, each of which corresponds to one of the four elements. Beyond the layer of fire which encircles the layer of air, there is ether "so resplendent and pure that it offers no obstacle to light. The angels cross through it when they come to bring messages to earth, but the eye of man could never stand the brilliance they bring with them, and this is why one usually sees angels only in dreams."[10] His description of the terrestrial paradise is consistent with the others of the period. It is found in Asia "where the famous Tree of Life stands, its entrance cut off by a curtain of flames which rises to the clouds."[11]

The notion of an earthly paradise, an inaccessible garden of perpetual spring, predates the Christian era. Homer alludes to the gardens of Alcinoüs, an immense orchard where the fruit "never fails nor runs short, winter and summer alike, it comes at all seasons of the year, and there is never a time when the West Wind's breath is not assisting, here the bud, and here the ripening fruit; so that pear after pear, apple after apple, cluster on cluster of grapes and fig upon fig are always coming to perfection."[12]

The Christian paradises of the Middle Ages continued to be reminiscent of the classical *locus amoenus*. Ovidian, Horatian, Claudian and, most especially, Virgilian accounts influence Christian writers, who, however, prefer to place paradise on a mountain top so high that it touches the sphere of the moon. In the center of the garden stands the Tree of Life and the four rivers flow out of it.

One of these evocations, a long poem by Alain de Lille written in 1183, is remarkable for its elaborate detail: "flowers, breeze, eternal springtime, all kinds of fruit and trees, singing birds and sweet water – all exist in harmony." In the midst is the Palace of Nature "which is on tall columns, gleaming with gems, burning with gold, and shimmering with silver."[13]

Such allusions are commonplace in both the Middle Ages and the

Renaissance. Milton, for example, puts emphasis on fragrance. The pure air inspires:

> Vernal delight and joy, able to drive
> All sadness but despair: now gentle gales
> Fanning their odoriferous wings dispense
> Native perfumes, and whisper whence they stole
> Those balmy spoils. As when to them who sail
> Beyond the Cape of Hope, and now are past
> Mozambic, off at sea north-east winds blow
> Sabaean odours from the spicy shore of Arabie the blest . . .[14]

Poets took their inspiration from the navigators and explorers who continued to search for this rich paradise. Long before they began circling the globe, people had had in their possession "maps and treatises describing its position, now east, now west, now on an island, now behind or upon a mountain – but always remote, always inaccessible."[15] Then, with the age of exploration "the Garden of Eden was removed from a distant past to a distant present, from something remote in time to something far away, but still conceivably discoverable."[16]

Christopher Columbus, like so many of the navigators who would follow him, was convinced that he had discovered Eden. Some historians suggest that its discovery was the real purpose of his voyage. One of his men, Luis de Torres, was assigned to "a reconnaissance mission . . . chosen because as a converted Jew he knew Hebrew, Arabic and Chaldaic – the languages that would certainly be required in these circumstances, and in describing the flora and the fauna, and the manners of the inhabitants, Columbus had recourse to the language of Ovid's description of the golden age."[17] With each successive voyage, Columbus became more convinced that Eden lay just below the equator in the extreme Orient which he had reached by sailing West:

Eden had a temperate climate; and the fleet had encountered no hot weather since escaping from the doldrums. In Eden grew every good plant and pleasant fruit; and had he not found strange but delicious fruits on the shores of Paria? . . . 'And a river went out of Eden to water the garden; and from thence it was parted, and became four' . . . had not his men reported four rivers at the head of the gulf? . . . Pierre d'Ailly said that the Terrestrial Paradise was lofty 'as if the earth there touched the moon'. And Columbus's observations of Polaris on the voyage proved that he was sailing uphill.[18]

Fernandez de Navarrete, another crew member, recorded Columbus's reactions, chronicling:

The freshness and beauty of the trees, the clearness of the water and the birds, made it all so delightful that he wished never to leave them. He said to the men who were with him that to give a true relation to the Sovereigns of the things they had seen, a thousand tongues would not suffice, nor his hand to write it, for that it was like a scene of enchantment.

And later, in a letter:

The lands are high, and there are many very lofty mountains . . . all most beautiful, of thousand different shapes, accessible and covered with trees of a thousand kinds of such great height that they seemed to reach the skies. . . . Some were in bloom, others bearing fruit. . . . There were palm trees of six or eight kinds, wonderful in their beautiful variety . . . fruits, and grasses, trees and plants filled us with admiration.[19]

The writer's enthusiasm shines through the words, conveying a freshness and vividness that is often missing from the purely literary evocations of this period.

After Columbus, explorers and geographical writers tend to express themselves in less optimistic terms, evincing rather "homesickness for the perfection that might have been possible without the meanness of men."[20] For many of these authors, the Garden of Eden like "the golden age was not only the vision of an ideal, but the literary expression of an experienced loss."[21] Like Columbus, many of them believed fervently in the perfection they had discovered which, upon their return, seemed to pale. Others watched with dismay as their newly discovered worlds were corrupted by European contact. One of them writes:

The people of Iceland seek only what nature grants them. For instead of cities they have mountains and fountains for their delight. They are indeed fortunate, all the more because no one envies their poverty. But the English and Danish merchants will not leave these poor people in peace and cannot tolerate that they are content with what they have. Thus, in order to trade with them for fish, which [the Icelanders] have in great abundance, they associate with them and in trading they have brought with them all kinds of vices from home.[22]

Elsewhere, these geographical authors seldom display sensitivity, evincing instead an indifference which borders on cruelty. Their unfeeling accounts of events and episodes strike us today as heart-rending or heroic, and, as Atkinson observes, their lack of pity was accompanied by a singular absence of imagination and intellectual curiosity. The first wave of geographical authors "embellished less than their literary ancestors and less than their descendants."[23]

Nonetheless, optimism and the passion for distant places of perfection had not yet been extinguished. When at last it was realized that neither Columbus nor his followers had discovered paradise, or even Cathay, a new attitude arose. Instead of searching for the Garden, people thought of re-creating it, of quite literally making heaven on earth. In a kind of magic spell wherein living plants took the place of words, the great botanic gardens of the Renaissance in Padua, Leyden and Montpellier were painstakingly laid out and assembled with Eden as their model:

> For the first time since the Fall, thanks to the discovery of America, a truly encyclopedic collection of plants could now be made that would offer a complete guide to the many faces of the Creator. Since each family of plants was thought to represent a specific act of creation, that scholar would come to understand God who best found room in a *pulvillus* for every *genus*. This, then, was the Garden of recreation into which the wise man would retire, and shut the door upon the busy, disfigured world outside. . . . Thus it was that, in a Botanic Garden, beside the fountain in the middle, a man could enter into communion with what was green and full of sap, recover his innocence, and shed his fear of decay.[24]

The discovery of the New World even permitted a reinterpretation of the Book of Genesis. It was believed that God in the age of discovery had finally seen fit to reveal the hidden part of creation, and from it, the Garden of Eden could be recreated "by gathering the scattered pieces of the jigsaw together in one place into an epitome or an encyclopedia of creation."[25] It seemed that God's creation had been broken apart rather than poisoned at the moment of the Fall. It followed then that if all the plants and animals of the earth could be gathered back together and arranged in a certain order as a kind of vast book, the world would at last be restored to its prelapsarian harmony. Men and beasts would live together forever after in peace, and would even be able to understand one another.

A complex geometrical arrangement formed the groundwork for spiritual understanding and harmony. The four corners of the botanical gardens were a microcosmic representation of the four continents of the world:

> In his account of the garden at Padua, Porro drew attention to the fact that the plants which came from the East (mentioning the cedar, the laurel and the myrtle among others) were to be planted on the eastern side of the garden. . . . [In] the gardens of Renaissance princes . . . trees and bushes might be laid out in rings to represent the orbits of the planets, and waterworks installed to illustrate the laws of hydraulics and mechanics – all revelatory of the laws of nature and the works of God.[26]

To an even greater degree than these carefully recreated gardens, the medieval theater, like the greatest medieval architecture, was a collective undertaking, and like the architecture, it reflected the genius and the passion of an entire society. Just as the botanical gardens were intended to restore Eden, the medieval drama also brought heaven to earth, albeit in a different way.

Begun in the church as part of the Mass, medieval plays did not merely enact the liturgy, they brought Christ to the world. During the Mass, Christ and the priest are one, and thus plays rooted in the liturgy are not plays at all; heaven and hell are not "impersonated", but made visible, actual and alive. For example, even in the semi-liturgical *Le Mystère d'Adam*, an Anglo-Norman play of the latter part of the twelfth century:

> The church itself served as God's heavenly dwelling, from which He and the prophets made their entrance. The top step or platform leading into the church represented terrestrial paradise where Adam and Eve remained until they were driven from the Garden of Eden. . . . to the lower level. . . after the Fall, and there the scenes involving Cain and Abel took place. It was from this lower level that the audience viewed the play, the devil and his demons making sorties among them. . . . The *infernus* of this play – more properly limbo than hell – seems to have occupied a separate structure [probably] to the right of the spectators, [jutting] out diagonally from the church steps in such a way that its gates would be visible to the audience.[27]

No longer vague notions, heaven and hell are present on stage, coexisting ideally with all other places and times. Simultaneous staging "allowed the action of the play to move from station to station without scene-shifting so that the sequence of events could proceed without breaking the illusion no matter where the action occurred. . . . Above all, in the religious plays such staging kept a synthesis of the play's meaning constantly before the audience."[28]

The simultaneous staging which resulted in the juxtaposition of distant places also determined the development of the drama, permitting the spectator to follow in a way that is unknown to us. In Rutebeuf's rather simple *Miracle de Théophile*, the movements of the character on stage reflect his state of mind. In his revolt, Théophile walks first toward Salatin and then toward Satan, who stand on his far left. Then as he repents, he moves symbolically toward his right, where the bishop and the Virgin await. By the fifteenth century, the simultaneous staging of heaven, hell and earth had become incredibly elaborate. In the *Incarnation et la nativité*, for example:

The action is divided between Paradise, Nazareth, Jerusalem, Bethlehem, Syria, Rome, hell, and limbo, and we are told where the seventy-eight characters involved are to be stationed. . . . In fact there were twenty-five *establis* [specific places] in all, besides six separate scaffolds for the prophets. Paradise adjoined the Holy Land; hell, with an entrance represented by the jaws of a dragon that could open and close, was placed next to Rome; and limbo, fashioned to look like a prison, formed part of hell.[29]

Poets, musicians, actors, directors, artisans and audiences alike were enthusiastically involved in the creation and production of these elaborate plays. The medieval theater, like medieval architecture and the intricate and carefully ordered botanic gardens, could only be a product of an age of faith: faith in God to be sure, yet, despite Christian precepts, a tireless optimism about the possibility of true and lasting happiness in this world. Re-creations of paradise were motivated by something more than mere greed or the desire for glory, and even something other than the love of God. Behind the collective efforts that for so many centuries gave rise to architecture, theater, the voyages of discovery, and the great gardens of the Middle Ages and the Renaissance, was the elemental passion for place, the desire for the innocence of Eden and the perfection of heaven.

University of Miami

NOTES

[1] François Rabelais, *Gargantua* in *Rabelais Oeuvres complètes*, ed. Pierre Jourda (Paris: Garnier, 1962), p. 190.
[2] François Rabelais, *Gargantua and Pantagruel*, trans. Burton Raffel (New York: W. W. Norton, 1990), p. 124.
[3] *Ibid.*, p. 117.
[4] *Ibid.*, p. 121.
[5] A. I. Gurevich, *Medieval Popular Culture* (Cambridge: Cambridge U. Press, 1988), p. 131.
[6] Charles V. Langlois, "Les Merveilles du Prêtre Jean" in *La Vie en France au Moyen Age*, v. 3 (Paris: Hachette, 1927), pp. 45–46 (my translation).
[7] John R. Hale, *Age of Exploration* (New York: Time Incorporated, 1966), p. 32.
[8] Langlois, *op. cit.*, p. 61.
[9] *Ibid.*, pp. 156–57.
[10] *Ibid.*, p. 164.
[11] *Ibid.*, p. 167.
[12] *The Odyssey*, trans. E. V. Rieu (Harmondsworth: Penguin, 1946), p. 115.
[13] A. Bartlett Giamatti, *The Earthly Paradise and the Renaissance Epic* (Princeton: Princeton U. Press, 1966), p. 55.

[14] John Milton, *Paradise Lost*, IV, ed. M. Y. Hughes (New York: The Odyssey Press, 1934), p. 115, pp 153–63.
[15] John Prest, *The Garden of Eden* (New Haven: Yale U. Press, 1981), p. 4.
[16] *Ibid.*, p. 30.
[17] *Ibid.*, p. 31 (see also Morrison).
[18] S. E. Morrison, *Admiral of the Ocean: A Life of Christopher Columbus*, 2 vols. (Boston: Little, Brown & Co., 1942), II, p. 283.
[19] Alfred Beise, *The Development of the Feeling for Nature* (New York: Burt Franklin, 1964), pp. 147–48.
[20] Geoffroy Atkinson, *Les Nouveaux Horizons de la littérature française* (Paris: Droz, 1935), p. 160 (my translation).
[21] *Ibid.*, p. 166.
[22] *Ibid.*, p. 167.
[23] *Ibid.*, p. 22
[24] Prest, *op. cit.*, p. 10.
[25] *Ibid.*, p. 42.
[26] *Ibid.*, pp. 46–47.
[27] Grace Frank, *The Medieval French Drama* (Oxford: Clarendon Press, 1974), p. 83.
[28] *Ibid.*, pp. 90–91.
[29] *Ibid.*, p. 190.

JADWIGA S. SMITH

THE CONCEPT OF SPACE IN MEDIEVAL DRAMA: TOWARD A PHENOMENOLOGICAL INTERPRETATION IN MEDIEVAL STUDIES

Until recently, the study of Middle English literature, particularly drama, was a bastion of traditional scholarly application: textual studies and manuscript editing, historical studies, economic and social studies, philosophy and theology, iconography (often used just to support historical explication or to add support to the typological focus of much of the scholarship). Medieval drama was treated as if it consisted of two entirely separate areas, the written dramatic texts on the one hand, and on the other the issues related to staging. The medieval stage as an object of scholarly interest was studied mostly from the point of view of history and archival studies, social arena, stage organization, iconography (mostly to solve problems concerning technical aspects of medieval staging). This paper will closely examine the shift in the studies of the medieval drama and its staging towards a more acknowledged phenomenological interpretation, towards semiotics and recent reception theories. It will also propose a secondary thesis for the purpose of illustration of this movement toward a different treatment of space in medieval studies. Thus the paper will comment on how the sense of space was translated by the medieval audience into the sense of place.

As a result of the shift, the division of the medieval drama scholarship into the analysis of dramatic texts and the relatively separate studies of stage production and theatrical logistics seems now to be narrowing. Granted, a definite conclusion to the on-going discussion concerning the priority of wagon pageants over stationary productions and the role of processions in the staging of the cycles is far from being final and agreed upon. Or for that matter, even the old staple of medieval studies, the role of trade guilds, is lately causing renewed interest and discussion. Thus, one should not really expect an expulsion of historical investigation or exclusion of the socio-economic context. However, the intricacies of staging, together with the complex iconographical data – involving not only traditional pictorial documentation and historical and figurative interpretation but, among others, phenomenological theories of perception – give rise to the new evaluation of some ever-present subjects in medieval studies, particularly drama. In other words, the medieval audience was involved in the theatrical spectacle to a much greater degree than later audiences. To understand, then, the principles behind such concepts as, for example, awareness of space as highly concretized experience of visual data loaded with meaning, can help us to see these concepts in relation to a larger context of religion, philosophy and ethics. To illustrate, left and right in relation to the position of God on stage, would be reversed in the eyes of the medieval audience, highly sensitive and accustomed to emblematic thinking. The resulting metaphysical confusion would force the audience to realize that their safe position is illusory. Their otherwise vague sense of space is transformed into hell, or heaven, or simply a place shared with good angels, or, for that matter, bad angels.

Pamela Sheingorn, when discussing the paradox of the relatively late representation of the Last Judgment – not until the twelfth century, despite its centrality to the Christian doctrine – comes to the conclusion that:

> By exploring the rise of visual languages in two media, the pictorial arts and drama, we are able to see how these two arts both resemble each other and differ in presenting a subject of central theological and psychological importance through images both formally sophisticated and visually memorable. ("For God Is Such A Doomsman", 16–17)

She goes on exploring the need to study "compositional principles such as symmetry, hieratic orderings, triangular arrangement of forms, and organization in bands or registers" (16).

At this point, let me further qualify my observation of the shift in the studies of medieval drama. Sheingorn's investigation of spatial organization both in iconographic material and in spatial interpretations of dramatic texts is symptomatic, if not altogether the most representative, of the recent interest in the modern theories of literature in medieval studies in America. To be sure, her writings are not on the fringes of scholarship, or bordering on the peculiar or unusual. Instead, there seems to be a rather harmonious atmosphere of cooperation and agreement among a diverse group of scholars of medieval drama, including Clifford Davidson and David Bevington.

Spatial organization as one of the phenomenological elements in the interpretation of an array of issues and problems in the medieval theatre, from purely theatrical to philosophical, has emerged relatively recently. This statement is not meant to imply that there had not been a substantial acknowledgement of space before the eighties. Let us recollect just a few works which had elaborated on the rule of space in explicating the medieval plays: *Drama and Imagery in English Medieval Churches* (1963) by M. D. Anderson, O. B. Hardison's *Christian Rite and Christian Drama in the Middle Ages* (1965), Stanley Kahrl's *Traditions of Medieval English Drama* (1974), V. A. Kolve's *The Play Called Corpus Christi* (1966), Robert Longsworth's *The Cornish Ordinalia: Religion and Dramaturgy* (1967), Alan Nelson's *The Medieval English Stage: Corpus Christi Pageants and Plays* (1974), Richard Southern's ground-breaking *The Medieval Theatre in the Round* (1957), William Tydeman's *English Medieval Theatre, 1400–1500* (1986), Glynne Wickham's three volumes of *Early English Stage, 1300–1600* (1959–1981).

This list is not intended to be any working bibliography for those researching the concept of space in relation to the medieval drama; neither is it intended to evoke a tangible impression of the amount of works interested, to some degree, in this concept. In some cases, the degree of interest may be, at first, unclear, but the main idea behind the selection of these works has been to indicate a sense of difference in approach to space as exhibited by the scholarship up through the seventies when compared with the eighties and nineties. Thus when Richard Southern discusses the staging of *The Castle of Perseverence* and builds up the case for his theatre-in-the-round model of medieval theatre productions, or Glynne Wickham describes pageant theatre of the streets or indoor theatres and entertainers, we are presented with obvious references to some theatrical spaces. Also, when G. R. Owst traces the historical and iconographical tradition of such popular stage elements as ship and castle, or William Tydeman acknowledges typological tradition in medieval staging, we should understand that in all these cases space is treated, at best, as one of the multiple dramatic elements.

The eighties, however, introduced a sense of the increasing importance of the recognition of stage spaces as ideologically potent in conveying medieval views, from morals to theology or concepts of history. Thus John W. Velz opens his 1982 article "From Jerusalem to Damascus: Biblical Dramaturgy in Medieval and Shakespearian Conversion Plays" with a statement about the far-reaching implications of stage space:

In medieval religious drama, the stage is a moral world – stage spaces leave moral significance which an audience perceives or apperceives as a complement to the action that takes place in and around them . . . consequently early drama worked for emblematic effects through use of stage space . . . (311)

Further, Velz is complaining that "the emblematic character of medieval stage space is not sufficiently stressed in standard commentaries; the aesthetic and the semiotic implications have not been closely examined" (311). He then proceeds to make a connection between an "essentially binary" organization of "typology through moral theology to eschatology" and suggests one possible use of emblematic space, namely in the analysis of "the metaphorizing of moral change as spatial move-ment in conversion plays" (312). In other words, in the movement from one space, across the *platea* to another, ideologically opposing spaces are an important emblematic feature of medieval conversion plays, enhancing the overall theological meaning.

Thus, the theological meaning emerges from such non-textual sources as, for example, the organization of space on stage in a typological manner. By facing actors on such a stage, the audience cannot see them as involved only in limited psychological conflicts and narrow, realistic situations. Hence the "actors' space" ceases to be their psychologically defined and narrow space and becomes a place shared with the audience, be it hell or heaven, Damascus or Jerusalem.

Also in 1982, Clifford Davidson published an article "On the Use of Iconographic Study: The Example of the *Sponsus* From St. Martial of Limoges". Although the article refers to a French text, the point Davidson formulates here is later on incorporated in his other works. The obvious need to consider the drama on the Continent as a necessary context to the English medieval drama, particularly to its earliest stages, should allow us to incorporate Davidson's article in our discussion, as well as a few additional articles about the Fleury *Playbook*, a Latin music-drama now in possession of the Bibliothèque Municipale in Orleans, France. Thus Davidson urges us to consider "the systematic study of the iconography" to determine the "dramatic structures", which are quite different from the self-contained sense of unity of actions, so familiar in later dramas. Davidson insists that:

Iconography . . . leads quite naturally to phenomenology and the recognition that perceived experience and observable structures need to be the focus of our attention as we attempt to place the individual medieval play . . . into its proper critical context. (43)

The study of texts, at the same time, will deliver "the necessary linkage of ideas that will piece together for us the meaning of a particular fragment of spectacle" (44).

Davidson discusses the iconography of the Wise and Foolish Virgins as leading to the understanding of the role of a spatial orientation for early productions of the *Sponsus*. His phenomenological analysis of the division of space into right and left together with iconographic evidence concludes that placing the Foolish Virgins at the viewer's left adds "a psychologically important factor which suggests the existential orientation of the source in relation to the viewer's own spiritual condition" (55). Davidson asserts that:

> The hermeneutic lesson of the *Sponsus* . . . is therefore quite clear. Through the play, the audience is enabled to come to terms with its own shortcomings as played out by the Foolish Virgins, but ultimately the drama has as its major purpose the task of bringing the audience "into the divine present". . . . Indeed, the *Sponsus* is a carefully structured work of theatrical art which may be approached through its iconography but ultimately it must been seen as a lesson in phenomenological hermeneutics. As a drama originally played by mortal actors, the play for the watchers looking on will illuminate not only Being but also test eternity which is beyond time. (58–59)

Thus Davidson's phenomenological stand is representative of the interest in the treatment of space as indicative of a larger context, a metaphysical space in what has otherwise been considered the domain of purely textual studies.

In one of his latest articles on the use of space in the medieval drama, "Positional Symbolism and English Medieval Drama", Davidson reaffirms his commitment to a phenomenological interpretation of dramatic texts and insists that they "fare far better when understood as dialogue to be fleshed out and made visible on the stage" (67); he also quotes Hans-Georg Gadamer that a "drama exists really only when it is played" (67).

Hence, we have to learn about the visual habits of the medieval audience through iconographic investigation of pictorial records as well as through a different focus on dramatic texts. In other words, we have to be able to read these texts with some degree of trust in our hermeneutic possibilities, if only we let ourselves acknowledge the sense of difference in the first place. The initial sense of paradox will dissipate, once we realize that the other alternative, that is, looking at the medieval stage only through the singular perspective of our contemporary visual habits, is not necessarily better.

This sense of urgency one gets from Davidson's insistence on the recognition of the visual aspects of medieval drama is certainly shared by Pamela Sheingorn in "The Visual Language of Drama". Her thesis sounds more like a manifesto when she says that her:

essay reflects the views of art historians who are dissatisfied with the extent to which the discipline has tolerated the separation of form and content; it seeks a universal, integrative approach in ways of seeing. I thus begin with the premise that these ways of seeing, as codified in perception theory, make a valid point of departure for visual analysis precisely because perception theory demonstrates that form and content are integrally related. (173)

Thus she proposes to examine the medieval visual arts and identify such elements as center, symmetry, hierarchy, balance, horizontal versus vertical axis. These elements, when defined, can be of utmost value to medieval drama studies. Again, let me emphasize how the illustrative point of the paper, the transformation of space into place in the medieval drama, can be corroborated by Sheingorn's investigation of "ways of seeing".

We can say, then, that space and the staging of medieval drama become all-inclusive from the point of view of the audience; the sense of belonging within a certain non-dramatic space becomes a sense of belonging to a certain clearly defined place, determined not only by a dramatic text but also by its visual rendition with all its metaphysical implications, in relation to such concepts as world order or spiritual beliefs.

R. W. Hanning recognizes this need to discuss a medieval drama as a stage performance in which the visual organization of stage space is an essential factor in an ideological interpretation of a play. He discusses the "Fall of Lucifer" plays from the four cycles "to see how they raise the problem of the dangerous imitations of God by his creatures" (141). Hanning comments on the implications of God leaving the scene of dramatic action, otherwise a "logical impossibility". As a result, a dramatic space emerges as "a place which is the locational equivalent of the metaphysical state of not-being-God", and thus inviting the audience to experience the world outside of order (146). Further, Hanning observes that the introduction of comedy into the action creates, "a universe of two 'spaces'", heaven and also non-heaven, eventually to include human kind, ultimately the audience. Hanning concludes: "Each space is also metaphoric, of course, expressing tropologically and anagogically the moral significance and ultimate consequences of loving or not loving God" (150–51).

Thus the role of space as a significant factor in analyzing medieval drama seems to be gaining momentum. If we can judge by the sheer number of those who have expressed an interest in this issue so far, we can certainly expect even more publications. Let me close this discussion with a brief acknowledgement of two collections of essays, since several of these essays comment on the role of stage place in recent medieval studies. First, in the 1985 volume on the Fleury *Playbook,* C. Clifford Flanigan discusses the traditions of medieval Latin drama in relation to modern scholarship, warning against indulgence in a text. Instead, he urges the scholars of liturgical drama to consult recent reception theories stressing the changing perspective of the audience. He complains that "the visual effect or spectacle of the performance is ignored in much scholarship, so too the reader or audience of the work is almost entirely neglected" (15).

David Bevington's article in the same volume devotes a lot of attention to the use of "symbolic spatial effects". As a result of these effects, a juxtaposition of *sedes* and the use of the space between for processional movement prepare the foundations for a "meaningful spectacle for a congregation" (79).

In the same manner, Thomas P. Campbell discusses Augustine's concept of the Two Cities in twelfth-century drama, making use of the spatial orientation of Herod's throne in the church setting. What is achieved is a heightened sense of physical contrast between the City of God and the City of Man.

Cynthia Bourgeault's experience as a director of liturgical drama seems also to confirm my observations on the space versus place relationship in medieval drama. She comments on the role of processionals in involving the audience in the spectacle, forcing it to move "essentially from unsanctified to sanctified space"; and "the movement from the rear of the church to the altar area represents a 'centering down', a repeating in play of a primary liturgical action which carried tremendous power" (154). Also, she finds symmetry "a very effective principle of stylization" (150).

Finally, a collection of essays published in 1985, titled *Homo, Memento Finis*, takes into account many similar points concerning stage composition. Several articles in the volume are written by David Bevington, and one is a product of his cooperation with Pamela Sheingorn. Both authors make extensive use of certain elements of form in the iconography of the Last Judgement, such as: symmetry, vertical arrangement, symbolic differentiation of right and left. These spatial arrangements have "spiritualized meanings", elaborated by the pictorial arts (Sheingorn and Bevington, 124). For example, Bevington finds the vertical dimension particularly effective in a stage representation of spiritual fall and rise ("Man, Thinke", 171).

In conclusion, these various treatments of space provide an important contribution to medieval studies – a proof that an area, which seemed to be quite impervious to newer theoretical approaches to literary studies, is now quite open to the latest thought in theory and philosophy of literature. This phenomenological angle in much of recent work is certainly an interesting and welcome development.

Bridgewater State College

REFERENCES

Bevington, David. " 'Man, Thinke on Thine Ending Day': Stage Pictures of Just Judgment in *The Castle of Perseverance*". *Homo Memento Finis: The Iconography of Just Judgment in Medieval Art and Drama.* Early Drama, Art, and Music Monograph Series, 6. Kalamazoo, Michigan: Medieval Institute Publication, 1985, pp. 147–178.

Bevington, David. "The Staging of Twelfth-Century Liturgical Drama in the Fleury *Playbook*". *The Fleury* Playbook: *Essays and Studies.* Eds. Thomas P. Campbell and Clifford Davidson. Early Drama, Art, and Music Monograph Series, 7. Kalamazoo, Michigan: Medieval Institute Publications, 1985, pp. 62–81.

Bourgeault, Cynthia. "Liturgical Dramaturgy and Modern Production". *The Fleury* Playbook: *Essays and Studies.* Eds. Thomas P. Campbell and Clifford Davidson. Early Drama, Art, and Music Monograph Series, 7. Kalamazoo, Michigan: Medieval Institute Publications, 1985, pp. 144–200.

Campbell, Thomas P. "Augustine's Concept of the Two Cities and the Fleury *Playbook*". *The Fleury* Playbook: *Essays and Studies.* Eds. Thomas P. Campbell and Clifford Davidson. Early Drama, Art, and Music Monograph Series, 7. Kalamazoo, Michigan: Medieval Institute Publications, 1985, pp. 82–99.

Davidson, Clifford. "On the Use of Iconographic Study: The Example of the *Sponsus* from St. Martial of Limoges". *Drama in the Middle Ages: Comparative and Critical Essays.* Eds. Clifford Davidson, C. J. Giauakaris, and John H. Stroupe. New York: AMS Press, 1982, pp. 43–62.

Davidson, Clifford. "Positional Symbolism and English Medieval Drama". *Comparative Drama* **25** (Spring 1991): 66–76.

Flanigan, C. Clifford. "The Fleury *Playbook:* The Traditions of Medieval Latin Drama, and Modern Scholarship". *The Fleury Playbook: Essays and Studies.* Eds. Thomas P. Campbell and Clifford Davidson. Early Drama, Art, and Music Monograph Series, 7. Kalamazoo, Michigan: Medieval Institute Publications, 1985, pp. 1–125.

Hanning, R. W. " 'You Have Begun a Parlous Pleye': The Nature and Limits of Dramatic Mimesis as a Theme in Four Middle English 'Fall of Lucifer' Cycle Plays". *The Drama in the Middle Ages: Comparative and Critical Essays.* Eds. Clifford Davidson, C. J. Gianakaris, and John H. Stroupe. New York: AMS Press, 1982, pp. 140–168.

Sheingorn, Pamela. "'For God Is Such a Doomsman': Origins and Development of the

Theme of Last Judgment". *Homo, Memento Finis: The Iconography of Just Judgment in Medieval Art and Drama.* Early Drama, Art, and Music Monograph Series, 6. Kalamazoo, Michigan: Medieval Institute Publications, 1985, pp. 15–58.

Sheingorn, Pamela. "The Visual Language of Drama: Principles of Composition". *Contexts for Early English Drama.* Eds. Marianne G. Briscoe and John C. Coldewey. Bloomington and Indianapolis: Indiana UP, 1989, pp. 173–191.

Sheingorn, Pamela and David Bevington. "'Alle This Was Token Domysday to Drede': Visual Signs and Last Judgment in the Corpus Christi Cycles and in Late Gothic Art". *Homo, Memento Finis: The Iconography of Just Judgment in Medieval Art and Drama.* Early Drama, Art, and Music Monograph Series, 6. Kalamazoo, Michigan: Medieval Institute Publications, 1985, pp. 121–146.

Velz, John W. "From Jerusalem to Damascus: Biolocal Dramaturgy in Medieval and Shakespearian Conversion Plays". *Comparative Drama* **15** (Winter 1981–82): 311–326.

PART FIVE

PLASTICITY OF PLACE
IN CREATIVE IMAGINATION

Jorge García-Gómez and Anna-Teresa Tymieniecka at the reception in the Institute.

WILLIAM S. SMITH

MEDIEVAL RUINS AND WORDSWORTH'S *THE TUFT OF PRIMROSES*: "A UNIVERSE OF ANALOGIES"

In *The Tuft of Primroses*, an 1808 poem, though not published until 1949, we find an excellent opportunity for grasping the essential analogousness of Wordsworth's treatments of experiences superficially so different as the gazing on a tuft of primroses, the contemplating of the ruins at Tintern, the sudden glimpsing of a cross high above the devastated monastery at the Grande Chartreuse, the reading of heroic tales, and the recollecting of saints' lives. The poet's quest, in all of these encounters, is invariably for those "privileged moments," which he treasures, those "spots of time" "that with distinct pre-eminence retain / A renovating virtue" (*Prelude* XII, 208–10). It is to the fact of the analogousness of these experiences, presented in this poem in terms of the poet's views of perception, knowledge, history, poetry, and language that this paper seeks to draw attention. The discussion of the "spots of time" also attempts to show the similarity between Wordsworth's treatment of these moments of insight and Platonic/Augustinian ascent patterns, Wordsworth's relationship to a continuing tradition being a sub-theme of the paper.

Wordsworth's medievalism is quite different from that of any other English writer of the nineteenth century, with the exception of Tennyson. It is different from that of Scott, for instance, who set many of his novels in the Middle Ages, and it is clearly different from the decorative use to which the Pre-Raphaelites, Millais, Burne-Jones, and the Rossettis put medieval materials. Wordsworth's medievalism is even more organic, more entirely assimilated into a theory of mind and mental growth. The image of the cathedral and of other medieval ecclesiastical structures haunts the poet's imagination all his life. Abbeys, monasteries, and cathedrals were loci of major importance to him in stimulating the development of his own visionary, synthesizing power of imagination. Time and again, these ruined structures are the occasions for those "privileged moments" which he treasures; these "confrontations" with several relics of the Middle Ages are used by the poet in working out his view of perception and poetry, which underlies the wonderfully homogeneous body of his poetic work.

The initial meditation in *Tuft* is on a work of God, the tuft itself, which brings the poet great relief from dejection and a sense of permanence. He moves then, by a natural progression, habitual with him, to meditations on the works of man. The main point is that for Wordsworth all the works of man: the domestic accomplishments of humble men; the ruins of great ecclesiastical structures which rise by English rivers; all the languaged works of man – his exalted poetry, his fairy tales and romances, doctrinal systems themselves (like that of St. Basil, to which a long section of the poem is given) – are to be seen as being produced out of that same imaginative insight which made possible his understanding of the tuft as symbol. The fact that all such works function for Wordsworth as meditational symbols through which the mind of man grasps and expresses his relation to time and eternity is emphasized in a discussion of Wordsworth's theories of mind, perception, and poetry, as implicit in the passages of the poem.

My approach to each subject of the poet's meditation is to open out the passage into backgrounds and into other poetic treatments of the same subject. Attention is also given to the nature of the links between the various sections of the poem, whose subject matter seems to shift, but never really does. The joy which he feels in the vision of the permanence which the tuft evokes fades as he considers how soon the humble works of unambitious lives have perished. He mourns to see them changed as if a "gulf / Hath swallowed them which renders nothing back" (214–215). From this abyss he brings himself back through the meditation on lives of hermits who, like himself, in response to a universal instinct for repose, were drawn to lonely places to find there what he has found in contemplation of the primrose.

In this poem Wordsworth's mind, in dwelling on time and change, is drawn to the churchyard and to the primrose itself. As the poem unfolds, the fact that the flower and church are analogous loci for the poet becomes increasingly evident. To the hermit, who spends much of his life "Fast anchored in the desert" (266), he attributes motivation like his own. The desire to escape from the world, from "the persecuting sword, [from] remorse" (267), could not be the sole nor the chief motivation of such a life. (In Wordsworth the solitary place can never serve as an escape from the world – withdrawal, whether to a grave or to a monastery, never becomes the goal of a pursuit of death. Withdrawal is invariably temporary – a respite for the soul which is also to use such quiet solitude to come to better knowledge of itself and its real situation. Wordsworth desires withdrawal to solitary places only when they are accompanied by such genuine illumination and followed by a resolute return to the active world.) There is always this reciprocity between the active and passive powers of the mind at work in his poetry.

He continues to reflect on those "Unambitious lives" (190) which have perished and so soon their humble works: The shrubs, the garden, "garish tulips," "fruit trees choice and rare / And roses of all colours" (195–196), all are ravaged so soon. The poet mourns to see "that these works / Of love and diligence and innocent care / Are sullied and disgraced" (212–214) – that all are changed as if a gulf "Hath swallowed them which renders nothing back" (212).

But the little primrose "remains, in sacred beauty" (220). And Wordsworth remembers how he, himself, had seen the flower, at evening after vespers, in that half-light which so often accompanies the visionary experiences in his poetry. In such moments the primrose becomes for him an image of permanence, of changelessness and security, a sight that for him holds the world still, all edging time and change in that moment of imaginative insight in relation to changelessness, itself. Thus, clearly the primrose has become for him an *axis mundi*. This experience is much like the *axis mundi* vision in the Grande Chartreuse section of the poem, which follows.

However, the next major section of the poem is a meditation on St. Basil, who is considered the founder of monasticism. Wordsworth describes St. Basil as an intellectual champion of the faith who, after many solitary years of meditation on his lovely mountain, "went forth / To a station of authority and power" (449–450), laying the foundations of monastic life "by written institutes and rules" (458), to which "he gave a solid being" (459).

By thus referring to the creative process whereby he sees St. Basil as having produced institutes and rules, Wordsworth indicated the analogue between religious and poetic language, which he had always assumed and which anticipates the explicit identification of imagination and faith which he makes in the 1815 "Preface" to *Lyrical Ballads*. Some brief attention must be given to that other kind of languaged work, the fairy tale and heroic tale, which also operate to lift the poet's mind to true aspiration. The account of the memorable experience at the Grande Chartreuse further supports the imagination/faith parallel.

What happens to Wordsworth at the Grande Chartreuse is that he comes up against his own willful refusal to enter into the process of fusion. This process, which he is always seeking and always describing, is drawn from a view of the subject/object relationship in which the border between the world and the subjective self dissolves. But the objective world does not dissolve. It is always there for Wordsworth, for if it were not, our recollections of past contacts with it could have no meaning and no power to illuminate and to repose. Subjectivism and solipsism have no place in Wordsworth's world-view. When we speak of his idea of the self creating a world by its own vision, we must never make the mistake of attributing to him the skeptical notion that thought is churned out of itself and has no real object. All of his confrontations of subject/object reciprocity involve the interaction of two existent realities with which he is concerned. Out of this interaction, self and knowledge are born. The self "assimilates the world – into itself as part of itself, and becomes its own object" (Engell 248).

So at the Grande Chartreuse the poet confronts his own will and the contrariety of possible views of the objects before him. In all of the versions of the Grande Chartreuse sequence (*Descriptive Sketches*, 1793, *The Prelude* 1850, *The Tuft of Primroses*), we also see the poet's awareness that the mind may utilize loci not to lead itself into glimpsing the possibilities of progressive growth in life, but rather into seeing all too clearly the possibilities for mental anguish and self-destruction.

Wordsworth's description of his own state of mind as he stands before the ruin is clearly built on an opposition between two modes of thought. He sees "the reverential pile / . . . not by reverential touch to time / Dismantled, not by violence abrupt" (*Prelude* IX, 467–469). He also now admits his own revolutionary zeal as having been only in part "real fervour." The rest he perceives as "less genuine," for he realizes that he had "wrought upon himself," had worked up his own emotions out of some vague desire to improve, to please his friend Beaupuy. But the real nature of the French Revolution and the actual plight of the French people are things he was not at that time able to understand. What he is saying is that in his immature state he was incapable of applying real thought to the real situation. In terms of theories of mind and language, he had followed abstract ideas and empty slogans, which interposed between himself and present reality. He records that, for him, the cross high above the Grande Chartreuse was a sign admonitory to the traveler, because it spoke to him (and to others) as "if from another world," as does the voice of the Leech Gatherer on the moor in "Resolution and Independence" or the voice of the Old Soldier on the road in *Prelude* IV. The actual situation in life, as Wordsworth epitomizes it at the Grande Chartreuse, is to be caught between the inward admonitory voice of truth, and the outward voice of the world's business and distraction, just as the voices which prevailed in France, at that time, proved tragically to be. A whole nation followed false prophets into the Reign of Terror and beyond into that renewed tyranny. In the succession of his treatments of the confrontation at the Grand Chartreuse, Wordsworth shows us his own mind gradually coming to be able to "read" what is before it – his symbol-making powers of mind have been used properly.

All of the medieval structures which appear in Wordsworth's poetry are in ruins, and it is always the poet's desire to seek out the aspects of permanence which they still manifest. It is true that all ruins may set in motion such trains of thought, and that English Romantic poetry abounds in such meditations on past and present. But in Wordsworth, the fact that the ruin is of an ecclesiastical structure has vast import, both for thinking about the growth of his mind and for thinking about the nature of historical development.

A general discussion of the imagination/faith question is supported in part by a consideration of the Grande Chartreuse passage, which comes near the end of the poem. His gradual coming to an understanding that it was the voice of nature herself which admonished from the Alpine throne is traced in this poem, and also his ultimate understanding that the "sin against nature" unto which he records himself as having succumbed almost immediately after the confrontation at the Grande Chartreuse is discussed as the poet's realization that his sin was against his own imaginative powers. This sin was his repression of the knowledge of the destruction of that venerable house, which had for so long provided nurture for the contemplative powers of man. This sin against his true imaginative powers was committed in order to maintain his zealous devotions to the abstractions of the revolution, which had taken hold of his mind.

When we come to recognize the analogousness of such superficially different experiences as the viewing of the primrose and the sight of the aerial cross above the Grande Chartreuse, we have come to the basis of the same analogousness of all such unitary experiences in the symbol-making powers of the mind. But in *The Tuft of Primroses*, the dread possibility of our falling off from such insight and such responsiveness to the symbolic meaning of things is very much with the poet, and he acknowledges himself vacillating between the serenity of the unitary vision and the despair of disjunction and bifurcation. He knows that such "dearest resting-places of the heart / Vanish beneath an unrelenting doom" (262–63). But he moves immediately toward the opposing view and in a long expatiation on the nature and meaning of the lives of hermits, Wordsworth discovers the hermits were drawn to their lonely cells for the reasons the poet is drawn in his walks to the primrose: for the universal instinct to repose, for a state of the soul "consistent in self-rule, and heaven revealed / To meditation in that quietness" (294–95).

This poem has importance in our effort to characterize Wordsworth's medievalism because here the encounters at the Grande Chartreuse and also at Tintern and Fountain Abbies appear in the context of a number of encounters with other kinds of objects, all of which have, at some time, provided the poet with those precious moments of unitary vision. The tuft of primroses, a churchyard, tales of Robin Hood, all function as meditational symbolic systems through which we express and grasp our relation to time and eternity. Architectural works, doctrinal religious systems, and languaged words, such as fairy tales, are expressions of creative power and reposition, and are the vehicles whereby the lasting vitality of such thinking is carried into the continuum of history. All are means whereby mind converses with mind. The parallel between faith and imagination which Wordsworth develops in the 1815 "Preface" grows out of this whole view of the contemplative life of the Middle Ages, which he seizes at the Grand Chartreuse and elaborates in the St. Basil sequence in *Tuft*. A resonant fabric of analogous, imaginative loci is presented in *The Tuft of Primroses*: A flower, a monastery, a hermit's life recalled, a tale of Robin Hood, all provide the poet with that significant experience of insight and repose he yearns for.

Bridgewater State College

REFERENCES

Engell, James. *The Creative Imagination: Enlightenment to Romanticism*. Cambridge: Harvard U.P., 1981.
Wordsworth, William. *The Prelude. 1799, 1805, 1850*. Norton Critical Edition. Eds. Jonathan Wordsworth, M. H. Abrams, and Stephen Gill. New York: Norton, 1979.
Wordsworth, William. "The Tuft of Primroses". *The Poems*. Vol. I. Ed. John O. Hayden. New Haven: Yale U.P., 1977, pp. 799–815.

ELDON N. VAN LIERE

MONET AND THE PILLARS OF NATURE: ARTICULATION AND EMBODIMENT

> La Nature est un temple où de vivants pilliers
> Laissent parfois sortir de confuses paroles;
> L'homme y pass à travers des forêts des symboles
> Qui l'observent avec des regards familiers,
> Baudelaire, *Correspondances*[1]

From the very beginning of the painter Claude Monet's career there was an emphasis on the experience of seeing, and this led Monet to the coloristic style known as Impressionism which embodied the fugitive aspects of contemporary life and the light that revealed it, but this outward directed Impressionism became for Monet a means of inward investigation. His paintings express what it means to have one's senses in tune with the world of nature, to make it a part of oneself both consciously and subconsciously. In his late years Monet tried to emphasize that it was light and light-shot atmosphere that was his fascination and nothing else. It was this and this alone, he would have us believe, that resulted in an emphasis being placed on color as it never had been before. Notwithstanding what was at times a nearly scientific attitude toward his investigations into color and light, color remains the most emotionally potent aspect of painting.[2] The cool dispassionate investigator that Monet made himself out to be by self-consciously and diligently avoiding revelatory statements regarding his personal and private life contradicted the passionate man he in fact was, and what he obscured verbally was not to be denied altogether in paint. Had he been successful in keeping his paintings free of passion, with no hints of his private inner life, Monet's work would have lost its dimension of underlying intrigue which serves to continually fascinate even if remaining unexplained.

Given the length of his career and the stylistic changes that occur in it, a painting taken from early in his career placed adjacent to one from his last years could well be seen as being by two different artists. Despite this he consistently sought out and focused on those things that mattered to him, and this often took on the character of self-set challenges that tested his strength and sensibility. Monet's subjects ranged from the suburban world of Argenteuil, where Impressionism was developed, to sites on the coasts of Normandy and the Mediterranean, the ravine of the Creuse river in the Massif Central, the spiky rocks of Belle-Île, the fog-shrouded bridges and government buildings of London and snow-covered Norway. Then there were the series paintings of Grainstacks, Poplars, Rouen Cathedral in which he sought to capture the evanescence of the moment and the elusive *enveloppe* that exists between the viewer and the object observed, and finally subjects drawn from his garden at Giverny. With any one of these I could have made a case for the "passion of place", but instead I have selected the motif of the lone tree which serves Monet as a focal point in paintings that deal with varied sites throughout his career. By doing so I am able to juxtapose the dramatic and the domestic aspects of the painter while revealing how the singling out and contemplation of a tree makes it more than a pictorial motif. As his career progressed the idea that the tree embodied something of the painter's self metamorphoses into a concentration of diverse aspects of nature.

Many of Monet's early landscapes depict laborers going about their daily round. *The Road from Chailly to Fontainebleau* of 1864 presents a view down a long forest-lined avenue with loggers and their equipment making use of the way.[3] This is a labor indigenous to the site and one that had been carried on here for centuries. This focus on labor echoes the kind of subjects employed by a group of painters a generation older than Monet whom he admired and who would come to be known as the Barbizon School.[4] Returning to the forest the following summer Monet executed two paintings of *The Road from Chailly* in the Forest of Fontainebleau which eliminate the laborers, leaving the open perspective to compete with a grand tree which is isolated from the others.[5] In making this change, Monet appears to be seeking a monumental power in the landscape that can stand on its own without references to Barbizon-like labor. At the same time he was painting these Monet was caught up by the idea of painting a figurative work which would not only have to be noticed, but surprise and unsettle by its very modernity.[6] His large (15' × 20') *Le Déjeuner sur l'herbe* clearly builds on these landscapes.[7] In *Le Déjeuner* his position was closer to the isolated tree, and by dropping a screen of foliage down behind the added figures he masks the deep perspective view (which is still barely visible). What started out as a landscape has been so altered that it has become a figure painting in a limited outdoor setting.[8] The patchy application of paint serves Monet well in achieving a brilliant immediacy in the image, and while this was radically modern there is a unique relationship with a well-known painting of the previous century: Watteau's *Pilgrimage to the Island of Cythera*.[9] The fashionable gowns worn by the women in Monet's painting, which make it so emphatically a depiction of modern life, were inspired by 18th-century fashion. This, and the fact that these people take their leisure out-of-doors in a country setting, begs the relationship with Watteau. To be sure, Monet's pairing of men and women is not as obvious as in the Watteau, nor is the balletic compositional flow. Cupids and statues of Venus could have no place in Monet's painting, and Watteau's poetic haze would have been counter to his concern for a sunlit immediacy. Yet for all these differences they both have figures arranged across the canvas in a horizontal sweep with a dog standing at the center. Venus may have been rejected in *Le Déjeuner*, but in her place stands a great tree trunk, and clearly carved into it's bark is the common emblem of love, a heart with an arrow piercing it.[10] In general way this sign suggests a human relationship and the union of opposites, which is re-enforced by the young people spread out around it. But for Monet to represent a heart carved into the bark of the tree was to connote his own love for his mistress Camille, who posed for all of the women, in a way that would have been recognized by those privy to the relationship. This, too, identifies the tree with Monet. This tree and others of this period such as *The Bodmer Oak* of the same year suggest that Monet in focusing on the isolated tree discovered significance in it.[11] In the case of *The Bodmer Oak* it was a tree associated with an artist who had frequently painted in the forest and thereby came to be given his name. That Monet would seek out this particular oak and not be satisfied with any one of thousands of impressive trees to be found in the forest, while at the same time he was denying the depiction of Barbizon-style peasant activity, implies that a tree can carry a human identification, in this case the artist's. All the isolated trees painted in the forest of Fontainebleau from 1864–65 are powerfully independent, which is exactly the way Monet saw himself then and throughout the whole of his career.[12]

In *Le Déjeuner* Monet rejected mythological references for a one-time use of a popular and easily recognized symbol. By the end of his career he had not only eliminated the use of such devices, but the human form as well, and yet there is a richness of meaning that is common to both this early work and the late *Water Lilies*. The tree that indicates a human relationship early on, with time comes to suggest a union of nature's opposites. Here it is firmly planted in the earth and suggests a height far beyond the limits of the canvas, thereby serving as a means of unifying earth and sky, with humankind occupying that point of transition, the earth's surface. In the late paintings the trunks of willows serve as vertical dark accents in what is otherwise a spreading horizontal world of suggestive water and fugitive reflections.

Le Déjeuner was never completed for the Salon exhibit of 1866 and Monet abandoned it. Still he was determined when he began *Women in the Garden* in the spring or summer of 1866 to paint this large canvas *en plein air*.[13] Thus the painting was pursued in the garden of his rented house with his mistress posing for all the figures, wearing a different dress for each. Convenience, at least in part, drove Monet into a garden, but no matter how fortuitous, it was a deeply significant event. *Women in the Garden* drew him to flower gardens for the first time and in the center of this garden stands a lone tree. From this time on gardens became a growing obsession, both the creating of them and the exploitation of them as subject. This intimate relationship culminates in his last years at Giverny where the water gardens, which were excavated to plan, become the source for the all-embracing apotheosis of his career.[14]

The tree in the center of this composition is not as grand a presence as the one in *Le Déjeuner*, but that is not to say that it is not as important, for the whole composition revolves around its trunk: as the limbs above shoot out from it the figures are deployed around it below. The vertical element is solidly rooted in the very heart of a paradise garden, surrounded by women and flowers. Blooming love with its many facets of joy and mystery is embodied in the use of Camille in several guises – the many in one. From the tree's protective shade Camille's dark and sensual eyes look seductively out over a bouquet held up to her face at the left, and from this point our attention is drawn down to front center where the seated Camille is found once again. The eye is inevitably drawn through the glow of the shaded area to sunlight tempered by the shadow cast by the parasol held by this central figure. The diagonal slash of light in the foreground directs the eye to the right of the tree where we find the most active of the figures, who is the only one in full sun. There is a sense of gradual awakening in the progression around the tree, from calm at the left to sunlight and dynamic movement at the right. The woman lunging forward is thereby related to the tree and implies a "crack the whip"-like movement around it, connecting with the left side. Monet's unquestionably clear association of women and flowers in *Women in the Garden* makes it a seminal image in his career, for once this connection was made it was to be a lasting one; he seldom thereafter depicted Camille without flowers accompanying her, and even after her death the evolving metamorphosis of this motif continued to the late water garden paintings, where the flower motif is wedded to the tree.

The motif of the lone tree does not recur again for fourteen years. In that time Monet marries, has two children, develops his Impressionist style, struggles for recognition, and with other young painters establishes an independent means of exhibiting work outside the Salon. The combination of financial hardship, the death of his wife and a complicated relationship with the wife of one of his patrons altered his world beyond recognition. His reaction to this was to throw himself into a fray offered up by nature that paralleled his own agitated life situation. In the spring of 1881 Monet went to the Normandy coast and began painting strikingly vertiginous images of cliff edges cutting across the canvas, evoking something of that frisson that comes from a danger and a power that fascinatingly draws one to it while at the same time causing a self-preserving recoil.[15] These paintings mark the beginning of a program of creating images that are awesome in their interpretation of natural power, many of them infused with agony wedded to a sense of joy through coloristic beauty. Monet did not simply let his responses to the multitudinous aspects of earth and sun, wind and water filter through the crevices of his practical consciousness. Instead he constantly sought to heighten these responses. The paintings of the 1880's reflect Monet's search for the intimate relationship to nature that had stirred the emotions of others before him, from the primitive races to the explorers and inveterate travellers of more modern times. Monet may have turned his back on his dream of suburban domesticity, but it was too strong to allow him to run off to the South Seas as did Gauguin, Robert Louis Stevenson, or Pierre Loti. His seeking out of nature's drama has inherent in it a sense of danger that suggests a catharsis and an escape from the domestic, commercial, and financial problems that had plagued his life up to this time. *The Sea Coast at Trouville* (1881) is the first of a series of images he would paint over the course of the next several years, of lonely isolated objects on the brink, and significantly it is a tree.[16] Here the wind-buffeted tree clings tenaciously to a bleak but vibrant cliff top, while its crown is silhouetted against the sea and sky. This curious form perched atop a cliff echoes Monet's view of himself, struggling alone before nature, buffeted by a hostile art world, and life in general.

The next year (1882) Monet returned to the Normandy coast and in exploring the coast west of Pourville he discovered the small lonely church at Varengeville, perched atop the cliffs. In his first four views of it Monet positioned himself some distance away on the slope of an intervening gorge, looking over it to the church silhouetted against the sky on top of the opposite incline, in the upper left corner of the canvas. The time of day is different in each painting, affecting the color harmony and the moods. The isolation of the church in these paintings, with the cliff edge rippling downward to the lower right to reveal the expanse of the sea, creates a strikingly poignant sense of loneliness. The only company Monet gives this church are two fragile but obviously tenacious pines that stand in the foreground of three of the four paintings, but both church and trees offer little sense of sanctuary in the face of immensity.[17] One is tempted to see Monet very much at the heart of these pictures, for while the lonely vulnerability of these forms is acute so, too, is the sense of tenacity. It is significant that this structure is a church, and it cannot be totally divorced from its traditional meanings.

Monet's domestic situation was now dominated by Alice Hoschedé. She had done much to take charge of the children and Camille in the latter's last months, and the liaison that Monet and Alice had entered upon before Camille's death continued. Monet, unlike Alice, was not religious, although he did consent to have his son baptized to please her. Still, Monet grew up controlled to a degree by church holidays and by tolling church bells. The church stood in every French town and city as a kind of stabilizing presence, a sign of security even if the faith and ritual were not accepted. As modest as this church is it carries rich and complex associations and the resonances of the centuries. To see this pairing of trees in three of these paintings is to suggest a metaphorical reference to the painter and Alice. The trunks stand distinct while their foliage merges into a unified whole. The fact that they stand close at hand and yet separated from the church, not only by distance, but by a gorge as well, is very suggestive of the problems the couple faced in relationship to Alice's profound Catholic faith. Alice, who was still married, had chosen to live with Monet even though it was against the tenets of her Church and her pious nature, which in turn made divorce out of the question. One will never know how many or the nature of the discussions that occurred between the two on this subject, but it can easily be assumed that never before had Monet given more profound consideration to the Church than he did in the period from 1880 through 1882, for it had a very real effect on his personal life. In the one painting where the trees are not included, the shadow of the church creeps down the slope and suggests, when taking the four pictures as a group, that the Church has powers that can eliminate dreams and desires that go counter to its dicta.[18]

In 1884 Monet made his first painting trip to the Mediterranean coast which he found fascinating as well as frustrating – as he expressed in a letter to Alice: "The broad, general views are rare. Its too thickly wooded – its all fragments with many details, a confused mass of foliage which is terribly difficult to render, while I am really a man for isolated trees and broad spaces."[19] Four years later he returned to the South and found several isolated trees to paint. *Stone Pine at Antibes* is one of a number of paintings where the hill the painter stands on establishes the foreground plane against which more distant ones are played.[20] The band with the pine to the left and the bush to the right cradles the bay, above which the town sits illuminated by late afternoon light. Rising in the distance, the blue mountains, touched with pink, sweep up to merge with the contour of the pine and drop away to the left in the same conforming manner. Thus the closest and furthest geometric shapes have been interlocked in a disarmingly straightforward and, if taken superficially, simple-minded fashion. The composition serves not only to unify the pictorial features formally, but also the elemental aspects of nature symbolically. The stately, but temporal, stone pine appears to have absorbed its stateliness from the eternal mountain behind it.

The last major sojourn Monet took in the 1880's was to the Creuse ravine in the Massif Central. The isolation he found there in the spring of 1889 was far different from that on the sparkling southern coast, for it is a lugubrious landlocked site. The works executed here have a brooding quality which resulted from Monet's point of view, down in the valley looking up the river, which quickly disappears in the high overlapping hills leaving only a narrow band of sky at the top. In three of the paintings Monet did here he selected the confluence of the Grande Creuse and the Petite Creuse, where a lone tree standing on a point serves as the focus for this group of paintings.[21] In the Boston version of this composition the sunlight rakes down the slopes, picking out the tops of boulders and shrubs and leaving flashing brilliant streaks along the otherwise dark slopes. There is a fascinating glow in these "dark" areas, for the blues and purples have an eerie atmospheric haze which reminds one of a photographic negative, where what is expected to be dark is just the opposite yet, despite this reversal, still comprehensible. Everything in this painting seems drawn, with the inevitability of a driven snowstorm, downward in broken rippling touches, as if seeking the horizontal level of the river's agitated surface. Darkness becomes a shivering mix of cold tones engaged in a kind of battle with touches of warmth, and only in the broad view of the whole does it all fall together to give a sense of a lugubrious recognizable world full of an unexpected life. The inhospitable character of these landscapes, combined with Monet's rich and complicated brushwork, give them a writhing uncomfortableness, as if the volcanic forces that had heaved this land mass up, to then be shaped by the river into hills, were felt and expressed. Rocks and river, time and light, are embodied in a dense and charged brushwork and symbolically united in the life of an isolated tree.[22]

If the excursions to dramatic and challenging sites in the 1880's were affirmations of that dimension of lonely independence that was an essential aspect of his art, the equally important domestic dimension of Monet's life and art was being carefully cultivated and protected at Giverny. The gardens around Monet's house at Giverny had by now taken on much of the character of an enclosed paradise garden. Within this world of Monet's making, insulated from the outside by a wall, there roamed, conversed, grew up, married, became ill, and died, members of Monet's large family (Monet, Alice, whom he married in 1892, Monet's two sons, and Alice's six children). The domestic dream he had coveted during years of struggle, and which he had sought to create and capture in both the gardens he cultivated and the paintings he executed from the 1860's on, was realized at Giverny. Having attained success by 1890 it became a secure reality. The realization of his dream may have left this restless pugnacious painter with a nostalgia for certain aspects of the years of struggle, but Monet's interests were closing in on Giverny itself. With success he was able to create the world he longed for, and eventually he discovered it as a subject for his art; but this did not mean he was liberated from doubt and acute dissatisfaction, for these continued to both plague and drive him.[23]

In March of 1898 a journalist visited Monet and noted that he saw studies of water lilies and that Monet had spoken to him of the idea of a large decorative scheme making use of the pond and its floating blossoms as the subject.[24] Right from the start of considering his pond as a subject, then, Monet had the notion that would take the last thirty years of his life to come to fruition. But although the idea was in hand, a preceding period of investigation and experimentation was necessary. To be sure he painted a few works that focused on the water's surface and its lily pads, of which *Nympheas*[25] is an example, but then he backed off from looking at what was at his feet when standing on the bank and began his first series using the water garden as his motif, which included the only architectural element at this site, the Japanese footbridge.[26] The water garden with its footbridge was a picturesque idyll, where planned irregularity inspired relaxation and contemplation. To create this, Monet literally captured part of the river by means of sluice gates, and domesticated it further by means of planting in and around it.

He had said of his garden, "I planted my water lilies for pleasure; I cultivated them without thinking of painting them. A landscape does not get through to you all at once. And then suddenly, I had the revelation of the magic of my pond".[27] The magic Monet discovered here is difficult to define, for much of it has to do with what Monet had become as an artist; thus he was able to look at this pond of his own making and see worlds to paint in it, worlds that would fascinate. The years of creating the pond itself and then painting the series of the *Japanese Footbridge* were years of active confrontation with, and contemplation upon, the water garden, and one suspects that without this its significance might very well have never been perceived. In the course of his deliberations he dispensed with the specifics of form, concluding his career with images of suggestive intangibles implying universal and timeless meanings. From the raw materials offered by nature Monet created, to his own design, an elaborate garden to take advantage of the blooms that the warm months offered; so in a sense we see in his paintings of Giverny a nature which has been manipulated twice. As a result the naturalist underpinnings of Impressionism become less direct, and the vision is now more the result of a personal world doubly arranged by the creative imagination. These images do not bear the stamp of the materialist's hand; instead they are a matter of sensation, feeling and idea. In focusing on the ungraspable elements of water reflecting sky and clouds, they become even less tangible than they are when viewed directly. The two infinities of aerial space, seen only as reflection, and aqueous depths, merge in Monet's pond, bound by intangible light. The cycle of life is contained here, for beneath this surface of life-giving light and reflective play which obscures like a veil, there exists a dank decay in those suggestive murky depths, out of which the blossoms rise and into which they will sink in death and decay. Once he focused on this hypnotizing surface he never depicted it with autumn leaves floating on the surface or covered with ice. The cyclic aspect of nature Monet discovered in his pond was contained *within* each of the paintings and did not depend upon seasonal depiction. The depiction of an aspect of any one of the seasons, of necessity, denied all the others, leaving the cycle incomplete. In the water lily pond he found a cyclic unity free of seasonal change but paralleling it. The fragility that Monet depicts in his paintings of the pond has a poignancy which seeks to embody the impermanence of life and asks one to contemplate the fullness of their meaning.[28]

While Monet had throughout his career sought signs that would give his paintings a sense of powerful immaterial meaning and a sense of monumental, in the water lilies he did away with the signs and created monumentality from the elusive. The depiction of light, its reflections off various objects, and the transformation of it by atmosphere had been a constant fascination throughout his career. This meant for Monet a world of color, with its myriad elusive harmonies that have inherent in them emotional responses. The colors Monet chose in painting pictures which denied form, with its inherent intellectual lucidity, were attuned to his inner nature. It is the reflection on his feelings and reactions to observed facts that give his paintings their poetry. Water had meant much to him in one form or another throughout his life, both personally and as a painter: it was by the sea that he discovered *plein-air* painting, it was in a river that he once made an attempt on his life, in its choppy reflective surface he discovered the elements of the shattered color of Impressionism; and the sea was a place where he not only sought renewal off and on throughout his life, but once thought of being buried on in a buoy. In creating these great paintings which were to ultimately form an ensemble that would surround the spectator in the Orangerie, Monet, in essence, immersed himself in a world that embodied all these aspects of the artist's understanding of water. These late paintings of reflections are, in a way, narcissistic, for Monet's long life and career had progressively contributed to a self-knowledge that culminates in these images, reflecting his self-discovery back at the artist as in a mirror.

Among the many studies Monet painted for what would ultimately become the Orangerie decorations were those of the weeping willows growing beside the pond. In all of the studies dating from 1916 to 1919

Monet stood beneath the "skirt" of the tree.[29] In a group of ten which can easily be seen as a series in itself, Monet looked up and down the trunk of the tree, which would have nearly been obscured had he stepped back outside the "skirt" of foliage.[30] Cut off by this foliage from the outside world except for a glimpse of the pond to the right and the path to the left, Monet was alone with the tree trunk that dominates the series. The vivid trunk in *Weeping Willow*, built up predominantly by complex touches of blue and purple, writhes through the rippling foliage which fills the canvas (except for the narrow undulating ground plane), creating a sense of nature's pulsating insistence coursing through the tree.

In *Weeping Willow and the Water Lily Pond* Monet moved in much closer to the tree trunk, presenting only its lower portion.[31] While the previous group of paintings was clearly a series this was a study for his grand conception which would ultimately be installed in the Orangerie, for there is a similar arrangement of grassy bank, tree trunk, hanging foliage, and pond at the left of *Morning with Willows*. Isolated as he was beneath this dome of foliage that hung down to the ground all around him, there must have been a kind of psychological isolation which was the only sort the aging painter would be able to manage. With his troubled eyesight shaded by this natural umbrella he first painted from a position just inside the limits of the enclosing circle and only subsequently moved in closer to the trunk, in much the same manner as he had done when exploring more expansive subjects. Sitting in this environment and turning to the right Monet would no longer have had the tree trunk included in his line of vision, but the dripping foliage of the weeping willow would still reach down towards the pond, as it does in many other of these late studies of the pond as well as in the Orangerie murals.[32]

The association of water and the willow trees has powerfully complex implications in Monet's late work. He does not give them obvious attributes, despite the fact that they have been seen to possess powers and characteristics meaningful to cultures throughout history. Monet's concern for the moment does not mean that these trees and the water lily pond are simply facts of momentary recognition, for he sat before them with brush in hand again and again, resulting in images that are rich in accumulated experience. The feeling of being sheltered by this tree that "weeps", that embodies the notion of strength in weakness, and that is a synthesis of heaven, earth, and water as it grows on the bank of his pond where the celestial and the terrestrial mingle in shivering reflections, makes these paintings rich syntheses of the dynamics of a primeval existence discovered and presented in a fragmented view. The decorative aspect of the actual pond is in large measure denied as a result of this. In developing these fragmentary views into the great sweeps of the reflective plane of water dappled by clumps of water lilies and interrupted by tree trunks that are the Orangerie murals, Monet evoked a resonant suggestiveness that could not have been created in any other way. Geffroy in his biography of Monet wrote of him late in life as having "discovered and demonstrated that *everything is everywhere*, and that after running around the world worshiping the light that brightens it, he knew that this light came to be reflected with all its splendors and mysteries in the magical hollow surrounded by foliage of willows and bamboo, by flowering irises and rose bushes, through the mirror of water from which burst strange flowers which seem more silent and hermetic than all the others".[33]

Once the arrangements for the donation of the *Nympheas* murals, and the two oval rooms in the Orangerie which would house them, were finalized, Monet could set about fine-tuning the layout of the separate panels.[34] When they were completed is difficult to pin down, for Monet was not going to let them out of his possession whilst he lived. They were installed in 1927, one year after the artist's death. The first and smaller of the two connecting rooms contains four murals, the largest on the north and south sides with the smaller ones at each end. The four are separated by arched doorways, one pair serving as entrances to the space and those opposite giving access to the second room. Upon entering *Setting Sun* is at one's back, *Clouds* to the left, *Morning* to the right, and *Green Reflections* at the far end of the room. *Clouds* and *Morning* face each other across the narrow dimension of the oval room and echo one another, for both bracket brightness between mysterious dark areas at each end. The center of *Morning* is a fresh bright blue dotted with water lilies, while in the other reflections of great white billowing clouds push down from the top.

Setting Sun on the west wall is a striking image with a great swatch of yellow and pink building towards the left from the lower right as a coloristic crescendo. When it reaches its greatest intensity at the center it abruptly ends, and the right side of the mural is a mysterious dimly-lit world where one has to peer into the gloom to discover the relaxing forms of the floating water lily pads, set in a surface of vertical strokes that represent the reflections of the unseen weeping willows. Here in the reflective surface of the pond the colors of a vivid sunset are dramatically contrasted with the dark reflections of foliage made darker by the waning light of evening.

Green Reflections on the east wall is the first mural one sees on entering the room and the last as one passes by it into the second room. It is a generally dark painting with glowing water lily blossoms spotted across it along with the shimmering pads. These stand out against the dark reflections of the foliage that rises above the banks of the pond, which are represented by vertical paint strokes, thus hinting at the depths below. There is a very general sense of sequence with the murals in this room, but the oval shape tends to replace it with a sense of immersion. The only tangibles in this room are suspended blossoms which seem to ask one to let the mind float as they do.

The most striking difference between the murals of the inner room and those in the preceding one is that the waterscapes are punctuated by the vertical trunks of weeping willow trees. The soil from which they spring is absent except in one case and so, too, are their fulsome crowns which are only suggested by the tendril-like fronds that hang down from the upper limits of the paintings on either side of each of the trunks. In each of the long side murals (both of which depict morning) there are massive trunks placed near each of the lateral limits, with the sweep of the pond in between. Those on the north do not match exactly those on the south, but their position and character are similar enough to create a sense of an architectural symmetry. The one willow which is depicted as growing from the grassy bank is in the north mural and is very reminiscent of the studies Monet completed in the years 1916–19, and the areas where the hanging willow foliage is played against the water and the water lily pads are similar to other studies of the same period.[35]

With two willows in each of the flanking murals and those at each end of the great end mural, which is titled simply *Two Willows*, there is a strong sense of orientation in this room that does not exist in the first. There everything floats, and the sense of being cut loose from the outside world is immediate and poetically puzzling. In this second room, surrounded again by a series of even larger murals, the viewer is isolated in an island-like situation with one's head, figuratively speaking, perpetually bowed, for it is impossible to look up to see the opposite bank. As a result there is a sense of limitless extension to this watery world and quiet isolation. Monet created these from a synthesis of views and impressions from the bank that surrounded his pond, and by surrounding the viewer with these murals things are reversed, for where the land surrounded the water at the outset, water now surrounds. If the land is almost totally missing, the trees and their nearness to us (made very clear by the fragmented view we have of them) create a sense of security that solid earth is beneath our feet. Isolated we may be and surrounded by the suggestion of limitless extension, but there is no thought of threat in this. It is a quiet world, even a protected one, for we must be under the sheltering canopy of these willows as we reflect on reflections. Isolation and security, which run like leitmotifs through Monet's career, are to be found here in this late life summa.

The brightest of the murals in this room is also the longest, filling the apsidal east end and extending far enough to occupy part of the flanking walls. As one approaches it, the slender curving trunks of the two willows, which are clearly younger than those in the side murals, are to one's left and right at the extreme limits of the painting, therefore standing opposite one another. From these the mural curves away, exaggerating the sense of an opening up of space and air, and at the center, and deepest part of the apse, atmospheric light, water, reflected clouds, and flowers, collectively seem to breath a quiet visual sigh. This light-filled unformed area is the climax of the sequence of murals. From here there is nowhere to go but turn and retrace one's steps, and in so doing a sequence is made apparent. In this inner sanctum the beginning is at the end, and as we move away from it we pass the youthful trees and then the heavy mature ones. In doing this one gradually approaches a dark mural flanked by the two doors giving access back into the first room. The title *Reflection of Trees* reveals little, but it is the most disturbing of them all. Plainly evident in the exact center of this painting is a sinuous tree trunk which Monet, late on in the course of his many reworkings, painted over, so that it exists as a ghostly presence. While this, like all the murals, is made up of a richly complex accumulation of individual paint strokes and subtle color harmonies, the overall effect is a shivering monochromatic darkness punctuated by the rare flash of a blossom with blue lily pads, so close in value to the shaded water upon which they float that they almost disappear. By removing the willow the sense of security is lost and darkness pervades, with only a few touches of life in the spark-like blossoms. Monet has opposed a darkly lugubrious formlessness at one end of the room with the glowing sanctuary with its guardian willows at the other. Light and dark do not collide here as they did in *Setting Sun* in the first room, but confront and oppose one another. The cycle could be said to end here, in the shaded damp darkness of this mural, but the oval room with its sense of sweep facilitates the sense of continuum and the cycle easily repeats. This pantheistic painter, through a life of confronting and contemplating nature, created a cycle that passes from darkness to light and from a formless end to a formless beginning.

We have seen something of Monet's career as it evolved from the depiction of contemporary life to a primal elementalism, and in this, too, beginnings meet endings and endings denote a new existence. Monet rejected organized religion along with its rich tradition of visual images, spending a lifetime in active comtemplation of nature. His constant questioning of what he observed in his pursuit of light was the key to his discovery of the artistic means by which he could depict the essential cyclic mystery of elemental nature. Monet was reported as saying, "the only virtue in me is my submission to instinct; it is because I rediscovered and allowed intuitive and secret forces to predominate that I was able to identify with creation and become absorbed in it. My art is an act of faith, an act of love and humanity".[36]

To be in these rooms is to be embraced by a drenched luxuriance, and if one gives in to this gentle welcome, one is drawn into its spell of formative beginnings. Despite the fact that these water murals are often referred to as decorations, they cannot be said to decorate these rooms as Puvis de Chavannes' murals decorate a museum or library stairwell, for people go to such buildings for the complex variety of experiences and functions they offer. Such decorations contribute to the grand sum of the structure but are not the *raison d'être* for it. These two rooms of the Orangerie do not function like an art gallery with changing displays; instead they have no other purpose than to permanently house these murals and to allow for their contemplation. By having the arrangement fixed, it embodies, like a religious chapel, the notion of the eternal. That Monet manipulated fragments, which by their incomplete nature become mysterious, and arranged and rearranged them until a final program was settled on, implies that a mystic environment was intended, where one could contemplate the suggestive meanings evoked by these images. The tree trunks that punctuate the murals in the inner sanctum can be seen as great piers holding up an unseen vault.

Monet's fascination with the moment and light is still here, the broken touches of color and loss of specificity that are integral to this aspect of Impressionism are obviously present, but the moment is meaningless without the idea of time, and when one looks back over his vast output time was inseparable from weather. There is no trace of weather in these murals, just as in eternity there are no seasons. Baudelaire had long ago noted that imagination consisted of recognizing analogies, and when he said that painters should "see the eternal in the transitory" he was asking that an analogy be made between the present and the eternal. When Monet referred to "mystery" he was suggesting that beyond the immediate pleasure afforded by a painting there is a richer meaning, something that belongs to eternity. Here at the end of his career Monet, by his empathy with the primitive universal and a fascination with the momentary, transforms the myth of nature into a timeless continuum. These two oval rooms of horizontal sweep are full of a moist potential – rich, complex and mysterious. Looking down into and onto this most feminine of elements to see the celestial bedecked with flowers is to know the amorphous power of water to absorb all things. Monet's profound lifelong visual contemplation of this phenomenon went through a process of penetration beyond surfaces that led to a metamorphosis of the past and the momentary present. To reach the innermost room of the Orangerie is to confront assertive forms that stand in emphatic opposition to the suggestive mix of beginnings and conclusions which is water. The man of lone trees achieved a cosmic summation of opposites in balanced harmony.

Michigan State University

NOTES

[1] "The pillars of Nature's temple are alive and sometimes yield perplexing messages; forests of symbols between us and the shrine remark our passage with accustomed eyes."

[2] Charles Blanc in his *The Grammar of Painting and Engraving*, tr. K. N. Doggett (New York, 1874), p. 144, noted that color was a feminine element in painting for it depended on instinct.

[3] *The Road from Chailly to Fontainebleau*, 1864, 98 × 130 cm, Private Collection.

[4] This group of painters, which included Rousseau, Millet, Díaz and Dupré, was named after a town on the edge of the Fontainebleau forest where many of them lived; see Robert L. Herbert, *Barbizon Revisited* exhib. cat. (Boston, Mass.: Museum of Fine Arts, 1962). For his part Monet never sought to monumentalize the laborer, as Millet had in *The Gleaners* or *The Man with the Hoe*.

[5] *Le Pavé de Chailly*, 1865, 42 × 59 cm, Musée d'Orsay, Paris and *Le Pavé de Chailly dans la Forêt de Fontainebleau*, 1865, 97 × 130 cm, The Ordrpgaard Collection, Copenhagen.

[6] The title he gave it was the same one Manet had given his scandalous 1863 work, *Le*

Déjeuner sur l'herbe. In so doing Monet was not only paying homage to Manet but competing with him.

[7] The large version of this painting was never finished and now exists in two fragments both of which are in the Musée d'Orsay, Paris. The small version of *Le Déjeuner sur l'herbe* (130 × 181 cm) is in the Pushkin Museum, Moscow.

[8] A preparatory drawing for this painting showing the figures set against the deep perspective is reproduced in J. Isaacson, *Monet: Le Déjeuner sur l'herbe* (New York, 1972).

[9] Georges Clemenceau noted that this was Monet's favorite painting; see G. Clemenceau, *Claude Monet, les nymphéas* (Paris, 1928), p. 68. Also Gerald Needham makes a passing connection between Monet's *Déjeuner* and the Watteau in his Ph. D. dissertation, *The Paintings of Claude Monet, 1859–1876* (New York University, 1970), p. 55.

[10] A charming painting by Fragonard, *The Souvenir*, in the Wallace Collection rounds out the 18th-century connection, for in it a young woman has begun to carve an inscription into the bark of a substantial tree while her dog looks on with great interest.

[11] *The Bodmer Oak, Fontainebleau Forest*, 1865, 97 × 130 cm, The Metropolitan Museum of Art, New York, Gift of Sam Salz and bequest of Julia W. Emmons by exchange, 1964.

[12] Monet's teenage success as a caricaturist in Le Havre where he spoofed those who were important within the community was the first outward indication of his independence, and the fact of the cartoon-like sign of a pierced heart on this tree adds credence to the tree/Monet identification.

[13] *Femmes au jardin*, 1866, 259 × 208 cm, Musée d'Orsay, Paris.

[14] Roger Shattuck observed in "Approaching the Abyss: Monet's Era", *Art Forum*, March 1982, pp. 35–42, that "At the end of letter after letter to Paul Durand-Ruel and Frédéric Bazille and Georges Clemenceau, he (Monet) habitually employed two down-to-earth words to describe his daily activity: *Je pioche* (I'm hoeing my row. I'm opening new ground with my mattock. I'm hacking away.) In other words, he unconsciously associated wielding a brush with wielding a gardening tool. That association helped to liberate him as a painter."

[15] For cliff edges seen from an elevated position see Daniel Wildenstein, *Claude Monet: biographie et catalogue raisonné*, Vol. II (Pairs, 1979), catalogue numbers 647–50 and 653–56.

[16] *Sea Coast at Trouville*, John Pickering Lyman Collection, Gift of Theodora Lyman (19.1314), Boston Museum of Fine Arts. For a discussion of the other paintings done by Monet at this time that deal with other isolated objects, see my "On the Brink: The Artist and the Sea" in *Analecta Husserliana*, Vol. XIX, pp. 269–286, 1985.

[17] *The Church at Varengeville, Sunset*, 1882, 65 × 81 cm, Private Collection. *The Church at Varengeville, Cloudy Weather*, 1882, 65 × 81 cm, J. B. Speed Art Museum, Lexington, Kentucky. *The Church, Varengeville*, 1882, 65 × 81 cm, Barber Institute of Fine Arts, University of Birmingham. Interestingly, Renoir painted this church several times in the early 1880s. (See Sothby-Parke Bernet, Inc. London, sale catalogue for Tues. 28 November 1989, item no. 35, *Varengeville Church*.) Renoir apparently came upon this site independently, while exploring this area as a guest at Paul Bérard's chateau at Wargemont (Renoir met Bérard in 1879).

[18] *The Church at Varengeville*, 1882, 65 × 81 cm, Columbus Gallery of Fine Art, Columbus, Ohio.

[19] See Wildenstein, Vol. II, letters nos. 392, 94 and 95. Wildenstein, Vol. II, letter no. 415, dated 11 February 1884.

[20] *Stone Pine at Antibes*, 1888, 65 × 81 cm, Museum of Fine Arts, Boston, Juliana Cheney Edwards Collection.

[21] Wildenstein, Vol. III, catalogue numbers 1230–32.

[22] The term *dynamic imagination*, which has been defined as a quality of mind "that neglects the substance of the element to see in particular a force or principle of transformation", might well be used to express what Monet does in painting. This is opposed to the *material imagination* "that unites with the substance of an element and looks for contemplative rest there". Suzanne Hélein-Koss, "Gaston Bachelard: Vers une nouvelle méthodology de l'image littéraire?", *French Review*, 45 (Dec. 1971), pp. 353–64. While such a quality describes nearly all of Monet's painting it becomes progressively more profound during the 1880s.

[23] Gustave Geffroy, *Monet: sa vie, son oeuvre* (Paris, 1922), p. 238 describes one such occasion of profound dissatisfaction.

[24] Maurice Guillemot, "Claude Monet", *La Revue Illustrée*, March 15, 1898; see Charles E. Stuckey, *Monet: A Retrospective* (New York, 1985), pp. 195–201 for translation.

[25] *Water Lilies*, © 1897–8, 66 × 104 cm, Los Angeles County Museum of Art.

[26] See my "Monet's Revealing Light: Evolution and Devolution" in A-T. Tymieniecka (ed.), *Analecta Husserliana*, Vol. XXXVIII, pp. 85–99.

[27] Marc Elder, *Chez Claude Monet à Giverny* (Paris, 1924), p. 12.

[28] With the death of Alice in 1911, Monet's attention for the remainder of his artistic life was to be predominantly focused on his garden and, more specifically, on the water lily pond. Emily Apter in "The Garden of Scopic Perversion from Monet to Mirbeau", *October*, Vol. 47 (Winter 1988), pp. 91–155 observes that the two major cycles of Nymphéas were "precipitated by the death of a beloved muse", p. 111. As Gaston Bachelard would have it, "To contemplate water is to slip away, dissolve, and die." *Water and Dreams*, tr. Edith R. Farrell (Dallas: The Dallas Institute of Humanities and Culture, 1983), p. 47.

[29] Wildenstein, Vol. IV, catalogue numbers 1848–53 and 1868–1877.

[30] *Weeping Willow*, ©1919, Musée Marmottan, Paris.

[31] *Weeping Willow*, ©1918, Michael Monet Bequest, Musée Marmottan, Paris.

[32] Wildenstein, Vol. IV, catalogue numbers 1850–53 an 1866–67.

[33] Gustave Geffroy, *Monet: sa vie, son oeuvre* (Paris, 1922), chapter 36.

[34] In 1918 Monet wrote his old friend Georges Clemenceau, who was Prime Minister of France, asking him to use his "good offices" to facilitate the gift of two of his decorative murals depicting water lilies to the state for placement in the Musée des Arts Décoratifs (Daniel Wildenstein, *Claude Monet: biographie et catalogue raisonné* [Paris, 1979], Vol. IV, letter no. 2287). This was a symbolic gesture of thanksgiving for the conclusion of the First World War, but Clemenceau took the idea and augmented it into what amounted to a monument to Monet himself. It was to entail a special architectural space which would be filled with a far more ambitious donation of *Nymphéas* (for accounts of the complicated negotiations regarding this gift, see Robert Gordon and Andrew Forge, *Monet* (New York, 1983), chapter 8). In 1926, while Monet was negotiating the gift of the murals that would become the Orangerie cycle, he was also negotiating with the state for the sale of the *Women in the Garden*. This was the painting that the official Salon jury had rejected in 1867, and now representatives of the French government had

agreed to pay the incredible price of 200,000 francs for it. He told René Gimpel that it was a "special" painting and that he was being paid the sum in compensation for the *Nymphéas* paintings he was offering to the state as a gift (René Gimpel, *Diary of an Art Dealer* (New York, 1966), p. 153 – entry for October 1926). That Monet finally sold this painting in the manner he did makes the connection between it and the *Water Lilies* unavoidable and establishes still another of those fascinating symmetries that occur throughout Monet's career. The eighty-one year old painter could at last let this figurative work, which had led him to gardens and the association of women and flowers, go out of his possession, for he was now thinking of his place in history, and the beginning and the end would be preserved by the state very close to one another.

[35] Wildenstein, Vol. IV, compare catalogue numbers 1848–49 with 1850–53.

[36] C. Roger-Marx, "Claude Monet's Water Lilies", *Gazette des Beaux-Arts*, June 1909, translated in Charles E. Stuckey, *Monet: A Retrospective* (New York, 1985), pp. 255–66.

MICHAEL LOSCH*

A VICARIOUS VICTORY: CÉZANNE'S PAINTINGS
OF MONT SAINTE-VICTOIRE AND THE
DUAL NATURE OF LOVE**

Cézanne's painting of Mont Sainte-Victoire (c.1904–6) in Philadelphia, stands as a "summa" of the painter's twenty-year obsession with what he called "le motif" (Figure 1). Perhaps the last painting to come from the painter's brush, it is nevertheless typical of the numerous other versions Cézanne painted of his beloved mountain during the final years of his life. Seen from the high vantage point of Cézanne's studio just north of Aix-en-Provence in southern France, the mountain rests atop an expansive horizon. Never had the mountain seemed so majestic and immobile, yet alive and organic; at once rooted firmly to the countryside of Aix while seeming at the same time to disappear into the ethereal blueness of the heavens above.

Such a tug between the celestial and earthly, order and chaos, is echoed throughout the canvas by a flurry of brushstrokes both frantic and controlled. While the passionate freedom of the brushstrokes that define the sky suggests an outpouring of emotional torment from the painter, we simultaneously detect an element of control in the occasional application of vertical parallel strokes superimposed upon the diagonal or freely applied paint underneath.

The foreground's predominently cold violet-blue band mirrors in its cool tonality the mountain and sky above, separated by a broad strip of warm greens and ochres defining the broad plains of the Aixois landscape. This juxtaposition of warm and cool tones serves a dual, apparently contradictory function: it suggests depth while simultaneously unifying the two-dimensional surface of the canvas which, not accidentally, shows through in several spots. No secret to those who prefer a strictly formal reading, Cézanne has, in effect, done away with the notion of linear perspective as practiced in Western art since the Renaissance. By the simple juxtaposition of cool and warm colors (which, respectively, have an optical tendency to recede from the beholder's point of view and to approach it), Cézanne was able to preserve the integrity of the two-dimensional flatness of the canvas while creating, at the same time, the illusion of the phenomenally observed third dimension found in nature.

Fig. 1. © Philadelphia Museum of Art: George W. Elkins Collection.

The resulting push-pull effect is ultimately reconciled by Cézanne's insistent inversion of colors describing the earthly and celestial realms (notably the greens and blues) found in virtually all his late paintings of Mont Sainte-Victoire, thereby further unifying his pictures' surfaces. This curious phenomenon has been noted by scholars but has rarely been discussed in depth. Why do we find, particularly in Cézanne's representations of Mont Sainte-Victoire, slashes and smudges of green, which should normally define the earthly realm below, oddly combined with strokes of blue defining the sky above, as we see quite clearly in our picture? Why this inversion of the celestial and earthly realms? This quest to merge the three-dimensional with the two-dimensional? The tension between the vertical and horizontal? Why, indeed, was Cézanne drawn to Mont Sainte-Victoire?

Max Raphael has perceptively noted that, "To interpret his work as intellectual constructivism is to overlook the tremendous significance nature had for Cézanne . . . [T]he artist himself was concerned with gaining insight into the essence and laws of being."[1] Cézanne seems to be attempting, via formal and aesthetic means, to reconcile or "to realize his inner struggle in form and color",[2] a conflict that plagued him his entire life, namely, that of the dual nature of our existence.

Among modern art historians, it was Bernard Dorival who first suggested that Cézanne was consumed by conflicting impulses when he quoted Jean Racine's famous line in order to characterize the painter's psyche: "Oh God! What cruel conflict, I find two men in me." Little did Dorival realize at the time that Racine was a writer whom Cézanne held in particularly high esteem. "No doubt", Dorival continued, "there were several Cézannes in Cézanne: a realist and a man of imagination, a sensualist and an intellectual".[3] But it was really Cézanne's conflicting views of the nature of love that formed the real root of his dilemma. His letters to his friend, the novelist Émile Zola, paint a picture of a man torn between the contradictory impulses to satisfy his carnal desires on the one hand, and his wish to enjoy a relationship that fulfilled his platonic dreams on the other. In fact, it was Zola's portrayal of Cézanne as the artist Claude Lantier in his novel of 1886 entitled *L'Oeuvre* – the publication of which ended their thirty-year friendship as Cézanne was deeply hurt over Zola's characterization of him as a failed painter – that perhaps best characterizes Cézanne's attitudes toward the opposite sex. In the novel, Zola describes Cézanne/Lantier: "chaste as he was, he had a passion for the physical beauty of women, an insane love for nudity desired but never possessed, but was powerless to satisfy himself or create enough of the beauty he dreamed of enfolding in an ecstatic embrace. The women he hustled out of his studio he adored in his pictures."[4] His paintings of Mont Sainte-Victoire, as we shall see, are expressions of his attempt to reconcile his conflicting feelings toward the opposite sex; his quest to somehow meld the sacred and the profane aspects of love via his dual association of his mountain with both Venus, the ancient Goddess of Love, and the Virgin, the embodiment of spiritual love.

In order to uncover the reasons why Cézanne was so passionately drawn to his mountain as a subject for pictorial representation, we must take into account a broad range of both personal and internal factors, as well as a myriad of external forces that fed Cézanne's attraction to Mont Sainte-Victoire. I will rely upon the following: the objective geographic and aesthetic appeal of the mountain as a subject, the biographical facts of the artist's life that coincide with his first concentrated efforts to paint the mountain, the local historical facts, and popular legends and lore that were associated with the mountain, a disclosure of the mystery surrounding the enigmatic origin of the name of the mountain, as well as an examination of the numerous literary influences, both contemporary and distant, that influenced Cézanne. Particular attention will be paid to the writings of his friend Émile Zola, as well as to the works of other luminaries of literature, criticism, and music such as: Gustave Flaubert, Jules Michelet, Goethe, Wagner, Baudelaire, and Dante. The works of each were known to Cézanne and all played an important role in reinforcing Cézanne's otherwise instinctive obsession with Mont Sainte-Victoire. Finally, a formal and thematic analysis of some of the important pictures wherein Mont Sainte-Victoire plays a prominent role will support the proposed underlying reasons I believe Cézanne devoted so much time, paint, and canvas to the representation of a place.

For Cézanne, duality, the conflict of opposites, was a real and troubling force. And his paintings are, in part, expressions of his attempt to come to grips with this dilemma. Yet, Cézanne expressed the desire to shield the soft underbelly of his emotional conflict (a relatively impossible task for any artist of strong character) so that the painter would remain hidden.[5] It is for this reason that he was so fond of the genre of landscape, because it offered him the vehicle to express those contradictory feelings without drawing attention to the more private aspects of his personal life. The notion of duality so blatantly expressed in

Cézanne's early letters and poems does not disappear in such seemingly "contentless" paintings as his Mont Sainte-Victoire series. Instead, they are revealed in sublimated form and under a new guise, where the conflict of dualities is veiled by the silhouette of a mountain.[6]

Mont Sainte-Victoire, the western face of which is located about eight miles east of Aix-en-Provence, attains a height of 3,315 feet. As the dominant geological landmark in the Aixois countryside, Mont Sainte-Victoire is nonetheless only visible from the extreme western or eastern boundaries of Aix. In the city itself – which rests in a shallow valley – the mountain is all but lost behind the screen of plane trees that line the Cours Mirabeau. One must either ascend the gently rising slopes west of Aix or venture into the gradually descending plains to the east of the city to catch a glimpse of what is perhaps the most famous mountain in the history of modern Western painting.

The extent to which Cézanne was attracted to Mont Sainte-Victoire as a subject is evidenced by the numerous drawings, prints, watercolors, and paintings of it that have survived. Approximately eighty images of Mont Sainte-Victoire are found in Cézanne's *oeuvre* in various media, the majority of which are paintings. While it may be argued that Cézanne was attracted to Mont Sainte-Victoire by virtue of its majestic, ubiquitous presence, it seems unlikely that this was the sole reason for his obsession with the mountain, an obsession that intensified with the years as he felt himself increasingly isolated from both his friends and the outside world. Unfortunately, Cézanne himself is silent on the subject. In his surviving correspondence, Mont Sainte-Victoire is mentioned only once, in a letter to his friend Émile Zola. Yet this single passage reveals a subtle insight into a crucial dimension of Cézanne's response to Mont Sainte-Victoire: he was attracted to the *motif* for reasons that went beyond mere interest in the mountain as an impressive geological monument. His letter recounts a train journey he took from Aix to Marseilles with one Monsieur Gilbert. As the train passed by Mont Sainte-Victoire, Cézanne commented that the mountain was such a "beautiful motif". According to Cézanne, Monsieur Gilbert's only response was that "the lines are too well balanced". Cézanne prefaced this tale by stating that "these people see well, but they see with eyes of professors", as if to suggest that his own response to Mont Sainte-Victoire as a subject included, but ultimately transcended, a purely formal or aesthetic attraction.[7] Later, in 1883, while Cézanne was painting in L'Estaque, he echoed these sentiments when he again told Zola, "there are some beautiful views here, but that does not necessarily make a good *motif*."[8]

Given the artist's response to the aesthetic appeal of this natural landmark, his fascination with Mont Sainte-Victoire does not exclude his equally important emotional response to the mountain. The absence of documented evidence makes arriving at any certain conclusion as to the meaning behind Cézanne's compulsion to paint Mont Sainte-Victoire a difficult endeavor. Yet, by examining the circumstances which surround Cézanne's first concentrated efforts to devote himself to the depiction of Mont Sainte-Victoire, as well as the traditional, mythological, and historical role of mountains in general – and Mont Sainte-Victoire in particular – one may surmise in what ways this mountain was, for Cézanne, a personal symbol. It was imbued with a meaning indelibly stamped by local tradition and informed by the more universal associations he encountered in the literature and culture with which he was most familiar.

The impetus for Cézanne's devotion to Mont Sainte-Victoire was triggered, it would seem, by a period of intense emotional and spiritual crisis. From about the year 1885 or 1886 until the end of his life he embarked upon the painting of numerous depictions of the mountain as an autonomous landscape object, devoid of intrusive human figures. The years 1885 and 1886 were full of frustration and disappointment for Cézanne. Early in 1885 he suffered from a severe case of neuralgia, followed in the spring by a painfully unrequited love affair with a mysterious woman. As his letters to Zola at this time reveal, Cézanne went to great lengths to conceal this affair from both his future wife, Hortense, and his family. The guilt he suffered from the mere thought of infidelity was mournfully expressed to Zola in a letter in which Cézanne, quoting from Virgil, wrote, "Trahit sua quemque voluptas!" (We are all prey to our passions!)[9]

The following year was just as crucial for him: Zola published his novel *L'Oeuvre* and, deeply hurt by the personal reference to him in the character of the artist Claude Lantier, a failure, Cézanne broke off his life-long relationship with his boyhood friend. Equally distressing was his concealment from his parents of the affair with Hortense and their illegitimate child, Paul *fils*. These tensions were only marginally relieved when Cézanne agreed to marry Hortense in the presence of his parents in April of 1886, only to witness the death of his domineering and moralistic father, Louis-Auguste, six months later. These events were compounded by his continued misfortune at the annual Salon, where his works were firmly rejected in both 1885 and 1886.[10]

That Cézanne, during this time of intense personal strife, should direct his attention to Mont Sainte-Victoire is not surprising. For it was in the contemplation of nature that he felt that truth would ultimately reveal itself. Nature, particularly the landscape of his beloved Aix, was imbued with personal and historical significance for Cézanne, and he believed the artist need only see and uncover these truths. In 1886 he wrote to his friend Victor Chocquet and, in his characteristically oblique manner of expression, attempted to describe these thoughts. He complained of his lack of "balance" and "serenity", and that this was "the only regret he had concerning the things of this earth". "As to the rest", he continued, "I have nothing to regret. It is always the sky, the limitless things of nature that attract me, and bring me to the opportunity to look with pleasure". Later he added, "there still exist treasures in this countryside, that have not yet found an interpreter equal to the wealth that it displays."[11] In short, Cézanne saw in his countryside secrets and truths that awaited discovery. As such, the artist's examination of nature provided a suitable path toward self-discovery, a means by which he might achieve serenity, balance, and ultimate truth. As John Wetenhall has noted, he saw in Mont Sainte-Victoire "the means of looking within, to know himself".[12]

Yet, Cézanne's attraction to Mont Sainte-Victoire was not merely the result of an idiosyncratic emotional response to a mountain. It is likely that he was also influenced by the local, historical, and legendary associations surrounding the mountain. By considering these historical events, facts, legends, and lore associated with Aix's natural wonder, as well as by analyzing the context within which the mountain appears in his early work, we will discover the underlying reasons why Cézanne might well have looked to Mont Sainte-Victoire in this time of crisis.

Mont Sainte-Victoire first entered the annals of recorded history in Plutarch's recounting of a famous battle of 102 B.C., which took place at the base of the mountain between the victorious Roman legions, under the command of Gaius Marius, and the barbarian forces of the Teutones and Ambrones.[13] To this day, the Aixois attribute the reddish color of their landscape to the blood that was shed two thousand years ago during this fierce struggle. Mont Sainte-Victoire, as the name would seem to imply, commemorates this victory. Yet the question remains: why

"Sainte-Victoire" (Holy Victory), if the name memorializes a pagan military victory?

Much discussion centers on the deciphering of the name Mont Sainte-Victoire itself. Carol Kiefer, in her dissertation *Paul Cézanne, François-Marius Granet and the Provençal Landscape Tradition*, claims that the mountain is named after a martyred fourth century Roman soldier, Saint Victor, who refused to renounce his conversion to the Christian faith.[14] As tempting as this theory may be, it is most unlikely: the name Victor (which is masculine in French) has little to do with Victoire (which is feminine), and the former is a proper name while the latter is a noun. Furthermore, the feminine French form of Victor is not Victoire, but Victorine. The name Sainte-Victoire must therefore refer to spiritual victory, an appellation which must have been adopted during the Middle Ages.

How well known this legend was in Cézanne's time is born out by the testimony of various travellers and tourists who passed through Aix. One Archibald Marshall, for example, explained in 1914 that, "on the top of Mount Victoire, which overlooks the scene of a terrific battle, a temple was erected and dedicated to Venus Victorix. This became a Christian church and Venus Victorix became St. Victoire."[15] Marius's dedication of the temple in antiquity to Venus Victorix, or the Venus of Victory, after his defeat of the barbarians, was an obvious reference not only to Venus as victor in the mythic Judgment of Paris, but also to her patriotic role as the mother of Aeneas, the legendary founder of the city of Rome, the very city Marius courageously defended from the barbarian attack.

Once Aix had been thoroughly Christianized, the former pagan dedication to Venus as victor was seemingly replaced with a dedication not to a secular or military victory, but to one that conformed to the Christian faith. Pagan (military) victory became Christian (spiritual) victory. Such continuity of meaning between the two different senses of the concept of victory (military and spiritual), as demonstrated in the naming of Mont Sainte-Victoire, was commonplace in regions throughout Christendom where there was once a strong pagan influence. This is particularly true of Aix-en-Provence, which is a region rich in Roman antiquities and classical influence.

How enduring this Provençal connection is between the two eras – pagan and Christian – is demonstrated by the fact that an ancient sacrifice and offering of thanks, which was held in pagan times atop Mont

Sainte-Victoire, survived well into the eighteenth century. According to Amédée Thierry, writing in 1870, the sacrifice of thanks offered by Marius in the temple he erected atop the mountain was not abolished by the Christians. Instead, the nature of this feast was merely tranformed through time and became a Christian celebration. Moreover, it was perpetuated every year since antiquity, according to Thierry, in the month of May up until the French Revolution, when this Christian celebration was, apparently, abolished.[16]

Both the nature of this celebration and the character of the new Christian church that replaced the pagan temple, is not entirely clear. The celebration was originally an offering of thanks for Marius's deliverance of the environs of Aix, and hence the Italian penisula, from the barbarians, it was then later converted into a processional following the rites of the Catholic Church.[17] The church that replaced the pagan temple was simply referred to as "l'église de Sainte-Victoire".[18] Any further knowledge as to its specific affiliation – the particular Christian order or religious community – is lost. However, in the seventeenth century, a priory called Nôtre Dame de Sainte-Victoire was erected and inhabited from 1656 to the time of the French Revolution by various religious orders, among them the Camaldolese and the Carmelites, the latter specifically devoted to the Virgin Mary.[19] It appears that Mont Sainte-Victoire during the period of Christian domination possessed a Marian connotation, as "Our Lady of Holy Victory" suggests.

Cézanne himself had made many excursions to the ruins of this abandoned chapel. Émile Solari, the son of Cézanne's friend Philippe Solari, tells us how, on one specific hike up the mountain, his father lunched within the ruins of the chapel atop Mont Sainte-Victoire. Moreover, Émile mentioned that the chapel was the site of an episode in Sir Walter Scott's historical novel *Anne of Geierstein*.[20] If one examines the pertinent passages in Scott's novel, the nature of the chapel and of its dedication is revealed: according to Scott, it was dedicated to the Virgin Mary.[21]

The association of Mont Sainte-Victoire with the Virgin is strengthened by the fact that the traditional annual celebration that took place until the time of the French Revolution on Mont Sainte-Victoire, according to Thierry, took place in May. According to Catholic tradition, May is the month of the Virgin, and May 31 is the feast-day celebrating the Queenship of the Blessed Virgin Mary. That Mont Sainte-Victoire was identified with the Virgin is further reinforced by Engeurrand Charonton's altarpiece *Le Couronnement de la Vierge*, dating from the mid fifteenth century. According to Charles Sterling, Charonton, who worked in Aix as early as 1444, painted what is most certainly Mont Sainte-Victoire in the background on the horizon below the scene of the Virgin's Coronation depicted in the heavens.[22]

For Cézanne, who must have been aware of the dual dedication of Mont Sainte-Victoire to Venus in antiquity and to the Virgin in the Christian era, this conflation must have struck a vital chord in his imagination, one that helps to explain his attraction to Mont Sainte-Victoire. In the mind of a painter most interested in the conflation of pagan and Christian themes, the mountain carried with it a twin association: one a goddess of sensual love, the other a personification of divine love. Thus, the mountain became a symbol of the duality of life and of Cézanne's own conflicts: his simultaneous attraction to the sacred and profane, fused here into the natural landmark of Mont Sainte-Victoire. As its very name suggests, Cézanne probably saw in it a symbol of his own victory over the conflicting forces that troubled his soul. Even the French word *victoire*, according to the nineteenth century lexicographer Emile Littré, has a dual meaning, referring as it does to both a mundane victory or achievement as well as a "victory over one's passions, over oneself".[23]

The identification of Mont Sainte-Victoire with the Virgin was a conjunction in relation to which Cézanne hardly needed prompting, for Marian doctrine reached its apogee in nineteenth century France. Not since the Middle Ages, when virtually every cathedral in France was dedicated to the Virgin, had there been such an intense veneration bestowed upon the Queen of Heaven. The papacy encouraged Marian piety, and it was in 1854 that Pope Pius IX decreed the doctrine of the Immaculate Conception. Furthermore, the most popular and important Catholic confraternity in France at the time was the Archconfraternity of Nôtre-Dame des Victoires, whose chief function was the conversion of sinners. According to Thomas Kselman, the Virgin's popularity was chiefly due to "her unique ability to symbolize the contemporary feminine ideals of maternity *and* virginity."[24] As such, Cézanne's interest in the Virgin was a result of her unique ability to remain pure and, at the same time, give birth to Christ. Moreover, in nineteenth century literature, the feminine ideal was a woman who was at once bearer of children, virgin, and spiritual protectress, and the Madonna served as a model of this ideal. The extent to which nineteenth century men were preoccupied with this idea is perhaps best, though incredibly, revealed by Auguste

Comte's astonishing proposal to solve the dichotomy by means of artificial insemination. Such a method of impregnation would, according to Comte, sustain a woman's life-giving function while at the same time maintaining her virginal virtue and role of familial spiritual priestess.[25]

Cézanne undoubtedly shared history's dichotomous view of women. And this attitude was only reinforced by his reading of an important, but now obscure, novel written his friend, Émile Zola, entitled *La Faute de L'Abbé Mouret*, published in 1875. In this novel, the protagonist Father Mouret, is a country priest who, while remaining steadfastly devoted to the virtues of chastity and the Virgin is, nevertheless, enticed by the charms of a local girl named Albine. His conflicting impulses are revealed while he waits with "glad hope" for the coming of May – which according to the Catholic calendar is Mary's month. In the novel, while spiritually preparing himself with litanies of prayerful devotion and meditations before a sculpture of the Virgin in his country parish, Father Mouret painfully, and for the first time, recognizes a disturbing aspect of the Mother of Christ:

But he could not slide into prayer's half-sleep with the customary joyous ease. Mary's maternity, glorious and pure as she revealed herself, this round body of a mature woman carrying her naked child on one arm, upset him profoundly; she seemed to be a heavenly continuation of the overflowing outburst of generation through which he had been walking since morning . . . Mary gave birth and engendered life . . . he was distracted and lost his train of thought; he saw things he had never seen before . . . .[26]

The month of May is not only Mary's month, but the beginning of spring and the renewal of life, when all of nature is teeming with regenerative forces in a reaffirmation of the reproductive powers of life. As spring necessarily confirms the sexual powers of human existence, it is repugnant to Father Mouret, who consciously seeks to deny the human appetites of life. His sudden discomfort during his contemplation of the Virgin is the direct result of his recognition of the Virgin's dual nature. In his eyes, the Virgin had subsumed and incorporated the role generally reserved for Venus, the pagan goddess of love and fecundity.

Father Mouret's spiritually distressing revelation is foreshadowed earlier in the novel when he subconsciously conflates Mary with her pagan counterpart, Venus: "Often, on peaceful nights, when Venus shone blond and dreamy through the warm air, he gave himself up to contemplation, the *Ave maris stella* dropped from his lips as an emotional hymn revealing . . . gentle seas . . . lit by a smiling star . . ."[27] The *stella maris* (Star of the Sea) has traditionally been linked with the Virgin and her ability to guide and protect sailors on their course.[28] It is also variously associated with Venus as both morning and evening star. Like the *stella maris*, Mont Sainte-Victoire at one time also served to guide sailors entering the nearby port of Marseilles.[29] Moreover, Mont Sainte-Victoire was conversely associated with the Star of Venus, for the feast of the *Bello Estello* (Star of Venus) was held every seven years on the summit of the mountain in commemoration of the symbolic marriage of Maguelone and Pierre de Provence.[30] The mountain was itself, therefore imbued with a rich and complex history of serving the divergent traditions of paganism and Christianity, and as such became a perfect symbol for Cézanne of his personal quest to harmonize his own conflicting impulses.

If Cézanne's concentrated interest in Mont Sainte-Victoire as a subject was triggered by a period of intense self-reflection, it only increased with age, particularly after he returned to the Church as a devout, God-fearing Catholic in 1891. Perhaps the smell of fire and brimstone, combined with his increased awareness of his own failing health and mortality, fed his need to turn to nature, and to Mont Sainte-Victoire, as a symbol of harmony and victory over discord. Like the Virgin, the mountain was a natural symbol of the intercessor, partaking as it does of both the phenomenal world and the heavens above.

The historical and legendary associations informing the symbolic meaning of Mont Sainte-Victoire were certainly enough to capture Cézanne's attention, but the painter's attitude toward the mountain was also fueled by a long-standing interest in it that dates back to his early paintings. Whilst it is true that Cézanne focused and narrowed his view of Mont Sainte-Victoire from about 1886 until his death in 1906, he had always been aware of its presence. His early paintings demonstrate that, while the mountain often seemed to play a subservient pictorial role, it was, in reality, a looming force that informed the symbolic significance of his pictures. An analysis of the instances where Mont Sainte-Victoire appears in Cézanne's early work offers further clues as to how pervasive a symbol it was for him throughout his life. One such early painting is his *La Tranchée* (V. 50) of about 1871.

Also known as *The Railroad Cutting*, the painting depicts a train pass cut through a hillock in the center of the composition. Flanking the cutting is a house to the left, and Mont Sainte-Victoire to the right. To the casual observer, this may be read as a youthful study of the landscape near the Cézanne family estate at the Jas de Bouffon, but as Sidney Geist has discovered, the painting hardly conforms to the local geographical realities. According to Geist, the view of the cutting could in no possible way include Mont Sainte-Victoire in the background as it clearly does in the painting. Cézanne therefore, has gathered disparate geographical realities and assembled them within a single canvas. Geist interprets the painting as a veiled allusion to Hortense's recent pregnancy via a play on words. The cutting, which in French is *tranchée*, the "trench", also means the "female pudendum", and the retaining wall behind, *"enceinte"*, also means "pregnant". Moreover, Geist observes in the configuration a prone nude woman cleverly defined by the landscape, with her head expressed in the "physiognomy" of the house to the left, the small hillocks as breasts, and the cutting as her splayed legs.[31]

If Geist's interpretation appears excessive and improbable at first, it gains in credence when related to a certain passage in Zola's *La Faute de L'Abbé Mouret*, where we read this description of the Provençal landscape:

> At night, this ardent country assumed the tortured arch of a woman consumed by lust. She slept, but the covers had been thrown aside; she swayed, twisted, passionately spread her legs, exhaled in great warm breaths the powerful smell of a beautiful, sleeping woman dripping with sweat. It was like some strong Cybele . . . forever dreaming of impregnation.[32]

Zola's description of the landscape serves as a mouthpiece for Father Mouret's reaction to a nature teeming with fecundity. For him, nature is a tempting force that threatens his self-imposed state of physical and psychological virginity. Whether or not Cézanne's *La Tranchée* is a reference to Hortense's pregnancy, as Geist maintains, is difficult to verify, but it is clear that this rather unassuming subject is imbued with allusions to sexuality and to the forces of nature as they were personified, in the nineteenth century, by woman.

However, the question remains as to the role played by Mont Sainte-Victoire. Why did Cézanne place it above the cutting in defiance of the realities of the actual scene? The answer can only reside in the spiritually redeeming association of the mountain's Marian symbolism. As a symbol of the Virgin, Mont Sainte-Victoire presence offers the painter a symbol of purity and fecundity in direct contrast to the landscape's beckoning call to sensuality. The mountain's ethereal blueness also contrasts symbolically with the rich ochres defining the earth below.

Moreover, as Geist has observed, Cézanne has brought the tower of Saint Sauveur cathedral to the right of Mont Sainte-Victoire,[33] thereby further emphasizing the spiritually symbolic function of the mountain.

It can hardly be a coincidence that Mont Sainte-Victoire first makes its appearance in Cézanne's work at about the same time as the publication of Michelet's popular *La Montagne* in 1868.[34] Given Zola's fascination with Michelet, it seems unlikely that Cézanne could have been unaware of this treatise.[35] On a superficial reading *La Montagne* appears to be a study in natural history. But, in reality, it transcends that purpose, and is a study of the complex relationship between man and nature and the duality of life. For Michelet, the mountain was symbol of the harmonious relationship of opposites. Describing his experience on mountaintops, he exclaims, "Beautiful agreement. Noble harmony. All that which is elsewhere obscured is here clear."[36] For him, the mountain was symbolic of our aspirant nature, the quest to understand life's complexities and to seek a resolution to its conflicts. In *L'Amour*, which Zola discussed at length with Cézanne, Michelet refers to a mountain's ability to "pacify my mind, by permitting me to embrace, in one great simplicity, all the apparent contradictions of things, and to recognize the profound concord in all that seems discordant."[37] Although Michelet makes few specific allusions to Christian spirituality, he does echo Cézanne's perception of the mountain as symbol of an intermediary which, theologically, is also the role fulfilled by the Virgin.

Perhaps the most important and symbolically significant of the early paintings in which Mont Sainte-Victoire appears is an oil from about 1877 entitled *L'Eternel féminin* (Figure 2). Under the shelter of a canopy, Cézanne has painted a fair-haired, nude woman seated before a group of male admirers from various occupations and walks of life. Among them is a mitred bishop, gift bearers, musicians, workers and, to the right, a painter poised before an easel. A wide spectrum of humanity is shown offering homage to the enthroned woman. Yet the painter to the right seems to look not at the woman, as the rest assuredly do, but across the scene at a mountain, which he has begun to paint upon his canvas. If this painter is Cézanne – as has been proposed – why then is he steadfastly refusing to paint what is before his eyes? The answer lies in the title *L'Eternel féminin*. As Gary Wells has discovered, the title comes from the last lines of Part Two of Goethe's *Faust*:[38]

CÉZANNE 285

Fig. 2. From the collection of the J. Paul Getty Museum, Malibu, California, Paul Cézanne, L'Eternel feminin, ca. 1877, oil on canvas, 17 × 21 in.

> What is destructible
> Is but a parable;
> What fails ineluctably,
> The undeclarable,
> Here it was seen,
> Here it was action,
> The Eternal-Feminine
> Lures to perfection.[39]

The theme of Goethe's concluding words can be interpreted as a "mystical expression of the relation between the earthly and heavenly spheres."[40] According to Goethe, the ideal is expressed in feminine terms on earth as a symbol or reflection of the "higher spheres". Only woman is capable of this. Significantly, the final scene is dominated by the presence of the Virgin as voiced in the adoring words of Doctor Marianus – whose very name refers to his Marian devotion – uttered immediately before the close of the play:

> Penitents, behold elated
> The redeeming face;
> Grateful, be regenerated
> For a life of grace.
> That all good minds would grow keen
> To serve thee alone;
> Holy Virgin, mother, queen,
> Goddess on thy throne!
> (12096–12103)

The end of *Faust*, with its emphasis on the redeeming power of love through the grace of the Virgin, would have had an immediate appeal to Cézanne on several levels. In the Doctor's words, Goethe refers to Mary as "Virgin", "Mother", *and* "Goddess" in such a way as to suggest that she embodies the archetypal notion of woman in all her manifestations. According to Hans Eichner, the Eternal Feminine is a symbol of the purity of the Virgin who hovers above, a "purity, that by a miracle, is not sterile: Virgin and Mother." Furthermore, it refers also to "Gretchen, who precedes Faust in his ascent to higher regions . . . ."[41] In *Faust*, earthly love is a symbol of the divine love found in "higher spheres", and it is woman who is capable of communicating and drawing man to the divine realm, the only place where love can find true fulfillment.

Goethe's words are thus paraphrased in Cézanne's painting in his own idiosyncratic fashion. Without relying on any direct depiction of the poetic text, Cézanne has his own, personal response to the final message in *Faust*. He has shown himself painting the very symbol of the Eternal Feminine – Mont Sainte-Victoire – which, as I have suggested, metaphorically embodies the dual notion of love and symbolized both the Virgin and Venus. The woman under the canopy – whose configuration Schapiro has, significantly, likened to an *Hommage to Venus* – is a Faustian symbol of the means by which one achieves this end.[42] Woman alone can lead one's soul upward to the redeeming, all-pervasive power of sacred love. That the mountain embodies and reconciles these opposites is reflected in the similarities between the shape of the mountain on the canvas, the canopy sheltering the woman, and in the pose of the woman herself.

As Schapiro suggests, if the woman under the canopy is a Venus type, then again Cézanne has blended the Virgin with her pagan counterpart. Such a seemingly odd pairing is justified if we turn to two other sources familiar to Cézanne, both of which use as their dominant themes the juxtaposition of the sacred and profane in the guise of the Virgin and Venus and include a mountain as a symbolic vehicle expressive of this idea: Richard Wagner's opera *Tannhäuser* and Dante's *Purgatorio*.

Cézanne admiration for Wagner was shared by many of his fellow artists. During the mid-eighties, when he began to paint Mont Sainte-Victoire, there appeared an influential, albeit short-lived, journal devoted to the music and philosophy of Wagner, *La Revue wagnérienne*, published between 1885 and 1888. While Cézanne's love for Wagner's music predates the journal's arrival by some twenty years, his interest in Wagner, and Mont Sainte-Victoire, was undoubtedly rekindled by its publication.

While no direct evidence exists that Cézanne ever attended a performance of a Wagner opera, it is certain that he was familiar with both the music and libretto as well as the critical responses to the scandalous *Tannhäuser*. As a young artist, Cézanne arrived in Paris exactly one month after the opera's premiere there, and the various popular Parisian newspapers and journals were abuzz with mostly negative reviews of Wagner's unorthodox operatic form. However, there exists not only documentary but also pictorial evidence attesting to the young Cézanne's admiration for Wagner.

Cézanne devoted three canvases to the theme of *Tannhäuser* each entitled *The Overture to Tannhäuser*, dating from between 1864 and 1869. Unfortunately, only one version survives dating from about 1866–69 (V. 90). The painting is rather prosaic in its proposed treatment of the complexity of the opera's libretto and score. Yet, the models may have been Cézanne older sister Marie, at the piano, and Mme. Cézanne, who listens in the background. If this is so, then Cézanne has again juxtaposed two contrasting images of woman: his virginal sister and his mother.[43] Though the painting scarcely illuminates Cézanne's reaction to the opera, the title of the painting refers specifically to Wagner's overture, which received much critical attention, particularly from Cézanne's favorite poet, Charles Baudelaire. And it is to him that we must now turn our attention, as Cézanne assuredly did.

Baudelaire's article in defense of Wagner's *Overture* appeared after its controversial performance in 1860 in Paris. In his eloquent article, he devotes considerable space to Wagner's thematically rich overture. Baudelaire's articulation of the themes of Wagner's opera had an immediate, vitally resonant, appeal to the sensibilities of Cézanne's personal and artistic philosophy. Baudelaire emphasized the theme of duality as expressed in the overture, which represented for him "the battle of two principles which have chosen the human heart as their field of battle, that is to say the flesh with the spirit, hell with heaven, Satan with God." These conflicting forces are in turn expressed in the music. In Baudelaire's words, the drama is echoed by the two melodies, "the religious and the sensual, which, to borrow Liszt's formula, 'are here posed as two terms which, in the finale, are resolved.' "[44]

Baudelaire's analysis of the overture was so well known that it was paraphrased in a conversation between Gagnière and Claude Lantier in Zola's novel, *L'Oeuvre*. In the novel, Gagnière speaks of the profound religious motif of Wagner's Pilgrim's Chorus, which slowly gives place to "the voices of Sirens that, little by little, give way to the voluptuousness of Venus" only to be taken over by the sacred theme, which welds them into one "supreme harmony . . . in order to carry them away on the wings of a great triumphal hymn!"[45]

The story of Tannhäuser – a man caught between his desires for sensual pleasure and spiritual salvation – surely interested Cézanne. Even more significant is the fact that the hero is more specifically poised between Venus and the Virgin as revealed in the opening dialogue in Act One. The scene is the grotto beneath the Venusberg mountain where the pagan goddess, now banished, keeps her abode. Tannhäuser, after submitting to the powers of Venus, is suffering from a spiritual crisis. He wishes, against the demands of Venus, to flee the subterranean grotto. The ensuing dialogue magnifies the opposition between Venus and the Virgin:

VENUS: Repose will never be your lot,
neither will you find peace!
Come again to me, if, some time, you should seek your salvation!

TANNHAUSER: Goddess of pleasure and delight, no!
Oh, not in you shall I find peace and repose!
My salvation lies in Mary![46] (Act One, Scene One)

Baudelaire's essay addressed the transformed character of Venus as she appeared in Wagner's opera, when he observed that the goddess "has not traversed the horrific shades of the Middle Ages with impunity. She no longer inhabits Olympus . . . She has retired to the depths of a magnificent cave . . . By descending underground she has brought herself closer to Hell . . . ."[47] It is easy to ascertain the extent to which Cézanne would have absorbed Baudelaire's assessment of the place Venus now occupies in modern culture. Venus, who used to occupy mountaintops, has now been cast down to earth, and the implication in Wagner's opera is that she has been replaced by the Virgin, to whom Tannhäuser turns for absolution and salvation. The implications of this transformation are self-evident with respect to the dual meaning Mont Sainte-Victoire held for Cézanne. The *mons veneris* with all of its sexual connotaions had now, in his imagination, become Mont Sainte-Victoire.

The Wagnerian and Baudelairian equation of Venus and hell, an identification not lost on Cézanne, calls for a new interpretation of one of his most celebrated images of Mont Sainte-Victoire: *Mont Sainte-Victoire Seen From the Bibemus Quarry* (V. 766), from about 1898, now in Baltimore. Never before in Cézanne's images of Mont Sainte-Victoire has the mountain so emphatically imposed itself upon the beholder. Cézanne chose to depict the mountain as close to the frontal plane of the canvas as possible, while at the same time, through the juxtaposition of warm and cool tones, suggesting spatial depth. The most striking feature of this particular canvas is the starkly rendered opposition of the cool blueness of the mountain and the infernal reddish ochres of the quarry. From Cézanne's vantage point, he seems to be perilously poised before an abyss, with the mountain soaring into the sky behind. It seems inconceivable that this particular compositional arrangement is an abstracted formal construct. The opposition of up (mountain) and down (quarry) vibrates with symbolic significance. We have already witnessed, in the case of Cézanne's earlier *La Tranchée*, the juxtaposition of the sexuality (death) of the earth with the aspirant form of Mont Sainte-Victoire, which yearns for the blue sky above.[48] There is little doubt that the same guiding impulse is at work here in the Baltimore picture, but the crucial difference between the two pictures rests in Cézanne's artistic decision, in the later picture, to manipulate the canvas to such an extent that the near and the far, the quarry and the mountain, the accessible and the elusive, and the real and the ideal are amazingly welded together into a harmonious ensemble through the ingenious manipulation of the two-dimensional surface of the canvas. Cézanne's coercion of nature to conform to the realities of his canvas was a deliberate artistic device directly related to, and an expression of, his desire to resolve the conflicts which laid siege to his troubled inner self.

Cézanne was far from alone in devoting so much of his attention to a mountain towards the end of his life. This was something he shared with other painters who, like himself, turned to the painting of mountains as they sensed their own mortality. One need only observe the monotypes of Degas, Hodler's Alpine pictures, and the *Tannhäuser* paintings of Fantin-Latour, all created in the artists' later years.

While these painters may not have turned to the mountain for precisely the same reason as did Cézanne, they certainly saw in this subject something psychologically or spiritually comforting. The mountain constitutes, therefore, an archetypal symbol of hope and harmony, as the abundant allusions in literature attest. For example, Balzac in his *Seraphita*, whose central theme is that of the harmonious fusion of opposites, claimed "There beneath us I hear the supplications and wailings of that harp of sorrows . . . Here I listen to the choir of harmonies. There, below, is hope, the glorious inception of faith; but here is faith – it reigns, hope realized." Carus claimed that mountains allowed one to "lose yourself in space; your whole being undergoes a quiet refining and cleansing; your ego vanishes . . .".[49]

The association of the ascent of a mountain with a cleansing or purifying process is a very old one, one embraced by every Alpinist. For Cézanne this surely dates back to his youthful readings of Dante, particularly of the *Purgatorio*.⁵⁰ Dante's Mountain of Purgatory as a symbol in the second part of *The Divine Comedy* is a complex subject about which much has been written and need not be reiterated here. Yet there are several aspects of Dante's epic poem that bear a significant relationship to our present discussion.

Dante's Purgatorial mountain stood as a symbol of the purification of the penitent's soul in preparation for the entry into the Earthly Paradise. As Dante and Virgil are about to begin their ascent of the mountain, one of the first things they notice is Venus as the morning star, a symbol of the human love ⁵¹ that, according to Dante (and similarly Goethe), leads to divine love in the guise of Beatrice/Mary. The higher Dante ascends, the more frequent are the references to Venus's opposite, Diana (the chaste goddess of the hunt and, therefore, a pagan counterpart to the Virgin), here associated with both Beatrice and the Virgin in one of many examples of Dante's adaptations of pagan themes to Christian belief. It is only after Dante reaches the summit of the mountain that he is completely purged of sin and ready to mount to the stars and the Virgin in Paradise. Once again, we find associated with a mountain the duality of the Virgin and Venus, or human and divine love. The path to the divine is paved by human love – or the Eternal Feminine – symbolized by Beatrice who, by implication, will lead Dante to the Virgin.

The mountain as a symbol of the Dantesque quest for the ideal and the purity of the spirit was not unknown amongst nineteenth century painters. The most prominent example is found in a poster announcing the first exhibition of the *Salon de la Rose-Croix* designed by the artist Carlos Schwabe in 1892. The format of the poster is appropriately tall and narrow. It depicts three female figures, two of whom are clothed and ascend a flight of stairs. The other figure, who is shown nude and covered with a muddy substance, crouches at the bottom of the composition. The figure in the middle ground is offering a lily to the figure above who is depicted as an ethereal being. She represents, according to Pincus-Witten, "pure Idealism". The steps upon which these two figures stand are strewn with lilies and roses, both of which are traditional attributes of Mary.⁵² In the background is a towering mountain. Schwabe's poster is indicative of the trend in the nineties in France toward a new spiritual revival which sought to combat the positivism and materialism dominating French nineteenth century culture. The poster may well have been known to Cézanne, for he was in Paris in 1892, where it was highly visible. Furthermore, Cézanne would have been familiar with Schwabe's work since he illustrated Zola's novel *Le Rêve* in the same year.[53]

Cézanne's paintings of Mont Sainte-Victoire are visual expressions of his immersion in nature as a vehicle toward self-expression. Our Mont Sainte-Victoire (Figure 1) is a fully developed manifestation of his response to his mountain. The mountain at first recedes from the frontal plane of the canvas only to be pulled back to the foreground by Cézanne's characteristic horizontal banding of warm and cool tonal juxtapositons. The neat formal stratificaion of the picture's two-dimensional surface is accompanied by a flurry of brushstrokes, resulting in an artistically expressive ensemble that partakes of both an ordered and seemingly chaotic response to nature. The unification of the painting's surface, by extension, welds these divergent formal aspects in the same way that Wagner's overture to *Tannhäuser* conjoins two opposing musical themes.

While the manifest themes found in the works of Zola, Goethe, Wagner, Dante, and Baudelaire echo Cézanne's quest toward wholeness and inner reconciliation, they merely reflected his dreams, not his reality. The duality that so characterized Cézanne's entire existence was eased only by his ability to reconcile on canvas that which he could not in life. These last paintings of Mont Sainte-Victoire represent Cézanne at the height of his artistic powers. Both the choice of subject matter (and its attendent associations) as well as the formal means by which Cézanne constructed these pictures, facilitated the expression of his desire to fuse opposites: earth and sky, order and chaos, emotion and intellect, pagan and Christian, the Virgin and Venus, the sacred and the profane. The duality of his life was pictorially and symbolically reconciled by the dualism that characterizes his Mont Sainte-Victoire pictures.

Cézanne's paintings, particularly his Mont Sainte-Victoire series, have often been seen as the crucial link between the nineteenth century and the Cubism of Picasso. As such, Cézanne has often been referred to, and with much justification, as the "father of modern art". While there is no doubt that the flat, faceted, and semi-abstract formal qualities found in Cézanne's pictures anticipated and fed Picasso's Cubism, it is a mistake to see Cézanne as a willing participant in such an art historical game. For Cézanne, form was a means toward an end, not an end in itself. Cézanne painted the way he did not becuase he was interested in contributing something new and novel to the history of art, but because it was the means by which he could express his innermost desire to reconcile conflict. It was, in short, the only way he could paint.

NOTES

* I would like to thank Profs. Mary Louise Krumrine, George Mauner, Eldon Van Liere, and my wife Amy Yerkes for their support and helpful suggestions in the writing of this article.
** Throughout this article I mention and describe works that are not accompanied by illustrations in the present text. In such cases, I either direct the reader to the appropriate source of said illustrations via a footnote or, in the case of Cézanne's works, I will direct the reader to the standard Catalogue Raisonné reference number(s) found in Lionello Venturi, *Cézanne, son art, son oeuvre*, 2 volumes (Paris, 1936). Such works mentioned in the text will be followed, in parentheses, by the designation V. and the appropriate number.

[1] Max Raphael, *The Demands of Art* (Princeton, 1968), p. 11.
[2] *Ibid.*, p. 11.
[3] Bernard Dorival, *Cézanne*, trans. H.H.A. Thackthwaite (New York, 1948), pp. 94–95. In an undated questionnaire Cézanne responded that the writer he most admired was Racine. This document is reproduced in Adrien Chappuis, *The Drawings of Cézanne: A Catalogue Raisonné* (Greenwich, 1978), pp. 25–28.
[4] Émile Zola, *The Masterpiece*, trans. Thomas Walton (Ann Arbor, 1983), p. 52.
[5] Paul Cézanne, *Correspondance*, ed. John Rewald (Paris, 1978), p. 249. See letter to Gasquet of 30 April 1896. Cézanne stated, "Certes, un artiste désire s'élever intellectuellement le plus possible, mais l'homme doit rester obscur."
[6] Meyer Schapiro, *Cézanne* (New York, 1952), p. 11. Schapiro was the first to recognize Cézanne's sublimation of the themes of his early "literal" paintings into the less obvious genres of landscape and still life. See especially his article, "The Apples of Cézanne: An Essay on the Meaning of Still Life", reprinted in his *Modern Art: 19th and 20th Centuries* (New York, 1982), pp. 1–38.
[7] Cézanne, *Correspondance*, p. 165. Letter to Zola of 14 April 1878.
[8] *Ibid.*, p. 211. Letter of 24 May 1883.
[9] *Ibid.*, p. 217. Letter of 14 May 1885.
[10] Rewald, p. 269.
[11] Cézanne, *Correspondance*, pp. 226–227. Letter of May 1886.
[12] John Watenhall, "Cézanne's *Mont Sainte-Victoire Seen from Les Lauves*", *Pantheon*, I, 1982, p. 48.
[13] Plutarch, *Plutarch's Lives*, Vol. 9, trans. Berandotte Perrin (Cambridge, 1959), p. 511.
[14] Carol Solomon Kiefer, "Paul Cézanne, François-Marius Granet and the Provençal Landscape Tradition", Ph.D. dissertation, University of Pittsburgh, 1987, p. 11. See also Michel Hoog, "Le Motif de la Sainte Victoire", in *Cézanne ou la peinture en jeu*, ed. Denis Coutagne (Aix, 1982), pp. 93–105. Hoog acknowledges the confusion surrounding the etymology of Sainte-Victoire but claims that, in any case, the name evokes both the sacred and the victorious, p. 101. He also mentions that it has been suggested that Sainte-Victoire may refer to one Saint Victurien – a proposal that, in my mind, is as unlikely as the association of the mountain with Saint Victor. Since the completion of my dissertation

an important exhibition has been held, and its catalogue published, on Cézanne's Mont Sainte-Victoire pictures. Much of the information I offer here concerning the history of the mountain and origin of its name was independently presented in this catalogue. See: Paul-Albert Février, "Histoire de Victoires", and Nicole Martin-Vignes, "Pèlerinage", in Denis Coutagne and Bruno Ely (eds.), *Sainte-Victoire Cézanne 1990* (Aix-en-Provence, 1990), pp. 63–72.

[15] Archibald Marshall, *A Spring Walk in Provence*, 2nd ed. (New York, 1920), p. 94.

[16] See Amédée Thierry, *Histoire de Gaulois depuis les temps les plus reculés jusq'à l'entière soumission de la gaule à la domination romaine*, Vol. 2, 18th ed. (Paris, 1870), pp. 29–30. See also M. Fauris de Saint-Vincens, "Topographie", *Le Magasin encyclopédique, ou journal de sciences, des lettres et des arts*, Vol. 4, 1814, pp. 320–321. Fauris de Saint-Vincens claims that the dedication of the temple erected by Marius was at some point rededicated and that "Sainte-Victoire fut nommée la patronne de ce temple". The identity of this "patronne" is unclear. As there exists no Saint Victoire in the lexicon of saints, the only certainty is that this "patronne" is indeed female. I assert that the patroness of the new "temple" was the Virgin herself.

[17] Fauris de Saint-Vincens, pp. 321–322.

[18] Thierry, p. 30.

[19] Claude Alleau, *Les Guides Noirs: Guide de la Provence mysterieuse* (Paris, 1965), p. 350. The Carmelites were especially devoted to the Virgin.

[20] Quoted in Gerstle Mack, *Paul Cézanne* (New York, 1935), pp. 328–329.

[21] Sir Walter Scott, *Anne of Geierstein* (London and New York, 1880), pp. 354–357. In Scott's historical novel, which was most popular in France in the nineteenth century, the character Thiebault explains the origins of the name Sainte-Victoire. According to him (Scott), the mountain derived its name "from a great victory which was gained by a Roman general, named Caio Mario . . . in gratitude to Heaven for which victory Caio Mario vowed to build a monastery on the mountain, for the service of the Virgin Mary, in honour of whom he had been baptized", p. 354. Despite the obvious anachronism (one which Scott himself acknowledges) it is clear that, in the nineteenth century, Mont Sainte-Victoire was associated with the Virgin. Unfortunately, I have been unable to locate Scott's source of information.

[22] See Charles Sterling, *Le Couronnement de la Vierge* (Paris, 1939), pp. 17–18 and the corresponding illustrations.

[23] Émile Littré, *Dictionnaire de la langue française*, abrégé par A. Beaujean (Vernoy, 1981), p. 1267.

[24] Thomas Kselman, *Miracles and Prophecies in Nineteenth-Century France* (New Brunswick, N.J., 1983), pp. 89, 102, and 166–168. Emphasis mine.

[25] See Bram Dijkstra, *The Idols of Perversity* (Oxford, 1986), pp. 15–24, especially p. 19.

[26] Émile Zola, *The Sin of Father Mouret*, trans. Sandey Petrey (Lincoln, Nebraska, 1969), p. 79.

[27] *Ibid.*, p. 73.

[28] The *Stella Maris* was one of the most enduring epithets of the Virgin. According to Albert Boime, *Thomas Couture and the Eclectic Vision* (New Haven, 1988), p. 249, the image of Mary as Star of the Sea was a prominent image among the Romantics and probably, in part, inspired Couture's mural *Stella Maris* in the church of Saint-Eustache

in Paris. See Boime, fig. VIII.2, p. 234. I am indebted to George Mauner for leading me to this source.
[29] Fauris de Saint-Vincens, p. 321.
[30] Alleau, p. 568.
[31] Sidney Geist, *Interpreting Cézanne* (Cambridge, 1988), pp. 69–73.
[32] Zola, *The Sin of Father Mouret*, p. 91.
[33] Geist, p. 73.
[34] Michelet's *La Montagne* was a huge popular success and went through several editions in its first year. See Edward K. Kaplan, *Michelet's Poetic Vision: A Romantic Philosophy of Nature, Man, and Woman* (Amherst, MA, 1977), p. 94.
[35] Apparently, while reading Michelet's *L'Oiseau, L'Insecte,* and *La Montagne,* Zola underwent a near mystical experience. See Philip Walker, *Zola* (London, 1985), p. 79.
[36] Jules Michelet, *Oeuvres complètes*, ed. Paul Viallaneix (Paris), p. 108.
[37] Quoted in Kaplan, p. 137.
[38] Gary Neil Wells, "Metaphorical Relevance and Thematic Continuity in the Early Paintings of Paul Cézanne", Ph.D. dissertation, Ohio State University, 1987, p. 214.
[39] J.W. Goethe, *Faust*, trans. Walter Kaufman (Garden City and New York, 1963), p. 502. All quotations are from this edition.
[40] Goethe, J. W., *Faust*, trans. Bayard Taylor, eds. Marshall Montgomery and Douglas Yates (London, 1963), p. 446.
[41] Hans Eichner, "The Eternal Feminine: An Aspect of Goethe's Ethics", *Transactions of the Royal Society of Canada*, ser. 4, no. 9, 1971, pp. 234–244. Reprinted in *Faust*, trans. Walter Arndt, ed. Cyrus Hamlin (New York, 1976), p. 624.
[42] Schapiro, "The Apples of Cézanne", p. 38, 91 n. Schapiro likens Cézanne's picture to J. A. Van Dyck's *Hommage to Venus* in Karlsruhe. Both compositional and thematic similarities between the two works suggest familiarity and an influence must be assumed. However, I have not been able to uncover direct evidence that Cézanne had actually seen this work. Moreover, Wells has discovered that Cézanne's painting conforms fairly closely to an episode in *Faust* where Helen is described before a canopied throne surrounded by admirers. See: Wells, pp. 214–218. If this is indeed the case, then it would be highly probable that Cézanne would see Helen as a Venus type and conflate the symbolic meanings of the two.
[43] Rewald, p. 123. According to Rewald's research, Marie was apparently a "devout spinster".
[44] Charles Baudelaire, *Oeuvres complètes*, ed. Y.-G. Le Dantec, rev. by Claude Pichot (Paris, 1961), p. 1223.
[45] Émile Zola, *Les Rougon-Macquart*, ed. Henri Mitterand, Vol. 4 (Paris, 1966), p. 201.
[46] Richard Wagner, *Tannhäuser*, cond. Erick Leinsdorf, The Metropolitan Opera, Decca, 1971. English translation by Peggie Cochrane.
[47] Baudelaire, *Oeuvres complètes*, p. 1219.
[48] That Cézanne in this picture has associated the earth with death via the stark tonal juxtaposition of the quarry and the mountain may be, in part, explained by a local Aixois tradition. Mary Tompkins Lewis has discovered that there was a long-standing fascination in Aix with death imagery. In the nineteenth century several archeological excavations of the environs of Aix uncovered evidence of a primitive "Celtic Ligurian culture in which

the *tête de mort* was venerated and thought to protect its worshipers." Lewis goes on to say that pillars hewn from the Bibemus quarry (the very quarry depicted by Cézanne) were decorated with death's heads. These artifacts were exhibited at the Musée Granet during the artist's lieftime. See Mary Tompkins Lewis, *Cézanne's Early Imagery* (Berkeley, 1989), pp. 40–43.

[49] Quoted in Roald Nasgaard, *The Mystic North: Symbolist Landscape Painting in Northern Europe and North America, 1890–1940* (Toronto, 1984), pp. 138–139.

[50] The early letters between Cézanne and Zola contain numerous references to Dante. See, for example, Zola, *Correspondance*, pp. 130 and 140.

[51] According to Ciardi, "Venus represents love [and] leads the way and that Divine illumination follows it." See Dante, *The Purgatorio*, trans. John Ciardi (New York, 1961), p. 37. See Canto I, 19–21. Moreover, later in the *Purgatorio*, Virgil and Dante encounter two trees (one in Canto XXII and the other in Canto XXIII). According to Francis Fergusson, *Dante's Drama of the Mind* (Princeton, 1953), p. 141, these trees are an obvious allusion to both the Tree of Knowledge and the Tree of Death which "symbolize, both in their natural and historic aspects, the paradoxes of human nourishment: nourishment for the flesh and for the spirit; delight and renunciation, feast and sacrifice in one."

[52] See Figure 8, p. 246, in Robert Pincus-Witten, *Occult Symbolism in France: Joséphin Peladan and the Salons de la Rose-Croix* (New York, 1976), p. 102. The rose was also, not surprisingly, a traditional attribute of Venus as well. See, for example, J.C. Cooper, *An Illustrated Encyclopedia of Traditional Symbols* (London, 1987).

[53] *Ibid.*, p. 103.

ALAIN LAFRAMBOISE

LES PORTRAITS EMBLÉMATIQUES DE BRONZINO, AUX MARGES DES PRATIQUES SYMBOLIQUES CONSACRÉES DANS LES ARTS VISUELS*

Parlant de certains éléments qui apparaissent dans les portraits de Lorenzo Lotto, John Pope-Hennessy écrivait:

Par nature les emblèmes sont envahissants et même des peintres de l'envergure de Lotto n'arrivaient pas à les intégrer de manière satisfaisante à leurs compositions.[1]

Si les «emblèmes» se révèlent moins gênants dans les portraits de Bronzino, ils n'ont pas moins d'envergure et c'est la nature de leur invasion, dans ce qu'on pourrait appeler une galerie de portraits, que je voudrais aborder ici.

Mais d'abord un préambule en forme d'aide-mémoire. Cesare Ripa annonçait dans la préface de son *Iconologia*, parue à la fin du XVIe siècle (1593), que les images dont il traitait étaient «faites pour signifier une chose différente de celle que voit l'œil» (*Le imagini fatte per significare una diversa cosa da quella, che si vede con l'occhio*). Il appelait *l'arte dell'altre imagini*, l'art des autres images, la réalisation des allégories.

Ripa, qui souhaitait être perçu comme un lettré et un érudit[2] n'entendait pas proposer un code dépourvu de toute subtilité. La preuve en est qu'il n'hésitait pas à rapprocher ses allégories des jeux concettistes des auteurs d'*imprese*. Ces images dont il disait qu'en peu de corps et en peu de mots (*con pochi corpi, & poche parole*) elles faisaient surgir un concept (*concetto*).

Il expliquait que celles-ci devaient avoir forme humaine puisque c'est de l'âme humaine qu'il était question — reprenant aux philosophes l'idée que l'homme est la mesure de toutes choses — et que tous les éléments de l'image contribuaient à sa signification. Ajoutant que dans ces images la position de la tête et l'apparence du visage permettaient d'afficher telle ou telle passion, que les bras, les mains, les jambes, les coiffures, les vêtements jouaient leurs rôles, que la couleur, les proportions, l'âge, toutes ces données qui ne pouvaient se séparer de l'ensemble contribuaient à définir l'allégorie, la rendant «conforme à la chose» et témoignant du bon jugement (*il buon giudizio*) de celui qui avait su la constituer en une «chose parfaite et agréable» (*una cosa sola, ma perfetta, & dilettevole*). Ainsi, comme avec l'*impresa*, le jugement et l'ingéniosité concettiste de l'inventeur demeuraient un aspect essentiel de ce jeu consistant à produire des images articulées sur le mode d'une définition.[3]

Cette conformité avec la chose faisait que la définition produite en peinture devait être à l'imitation de la définition écrite (*definitione scritta*) et semblable à la description dont se servaient les orateurs et les poètes. Connaissant la «chose» (*le qualità, le cagioni, le proprietà, & gli accidenti d'una cosa definibile*) dont il traitait, l'auteur de l'allégorie devait chercher quelque similitude (*similitudine*) avec des objets matériels qui allaient lui servir à figurer son concept.[4] Similitude de proportion, précisait Ripa, entre deux objets distincts. Ainsi la colonne servait à figurer la Force puisque la colonne soutenant tout l'édifice sans vaciller est comme la force de l'homme qui résiste aux fatigues et difficultés diverses qu'il rencontre; ainsi l'épée et l'écu, outils du soldat qui défend sa propre vie et attaque autrui conviennent-ils à un rapprochement avec la Rhétorique, car l'orateur avec ses arguments sait se rendre les choses favorables et repousser celles qui lui sont contraires. Il admettait aussi qu'on ait recours à «une autre sorte de similitude quand deux choses distinctes se rejoignent dans une chose différente d'elles»; ainsi, pour dénoter la magnanimité, on prendra le lion, «cette façon de procéder qui doit déjà moins à l'analogie, mais associe encore deux idées dans un signe unique, étant de l'avis de Ripa moins louable, encore que plus usitée».[5]

Il peut sembler paradoxal, alors qu'on aborde un corpus de portraits, de parler d'un ouvrage appartenant à la théorie de l'expression figurée. On sait cependant que les théoriciens de l'*impresa* allaient jusqu'à dire qu'à la limite tout tableau pouvait être entendu comme une *impresa*. Sans trop m'éloigner de ces propositions, mon objectif sera de lire les portraits de Bronzino comme s'il s'agissait d'images symboliques, sachant que Bronzino avait, par ailleurs, réalisé de remarquables allégories conformes, avant la lettre, aux prescriptions de Ripa. On sait à quel point, encore aujourd'hui, l'*Allégorie de Londres* a le pouvoir de solliciter l'*ingegno* des historiens de l'art.

Les portraits de Bronzino ne correspondent pas à l'objectif premier du portrait à la Renaissance, soit à un énoncé de l'artiste sur la personnalité de son modèle à un moment où l'on considère que le visage parle, qu'il peut exprimer ou masquer des émotions[6]. Depuis la Renaissance, «L'individu est [...] indissociable de l'expression singulière de son visage, traduction corporelle de son moi intime.»[7]

Cet énoncé du peintre qui trace un portrait peut être appuyé ou renforcé par des procédés littéraires ou symboliques, soit l'inscription qui accompagne le portrait sur une médaille (avers ou revers), soit les tableaux qui couvrent le portrait qu'ils recèlent un peu comme la page frontispice d'un livre et qui proposent une sorte de définition cryptée du sujet, à la manière de l'*impresa* (qu'on songe à l'allégorie peinte par Lorenzo Lotto qui recouvrait le portrait qu'il avait fait de Bernardo de' Rossi, évêque de Treviso)[8]. Le peintre peut aussi choisir une composition explicitement allégorique (les fresques de Botticelli à la Villa Tornabuoni qui font que Lorenzo Tornabuoni rencontre les figures des Arts libéraux), ou encore déterminer les attributs dont s'accompagne son modèle: il pourra s'agir d'un motif végétal ou architectural dans l'environnement du modèle, d'un élément floral brodé sur un vêtement et ayant un caractère emblématique, de divers objets et figures dont l'envergure et la transparence symbolique varieront.

On sait, par exemple, que Lorenzo Lotto a réalisé des œuvres qui faisaient se rejoindre l'aspect emblématique de l'image et le travail du portraitiste attentif aux expressions avec, on peut le croire, l'objectif d'en arriver à des portraits plus justes. John Pope-Hennessy disait à propos du *Portrait d'Andrea Odoni* que cette peinture était une construction et que son sujet n'était pas d'abord le portrait d'un collectionneur, fier de montrer sa pièce, comme c'est le cas avec le *Portrait de Jacopo Strada* par le Titien. Odoni tend de sa main droite au spectateur une statuette représentant la Diane d'Éphèse, symbole de la Terre ou de la Nature. Pope-Hennessy rappelle qu'on retrouve la déesse au plafond de la Chambre de la Signature et que Ripa l'a décrite ainsi qu'on peut la voir. Burckhardt avait supposé que dans ce portrait il fallait plutôt l'entendre comme une figure de l'antithèse entre la nature et l'art. L'air méditatif d'Odoni suggérerait des pensées tournées vers les pouvoirs destructeurs du temps et les outrages qu'a subis la culture du passé.

Fonctionnant tout à fait suivant les mêmes modalités, ce *Portrait d'une veuve* par Bronzino qui a été souvent commenté[9]. Le modèle est flanqué d'une version réduite de la *Rachel* du *Tombeau de Jules II* de Michel-Ange et les figurines qui ornent le rebord de la table reproduisent les sculptures de la Chapelle Médicis. La *Rachel* représente évidemment la vie contemplative qu'a choisie cette jeune femme et les figures allégoriques du tombeau des Médicis étaient interprétées par Vasari et Condivi comme des figures des Heures (l'*Aurore*, le *Jour*, le *Soir* et la *Nuit*)[10] signifiant le pouvoir destructeur du temps, bien que Varchi y ait plutôt vu une déclaration affirmant que non pas un hémisphère mais le monde devait être une tombe à la mesure de chacun des deux ducs. Quoi qu'il en soit, le caractère funéraire de ces figures ne fait aucun doute.

Mais que dira-t-on de ce *Portrait d'un gentilhomme* par Bronzino, maintenant au Musée des Beaux-Arts du Canada, qui, comme Andrea Odoni, a près de lui une statuette, cette fois celle d'une Vénus pudique? Comment doit-on interpréter cette figure et le portrait tout entier? Je vous propose donc de voir comment Bronzino a créé de nouvelles formules à l'intérieur d'un langage qui était celui de la peinture de portrait à caractère emblématique. Pour cela, il est nécessaire de considérer non pas les œuvres individuellement mais un ensemble de portraits de cet artiste. On verra alors qu'un autre type de discours est possible qui vient élargir la compréhension que nous avons de ce maniériste florentin.

Chez Bronzino, les figures sont inscrites à la fois dans un cadre physique (souvent architecturé) et dans un cadre intellectuel (le plus souvent indiqué par des sculptures (statuettes) et des livres). Mais les attributs qui leur sont octroyés par le peintre n'ont pas l'évidence qu'on leur reconnaît chez nombre de ses prédécesseurs ou contemporains. Par contre, là où on n'attendait que des portraits surgit un discours d'un tout autre ordre.

Agnolo Bronzino, *Portrait d'un gentilhomme*, Ottawa, Musée des Beaux-Arts du Canada, huile sur bois, 107 x 83 cm, v. 1550-55.

Avant de s'attarder à la galerie de portraits que je vous propose, il est nécessaire de relever un certain nombre de traits du contexte artistique florentin. Il y eut une controverse à Florence et à Rome au XVIe siècle à savoir lequel des deux arts, de la peinture ou de la sculpture, était supérieur à l'autre. Le débat portait sur l'imitation de la nature et sur la question de ce qu'on appelle aujourd'hui l'*Ut pictura poesis*. Question débattue depuis l'Antiquité, qu'on pense à Philostrate (*Eikones*), à Pline l'Ancien (*Histoire naturelle)*, à Alberti (*De Pictura*) qui écrivait: «qui douterait que la peinture soit la maîtresse parmi les arts», à Léonard et à Castiglione (*Il Cortegiano*, 1527), tous deux également en faveur de la peinture.

Mais c'est ici surtout Varchi qui m'intéresse, lui qui cherchait à définir la fonction morale de l'art en empruntant à l'aristotélisme, au néo-platonisme, à Pétrarque, à Dante, à Bembo, plus à la manière d'un amateur que d'un vrai philosophe, mêlant la théorie de l'imitation d'Aristote aux Idées platoniciennes. On sait que sa réflexion prenait pour point de départ le célèbre poème de Michel-Ange «*Non ha l'ottimo artista alcun concetto*».

Benedetto Varchi (1503-1565), humaniste florentin, un des intellectuels les plus éminents de la cour médicéenne, après deux conférences à Florence en 1546, eut donc l'idée d'une *Inchiesta* à propos du *Paragone* (cette comparaison établie entre la peinture et la sculpture et d'autres fois entre poésie et peinture). Il mena son enquête auprès de l'architecte Tasso, des peintres Vasari, Pontormo, Bronzino, des sculpteurs Francesco da Sangallo, Tribolo, Benvenuto Cellini, et de Michel-Ange qui lui répondit qu'il avait peu de temps pour ce genre d'amusements et qu'il avait toujours considéré que «la sculpture était à la peinture ce que le soleil était à la lune».

Dans ce contexte, Bronzino fut, bien sûr, un partisan de la peinture mais, paradoxalement, son œuvre est remplie de références à la sculpture.

Je vous propose de tenter de voir ce que peut signifier une telle pratique et les effets de cette pratique en ce qui a trait à l'iconographie bronzinesque.

C'est un lieu commun que de faire mention de la sculpture quand on parle de la peinture de Bronzino. En termes stylistiques on relève surtout le dessin marqué, insistant sur les arêtes vives, la stylisation des corps, l'impassibilité des traits des personnages, l'emphase sur la verticalité, sur la rigidité, la coloration des chairs qui rappelle le marbre, l'ivoire. Cela dit, il faut aller au-delà de ces constatations et les interroger. Le rapprochement peinture-sculpture opère donc sur des observations précises, la connotation sculpturale est claire, évidente[11].

On retiendra surtout les portraits de la période de 1535-1555 en se rappelant que l'*Inchiesta* de Varchi est de 1546. Si les portraits sont les tableaux où les influences sculpturales sont les plus marquées, on retrouve aussi ces dernières dans toute sa production.

L'insertion la moins apparente de la sculpture dans la peinture a lieu dans la mise en scène du personnage, dans sa pose. Le modèle est, évidemment, offert par la sculpture. L'insertion la plus explicite expose clairement des citations, des statuettes, répliques de sculptures souvent connues, dont le caractère emblématique ne fait aucun doute, ou alors elle consiste, comme on l'a dit, en des attributs sculpturaux: chairs marmoréennes, éburnéennes suggérées par des membres épurés, stylisés, des passages brusques de la lumière à l'ombre.

Les motifs empruntés à la sculpture sont le plus souvent michelangélesques. Ainsi:

— le *Cosimo de' Medici* portant l'armure, dont la posture rappelle celle du *Moïse* par son opposition de la tête et des épaules;
— le *Portrait d'Ugolino Martelli* ou celui du *Gentilhomme* du Musée des Beaux-Arts du Canada à Ottawa s'établissant sur le motif inversé du *Giuliano*;
— le *Jeune homme au luth*, bras droit en retrait, main gauche sur le genou, main droite à moitié fermée sur un objet, reprenant sans le renverser, cette fois, la pose du *Giuliano*.

Mais en dehors des portraits on retrouve dans la peinture sacrée de Bronzino les mêmes pratiques:

— la *Déposition du corps du Christ* de Bronzino emprunte un motif célèbre à la première *Pietà* de Michel-Ange. Dans les deux cas, on a la même silhouette et Bronzino a rendu l'aspect musculaire en insistant sur les articulations qui sont particulièrement soulignées et qui se ressentent de l'influence de la sculpture. Je n'insiste pas sur le motif du bras et la pose de la main;

— le motif bien connu de la *Vénus pudique*, fort répandu dans l'Antiquité grecque et romaine et repris à la Renaissance par plusieurs artistes, a été utilisé dans la représentation du personnage féminin (l'Ève) apparaissant dans *Le Christ aux limbes* et dans celle d'un ange de *La Résurrection du Christ*. La citation est claire.

S'il faut parler de citation dans les trois derniers cas, c'est le terme de métaphore figurative qu'il faut employer pour identifier le travail de Bronzino, observé dans les portraits qu'on vient de voir, au sens que lui donnait Robert Klein, soit un procédé «aussi commun que la métaphore du langage [et qui] remplit la même fonction: suggérer, sur la base d'une ressemblance formelle, une assimilation révélatrice.» Klein observait encore que «Ce type de signification possède un statut spécial. Il n'est pas véhiculé par les formes sensibles de l'image, sinon indirectement, à travers une référence à autre chose»[12].

Dans les portraits, on verra que la sculpture est, en outre, présente sous forme de citations (miniaturisées):

— dans le *Portrait d'Ugolino Martelli*, une réplique d'un *David*, attribué à Antonio ou Bernardo Rossellino, qui est maintenant dans la collection Widener à la Galerie Nationale de Washington, apparaît à l'arrière-plan;

— dans le *Portrait d'une gentildonna*, aux Offices, on a déjà remarqué la *Rachel* du *Tombeau de Jules II* par Michel-Ange, et dans celui du *Gentilhomme* d'Ottawa, il y a sur la table une figurine de Vénus mutilée;

— dans le *Portrait d'un jeune homme*, dans la collection Merser à Londres, on trouve la statuette à demi cachée par une draperie d'un Bacchus;

— dans le *Jeune homme au luth* de Berlin, on voit une Suzanne au bain, dont la pose rappelle celle des *ignudi* de Michel-Ange, servant d'encrier posé sur la table;

— le *Jeune sculpteur* du Louvre tient une figure de la Renommée.

On constate donc que ce parcours révèle, au-delà des associations iconographiques, un champ sémantique très serré, articulé, une problématique.

Précisons davantage. Le plus étonnant et le plus intéressant, c'est encore de retrouver dans la peinture de Bronzino non seulement des motifs ou des poses et des citations sous forme de statuettes mais aussi des attributs que l'œil n'accorde qu'à la sculpture, qu'il ne rencontre qu'en sculpture.

Dans L'*Allégorie* de Londres, *La Luxure dévoilée par le Temps* ou *Vénus, l'Amour et la Jalousie* de Budapest, les corps rappellent, par leur tonalité, le marbre. Les nus du premier plan sont d'une teinte blanchâtre et uniforme que seule la lumière anime en jouant sur les muscles.

Même chose encore pour l'*Éléonore de Tolède et son fils Don Giovanni*. Le visage et les mains ont cette coloration livide qu'atténue et souligne à la fois l'éclairage.

Le *Portrait de Lucrezia Panciatichi* aux chairs blafardes et le *Portrait de Bia* aux mains, visage et cou particulièrement pâles, sont à associer à la même série. On remarquera que les joues légèrement colorées de Bia font l'effet d'un fard sur un visage de marbre.

Dans tous ces tableaux, on a noté une tendance à la géométrisation, un éclairage des corps polissant, une lumière qui irradie là où elle frappe. Le contour du visage est lavé de toute imperfection, de tout accident, il se rapproche de l'ovale pur. Le cou est lisse, plein, sans le moindre accident. C'est un cylindre et le tronc aussi.

Ainsi Bronzino a composé ses tableaux et particulièrement ses portraits à partir de certains éléments spécifiques à la sculpture.

Il faut maintenant évoquer, trop rapidement, les discours en vogue de la théorie de l'art pour saisir la portée des enjeux de l'œuvre de Bronzino du point de vue qui m'intéresse ici, à savoir les traités sur la peinture et sur la sculpture dans le contexte de cette controverse concernant la supériorité de la peinture ou de la sculpture sur l'art rival.

D'abord rappelons-nous que Vasari fait du dessin le père de l'architecture, de la sculpture et de la peinture. Pour lui, «le dessin ayant son origine dans l'intelligence extrait d'une multiplicité d'objets particuliers un jugement général, il est comme la forme ou l'idée de tous les objets naturels, laquelle forme par rapport à toutes les autres formes de la nature se singularise dans ses dimensions. [...] et de cette connaissance naît un certain concept (*giudizio*) qui se forme dans l'esprit. [...] Le jugement se forme dans l'esprit et s'exprime par les mains.»

On sait que dans la pratique, le sculpteur emploie le dessin lorsqu'il réalise une étude préparatoire à une œuvre, il pose ce qu'on appelle les *contorni*.

En peinture, le dessin a plusieurs emplois. D'abord il sert à tracer les contours de chaque figure. S'ajoute à cela le modelé aux fins de la vraisemblance.

Pour Vasari les figures peintes ou sculptées sont exécutées plus avec le jugement qu'avec la main en considérant la distance, le point de vue, l'effet. En termes d'effets, Varchi insiste pour dire que tant en peinture qu'en sculpture, l'objet ne se donne vraiment qu'à voir. La vue étant le sens important qui permet une certaine connaissance des choses et des personnes qui nous entourent. Malgré sa tridimensionnalité, la sculpture ne s'adresse, elle aussi, qu'à la vue. Mais la vue est un sens qu'il est facile de tromper.

Varchi, dans ses *Lezzioni*, pose que peinture et sculpture, face à leur modèle, la Nature, sont mensongères. L'une s'en rapprochant par la couleur, l'autre par le relief. Il expose que la peinture se rapproche de la Nature par le rendu des accidents (*accidenti*), la sculpture par la substance (*sostenza*, le relief). L'une par la vue, l'autre par le toucher. Différence qui tient donc au matériau. Peinture et sculpture, donc, travaillent différemment.

La sculpture construit en extrayant (car on pense au marbre plutôt qu'au bronze) et beaucoup plus lentement. Elle demande un surplus d'effort, de fatigue physique et intellectuelle. Elle gagne en outre en durabilité et en permanence sur tout ce que peut attendre un tableau.

La peinture se construit en ajoutant et se fait rapidement. Elle est beaucoup plus fragile qu'une sculpture et n'offre qu'un seul point de vue alors que la sculpture en propose huit (ce qu'avait avancé Benvenuto Cellini). La spécificité de la peinture naît donc de ses restrictions physiques: son support, une surface plate recouverte de couleurs. Elle ne peut représenter d'une figure plus d'un seul point de vue.

Mais la peinture sait rendre les *accidenti*. Dans le même sens, Paolo Pino a écrit: «L'art de la peinture imite la nature dans les choses superficielles.» (*L'arte della pittura è imitatrice della natura nelle cose superficiali.*) La peinture, c'est l'art de tromper le spectateur par le rendu des choses dans leur surface et sous certains angles. Et Varchi de reprendre l'anecdote des raisins de Zeuxis et du voile de Parrasios.

Par conséquent, pour bien maîtriser son art, le peintre doit réussir l'expression des *artificii* avec ses moyens techniques et son *giudizio*, soit les textures autant que les raccourcis: toutes choses que maîtrise Bronzino.

Donc Bronzino sait tromper la surface: soit jouer avec la perspective, suggérer les textures, traiter la lumière. Il le fait avec une grande virtuosité dans ses portraits en utilisant des éclairages étudiés. Car l'éclairage a un rôle important dans le rendu du relief, de la tridimensionnalité des corps. Bronzino fait de l'éclairage une utilisation suggestive en ce qui concerne le relief aux fins d'un rapprochement avec la sculpture.

On voit que Bronzino rencontre toutes les exigences sauf une: pourquoi un peintre aussi habile ne rend-il pas la texture de la chair ou seulement sa couleur? La thèse de l'incapacité technique est insoutenable.

Du côté des traités consacrés à la sculpture, dans cette perspective d'un détournement du sculptural vers le pictural, on ne retiendra que le conseil de Gauricus à ses élèves.

Celui-ci expliquait que le dessin du sculpteur devait d'abord insister sur les contours, les lignes extérieures et ensuite sur les articulations des membres. Il devait, en somme, toujours accuser nettement la troisième dimension. Chez Bronzino, l'utilisation très marquée de la lumière donne une grande puissance plastique au dessin, une grande fermeté où se sent la forte influence des reliefs antiques et de l'œuvre de Michel-Ange, de son travail à la Sixtine.

Gauricus recommandait également au sculpteur d'éviter l'excès de musculature, il était sévère pour ce qu'il appelait «les écorchés» de Verrocchio. Il incitait aussi à tempérer l'imitation minutieuse de la nature par un souci de beauté idéale et ressortait, comme tant d'autres, cette histoire de Zeuxis et des cinq plus belles jeunes filles d'Athènes.

On pourrait augmenter les remarques visant à faire voir à quel point un peintre admirant la sculpture était confronté à un ensemble considérable de prescriptions. C'est avec celles-ci que Bronzino a composé.

On a là les deux pôles entre lesquels Bronzino oscillera constamment: celui d'une imitation, d'un réalisme poussé, celui de l'épuration, de l'abstraction. Même dans ses portraits, ce qu'on pourrait appeler une forme de stylisation est évidente dans le traitement des visages, des mains, du cou, du torse. Mais cette stylisation renvoie parfois à des observations concernant la difficulté pour le sculpteur à représenter les mains ou les chevelures. Souplesse artificieuse de la main, chevelures traitées sculpturalement.

La peinture de Bronzino n'en est donc pas à une ambiguïté près.

La plupart des portraits que nous considérons furent exécutés entre 1535 et 1555. En 1539, Bronzino devient peintre officiel à la cour de Cosimo de' Medici. C'est une période tout imprégnée de l'*Inchiesta* de Varchi, déjà en gestation bien avant 1546.

Pour les portraits de cette époque, la mise en scène et le traitement varient peu, on l'a vu. Les objets qui entourent le modèle aident à le percevoir «intellectuellement»; c'est ce que Pope-Hennessy appelle «the intellectual setting»[13]. C'est en fait le meilleur moyen pour Bronzino de singulariser le personnage, car chaque visage est lisse, plein, pâle, épuré, lavé de tout accident par la lumière et par la ligne.

Culturellement, socialement, le portrait, à la Renaissance, sert à immortaliser l'aspect physique d'un individu et, à travers ce dernier, l'homme lui-même, ses qualités morales, son importance dans son époque. Le portrait a à voir avec cette aspiration à l'immortalité dont on a tant parlé. Bronzino refuse le réalisme de la représentation et, de plus, il en arrive à priver le portrait pictural de toute forme d'expression. N'oublions pas que la *Joconde* représente une sorte de paradigme du genre portrait. Elle fut l'inspiration de Raphaël, d'Andrea del Sarto et de tous les artistes du XVIe siècle. C'est au XVe siècle que les problèmes formels du portrait avaient primé sur ceux de l'expression, mais Léonard avait vraiment cristallisé les règles du genre. Les trattatistes vantaient, par exemple, les mérites du Titien dont chaque portrait était extrêmement individualisé, autant physiquement que psychologiquement.

En fait, les portraits de Bronzino fonctionnent sur un autre registre. Ils n'obéissent pas au modèle proposé par Léonard. Ils sont davantage à entendre comme des images ambivalentes, à la fois portrait et image symbolique, expression figurée comme on le dit pour l'*impresa*. Le personnage, les objets qui l'accompagnent et leur traitement sont des signes à interroger de même qu'on décrypte ou lit une *impresa*.

Prenons le *Portrait d'un sculpteur* du Louvre. Ici la sculpture est au service de la peinture dans un jeu rhétorique. Le statut métonymique de la figure de la Renommée est facile à entendre. La statuette est là à la fois pour signifier la Sculpture et les ambitions du sculpteur. La Renommée lui tourne — encore — le dos (ou la tête) mais elle est tout de même entre les mains du jeune sculpteur, saisie par lui. En se faisant portraiturer par Bronzino, il devient d'autre part sa propre statue, ce qui déjà lui vaut une certaine gloire. Cela dit avec ou sans ironie.

Avec le *Portrait d'Andrea Doria* (à la Brera de Milan), on a une métaphore ennoblissante pour Doria (précisément une antonomase) présenté en Poséidon avec les attributs du dieu: la nudité, le trident, la barbe imposante. La représentation offre au regard un Poséidon de pierre. La sculpture assure un relais entre le modèle et la peinture. En outre, la figure est d'une plasticité michelangélesque. On notera surtout les mains aux index typiques de l'art du maître. L'hommage rendu à Doria est, de toute évidence, triple: d'abord Bronzino fait son portrait en peinture, mais de plus il le réalise à travers la représentation de sa «statue», et il l'associe à une divinité.

Lié moins évidemment à la question de la sculpture bien que le strict profil rappelle immédiatement les représentations de médailles, c'est le *Portrait de Laura Battiferri*, au Palazzo Vecchio de Florence. Elle est physiquement inaccessible, son regard se dérobe. Mais cette inaccessibilité est récupérée par un geste qui donne à lire. Elle tient un volume des *Sonnetti* de Pétrarque ouvert au sonnet LIV et au sonnet CCXL. On lit: «*Se voi poteste per turbati segni*» sur la page de gauche; et sur la page de droite: «*I ho pregato amor e nel repiego*». Elle présente son profil dantesque (entendre un profil de poète, *le* profil *du* poète), détourne son regard de celui du spectateur (comme elle l'a auparavant détourné de celui du peintre) mais dit autrement ses émotions et son trouble. Les historiens ont vu là une allusion à l'idylle platonique entre le peintre et son modèle.

Le *Portrait d'Éléonore de Tolède et de son fils*. Ici le caractère sculptural est très marqué au détriment du naturalisme qu'autoriserait le portrait: visages inexpressifs, blanchâtres, lisses, corps inanimés, froids, soit morts. Toute la vie est passée dans le costume. Personnage et costume sont en relation métaphorique l'un par rapport à l'autre. Les perles que porte Éléonore ne servent qu'à exalter un rapprochement avec sa chair minéralisée. L'usage de la lumière polissante est à souligner.

Le *Portrait d'Ugolino Martelli* à Berlin (Gemaldegalerie Dahlem).

Sa main droite désigne le Chant IX de l'*Iliade*, sa gauche est posée sur un volume du poète Pietro Bembo. Derrière lui le *David*. Au Chant IX, il est question d'un conseil nocturne chez les Achéens, d'une ambassade chez Achille, des offres d'Agamemnon, du discours d'Ulysse, de la réponse d'Achille... L'énigme attend d'être résolue.

Le gentilhomme, du Musée des Beaux-Arts du Canada à Ottawa, est une œuvre importante dans le contexte qui nous intéresse. C'est un tableau peint vers 1555, soit à la limite de la période que l'on vient de considérer. Luisa Becherucci et Andrea Emiliani croient qu'il pourrait s'agir de Cosme de Médicis aux environs de sa trente-cinquième année. En rupture avec les œuvres précédentes, ici les chairs autant que les vêtements sont d'une réalité convaincante: la lumière est absorbée plutôt que réverbérée par l'épiderme et les reflets dans le vêtement de soie noire sont rendus avec une virtuosité éblouissante. Mais l'insolite s'est déplacé: la statuette mutilée d'une Vénus pudique est d'une coloration bleutée surprenante et invraisemblable, ce qui gêne d'autant plus qu'elle se découpe sur un fond neutre d'une étrange couleur, gris-beige légèrement teinté de vert. Il suffit de comparer ce fond à l'arrière-plan du *Portrait d'Andrea Odoni* pour constater un total aplatissement du fond du tableau opéré par Bronzino: aucune modulation lumineuse, aucune profondeur atmosphérique, aucune ombre portée. Cependant le gentilhomme est, par ses chairs, ses cheveux, sa barbe, ses vêtements, ses mains, extrêmement présent et réel même si sa pose reprend en l'inversant, comme on l'a vu, celle de la figure de *Giuliano de' Medici* des tombeaux de la Nouvelle Sacristie de San Lorenzo à Florence.

À sa manière cette œuvre répond à l'*Inchiesta* de Varchi, elle termine la lettre laissée inachevée par Bronzino et qui s'interrompait au moment d'entreprendre la défense de la peinture après avoir énuméré les avantages de la sculpture mais en disant que si elle dure plus longtemps, cela tient au matériau qu'elle emploie, que si elle demande beaucoup de fatigue, c'est celle du corps, que si elle n'autorise pas l'erreur, car on ne peut recommencer après un mauvais coup de ciseau, cet argument n'avait pas de poids car il ne voulait considérer que les excellents maîtres. Il reprenait l'idée que ce qui comptait c'était l'imitation de la nature et que

ce qui seul tient de l'art, ce sont les lignes qui circonscrivent les corps lesquelles sont en surface [...].

Le rapport de ces trois éléments: fond, statuette et personnage, constitue une fort belle démonstration sur la peinture en illustrant les trois étapes majeures de la réalisation d'un tableau.

— Premièrement, l'*imprimitura*, à laquelle correspond le fond gris-beige du tableau, soit cette base teintée qui constitue l'apprêt du tableau (la couche supérieure de l'apprêt s'appelait l'*imprimitura)*;
— deuxièmement, le camaïeu, que la statuette bleu clair suggère de toute évidence (la couleur improbable prend alors son sens);
— et troisièmement, la phase finale, la couleur.

On a donc là un discours sur la peinture empruntant exclusivement la voie picturale. Mais la statuette — mutilée — figure aussi la Sculpture et devient, littéralement, un moyen pour faire de la bonne peinture. Alberti déjà recommandait aux peintres désireux de faire de la bonne peinture d'étudier la nature et de copier des sculptures plutôt que des œuvres peintes.

> Et si cependant il te plaît de copier les œuvres d'autrui, parce qu'elles ont avec toi plus de patience que les choses vivantes, il me plairait davantage que tu copies une sculpture médiocre qu'une excellente peinture, parce que des choses peintes tu n'acquiers que de savoir les imiter mais des choses sculptées tu apprends à les imiter et à représenter des lumières. [...] Et si je ne me trompe pas la sculpture reste plus certaine que la peinture; et rare sera celui qui peut peindre bien une chose de laquelle il ne *connaît* pas le relief [...].

La sculpture n'est plus qu'un moyen au travers duquel s'exprime le concept de la forme, du délinéament (du contour, car le sculpteur ne commence-t-il pas toujours par «*disegnare in carta*»?). La position intermédiaire de la statuette dans le tableau de Bronzino indique ce qu'est la sculpture pour Bronzino (en termes d'enjeux théoriques), une partie de la peinture, une étape dans le travail de peinture.

> Le dessin, père de nos trois arts, architecture, sculpture, peinture, procédant de l'intelligence, extrait de beaucoup de choses un jugement universel semblable à une forme ou une idée de toutes les choses de la nature [...] [Vasari].

Dans un contexte où le dessin est associé au jugement, à la juste appréhension de la forme, où le dessin est «une déclaration du concept qu'a formé l'esprit» (Vasari), la sculpture est entendue comme allant dans le sens d'une plus grande abstraction (elle est affaire de substance, d'être, d'essence). La peinture, elle, est vue comme étant dirigée vers l'imitation, le détail, la couleur (les accidents), elle imite la nature dans les choses superficielles. Mais pourquoi renoncerait-elle à être à la fois forme (soit lignes) et couleur?

Bronzino a répondu à Varchi. Et cela à travers une galerie de portraits à caractère emblématique. Il me semblait intéressant de souligner qu'il y avait en quelque sorte nécessité d'aller, paradoxalement, en deçà du registre symbolique le plus évident, où l'on considérerait les éléments du tableau un à un, en deçà d'un registre iconographique, au sens où l'entend Panofsky, pour être attentif à la facture même du tableau. Pourtant, c'est en s'arrêtant d'abord à ce niveau de lecture et en mêlant registre pré-iconographique, soit travail sur la forme, et lecture symbolique qu'on est à la fois au cœur des choses que l'œil est en mesure de voir mais aussi de ce que la raison est en mesure d'évaluer (*il buon giudizio*). Le caractère emblématique de chaque portrait sert de soutien, lorsque l'on passe ensuite à l'échelle de la galerie, à un discours sur les fins et les pouvoirs de la peinture que l'allégorie orthodoxe aurait difficilement pu tenir.

Ainsi donc, dans chaque tableau que l'on a trop brièvement regardé, et tout particulièrement dans le *Portrait du gentilhomme* du Musée des Beaux-Arts d'Ottawa, tous les éléments (position du modèle, couleurs, composition, objets) contribuent à constituer une image qui, au-delà de l'impressionnant portrait qu'elle constitue, signifie une chose différente de ce que voit l'œil. Cette «chose», c'est donc une réflexion de Bronzino sur la peinture, jouée à partir des propositions des trattatistes des *Quattrocento* et *Cinquecento*, une construction où chaque composante est à lire dans le registre même des discours de la théorie de l'art. Ainsi la statuette signifie métonymiquement l'art antique, une forme d'idéalité esthétique et elle peut fort bien être associée, dans le contexte humaniste florentin, à la famille Médicis, mais d'abord et avant tout elle figure la Sculpture en autant qu'elle est assimilable au dessin (*disegno-giudizio*); le personnage rappellera par sa pose l'art de Michel-Ange mais le rendu attentif des «accidents» et l'usage minutieux de la couleur l'opposent aux lignes épurées de la statuette plus proche d'un objectif d'abstraction.

À titre de renforcement, et comme pour étayer la lecture que je viens de proposer, un bref regard non point sur des portraits mais sur deux *istorie*.

Cette réflexion menée par Bronzino sur la question du *Paragone*, on la trouve déjà amorcée et de manière remarquable dans une œuvre de jeunesse, des années 1529-30, son *Pygmalion et Galatée* maintenant au Palazzo Vecchio de Florence[14]. Il est d'ailleurs intéressant de la considérer rétrospectivement, à la lumière de la lettre adressée à Varchi et des œuvres postérieures.

D'une part, ce tableau affirme le pouvoir de la peinture de raconter une histoire, celle-ci étant empruntée aux *Métamorphoses* d'Ovide. On sait qu'au moment des fêtes de Vénus, le sculpteur demanda à la déesse qu'elle lui fasse connaître une femme correspondant à ses vœux, c'est-à-dire semblable à son œuvre, et que Vénus anima la sculpture de Pygmalion. Bronzino a réussi à retenir et à illustrer l'essentiel du récit d'Ovide. Galatée, animée mais toujours sur son piédestal, regarde le spectateur alors qu'elle se tourne vers Pygmalion, contemplatif, mains jointes. Tous les moments essentiels du récit sont alors réunis: l'exécution de la statue indiquée par les outils du sculpteur visibles au sol, la prière à Vénus à laquelle renvoient l'autel où une génisse a été sacrifiée, la flamme dressant sa crête dans les airs, signe d'acquiescement de Vénus, la pose ambiguë de Pygmalion, signifiant autant l'imploration que l'action de grâces et l'animation de la statue. Ainsi Galatée est aussi Vénus: et par les condensations qu'impose la mise en scène picturale et par son aspect puisque Bronzino lui a donné la pose d'une Vénus pudique, s'adonnant à la métaphore figurative. (On notera en passant le motif principal de l'autel, sculpté, qui représente Pâris remettant la pomme d'or à Vénus...)

D'autre part, le même tableau affirme la priorité de la peinture sur la sculpture puisqu'il traite d'un sujet qu'essentiellement seule la peinture est en mesure de représenter. L'animation de Galatée ne peut se suggérer que par la coloration des chairs. Ce pouvoir qui dans le récit ovidien est réservé à la divinité, à Vénus, c'est, à un autre registre, celui de la couleur, de la peinture.

Le Martyr de saint Laurent à San Lorenzo, à Florence, fresque réalisée vers 1569, soit quarante ans plus tard, traite au fond du même sujet. Tout cet ensemble de figures michelangélesques passe progressivement d'un camaïeu de gris dans la zone supérieure à la couleur au fur et à mesure qu'on rejoint le bas de l'image où un saint Laurent évocateur de l'*Adam* de Michel-Ange «pose» sur le gril. Toutes ces figures sculpturales connaissent une invasion progressive de la couleur. C'est toute la fresque qui est devenue une Galatée. L'épisode de Pygmalion et Galatée a son revers ou son négatif dans un autre récit ovidien, celui de Persée et de Méduse. Mon hypothèse est qu'un dispositif méduséen travaille dans son ensemble l'œuvre de Bronzino. D'où cette galerie de visages et de corps pétrifiés.

À ce point, on peut maintenant s'arrêter au *Portrait d'un jeune homme* du Metropolitan Museum de New York et le penser dans la perspective de cette question du *Paragone* et de la galerie de portraits que l'on a amorcée. On peut plus particulièrement considérer la série de portraits où interviennent des représentations de sculptures. On est alors en mesure de donner aux éléments sculpturaux de ce tableau, qui pourraient passer pour secondaires, toute leur signification.

On peut, en effet, se concentrer sur le livre comme «attribut» unique du personnage et ignorer les éléments du décor qui ont pourtant ici une envergure et une situation tout à fait particulières. Et ce livre reste un accessoire un peu banal. Ce qui est, par contre, inusité, par rapport à l'importance qui leur est accordée dans le tableau, ce sont ces deux têtes qui ornent le mobilier. Elles sont employées à contrario de tous les enjeux que l'on a vus jusqu'à maintenant. Je dis têtes, il faudrait dire masques ou mascarons. Ces visages sculptés, employés comme ornements et servant à la décoration tantôt de portes, d'arcades, de fontaines, de corniches, d'entablements, de sarcophages, de meubles divers et auxquels on donne soit un caractère noble ou grotesque. C'est d'ailleurs aux figures grotesques ou ricanantes que l'on réserve le nom de mascaron. Pour les figures calmes et nobles on dit masques. D'autre part en peinture le masque est souvent employé comme un emblème de l'illusion. Bronzino le savait lui qui en a représenté deux dans son *Allégorie de la Luxure dévoilée par le Temps*. Il les a déposés au pied de Vénus comme un symbole de tromperie.

La tête parfaite, lisse, dépourvue de tout accident du jeune homme est alors confrontée à ces deux visages grotesques placés à la hauteur du sexe du modèle: dans la table-chapiteau d'un rose violacé, une tête sculptée et chiffonnée qui grimace. Chiffonnée comme l'est la peau du saint Barthélemy du *Jugement dernier* (1537-1541) de Michel-Ange.

De plus, la volute du chapiteau se dresse, pointe (comme un serpent) vers la braguette et le drapé de cette face sculptée pointe lui aussi le même objet. Sur le bras du fauteuil, une autre face monstrueuse, léonardesque (penser aux caricatures des *Carnets*). Cette tête est du même volume que la braguette et tournée vers elle également.

Un circuit s'établit alors entre l'animé et l'inanimé, entre le masque noble du modèle qui s'est pétrifié en sa propre statue et qui se garde de toute expression et les mascarons inanimés pourtant chargés dans le tableau d'exprimer de douloureuses grimaces. (Il y a encore des mascarons sur le fauteuil de *Lucrezia Panciatichi*.) Comme pour le *Portrait d'Éléonore de Tolède*, la vie passe dans l'accessoire et le corps reste figé. Ici pas d'épiderme sur ce visage lisse comme une sculpture mais une peau sur la face tordue d'un mascaron.

De plus, ce jeune homme louche. L'œil droit nous regarde, l'autre sort de l'image, va en coulisse. Ce deuxième œil qui s'écarte serait un œil admoniteur de la coulisse, suggérant des parcours moins convenus au spectateur. Cette schize du regard devenant figure d'une schize des émotions, d'une peinture tournée vers la sculpture, d'un système qui détourne les voies entendues de l'expression en peinture.

On voit donc que la question de la sculpture dans la peinture de Bronzino, celle des portraits par rapport à la peinture d'histoire, celle d'une iconographie élargie spécifique à l'artiste sont trois questions indissociables. Le travail sur la forme avec tous ses jeux de renvois, ses liens avec les problèmes d'expression et une iconographie «élargie», implique que l'on cartographie l'œuvre complet de Bronzino à la recherche d'une mémoire multilocalisée (mémoire artistique et mémoire individuelle en interaction). L'usage du masque n'en est qu'un exemple et on aura compris qu'il ne s'agit pas de le renvoyer à une signification mais à une aire ou à une chaîne de significations diverses et contiguës.

Université de Montréal

NOTES

* Cette réflexion s'inscrit dans le cadre d'un projet de recherche subventionné par le Conseil de recherche en sciences humaines du Canada (C.R.S.H.) que je codirige avec Françoise Siguret à l'Université de Montréal et qui porte sur la figure d'Andromède, du maniérisme au Baroque.

1 «Of their nature emblems are intrusive, and even painters of Lotto's stature could not always integrate them satisfactorily in their designs.», John Pope-Hennessy, *The Portrait in the Renaissance* (New York: Pantheon Books, 1966),p.231.

2 Ripa, qui se présente comme celui qui a compulsé les savoirs des Anciens, Latins et Grecs qui eux-mêmes n'ignoraient pas ce qu'il appelle la doctrine égyptienne, s'adresse aux poètes, peintres et sculpteurs dans sa première édition de 1593; aux historiens, poètes et à ceux désireux de découvrir la sagesse occulte de l'ancien monde dans la seconde édition de 1602, sans qu'il soit question des artistes; enfin il recommande sa troisième édition aux poètes, peintres et sculpteurs et à tous ceux qui devront représenter des figures allégoriques. Cf. l'introduction de Erna Mandowsky à l'édition fac-similé de l'*Iconologia* de Cesare Ripa de 1603 (Hildesheim, New York: Georg Olms, 1970).

3 Au sujet des *imprese*, cf. Robert Klein, «La théorie de l'expression figurée dans les traités italiens sur les *Imprese*, 1555-1612», *La Forme et l'Intelligible* (Paris: Gallimard, 1970),pp. 125-149; et à propos de l'allégorie, Hubert Damisch, *Théorie du nuage* (Paris: Seuil, 1972),pp.79-90. «Comment procédera donc le peintre qui veut signifier, par les moyens de son art, une chose différente de celle qu'il donne à voir? Il travaillera à former une figure dont les parties correspondent terme à terme à celles de la chose signifiée, tout en étant disposées dans un ordre conforme à celui des éléments de la représentation, de telle façon qu'elles constituent un ensemble si bien cohérent [...] qu'on ne sache ce qu'il faut le plus admirer, de l'exacte proportion qui existe entre les deux choses, ou du bon jugement de celui qui a su si bien ordonner les parties que le spectateur n'a à connaître que d'une seule chose, mais parfaite et délectable.», *Théorie du nuage*, p.82.

4 «Représenter une idée par une figure qui «participe» à l'universalité et à l'idéalité de son objet est, comme on sait, la fonction propre du symbole, telle que l'ont conçue les néo-platoniciens de la Renaissance», Robert Klein, *La Forme et l'Intelligible*,p.135.

5 Hubert Damisch, *Théorie du nuage*,p. 87.

6 Sur les liens entre sujet, langage et visage, cf. Jean-Jacques Courtine et Claudine Haroche, *Histoire du visage* (Paris: Rivage, 1988).

7 Jean-Jacques Courtine et Claudine Haroche, *Histoire du visage*,p.14.

8 John Pope-Hennessy, *The Portrait in the Renaissance*,pp.214-216.

9 Pour les reproductions de l'œuvre de Bronzino, je renvoie le lecteur à *L'opera completa del Bronzino* (Milano: Rizzoli Editore, 1973).

10 Erwin Panofsky, «Le mouvement néo-platonicien et Michel-Ange», *Essais d'iconologie* (Paris: Gallimard, 1967).

11 Ces observations se retrouvent sous la plume de nombreux historiens et étalées sur nombre d'années. Par exemple, Luisa Becherucci, Andrea Emiliani, John Pope-Hennessy et Charles MacCorquodale en parlent habilement. Gilles Godmer, dans un mémoire déposé en 1974 à l'Université de Montréal et intitulé *L'utilisation de la sculpture dans l'œuvre peinte d'Agnolo Bronzino* a, en quelque sorte, compilé lesdites observations concernant motifs, poses, textures, et y a ajouté ses propres analyses. J'emprunterai ce recensement de Godmer pour constituer le dossier de ces portraits où la peinture prend des airs de sculpture.

12 Robert Klein, *La Forme et l'Intelligible*, pp. 360-361.

13 John Pope-Hennessy, *The Portrait in the Renaissance*.

[14] Le *Pygmalion et Galatée* de Bronzino «recouvrait» un *Portrait de Francesco Guardi* par Pontormo (v. 1529).

PART SIX

POETIC ASSOCIATIONS, TRANSPOSITIONS, TRANSFORMATIONS

GEORGE L. SCHEPER

"WHERE IS OUR HOME?": THE AMBIGUITY OF BIBLICAL AND EURO-AMERICAN IMAGING OF WILDERNESS AND GARDEN AS SACRED PLACE

I. HOME THOUGHTS

Certainly a radical attachment to place, whether to features of an accustomed landscape, or to sites or monuments of personal, ancestral, legendary or historic associations, must be numbered among the "elemental passions of the soul". As Yi-Fu Tuan points out, such strong emotional attachments can form independently of any highly-charged associations with the sacred or the heroic, or with national or ethnic identity, and "may come simply with familiarity and ease, with the assurance of nurture and security, with the memory of sounds and smells, of communal activities and homely pleasures accumulated over time" (p. 159), so we need to be wary of overgeneralizing or essentializing this elemental passion, and to be attentive instead to expressions of cultural and personal difference. With that caveat in mind, this essay will explore the ambiguity encoded in the biblical imaging of sacred place, particularly in the images of garden and wilderness, and some of the ways in which this ambiguity has passed into Western conventions of art and literature. But first, in order to frame this investigation within a larger context of comparative cultural study, I should like to begin by referencing the widely perceived difference between the biblically inspired Western sense of *historically* significant place and the sense of *naturally* significant place common in many indigenous cultures. I should like, that is, to explore both the difference, insofar as it can be documented, and the perception of the difference, as an aspect of the history of consciousness.

A paradigmatic instance of indigenous cultural representation of natural landscape features as sacred places, of the phenomenology of natural forms presencing themselves as experienced numinous realities, is provided by the Aborigine traditions in Australia, as described by James Cowan:

Among Aborigines the earth embodies a culture of its own. It was formed, after all, by the explicit action of Sky Heroes at the time of the Dreaming. Thus the land is a geographical icon beacuse its very coming into being is of a mystical order, not a geological one. Its categories of sacredness, recognizable as they are by the intellect or soul, can be seen in the landscape. . . . In the Aboriginal context this is a 'Dreaming' landscape, an embodiment of mystical realities not easily explained by language. So that when an Aborigine speaks of his 'Dreaming' he is talking about the land as an icon which expresses his mystical attachment to it. His whole being, his cultural associations and knowledge of tribal law, which have been handed down to him from the Dreaming, becomes an extension of . . . visionary geography (pp. 16–17).

Yi-Fu Tuan elaborates, citing W. E. H. Stanner's study of Aboriginal territorial organizaton, distinguishing "range" and "estate"; "range" referring to the wider hunting/foraging orbit, where they can run or walk, "estate" referring to the place "where they could sit. . . . It is the home of ancestors, the dreaming place where every incident in legend and myth is firmly fixed in some unchanging aspect of nature – rocks, hills and mountains, even trees. . . . Landscape is personal and tribal history made visible" (p. 157). Similarly, the Maori of New Zealand revealed their deep-rooted sensitivity to homeland feelings even in their treatment of a prisoner, who might ask, prior to being slain, to be conducted to the border of his tribal territory so that he might look upon it once more before dying, or to be allowed to drink of the waters of some stream that flowed through his native territory (p. 155).

Similar attachment to sacred geography is a hallmark of various Native American cultures, to the point where it is widely perceived as being at the center of a virtually pan-Amerindian cosmovision. Although, as Åke Hultkrantz points out, Pan-Indianism is a recent, activist response to white domination, and traditional Indian cultures have had "a very diversified attitude to nature" (p. 124), ranging from animal ceremonialism among hunting groups like the Inuit, to food-grain ceremonialism among agriculturalists like the Pueblos of the Southwest. While such ceremonial traditions focus selectively on specific sources of vitality, whether salmon or maize, structurally underlying each of them is a "cosmo-theism" (p. 127, citing Hartmann p. 186) based not on romantic aestheticism but on a consciousness of a principle of harmony and beauty in the order of things. As Sam Gill summarizes the Navajo world-view, for instance: "The world was created in perfect beauty, but perfect beauty means a static order; since life is a dynamic process requiring movement, it risks destroying this beauty; so as disorder arises and life is threatened, one must be able to reconstitute order and beauty in the world; and this is done by ceremonial means, which recreate the pattern of perfect beauty" (*Native American Religions*, p. 34). Underlying Navajo ceremonialism, then, is the perception that all human activity, including farming, is to some extent disruptive of the natural harmony (*hohzho*), and the belief that traditional ceremony, offering a return of the sacred to the sacred, an action freed of any ego-invested individual interest, represents a restoration of that harmony. The popularity of Tony Hillerman's regional detective stories derives in no small part from his successful rendering of this Navajo sense of sacred place, as in this passage from *The Ghostway*:

> Outside . . . Chee stretched, yawned, and sucked in a huge lungful of air. It was cold here, frost still rimming the roadside weeds, and the snow-capped shape of the San Francisco Peaks twenty miles to the south looked close enough to touch in the clear, high-altitude air. . . . Beautiful to Chee. He was back in Dine' Bike'yah, back between the Sacred Mountains, and he felt easy again – at home in a remembered landscape. . . . "Memorize places", his uncle had told him. "Settle your eyes on a place and learn it. See it under the snow, and when first grass is growing, and as the rain falls on it. Feel it and smell it, walk on it, touch the stones, and it will be with you forever. When you are far away, you can call it back. When you need it, it is there, in your mind" (pp. 521–22).

Hillerman fictionally dramatizes what the interested reader can find in expositions of Navajo ceremonial life: that being "between the Sacred Mountains" is no mere figure of speech, but a lived reality, experienced kinaesthetically in the sacred races and pilgrimages to the mountains, in the gathering of the sacred substances from each mountain in the Four Mountains Bundle carried inside a Navajo's personal medicine bundle.

Classic statements of Native American "cosmotheism" are recorded from the period of encroachment by whites, and are the more poignant, and eloquent, from the pressure of the progressive loss of this sacred landscape – orations such as those of Smohalla (1885): "You ask me to plough the ground? Shall I take a knife and tear my mother's bosom? . . . You ask me to dig for stone! Shall I dig under her skin for her bones? Then when I die I can not enter her body to be born again" (Gill, *Mother Earth*, p. 54); or Chief Seattle (1854): "Every part of this soil is sacred in the estimation of my people. Every hillside, every valley, every plain and grove, has been hallowed by some sad or happy event in days long vanished. The very dust upon which you now stand responds more lovingly to their footsteps than to yours, because it is rich with the blood of our ancestors and our bare feet are conscious of the sympathetic touch" (*Portable North American Indian Reader*, p. 253) – although we need to be aware that the rhetoric of such orations comes mediated by white recorders and even, in the case of Chief Seattle's speech, modern paraphrase (see Kaiser; and Tuan pp. 223, n. 13; Gill argues that the specific metaphor of Earth as mother, far from being of great antiquity in Amerindian culture, is actually a product of the last hundred years or so [*Mother Earth, passim*]).

Certainly a passsionate attachment to the sacredness of specific landscape seems to be a constant in Native American testimonial literature, both traditional and contemporary. As Black Elk told Joseph Brown, "all things are the work of the Great Spirit. We should know that He is within all things: the trees, the grasses, the rivers, the mountains, and all the four-legged animals, and the winged peoples . . ." (cited in Hultkrantz, p. 126). Washington Matthews, the great nineteenth-century student of the Navajo, had noted that nostalgic crying stimulated by contemplation of the beauty of the landscape was regarded as the origin of song: "The hero of the Mountain Chant disobeyed his father by going to a forbidden place. From the top of a hill he beheld the beatuiful slopes of a mountain. Clouds hung over it; showers of rain fell. As he greeted the land with appreciation he was overcome with loneliness and homesickness and, weeping, he sang a song" (cited in Reichard, p. 285).

This "elemental passion" for emotionally and spiritually charged landscape could, we know, be documented in a worldwide context, on every continent. Certainly, it could be fruitful to compare the Native American expressions of attachment to landscape with, let us say, traditional Chinese expressions, whether in painting, poetry or religious text, for instance the Wang River sequence of the T'ang dynasty poet-painter Wang Wei, or his short lyric "Going at Dawn to the Pa Pass", ending with the lines, "The people spoke a peculiar dialect/ But the orioles sounded as in my own country/ And luckily I know about landscape/ And that abated my feeling of isolation" (p. 72; cf. pp. 63, 89 and 103); or, again, the many poems of nostalgia by the much-travelled Tu Fu. The Taoist tradition, in particular, fed the Chinese sensibility that it was above all in the untrammelled, irregular, seemingly chaotic manifestations of wild nature that the grain, the natural flow of things – the Tao – was to be apprehended (see Waley, pp. 43 ff.); and, as Nash points out, the same spirit pervades Shintoism: "In Japan the first religion, Shinto, was a form of nature worship that deified mountains, forests, storms, and torrents in preference to fruitful, pastoral scenes since the wild was thought to manifest the divine being more potently than the rural. In linking God and the wilderness, instead of contrasting them, as did the Western faiths, Shinto and Taoism fostered love of wilderness rather than hatred" (pp. 20–21). Nash continues, "Chinese and Japanese landscape painters celebrated wilderness over a thousand years before Western artists. . . . Wild vistas dominated this genre, while human figures, if they appeared at all, took secondary importance to cliffs, trees, and rivers" (p. 21).

Of course the theme of landscape-homesickness or *Heimweh* is common in the European poetic tradition as well. In fact, it is the theme of more than one official or unofficial national anthem, as in the poignant Czech anthem, "Where Is My Home?", a song which locates "home" in the beloved Bohemian landscape, but which also, by virtue of its interrogatory mode, reads as a question posed by a small nation surrounded and dominated by mighty neighbors to East and West – Germanic, Slavic and Magyar – and which seems supremely apt for the nation that produced the composers of "Ma Vlast" and the *Symphony from the New World* (although commonly abbreviated as *New World Symphony*, the work is not, as is commonly thought, "about" the New World; rather, it is a meditation on the Old World from the vantage of the New, and uses American folk spiritual melodies such as "Going Home" precisely in aid of this nostalgic reflection). Although it is not the national anthem, every American knows "America the Beautiful" as a hymn-like paean to the physical beauties of the continent. Most commonly in the West, the expressions of home-sentiments are couched in terms of history and ethnicity, as well as nature, as in the following entry for the term *Heimat* in a 1953 South Tyrolean almanac recorded by Leonard Doob:

> Heimat is first of all the mother earth who has given birth to our folk and race, who is the holy soil, and who gulps down God's clouds, sun, and storms so that together with their own mysterious strength they prepare the bread and wine which rest on our table and give us strength to lead a good life . . . Heimat is landscape. Heimat is the landscape we have experienced. That means one that has been fought over, menaced, filled with the history of families, towns, and villages. Our Heimat is the Heimat of knights and heroes, of battles and victories, of legends and fairy tales. But more than all this, our Heimat is the land which has become fruitful through the sweat of our ancestors. For this Heimat our ancestors have fought and suffered, for this Heimat our fathers have died (cited in Tuan, p. 156).

But this admixture of historic and ethnic elements with elements of nature lends a tone of exclusivity and combativeness to such expressions, which bear ominous reverberations in the context of twentieth-century history in Central Europe and the Balkans. The implicit sense in typical patriotic expressions that one's own homeland is inherently more blessed than another's is undercut by a modern ecumenical anthem set to the tune of *Finlandia*, Lloyd Stone's "This Is My Song" (1934), in which the familiar sentiments for "my home", praise of its beauties and prayers for its peace and blessing, are balanced with the acknowledgement that "other hearts in other lands are beating/ With hopes and dreams as true and high as mine", and that "skies are everywhere as blue as mine". Of course this idealism is strikingly untypical.

Among the innumerable poetic expressions of this "home thoughts" sentiment in European and American literature and extending from Homer and Hesiod, through Virgil, the seventeenth-century "country-house" poets, to Wordsworth, Longfellow, Whitman, Yeats, and such diverse modern voices as Hopkins, Thomas, Frost, Gary Snyder, or Wendell Berry, we could choose as characteristic Heine's "Nachtgedanken" (Night Thoughts), which incorporates the potent combination of thoughts of mother and German homeland. The poet says it has been twelve years since leaving both home and mother; but his sense of consolation that the "sturdy" and "hale" homeland will not fail or decay is undercut by the simple truth that "my mother, though, might pass away" (Heine, pp. 48–51). These "biedermeier" sentiments are paralleled by the archetypally British sensibilities of the persona of Robert Browning's "Home-Thoughts, from Abroad" ("Oh, to be in England/ Now that April's there. . . ." [*Norton Anthology*, p. 1195]), or by those of the intensely nostalgic narrator of "View From Charles Bridge" by Czech poet Jaroslav Seifert, which begins with a poignant evocation of a church service in Moravia, but ends with the heartfelt declaration: "I was homesick for Prague,/ even though I'd only briefly stayed/ outside her walls". He cannot tear his eyes away from that familiar image of Prague Castle and St. Vitus Cathedral as seen from Charles Bridge, but gazes on it in endless gratitude, because – no matter how often painted, photographed or otherwise appropriated – "It is mine/ and I also believe it is miraculous" (Seifert, p. 145). Bachelard, of course, has been the great explorer of such themes in *The Poetics of Space* and *The Poetics of Reverie*.

II. UPROOTEDNESS

As many cultural historians have noted, the theme of *patria* and sense of place in Western literature seems always balanced, if not in fact overbalanced, by the converse theme of uprootedness, which at least in part seems self-inflicted. Indeed, the story of a great circling adventure – from leave-taking, through critical encounters, to homecoming – whether of Odysseus or Parsifal, is what Joseph Campbell would call the "monomyth" of Western literature. What is implicit in Homer, that Odysseus delays his own homecoming for the sake of adventure, is explicit in Dante (*Inferno*, Canto 26), in Tennyson's "Ulysses" ("I cannot rest from travel . . . / I am a part of all that I have met;/ Yet all experience is an arch wherethrough/ Gleams that untravelled world whose margin fades/ Forever and forever when I move . . . / There lies the port . . . / 'Tis not too late to seek a newer world . . ." [*Norton Anthology*, pp. 1067–69]) and in Cavafy's "Ithaca" ("When you set out on the voyage to Ithaca,/ pray that your journey may be long,/ full of adventures, full of knowledge . . ." [*Modern Greek Poetry*, pp. 38–9]). It is the spirit of Kazantzakis's *The Odyssey: A Modern Sequel*, and of Whitman's "Song of the Open Road".

But what has been accepted as a paean to personal freedom can appear a very different thing when seen in its national guise. For this sentiment has been, in a sense, the special myth of America, founded on the legendary constructs of Columbus and Plymouth Rock and fulfilled in the frontier imperative of manifest destiny. Earlier generations of American scholars in effect "celebrated" the myth – notably in the famous "frontier thesis" promulgated by Frederick Jackson Turner in 1893 – that the frontier, with its wilderness challenge, has in effect promoted individualism and democracy (Billington, p. 16). More recent scholars, especially those informed by eco-feminist perspectives, have radically deconstructed the frontier thesis and focused on the disastrous environmental consequences and genocidal impact on Native Americans of the westward expansion. Notable in this revisionist project have been Leo Marx's *The Machine in the Garden*; Roderick Nash's *Wilderness and the American Mind*; Annette Kolodny's *The Lay of the Land*; Catherine Albanese's *Nature Religion in America*; and, especially, Frederick Turner's (no relation to his "frontier thesis" namesake) *Beyond Geography*, whose subtitle, "The Western Spirit Against the Wilderness", could well serve as a thesis statement for the second half of this paper.

The latter Turner's "anti-frontier thesis", if I may so designate it, is that unlike non-urban indigenous cultures, the West, like other urbanized cultures, has been in a millenia-long struggle "against nature" and therefore against any naturally defined sacred space as home. We could take as a starting-point of this thesis (although this is not a subject Turner himself takes up) evidence compiled by John H. Falk that human beings originally evolved with a sense of adaptation to a particular "favorite" (i.e., favorable) environment; that human beings are "hard-wired" to favor savanna settings like those of East Africa where humans first evolved: "So much of what defines humanness relates to that savanna – bipedalism, and advances that walking upright made possible, like the apposable thumb and the use of the hands for carrying and as tools. Habitat preference may be tied into our basic anatomy" (cited in Hiss, p. 37). Falk's thesis may be a bit too universalizing; recent archaeological research in Mesoamerica has suggested an alternative "ultimate homeland" image in the form of a horseshoe-shaped valley or cove, backed by mountains viewed as vessels of water, sited over caves and surrounding a fertile plain (Garcia-Zambrano, "*Teocomitl*").

Be that as it may, both Turner and Nash pick up with Lewis Mumford's thesis that the so-called neolithic revolution in agriculture also meant the beginnings of urbanization and the cultural preoccupation with demarcating the boundaries between "wilderness" and city, or "wilderness" and garden – that, in fact, it is urbanization that gives rise to the very construct "wilderness": as Standing Bear declared, "Indians know no wilderness" (Hultkrantz, p. 129). While much attention has been devoted to the well-documented conflict in the Bronze and Iron Ages between pastoral/nomadic cultures on the one hand, and urban/agriculturalist cultures on the other (e.g., between the Aryans and the dark-skinned *dasas*; or between the Hebrews and the Canaanites; or between the Dorian Greeks and the Minoan/Mycenaeans), both such groups had in common their mythic war against the "wilderness"; the nomads with their "aggressively masculine" mystique of vigilance, fortitude and will and correspondingly militaristic and vindictive sky-gods (Turner, pp. 24–6), and the agriculturalists, who at first apparently cultivated a fertility-based, goddess-centered religion, but by the time of the great city-states of the Ancient Near East had become purveyors of a masculinized mythos featuring the violent victory of a warrior sky god over a primeval female sea-monster representing chaos and wilderness. Paradigmatic of this pattern would be the myth of Indra's victory over Vritra (*Rig-Veda*, I.32), or Marduk's victory over Tiamet (*Enuma Elish*, in Pritchard, pp. 34–35), the latter paralleled in Yahweh's domination of *tehem*, "the deep" (Gen. 1:2) or triumph over Leviathan (Ps. 74:13–17; Job 26:5–14, 40:25–41; see Day).

For both pastoralists and agriculturalists in the Ancient Near East, the image of the ultimate good place – naturally enough for a people surrounded by desert and dependent above all on water and shade – was "paradise", the pleasure garden, full of natural imagery and bounty, but distinctly not nature, rather a *hortus conclusus*. The antinomy is clear in Genesis: paradise vs. the wilderness "east of Eden" to which Adam and Eve are exiled and cursed to live and work in sorrow and pain, setting up the fundamental hermeneutic of paradise lost/paradise regained of Christian original sin theology, against which Matthew Fox and Thomas Berry argue that the real loss has been the loss of the sense of "original blessing", the indigenous sense of nature as sacred home. (Again, this is not to imply that indigenous cultures "romanticized" nature; far from it, all the cultural evidence shows that indigenous cultures by and large have had a most unsentimental apprehension of nature, of the hardship and threat posed by natural processes – but without, as we have seen, losing the sense of that vast eco-surround as the source of all vitality.) By contrast, biblical theology, as represented both by patristic and modern expositors, has tended to define itself according to the dichotomy of the singular covenantal God whose interventions in history are experienced as redemptive *dis*continuities, vs. the nature-gods whose cyclical, seasonal *con*tinuities are viewed as a seductive temptation away from righteousness (see Brueggemann, p. 188; Santmire, *Travail of Nature*, chap. 9). An epitome of this "against the wilderness" theology is Karl Barth's declaration that "There is surely a realm of Nature which as such is different from the realm of Grace. But at the same time in the realm of Nature *all* properties which are not directed to Grace and which do not come from Grace amount to nothing. *There is nothing in Nature which may lead a life for itself and which may follow its own course*" (quoted in Santmire [italics his], *Brother Earth*, p. 128). Barth is anticipated in this sentiment, we may say, by one of Cotton Mather's pronouncements, to the effect that "what is not useful is vicious" (Elman, p. 6), in which biblical theology and utilitarianism meet. But just as with the frontier thesis, what once was lauded now comes under either attack – as critics increasingly trace the current environmental crises and urban pathologies to this anti-nature ideology – or revision – as contemporary eco-theologians strive to demonstrate that the biblical God is after all a God of nature, and biblical theology, properly understood, after all a creation-centered as well as redemption-centered theology (see Moltmann; Westermann; Brueggemann; Santmire; *Travail*, chap. 10; Fox).

III. PRECARIOUS GARDEN, MYSTICAL DESERT, HOWLING WILDERNESS

What we are left with, I propose, is a deeply ambivalent attitude toward nature in the biblically-grounded traditions of Western culture – whether Jewish or Christian, Catholic or Protestant, Capitalist or Marxist – traditions that, in effect, define the world as it is as a workplace, and our "home" as *elsewhere*. This ambivalence is deeply encoded in the biblical text, in its complex representations of paradise and wilderness. For the paradise-garden, the *terra beata*, is only precariously the place of divine favor, and after the expulsion becomes the *terra interdicta*, recoverable, according to medieval theology, only through the atonement of Christ and initation into the sacramental life of the Church. Gardens retain this ambiguity throughout medieval literature and art, and the modern reader must tread warily in them, because the garden "in malo" (for example, the literary garden of Deduit in the *Roman de la Rose*, or Bosch's painted *Garden of Earthly Delights*) can look deceptively indistinguishable from the garden "in bono". In fact, they may literally be the same place, as in Chaucer's "Parlement of Foules" (ll. 127–140), but with a gate that bears two opposing inscriptions, one indicating that this is the entrance to a paradise garden, the other indicating it is a gate to hell – for the garden of this world is indeed a heaven or a hell depending on whether one is living in charity or cupidity.

On the other hand, the wilderness, the symbol of expulsion from the garden, becomes, with prophetic irony, the very place of Israel's experience of special covenantal intimacy with God, indeed the place of betrothal between Israel the bride and Yahweh her divine bridegroom recalled by the prophets in constrast to the lapses of Israel too-comfortably ensconced in its kingdom (Hos. 2:14–15; Jer. 2:2). This is taken up in New Testament typology with the imagery of John baptizing in the wilderness and Jesus in the desert (also see John 3:44, 4:31–33; 1 Pet. 1:13–20, 2:1–10; 1 Cor. 10:1–11; Apoc. 1:9, 12:6, 17:3). In both the Old and New Testament contexts, the redemptive experience is located not at the urban center, we might say, but in the wild or eccentric periphery. But while there *is* a creation spirituality (theocentric, to be sure) in the Bible (see Brueggemann; Santmire; Fox), and this ambiguity about the "wilderness" exists in the texts, it does not eventuate in a wholesale sacralizing of untrammelled nature as a spiritual home; as Brueggemann admits: "The traditions of the wilderness prevent us from romanticizing landlessness as a time of resourceful faith. For Israel the wilderness period provided a double image and memory. It is a route on the way to the land, but it is also a sentence of death" (p. 8). Understandably, one of the greatest of blessings was still God's promise to turn a barren wilderness into a blessed and fruitful land of living waters where Israel could flourish (see Nash, pp. 14–15). As Turner puts it more pointedly: "Here then is the tangled but necessary truth of the Israelites' wilderness experience: though they were originally a desert people, though their god is a desert god, though their covenant with him is ratified for all time in the Sinai wilderness, yet they must *resist* the wilderness and its dark temptations" (p. 46). Nash concurs that in the Bible "Wilderness never lost its harsh and forbidding character. Indeed, precisely because of them it was unoccupied and could be a refuge as well as a disciplinary force. Paradoxically, one sought the wilderness as a way of being purified and hence delivered from it into a paradisiac promised land. There was no fondness in the Hebraic tradition for wilderness itself" (p. 16).

The same thematizing is evident in rabbinic and early Christian and patristic typological allegorizing, as the journey through the desert becomes a type of the soul's progress in the spiritual life and, especially for early expounders of mysticism (Philo of Alexandria, Gregory of Nyssa), a type of the mystical *via negativa* – just as paradise becomes the complementary allegorical image of Christian intitation and the sacramental life of the Church (Scheper, "Spiritual Marriage", pp. 103–106): no longer a garden except in the most stylized sense, the Byzantine ecclesiastical image of paradise becomes a mosaic-covered baptistry (and the tradition continues into the Renaissance with Ghiberti's doors to the baptistry in Florence designated as the "Gates of Paradise"). Meanwhile, the monastic version of an architecturally-defined paradise, the cloister, does at least retain features of a (very controlled) enclosed garden, an image that has passed into the general Western culture with the (no longer very cloistered or very controlled) tradition of the college campus.

It should perhaps also be pointed out here that the fascination with the literal earthly paradise never flagged, persisting, dramatically, right up through Columbus's third voyage and his belief upon reaching the mouth of the Orinoco that he had, indeed, discovered its location, a notion perpetuated in such "promotional" colonial enterprise literature as Sir Walter Raleigh's *Discoverie of . . . Guiana* (1596).

The theme of a paradisiac desert wilderness of course runs deeply through the literature of the early Christian ascetics and desert fathers (See Waddell; Brown; Santmire, *Travail*, chaps. 3–5; Scheper, "Spiritual Marriage", pp. 107–9), and continues on into the Cistercian mystics of the twelfth century and the Spanish mystics of the sixteenth (Teresa, for instance, speaking of bringing the desert into the city by founding Carmelite convents), but ever, as Santmire puts it, with a "heightening of the ambiguity", or, we might say, deepening of the contradictions. From Origen, through Jerome, Augustine, Gregory, Innocent III and Thomas Aquinas, the "De contemptu mundi" theme represents not only a repudiation of worldly corruption but an on-going sense of a deeply conflictual, if not outright alienated relationship to nature, the counter-current of the creation spirituality of Francis, Hildegard of Bingen and Julian of Norwich only highlighting the negativity of the mainstream tradition (see Santmire, chap. 6; Fox *passim*). Turner comments: "Even if we accept the postulate that the death of physical distractions opens the way to the true life of the soul, it seems unfortunate that so terribly much of human existence should have to appear under the guises of encumbrances, pitfalls, snares, or other terms of opprobrium. Especially the body. The mystical tradition is so replete with examples of twisted, cankered sexuality and physicality, of hatred and fear of the necessary conditions of animate existence, that this alone vitiated whatever spiritually regenerating influence it might have had" (p. 69) – although here he perpetuates an unfortunate tendency inherited from the Reformation and Enlightenment to lump together all modes of medieval spirituality as "monkish" and "mystical", for which Matthew Fox is an excellent corrective (also see Peter Brown).

We have spoken of the Spanish mystics, such as Teresa, for whom the founding of a Carmel was an act of bringing the desert to the city; and indeed the writing of Teresa and John of the Cross, especially, encompasses the fullness of this ambiguity, their Canticles-inspired prose and poetry filling their descriptions of this Carmelite desert with the most lavish and even sensuous pleasure-garden imagery (see Teresa, *Life*, chaps. 16, 18, 22; John of the Cross, "Dark Night of the Soul" & "Spiritual Canticle"). Perhaps even more dramatically privileging the wilderness as such as true spiritual home are the writings of the Flemish and Rhineland mystics (Eckhart; Tauler; Ruysbroeck), whose *via negativa* encompasses the desert or *Wüste* as the natural emblem of the perfectly emptied soul (Scheper, "Spiritual Marriage", pp. 118–19). An interesting prototype for this mystical embrace of the void in the form of utter "wilderness" is found in the solitary sea-journeys of the Irish monks, or in the Anglo-Saxon poem "The Seafarer", in which the wilderness of the sea is encoded not as an allegorical image of this harsh, transitory life contrasted with the safe harbor of heaven, as many critics have taken it, but as an allegorical image of the ascetic life contrasted with the soft, worldly "landlubber's" life. Or, as the poet Silesius expressed it:

Where is my biding-place? Where there's nor I nor Thou.
Where is my final goal towards which I needs must press?
Where there is nothing. Whither shall I journey now?
Still farther on than God – into a wilderness. (Leeuw, II, p. 493)

Certain of the separatist sects of the proto-Reformation, such as the Waldensians, actually enacted this flight into the wilderness, which they interpreted as the place prepared for them by God (Moreland, pp. vi–vii; cf. Scheper, *Spiritual Marriage*, pp. 120–21; Nash, p. 18); and later the Anabaptists (such as Melchior Hoffmann) and radical sects such as the Munsterites, Mennonites, Hutterites, Swedenborgians and Ranters viewed themselves as primitive Apostolic communities providentially dwelling in the wilderness God had prepared for them (Williams, *Radical Reformation*, pp. 92–4; see, e.g., Arndt, xiv, p. 169). On the Catholic side, the Observantine Franciscans who founded the missions in Mexico in the sixteenth century were similarly motivated by the millenarian vision that the Mexican "wilderness" would be the true home of a Christian Indian republic that would replace the corrupt "civilized" Christendom of Europe – a project completely at odds with the conquistador/colonial project of exploiting the El Dorado they expected to find in the "New World" (see Ricard; Phelan). The "barefoot narratives" of the millenarian Franciscans in Mexico are a remarkable record of this "errand into the wilderness" (see, for example, Motolinia's *The Indians of New Spain*, or the narratives gathered in the *Oroz Codex*), and the mestizo Catholic church remains richly nature-centered to this day, as evidenced in local traditions of fiesta and the decoration of churches.

For the most part, however, among the mainstream Protestant churches the "wilderness" lost most of its ambiguity, with writers such as Bunyan and Wesley specifically repudiating any positive, "mystical" connotation (Wesley, *Works*, III, p. 408). As for the New England Puritans, all they could say of the New World's natural environment was that it was a hideous wasteland; for Bradford "a hideous and desolate wilderness" (Turner, p. 208), for Mather a "sorrowful wilderness" (Nash, p. 26). The only alleviation of this relentlessly negative characterizaton of nature by the Puritans was the tradition of typological allegorizing, as in Jonathan Edwards' *Images or Shadows of Divine Things*. Surveying the writings of North America's English pioneers, Nash writes: "How frontiersmen described the wilderness they found reflected the intensity of their antipathy. The same descriptive phrases appeared again and again. Wilderness was 'howling', 'dismal', 'terrible' . . . the pioneers' situation and attitude prompted them to use military metaphors to discuss the coming of civilization [as] . . . a 'struggle with nature' for the purpose of 'converting a wilderness into a rich and prosperous civilization'" (*Ibid*, pp. 26–7). Winthrop, in his call for settlers, asked: why remain in England and "suffer a whole Continent . . . to lie waste without any improvement?" (*Ibid*, p. 31) As New England poet Michael Wigglesworth put it: on the eve of settlement the New World was "a waste and howling wilderness,/ Where none inhabited/ But hellish fiends, and brutish men/ That Devils worshiped" (*Ibid*, p. 36).

Thus, with the exception of a figure like Roger Williams who could contrast the natural righteousness of the American Indian with the corrupt hypocrisy of European "civilization" (Scheper, "Spiritual Marriage", p. 127), the story of American attitudes to wild nature in the eighteenth and early nineteenth centuries is a sad litany of antipathy fully documented by the studies of Nash (chap. 2), Turner (pp. 200–228), and Marx (chap. 4), and given classic literary expression in the fiction of Hawthorne, notably in "Young Goodman Brown", and the forest scenes in *The Scarlet Letter*. As Turner concludes, had these men been "other than they were, they might have written a new mythology here. As it was, they took inventory" (p. 256). In a sense, this was but an extension of a long-standing Western mind-set which seemed incapable of positive aesthetic response to wild nature – as is well known, mountain scenery held no recorded delights for European travelers, from the famous incident of Petrarch's Augustinian self-rebuke for almost admiring the natural beauty of a mountain scene, right up through Boswell and Johnson's rambles in the Hebrides (see Nash, pp. 19–20; Biese, pp. 109–20).

Until, that is, that great tidal shift in taste occurred sometime in the eighteenth century, involving the newly emergent taste for the picturesque and recognition of the "sublime" as an aesthetic category as codified by Shaftesbury, Burke and Kant (see sources cited in Nash, p. 46, n. 3), and manifest in the pre-romantic poetry of Joseph and Thomas Wharton and James Thomson, the naturalistic landscape garden movement in England, and the romantic painting and drawing of Caspar David Friedrich, Philip Otto Runge and Adolph Menzel in Germany, and Constable and Turner in England (see Honour, Chap. 2; Jonathan Wordsworth; *Romantic Spirit*). Constable's passionate localism, in particular, is perhaps as close an analogue as we can find in Western art to something like the Navajo sense of *Dine' Bike'yah*, except that for Constable the artifacts of human rural occupation are integral to that blessed landscape: "I even love every stile and stump, and every lane in the village, so deep rooted are early impressions" (Reynolds, p. 32); "I never saw an ugly thing in my life . . . for let the form of an object be what it may, light, shade and perspective will always make it beautiful. . . . The sound of water escaping from mill-dams, etc., willows, old rotten planks, slimy posts, and brickwork, I love such things" (Honour, pp. 92, 88). Of course this becomes in the nineteenth century the full flood tide of international romanticism – or, we should say, romanticisms – with its accompanying "religion of nature" (see Fairchild; Albanese). The first great American expression of this movement is found among the Transcendentalists, and particularly Thoreau, whose credo, "I believe in the forest, and in the meadow, and in the night in which the corn grows" (*Portable Thoreau*, p. 187), and whose declaration that in "wildness is the preservation of the world" ("Walking", in *Natural History Essays*, p. 112) could not be more diametrically opposed to the nature-hostility of the Puritans (Albanese, chap. 3; Nash, chap. 5).

Subsequently, with John Muir and the national park movement, Olmsted and the urban park movement, and the Hudson River school of painters led by Thomas Cole and Frederick Church (see Novak; Scheper, "Reformist Vision"; Nash, chaps, 6–9), a fully-fledged "wilderness cult" flourished, peculiarly American in character, and generating a whole distinctive genre of nature writing whose lineage includes Aldo

Leopold, Rachel Carson, Edward Abbey, Annie Dillard and Barry Lopez, and poets such as Robinson Jeffers and Gary Snyder. Such naturalist writers, along with the new generation of eco-theologians such as Thomas Berry, bring us back full-circle to the Native American idea of wild nature as spiritual home, as in the Navajo Beauty Way, the Way of *hohzho* or cosmic harmony, as it is expressed in the ceremonial blessing of a new hogan, a "house made of dawn": "This hogan will be a blessed hogan./ It will become a hogan of dawn. . . ./ It will be a hogan with beauty above it,/ It will be a hogan with beauty all around it" (Hillerman, p. 524).

Essex Community College, Baltimore, MD

REFERENCES

Albanese, Catherine L. *Nature Religion in America From the Algonkian Indians to the New Age.* Chicago: University of Chicago, 1990.
Arndt, John. *Of True Christianity.* Tr. Boehm. London, 1707.
Bercovitch, Sacvan, ed. *Typology and Early American Literature.* Amherst, 1972.
Berry, Thomas. *The Dream of the Earth.* San Francisco: Sierra Club Books, 1988.
Biese, Alfred. *The Development of the Feeling for Nature in the Middle Ages and Modern Times.* London, 1905.
Billington, Ray Allen, ed. *The Frontier Thesis/ Valid Interpretation of American History?* New York: Holt, Rinehart and Winston, 1966.
Brown, Peter. *The Body and Society/ Men, Women and Sexual Renunciation in Early Christianity.* New York: Columbia U.P., 1988.
Brueggemann, Walter. *The Land/ Place as Gift, Promise, and Challenge in Biblical Faith.* Philadelphia: Fortress Press, 1977.
Cowan, James. *The Elements of the Aborigine Tradition.* Rockport, Mass.: Element, 1992.
Day, John. *God's Battle with Sea and Dragon.* Cambridge: Cambridge U.P., 1985.
Doob, Leonard. *Patriotism and Nationalism: Their Psychological Foundations.* New Haven: Yale U.P., 1952.
Elman, Robert. *America's Pioneering Naturalists.* Tulsa: Winchester, 1982.
Fox, Matthew. *Original Blessing/ A Primer in Creation Spirituality.* Santa Fe: Bear & Co., 1983.
Garcia-Zambrano, Angel. "El poblamiento de México en la época del contacto: 1520–1540". *Mesoamerica.* Plumsock Mesoamerican Studies **24** (1992): 239–96.
Garcia-Zambrano, Angel. "*Teocomitl*: Clay Bowls and Sacred Basins in the Foundation of Indian Settlements in Sixteenth-Century Mexico". Author's MS; forthcoming in *Ancient Mesoamerica.*
Gill, Sam D. *Mother Earth/ An American Story.* Chicago: University of Chicago Press, 1987.
Gill, Sam D. *Native American Religions/ An Introduction.* Belmont, CA: Wadsworth, 1982.

Hartmann, Horst. *Die Plains – und Prarieindianer Nordamerikas*. Berlin: Museum fur Volkerkunde, 1973.
Heine, Heinrich, *Poetry and Prose*. Ed. Jost Hermand and Robert C. Holub. German Library 32. New York: Continuum, 1982.
Hillerman, Tony. *The Jim Chee Mysteries*. New York: Harper Collins, 1990.
Hiss, Tony. *The Experience of Place*. New York: Vintage/Random House, 1990.
Honour, Hugh. *Romanticism*. New York: Icon/Harper & Row, 1979.
Hultkrantz, Åke. *Belief and Worship in Native North America*. Ed. Christopher Vecsey. Syracuse: Syracuse U.P., 1981.
Hussey, Christopher. *The Picturesque: Studies in a Point of View*. London, 1927.
John of the Cross, St. *The Collected Works of St. John of the Cross*. Tr. Kieran Kavanaugh and Otilio Rodriguez. Washington, D.C.: Institute of Carmelite Studies, 1973.
Kaiser, Rudolf. "'A Fifth Gospel, Almost': Chief Seattle's Speech(es): American Origins and European Reception". *Indians and Europe/ An Interdisciplinary Collection of Essays*, ed. Christian F. Feest. Aachen: Rader-Verlag, 1987, pp. 505–526.
Kolodny, Annette. *The Lay of the Land: Metaphor as Experience and History in American Life and Letters*. Chapel Hill: University of North Carolina, 1975.
Leeuw, G. Van der. *Religion in Essence and Manifestation*. Tr. J.E. Turner. 2 vols. New York, 1963.
Marx, Leo. *The Machine in the Garden/ Technology and the Pastoral Ideal in America*. New York: Oxford U.P., 1964.
Miller, Perry, ed. *The American Puritans/ Their Prose and Poetry*. New York: Columbia U.P., 1956.
Modern Greek Poetry. Tr. & ed. Kimon Friar. Athens: Efstathiadis Group, 1982.
Moltmann, Jürgen. *God in Creation/ A New Theology of Creation and the Spirit of God*. San Francisco: Harper & Row, 1985.
Moreland, Samuel. *History of the Evangelical Churches of the Valleys of the Piemont*. London, 1658.
Motolinia [Toribio de Benavente]. *History of the Indians of New Spain*. Tr. Elizabeth Andros Foster, N.p.: Cortes Society, 1950.
Mumford, Lewis. *Technics and Civilization*. New York: Burlingame, 1963.
Nash, Roderick. *Wilderness and the American Mind*. 3rd ed. New Haven: Yale U.P., 1982.
Norton Anthology of English Literature. 6th ed. Vol. 2. Ed. M.H. Abrams. New York: Norton, 1993.
Novak, Barbara. *Nature and Culture/ American Landscape and Painting 1825–1875*. New York: Oxford U.P., 1980.
Oroz Codex. Tr. & ed. Angelico Chavez. Wasthington, D.C.: Academy of American Franciscan History, 1972.
Phelan, John Leddy. *The Millennial Kingdom of the Franciscans in the New World*. 2nd ed. Berkeley: University of California, 1970.
Portable North American Indian Reader. Ed. Frederick Turner. New York: Penguin, 1977.
Pritchard, James, ed. *The Ancient Near East*. Vol. 1. *An Anthology of Texts and Pictures*. Princeton: Princeton U.P., 1958.
Reichard, Gladys A. *Navaho Religion*. Bollingen Series XVIII. Princeton: Princeton U.P., 1977.
Reynolds, Graham. *Constable: the Natural Painter*. St. Albans, Herts: Panther/Granada, 1976.

Ricard, Robert. *The Spiritual Conquest of Mexico/ An Essay on the Apostolate and the Evangelizing Methods of the Mendicant Orders in New Spain: 1523–1572*. Tr. Lesley Byrd Simpson. Berkeley: University of California, 1966.
Romantic Spirit: German Drawings, 1780–1850, from the German Democratic Republic. Ed. Peter Betthausen, et al. 1989.
Santmire, Paul H. *Brother Earth/ Nature, God and Ecology in Time of Crisis*. New York: Thomas Nelson, 1970.
Santmire, Paul H. *The Travail of Nature/ The Ambiguous Ecological Promise of Christian Theology*. Philadelphia: Fortress Press, 1985.
Scheper, George. "The Reformist Vision of Frederick Law Olmsted and the Poetics of Park Design". *New England Quarterly* **62**.3 (1989): 369–402.
Scheper, George. "The Spiritual Marriage: The Exegetic History and Literary Impact of the Song of Songs in the Middle Ages". Diss. Princeton, 1971.
Seifert, Jaroslav. *Selected Poetry*. Tr. Ewald Osers. Ed. George Gibian. New York: Collier, 1986.
Stanner, W. E. H. "Aboriginal Territorial Organization: Estate, Range, Domain and Regime". *Oceania* **36**.1 (1965): 1–26.
Stone, Lloyd. "This Is My Song". *Everlasting Streams/ Songs for Worship*, ed. Ruth C. Duck and Michael G. Bausch. New York: Pilgrim, 1981. #23.
Teresa of Avila. *The Life of Teresa of Jesus* Tr. & ed. E. Allison Peers. New York: Image/Doubleday, 1960.
Thoreau, Henry David. *Portable Thoreau*. Ed. Carl Bode. Harmondsworth: Penguin, 1975.
Thoreau, Henry David. *The Natural History Essays*. Salt Lake City: Peregrine Smith Books/Gibbs M. Smith, 1984.
Tuan, Yi-Fu. *Space and Place/ The Perspective of Experience*. Minneapolis: University of Minnesota, 1977.
Turner, Frederick. *Beyond Geography/ The Western Spirit Against the Wilderness*. New Brunswick, NJ:1983.
Waddell, Helen, tr. *The Desert Fathers*. Ann Arbor: University of Michigian, 1960.
Waley, Arthur. *The Way and Its Power/ A Study of the "Tao Te Ching" and its Place in Chinese Thought*. New York: Grove, n.d.
Wang Wei. *Poems*. Tr. G.W. Robinson. Harmondsworth: Penguin, 1973.
Wesley, John. *Works*. Ed. John Emory. New York, 1856.
Westermann, Claus. *Blessing in the Bible and the Life of the Church*. Philadelphia: Fortress Press, 1978.
Wordsworth, Jonathan; Jaye, Michael C.; Woof, Robert. *William Wordsworth and the Age of English Romanticism*. New Brunswick: Rutgers U.P., 1987.
Williams, George. *The Radical Reformation/ 1520–1580*. Philadelphia, 1962.
Williams, George. *Wilderness and Paradise in Christian Thought*. New York, 1962.

JOAN B. WILLIAMSON

JERUSALEM: THE POETICS OF SPACE IN THE WORKS OF PHILIPPE DE MÉZIÈRES

People psychologically anchor themselves in the universe in terms of time and space. When an event occurs, they see it as a confluence of time and space, with the latter transformed into a particular place. To institutionally memorialize an event, to fix the fleeting moment which would otherwise be lost or remembered only hazily, rituals are enacted and then re-enacted periodically in either the place itself where the original event occurred or in re-creations elsewhere that recall a particular privileged space.[1] Perhaps no place on earth has been so much the object of this treatment, and has illustrated more passionately the workings of the poetics of place, than the city of Jerusalem. The focus of this presentation is the poetic of the city of Jerusalem in the work of Philippe de Mézières. Philippe, born ca. 1327, died 1405, was in turn soldier, diplomat, and politician, briefly a crusader, but a life-long propagandist for the Crusades; therefore this city occupied a dominant place in his thought. However, Philippe was very much a medieval man of learning, and as such borrowed extensively from his predecessors. It is therefore appropriate to first consider the earlier traditions that constituted his sources.

The Old Testament shows clearly that Jerusalem acquired a magical aura through the application of the poetics of space. For the biblical Jews this city had become a symbol of their land and their very selves. Its destruction and that of its Temple lay at the heart of their yearning for the Promised Land. Moreover, apocalyptic Judaism and the *Midrash* placed Jerusalem as their sacred center, the umbilicus of the world whence creation sprang.[2] Christianity was also to develop a detailed allegory of place concerning this city. Dorothea R. French, to whom I am indebted for the material from Jonathan Z. Smith and Mircea Eliade indicated in the last footnote, has magisterially discussed this development in her article "Journeys to the Center of the Earth".[3] Therefore I can do no better than summarize her presentation. French has shown how ritual journeys by Christians, the pilgrimages, helped claim all of Roman and Jewish Palestine for Christianity, thus transforming Palestine into a Christian sacred center. Christian pilgrims visited the Holy Land, particularly Mount Calvary, because they believed it was the place where Christ was crucified. But since it was from this act that redemption sprang, Mount Calvary acquired the allegorical sense of the center of the earth from which creation sprang. Thus we find Mount Calvary became the birthplace of Adam as well as his burial ground. These identifications are illustrated in religious iconography commencing in the sixth century with the placement of Adam's skull in a little cave beneath the Cross. And it was over this spot that the Church of Mount Calvary was built within the precincts of the Church of the Holy Sepulcher.

Tradition holds that the Byzantine emperor Constantine ordered the destruction of the temple of Venus, which had been erected by Hadrian over what was believed to be the site of the Holy Sepulcher. When this was done, the Holy Sepulcher was discovered, whereupon Constantine ordered that the Church of the Holy Sepulcher be built over it. The belief in the *inventio* of the True Cross helped attach allegorical meaning to the place. "The Cross, or Cosmic Tree, is an archetypical symbol of the center. All sacred trees are thought of as situated in the Center of the World, with roots that reach down into Hell and branches that reach into Heaven."[4] Legend credited Helen, the mother of Constantine, with the discovery of the three crosses on Golgotha. To discover which was Christ's, each cross was laid on a dead man, and the one on whom Christ's was laid came to life again. Thus the life-giving miracle of the True Cross, which formed a rupture or an opening to the cosmic levels, made of Mount Calvary in particular, and of the Church of the Holy Sepulcher generally, the allegorical center of creation, and this by virtue of being the place where Christ's redemptive sacrifice on the Cross had broken the power of the grave.

From this point on, Jerusalem was perceived as the literal center of the world. French has shown how practical maps, such as Ptolemy's second-century *Geographia*, became imbued with new meaning as they reflected this perception. While the fourth-century maps of Eusebius and Jerome are still to be considered as practical, they superimposed biblical place names on those of contemporary Roman Palestine, thus transforming profane into sacred space. Jerome's maps are oriented to the east (where the Garden of Eden was thought to lie), and their scale gives prominence to Palestine and Jerusalem. Eastern Church Fathers, such as the fourth-century Gregory of Nyssa, stressed the allegorical meaning of biblical sites, seeing them as symbols of Christ's salvific acts. In an eighth-century *mappa mundi* illustrating Beatus of Liebana's commentary on the Apocalypse, we see the completion of this appropriation of the world into sacred space. Sacred geography was considered the only real kind, as opposed to profane, which was seen as abstract. At the top of this map, in the extreme east, lies the Garden of Eden; and Palestine, although not at the center of the world, is dramatically oversized. From the eleventh through to the fourteenth century, Jerusalem was placed at the center of maps of the known world, as we see, e.g., in the Byzantine-Oxford T-O map (brought back to England or Ireland in 1110 after the successful First Crusade). The Holy Land dominates the center of the map, with Jerusalem replacing the bodies of water as the dividing line between Asia and Europe-Africa, and with the Cross, the symbol of salvation, placed at the exact literal center of the world.

Philippe de Mézières participated in this tradition that viewed Jerusalem as the center of the world, as we see in his *Songe du vieil pelerin*: Queen Truth admits to having visited the East and the center of the earth, which, she says, is where Jerusalem is "le centre de la terre".[5] The miniature accompanying his treatise, *Le Livre de la vertu du sacrement de mariage*, written between 1384 and 1389, features a crucifixion scene in which the torso of Adam rises out of a hole in the ground with arms upraised to receive Christ's blood.[6] While not a skull, Philippe's figure represents a resurrected Adam, the redeemed Adam, in keeping with the legendary belief that, "When the Messiah gained victory by the lance, blood and water flowed from his side, ran down into Adam's mouth and was his baptism and thus he was baptized."[7] Philippe's descriptions of a blessed and, in contrast, an accursed garden reflect the allegorical significance of the Cross and Mount Calvary, in that each of them has a fountain from which spring four rivers, producing, respectively blessed virtues and unremitting evils.[8] Tradition makes of Mount Calvary the source of four rivers, as exemplified in a sixth-century paten from Siberia, on which the Cross stands on the mount of Paradise from which flow four rivers, formed by the blood flowing from the crucified Christ's hands and feet.[9]

Philippe's description of the compass, used, as he says,[10] by sailors in the Mediterranean, but not those in the North Sea, makes the wheel or tablet, on which the lines indicating the four principal winds are drawn, the human body. The east wind represents the head, which is warm and moist; the west wind represents the legs and feet, which are cold and dry; the south wind represents the right shoulder, arm, and hand, which are hot and dry; while the north wind represents the left shoulder, arm and hand, which are cold and damp.[11] Philippe's symbol for humanity, created in the image and likeness of God, faithfully echoes the integration of Christ in the structure of the world, to show the cosmic importance of the crucifixion in the scheme of the salvation of the world, as seen in the Ebstorf map of ca. 1235.[12] In this map, as French describes it, Christ's head "emerges at the east, his wounded hands from the north and south, and his feet protrude from the edge of the world in the west. His body is comprised of the entire world."[13]

French closes her presentation of pre-Renaissance attitudes to literal and allegorical geography by citing John Friedman's conclusion that "the preoccupation of Christendom with the recovery of Jerusalem and the Holy Land no doubt reinforced the attitude that Jerusalem was the center of the world in this time period".[14] We see that this was indeed true from the remarks early crusade preachers made in their polemics for holy war. In 1095, Pope Urban II preached the first crusade sermon at the Council of Clermont.[15] Numerous accounts of this sermon survive, and from these we see the centrality of Jerusalem in the crusade preaching of both Urban and later preachers.[16] Fulcher of Chartres, himself a crusader, provides the earliest comprehensive account of Urban's sermon, in his work aptly titled *Historia Hierosolymitana*.[17] Another *Historia Hierosolimitana*, by the Benedictine monk Robert of Rheims, records Urban's pleas for Jerusalem, pointing out the shameful treatment of the Holy Sepulcher and the pollution of the holy places. Robert, in Cole's paraphrase, has Urban plead for the Franks to recover the Holy Land and Jerusalem, ennobled by Christ's life on earth, from its wicked possessor; Jerusalem is irresistibly attractive, "the center of the world, a land bountiful before all others, and, as it were, another paradise of delights".[18] Baudri of Dol also wrote a *Historia Jerosolimitana* in which he recorded Urban's pleas. According to Baudri, Urban referred to the calamitous events occurring at Antioch, where the blessed Peter first resided as bishop, but Jerusalem was the special object of Turkish atrocities. It is pity for this city, where Christ suffered because of human sinfulness, that Urban – in Baudri's words as rendered by Cole – seeks to invoke:

But I am on the edge of tears and cries; sighs and sobbing threaten to overcome me. Let us bewail, brothers, I beseech you, let us bewail, and lamenting from the depths of our being let us groan aloud with the Psalmist, for we are miserable and wretched in whose time that prophecy has been fulfilled: "God, the nations have come into your inheritance: they have polluted your holy temple; they have made Jerusalem guard the fruit trees;

they have put out the dead bodies of your servants to feed the birds and the flesh of your saints to feed the beasts of the land. They have shed blood like a river that runs around Jerusalem and there was no one to bury them." Woe upon us, brothers. Now "we have become a reproach to our neighbors, an object of derision and fun to those who live around us." Let us grieve with and suffer with our brothers, at least in our tears. Let us, who have become "despised by the mean" and worse than all men, weep for the monstrous devastation of the most Holy Land.[19]

Guibert of Nogent, who had not been at Clermont, completed his version of Urban's sermon ca. 1111–12. He begins by explaining why greater prestige is attached to a pilgrimage to Jerusalem than to other places associated with the Apostles or to Constantinople, the city of kings. As Cole paraphrases Guibert:

Jerusalem is the source from which Christians have received the grace of redemption and the origin of Christianity . . . . It is clear that the land and the city of Jerusalem are called sacred by Holy Scripture because of their association with the incarnate and suffering Christ . . . . For if, as we read in the sacred writings of the prophets, this land was the inheritance and the sacred temple of God before the Lord walked and suffered there, what reverence, what sanctity do we believe accrued to it when God became incarnate there, when he was nurtured, grew, and in human form, walked about or rode from place to place and where, briefly, the blood of the Son of God, more sacred than heaven and earth, was shed and where as the souls of the dead trembled, his body died and came to rest in the tomb; what veneration do we think it has earned?[20]

Cole points out that Urban, in Guibert's rendering, stresses the momentous importance of Jerusalem in the unfolding of sacred history. It is the source of the Old Law, but particularly the origin of Christianity, where men and women have received the Christian Gospel, the cleansing of baptism and the proof of faith.[21]

Among others, Henry of Albano (born in 1140) stressed the special sanctity of Jerusalem in his *De peregrinante civitate Dei*;[22] while Innocent III addressed the causes of the captivity and liberation of Jerusalem.[23] Jacques de Vitry, a preacher of the Fifth Crusade and bishop of Acre in 1216, recalls in his sermons, in a way that is reminiscent of the Clermont sermon, that Jerusalem is "the city of redemption, the mother of faith, the birthplace of the Old and New Law, and the center of the world, where God worked out man's salvation through his own humiliation."[24]

Philippe de Mézières echoes these views. Jerusalem, he says, is a holy city, the foundation stone of the Catholic faith and Christians' spiritual heritage on earth.[25] He also lends importance to Jerusalem by commenting on Helen's finding of the True Cross.[26] While he urges the French king,

Charles VI, to free Jerusalem in *Le Songe du vieil pelerin*,[27] in his *Letter to King Richard II*, he exhorts the English king to join with Charles VI in leading a new crusade to free the Holy Land, echoing the early crusade preachers when he urges his royal reader to avenge the wrongs done the Crucified One, and to remember that Mount Calvary, the Holy Sepulcher, and other sacred places which were watered by the precious blood of the Slain Lamb, are now befouled by the false followers of Mohammed.[28] He reminds Richard:

These enemies have burnt, destroyed and reviled to the utmost the sanctuary of your Faith, the Cross and holy relics of the Passion of your Redeemer and Saviour, Jesus Christ. O most excellent and puissant King, remember that you and your ancestors have been shamefully banished from your spiritual kingdom and inheritance, in that holy land purchased for you by Jesus at the price of His precious blood and death.[29]

Like Urban, he seeks to evoke an emotional response to Jerusalem's plight, as he asks with sincere emotion:

What man is there, baptised in the name of the blessed Jesus, whose heart is so steeled that he can here tell of these wrongs and not be moved to compasion, and so to offer in devotion to God his body, his goods and all that lies in his power, to remedy the great evils and this dishonour of Christendom, here briefly recited?[30]

Philippe himself was struck by compassion for the fate of Jerusalem, when he made his own pilgrimage there in 1347.[31] This experience first gave him the idea of preaching a new crusade, but when these attempts received no response,[32] he conceived of the idea of founding a military order to avenge the wrong done the Crucifix (i.e., the Crucified) and to free the Holy Land.[33]

His journey to Jerusalem was inevitable given his interests and the time in which he lived. Barbara Sargent has pointed out that in spite of the Arab conquests, by the eleventh century the pilgrimage to Jerusalem was already being made by the faithful in their hundreds and thousands.[34] Philippe reflects reality in his references to Jerusalem. When he urges Charles VI to go to the Holy City, he speaks in terms of a once-in-a-lifetime pilgrimage that corresponded to the actual number of times most Western travelers who made the pilgrimage to Jerusalem did go there.[35] He shows close knowledge of Jerusalem, which he informs us used to be known as Salem,[36] when he refers to the concession by the Saracens of free passage for Ethiopians traveling to their community in Jerusalem, for such a community existed.[37]

Jerusalem, however, was more than a place of pilgrimage for him; it was a place of epiphany. In it, in the Church of the Holy Sepulcher, he experienced a conversion, a vision that inspired him to found his military Order. He narrates how he saw in the spirit heavenly ladies who ordered him to found a new military Order.[38] Such a heady effect of this exalted place was not unique to him, e.g., Bridget of Sweden also experienced visions in this same church.[39] The idea of founding a military Order was also shared by others; e.g., his friend and master Pierre I of Lusignan, while still Count of Tripoli, was inspired by a vision to found his Order of the Sword.[40] Philippe's vision had a particularly exalted orientation. In the account of his inspirational vision that he gives in his *Oratio tragedica*, it is as another Moses that, after forty days and forty nights spent traveling to Mount Syon (that is Mount Sinai), he receives directly from the hand of God, as tablets of the law, the first part of the rules of his military Order of the Passion of Jesus Christ.[41]

Philippe had a special predilection for the figure of Moses. In addition to this presentation of himself in the guise of another Moses, he compares Richard II of England and Charles VI of France to Moses and Aaron;[42] and in consecration of Charles's divine mandate to lead the French people to salvation, he depicts him first as Moses in conversation with the Lord,[43] and then as Moses in apotheosis,[44] as I have pointed out elsewhere.[45] The early crusade preachers had used Old Testament warriors as exempla for their listeners; e.g., Pope Urban II, in the words of Guibert of Nogent, compared the suffering of the Maccabees with those of Christ,[46] and Jacques de Vitry cited the exploits of the Maccabees, Phineas and Mattathias.[47] Philippe also does this, but he makes such comparisons peculiarly his through extensive use of them.[48]

Guibert de Nogent recalls Urban's comparisons of earlier persecutions with that of the Turks, and Hrabanus Maurus endows the persecution of the Maccabees by Antiochus with Christian meaning.[49] But for Philippe time coalesces, and the Babylonian and Turkish dominations fuse. Between 1367 and 1368 he wrote a lamentation on the fate of Jerusalem. Although this work is now lost, we know of its composition from his own references to it, e.g., *Lamentation de Jerusalem sur la negligence des chrétiens*,[50] and *Libello lamentacionis Jherusalem*.[51] A copy of Philippe's text is perhaps the book referred to by Gilles Malet in his catalog of Charles V's Library as *Lamentatio super Jherusalem*.[52] While we cannot know its content, Philippe's Latin title recalls Jeremiah's *Book of Lamentations* and thus links the later fate of Jerusalem with the biblical events. Under Philippe's pen the ancient and the medieval Jerusalem become one city, for, while it is the Turkish threat that menaces Jerusalem in Philippe's time, he personifies it as the Sultan of Babylon.[53] Philippe calls Saladin – officially the Sultan of Egypt, who captured Jerusalem in 1187 – the Sultan of Babylon,[54] in metaphorical vein. Philippe also narrates an elaborate parable of Kings Vigilant and Ill-advised (Malavisé), where the former is the Sultan of Babylon and the latter the Christian kings who slept while Vigilant destroyed their banners, emblems, and arms (that is the Crucifix and other signs of the Christian faith), ousting them from Jerusalem and holding the people in subjection.[55]

Carrying further the analogy of the two Jerusalems, he presents the Western crusaders of the last forty years of his lifetime as the Israelites wandering in the desert, with his military Order constituting the manna from Heaven, paraphrasing Exodus 16:13–36 and Numbers 11:5 and 27:12–23, to concretize the comparison.[56] He makes of the Western Christians who refuse to go on crusade the children of Israel who preferred to stay in the Pharaoh's kitchens in comfort rather than travel through the desert in search of the Promised Land, with manna from Heaven as their sustenance; this is perhaps echoing Humbert of Romans' comparison of those who refused to go on crusade with the Jews who refused to leave Babylon for Jerusalem, preferring avarice, wine, gluttony, and luxury.[57]

Significantly, the physical geography Philippe presents in his works does not include a detailed Jerusalem. In *Le Songe du vieil pelerin*, the author, as his fractured personae of Ardent Desire and Good Hope, undertakes in dream a world journey in the company of the allegorized virtues of Truth, Peace, Mercy, and Justice. These divine ladies, having previously fled the world because of its wickedness, now returned to earth to seek a place hospitable to the installation of their forge, in which to once again mint their coin, a place sufficiently free from sin. The journey takes them through the countries of the West, the Near East, India, China, and Tartary; stops at important cities such as Avignon, Paris, Genoa, Rome, Venice, Prague, Naples, Barcelona, Burgos, Lisbon, Pamplona, London, and Ghent are described in great detail. Jerusalem, however, while on the itinerary as it must be in any world journey, is mentioned only in passing, receiving no description whatsoever. While the recapture of the earthly Jerusalem was Philippe's life's work, the mystical meanings he attached to the city precluded physical presentation.

The early crusade preachers had made of the earthly Jerusalem a metaphor for the Church Militant, positing a spiritual Jerusalem. For example, for the early thirteenth-century John of Abbeville the captivity of the earthly Jerusalem signified the captivity of the spiritual Jerusalem, the Church.[58] John sees a causal relationship between the Moslem occupation of the earthly Jerusalem and the loss of the spiritual Jerusalem, which for him symbolized Christian poverty of faith.[59] This metaphor also provided meaning for Humbert of Romans' inclusion, in his mid-thirteenth-century *De predicacione crucis*, of the conflation of the Babylonian and Turkish oppression of Jerusalem. According to Humbert, such destruction results from the faithlessness of Jerusalem's peoples, both the ancient Israelites and the sinful Christians.[60] Philippe, as we have seen, establishes the analogy of the Babylonian destruction of the earthly Jerusalem with the later Turkish domination. He also echoes these early preachers by attributing the loss of Jerusalem to the sins of the Christians:

> Through lack of good government, and, above all, through lack of justice, which includes the Faith of Jesus Christ and His holy works, and lack, also, of knightly discipline, first the capital city of all Christendom, that is the holy city of Jerusalem, the foundation stone of the Catholic Faith, and then the whole kingdom, the Promised land, have been lost, and conquered by King Vigilant, the Sultan of Babylon, who has held it for one or two hundred years, to the great shame and disgrace of Christian kings, alas, so ill-advised.[61]

Thus it is the spiritual Jerusalem that Philippe seeks to present. His *Livre de la vertu du sacrement de mariage* presents the sacrifice of Christ on the Cross as the marriage of Christ to the Church, figuratively presented as Mary, but also as Jerusalem.[62] However, the literal city is also a metaphor for salvation, for the heavenly Jerusalem, for the Church Triumphant. Referring to himself in his spiritual testament as a pilgrim, he hopes to achieve the end of his journey and arrive, through death, at the holy city of Jerusalem Triumphant.[63] Elsewhere he is more explicit when he expresses the hope that his military Order will achieve salvation for himself and its members by recovering the material city, the physical Jerusalem, which he calls "Jherusalem militant", to finally reach a triumphant Jerusalem on high, by which he means Paradise, where they will see God face to face: "Jerusalem la sus triumphant. C'est assavoir en Paradis et veoir Dieu en sa face".[64] In his explanatory table of the figures occurring in *Le Songe du vieil pelerin*, he makes it clear that the holy city of Jerusalem in Syria is figuratively Jerusalem Triumphant, that is, Paradise and the Kingdom of Heaven.[65]

Philippe thus moves from literal to anagogical meaning. We see that this Jerusalem Militant is the Church Militant, the Church of the Living God, which he identifies as the bride of the Slain Lamb.[66] In his *Livre de la vertu du sacrement de mariage* and *Epistre lamentable et consolatoire sur le fait de la desconfiture lacrimable du noble et vaillant roy de Hongeurie par les Turcs devant la ville de Nicopoli*, he frequently refers to Christ as the Lamb and the Slain Lamb.[67] His Jerusalem is the New Jerusalem of the Apocalypse (Apoc. 21:2),[68] the Jerusalem made of twelve jewels (Apoc. 21:9–27), allegorically echoed in Philippe's *Livre de la vertu du sacrement de mariage*;[69] the Jerusalem adorned as a bride for her husband (Apoc. 21:2–8), and her marriage to the Lamb (Apoc. 19:6–10), also allegorically narrated by Philippe in *Le Livre*.[70]

It is here that we comprehend the significance of the banner of Philippe's military Order of the Passion of Jesus Christ: the Lamb of God, a Lamb rampant, head encased in a halo, holding aloft with its right hoof a staff from which unfurls a white banner with a gold cross upon it, which is the Lamb of the Apocalypse (Apoc. 5:6–14). A lamb as the insignia of a military order seems incongruous until we realize that it is the Lamb of the Apocalypse (with all the connotations that name carries), and that for Philippe there could be no other. The Lamb of the Apocalypse arrays his troops on Mount Sion, and he marks them with his name (Apoc. 14:1). He fights the Ten Kings and we see how terrible an enemy he is, as he cuts off each of their heads (Apoc. 17:12–14). We see the force of his military power in an illumination for this passage in an early thirteenth-century manuscript of the Beatus of Liebana Commentary on the Apocalypse, in the Bernard H. Breslauer collection of manuscript illuminations.[71] Here the Lamb, with halo round its head and horns, stands upright on its hind legs like a man. It holds the shield of a crusader in one hand while it cuts off the heads of the Ten Kings with a sword held in the other. Above, in a semicircle of sky, is the Lamb of God, rampant, but instead of a staff held in its right hoof is a sword, from the blade of which unfurls the banner and round whose hilt is a halo. Philippe, who had spent time in Spain,[72] and for whom the Apocalypse is a much-quoted text, while not necessarily familiar with this particular manuscript, must surely have been familiar with such iconography and perception of the nature of the Apocalypse Lamb of God. However, Philippe was hardly the first to associate the crusader with the Apocalypse Lamb of God. As Cole points out, the Apocalypse would certainly have been in the library at Cluny, where Urban II passed much of his life, and equally certainly provided some of the inspiration for the first crusade sermon.[73] Also, accounts of the Christian martyrs, among whom crusaders were counted, contained motifs with strong Apocalyptic associates, such as the crown of victory and the Lamb.[74] The Lamb of God provided a potent and enduring image. How enduring we may comprehend from its survival among the modern descendants, "kakure Kirishitan", of the Christian Japanese converted between 1549 and 1639 as "anesutera" (from the Latin *Agnus Dei*), to denote the rank of saints who protect the world.[75] The Lamb of God was therefore particularly appropriate as a distinguishing sign for crusaders, whose military commander was Christ. Also, since the eternal Jerusalem that Philippe hoped to attain by the reconquest of the physical city, under the patronage of the Lamb of God represented on the banner of his Order, was the bride of the Lamb of the Apocalypse, the banner proclaimed both his fealty and his purpose.

We see that Philippe borrowed many of his ideas and imagery. He is important because he used these borrowings in a way that gave coherence and unity to his vision and his sacralization of the space that was Jerusalem, the scene of the Passion of the Lamb. Jerusalem represented, with all its significations, the passion of Philippe's life. Let us remember that this propagandist had also been a crusader, and had therefore been willing to sacrifice his life in the service of his passion. This propagandist's presentation is made, with the rhetoric of eloquence, yes; but also with all the passion of his soul. Jerusalem, the material place, signified so much more for Philippe than the physical space it occupied that no geography or *mappa mundi* could contain it. By omitting literal description, Philippe invites his readers to share what he himself sought, meditation on the ineffable, and it is here that he leaves us.

Long Island University

NOTES

[1] Nancy Regaldo has analyzed medieval pageantry as a way of fixing events in popular memory in "Marking Time: Performance and Public Memory", a presentation at the Memoria Conference: "The Memory Culture of the Middle Ages and the Renaissance", held October 11, 1991, at New York University under the sponsorship of the Faculty Colloquium on Orality, Writing, and Culture; Jonathan Z. Smith discusses how ritual activity transforms space into place in his book *To Take Place: Toward Theory in Ritual* (Chicago: U. of Chicago P., 1987), ch. 5.

[2] Mircea Eliade, *The Sacred and the Profane: The Nature of Religion*, trans. Willard R. Trask (New York: Harper and Row, 1961), pp. 42–47; and *The Myth of the Eternal Return*, trans. Willard R. Trask, Bollingen Series 46 (Princeton: Princeton U.P., 1971), p. 13.

[3] Dorothea R. French, "Journeys to the Center of the Earth", *Journeys toward God: Pilgrimage and Crusade*, ed. Barbara N. Sargent-Baur, Occasional Studies Series, Medieval and Renaissance Studies Program of the University of Pittsburgh 5, and Medieval Institute Publications SMC 30 (Kalamazoo: Western Michigan U., 1992), pp. 45–81.

[4] French, p. 54.

[5] Philippe de Mézières, *Le Songe du vieil pelerin*, ed. G. W. Coopland, 2 vols. (Cambridge, Eng.: Cambridge U.P., 1969), 1:233.

[6] Joan B. Williamson, "Paris B. N. MS. fr. 1175: A Collaboration between Author and Artist", *Text and Image*, ACTA 10 (Center for Medieval and Early Renaissance Studies, State U. of New York at Binghamton, 1983), pp. 77–92, esp. 82.

[7] French, p. 59, citing Gertrud Schiller, *Iconography of Christian Art*, trans. Janet Seligman, vol. 2 (Greenwich, Conn.: New York Graphic Society, 1971), p. 8.

[8] Philippe de Mézières, *Letter to King Richard II: A Plea Made in 1395 for Peace between England and France*, ed. and trans. G. W. Coopland (Liverpool: Liverpool U.P., 1975), pp. 128 and 130, for the French text, and pp. 55–57, for Coopland's English translation cited here.

[9] French, p. 56, citing Schiller, 2:8.

[10] Philippe de Mézières, *Le livre de la vertu du sacrement de mariage*, Paris, Bibliothèque Nationale, MS. fr. 1175, f. 142^v. The transcriptions of the text given in this article are from my forthcoming edition by the Catholic U. of America Press.

[11] *Le Livre*, ff. 143–143^v.

[12] French reproduces this map on p. 65, from Leo Bagrow, *History of Cartography*, ed. and rev. R. A. Skelton, trans. D. L. Paisley (Cambridge: Harvard U.P., 1964).

[13] French, p. 64.

[14] French, p. 67, citing John B. Friedman, *The Monstrous Races in Medieval Art and Thought* (Cambridge: Harvard U.P., 1981), pp. 219–20 n. 23.

[15] Penny Cole, *The Preaching of the Crusades to the Holy Land. 1095–1270* (Cambridge: Medieval Academy of America, 1991), p. ix.

[16] Cole, p. 3.

[17] Cole, p. 10.

[18] Cole, pp. 14–15, paraphrasing Robert of Rheims, *Historia Hierosolimitana*, Recueil des Historiens des Croisades, Occidentaux (RHC, Occ.) 3:729.

[19] Cole, p. 17, paraphrasing Baudri of Dol, *Historia Jerosolimitana*, RHC, Occ. 4:9.

[20] Cole, p. 23, paraphrasing Guibert of Nogent, *Gesta Dei per Francos*, RHC, Occ. 4:137.

[21] Cole, p. 24.

[22] Cole, p. 68.

[23] Cole, 80–101.

[24] Cole, p. 134, paraphrasing Jacques de Vitry, "Ad cruce signatos", *Analecta novissima spicilegii Solesmensis: Altera continuatio*, ed. Jean Baptiste Pitra, vol. 2 (Paris, 1888; repr. Farnborough: Gregg, 1967), p. 422.

[25] E.g., *Letter to King Richard II*, p. 99, for the French text, and pp. 24 and 29, for Coopland's English translation.

[26] *Letter to King Richard II*, p. 115, for the French text, and p. 41, for Coopland's English translation.
[27] *Le Songe du vieil pelerin*, 2:223, 296, 375, 410, and 498.
[28] *Letter to King Richard II*, p. 101, p. 28 for Coopland's English translation.
[29] *Letter to King Richard II*, pp. 101–102, for the French text, and p. 29, for Coopland's English translation given here.
[30] *Letter to King Richard II*, p. 102, for the French text, and p. 29, for Coopland's English translation given here.
[31] Philippe de Mézières, *Oratio tragedica*, Paris, Bibliothèque Mazarine, MS. 1651, f. 129^v.
[32] *Oratio tragedica*, f. 129^v–130.
[33] *Oratio tragedica*, f. 129^v.
[34] Sargent-Baur, *Journeys toward God*, p. vii.
[35] *Le Songe*, 2:410.
[36] *Le Songe*, 1:230.
[37] *Le Songe*, 1:221–22.
[38] Philippe de Mézières, *De la chevallerie de la Passion de Jhesu Crist*, Paris, Bibliothèque de l"Arsenal, MS. 2251, ff. 7^v–13^v.
[39] Johannes Jorgenson, *St. Bridget of Sweden*, trans. Ingeborg Lund, vol. 2 (New York: Longmans, 1954), p. 251.
[40] Nicolae Iorga, *Philippe de Mézières (1327–1405) et la croisade au XIVe siècle*, Bibliothèque de l'École des Hautes Études, Sciences Philologiques et Historiques 110 (Paris: E. Bouillon, 1896; repr. Geneva: Slatkine Reprints, 1976), pp. 76, n. 2, 83, and n. 2, 84–85, and n. 1, 120 and n. 3.
[41] *Nova religio milicie Passionis Jhesu Christi pro acquisicione sancte civitatis Jherusalem et Terre Sancte*, Paris, Mazarine, MS. 1943, second redaction, f. 45^v.
[42] *Letter to King Richard II*, p. 118, for the French text, and p. 47, for Coopland's English translation.
[43] *Le Songe*, 2:128.
[44] *Le Songe*, 2:284.
[45] "Les Songes et le processus onirique dans l'oeuvre de Philippe de Mézières: *Le Songe du vieil pelerin*" in *Revue des Langues Romanes* **96** (1992): 417–26, esp. pp. 420–21.
[46] Cole, p. 27.
[47] Cole, p. 134.
[48] E.g., the story of Judas Maccabee (Judas Machabeus) in *Epistre lamentable et consolatoire sur le fait de la desconfiture lacrimable du noble et vaillant roy de Hongeurie par les Turcs devant la ville de Nicopoli*, Brussels, Bibliothèque Royale MS. 10486, f. 8. This text has been partially published in vol. 16 of *Oeuvres de Froissart: Chroniques*, ed. Henri Marie Bruno Joseph Léon Kervyn de Lettenhove (Brussels: Devaux, 1872). However, the chapter (23) on Judas Maccabee was not published.
[49] Cole, p. 27.
[50] *De la Chevallerie*, f. 53^v.
[51] *Nova religio*, first redaction, f. 20^v.
[52] Nicolae Iorga reminds us of this possibility in his seminal book on Philippe de Mézières, *Philippe de Mézières*, p. 343, n. 2.
[53] *Le Songe*, 2:440.

54 *De la chevallerie*, f. 31ᵛ.
55 *Letter to King Richard II*, pp. 97–101, for the French text, and p. 27, for Coopland's English translation.
56 *De la Chevallerie*, ff. 1ᵛ–6ᵛ.
57 Cole, p. 209.
58 Cole, p. 153.
59 Cole, p. 154.
60 Cole, pp. 203–11.
61 *Letter to King Richard II*, p. 99, for the French text, and p. 26, for Coopland's English translation given here.
62 This is essentially the subject matter of Book Two of this text.
63 "*Le Testament* de Philippe de Mézières (1392)", ed. Alice Guillemain, *Mélanges Jeanne Lods: Du moyen âge au XXᵉ siècle*, Collection de l'École Normale Supérieure de Jeunes Filles 10, vol. 1 (Paris: École Normale Supérieure de Jeunes Filles, 1978), p. 302.
64 *De la Chevallerie*, f. 2ᵛ.
65 *Le Songe*, 1:112.
66 E.g., *De La Chevallerie*, f. 25ᵛ.
67 *Le Livre*, e.g, as the Lamb, ff. 17ᵛ, 20, and as the Slain Lamb, f. 26ᵛ; *L'Epistre lamentable*, as the Slain Lamb, pp. 455 and 475 of the partial Kervyn de Lettenhove edition.
68 To use the name of this text in the Latin Vulgate, the source of the references given here.
69 Particularly in Book Three.
70 Book Two.
71 Exhibited at the Pierpont Morgan Library, New York, Dec. 11, 1992 to April 14, 1993.
72 *Le Songe*, 1:385–91 and 518.
73 Cole, pp. 32–33.
74 Cole, pp. 30–31.
75 Ann M. Harrington, *Japan's Hidden Christians* (Chicago: Loyola U.P., 1993), p. 85.

CYNTHIA OSOWIEC RUOFF

HEAVEN: VAL-DE-GRÂCE, MOLIÈRE'S "LA GLOIRE DU VAL-DE-GRÂCE" AND ROTROU'S *LE VÉRITABLE SAINT GENEST*

The baroque, an international phenomenon emerging from man's "crise de conscience", is rooted in the last third of the sixteenth century, and it evolves as a reaction against the normative and rational precepts of order and harmony emphasized by the European Renaissance and modeled on Classical Antiquity.[1] As a result of the erosion of man's confidence in the correlation between knowledge and faith and the apparent dissolution of a unified and harmonious universe, architects, artists, and writers insist on freedom and turn to the diversity and disorder displayed in nature as the path to follow in their quest for permanence. Since an aesthetics of diversity dissociates itself from the order, harmony, and permanence represented by God, in an attempt to reunite God's representation with that of the world, theologians in the first half of the seventeenth century, such as Yves de Paris in *Theologia naturelle*, locate the roots of diversity in the Divine Essence composed of three persons in one God; for them the diversity and change seen in this world is an expression of God's infinity and omnipotence based on multitude and change.[2]

The baroque creators freely unfold their imaginations in new interpretations of reality; sense perception rather than reason expands their vision. They utilize movement, diversity, change, theatricality, illusion, and the "merveilleux" to awe the spectator or reader. Implied in the word "merveilleux" is a spectator who responds by expressing astonishment or surprise.[3] In *Le Baroque* Bernard Chédozeau notes that "le catholicisme de l'époque insiste puissamment sur l'inaccessibilité d'un Dieu présent-caché, incompréhensible à la raison mais sensible au coeur."[4] Baroque devotional artistic creation, therefore, arouses the spectator's passion, focuses attention on heaven, and moves him/her to yearn for man's final goal: eternal life in heaven.

A direct relationship exists between the baroque plastic arts and literature. Rubens, the Flemish painter, for example, was deeply inspired by the poet Du Bartas. We will examine the creative artists' depiction of the elemental passion of place: Heaven as represented in the baroque church Val-de-Grâce (1645–1667), in Molière's poem "La Gloire du Val-de-Grâce" (1669), and Jean Rotrou's play *Le Véritable Saint Genest* (1645).

VAL-DE-GRÂCE

The design of the church Val-de-Grâce specifically invites the spectator to feel God's presence. Philippe Minguet in *France Baroque* labels Val-de-Grâce as "l'église la plus baroque parmi celles qui subsistent à Paris."[5] Significantly, the young Louis XIV laid the foundation stone in 1645, the same year that Jean Rotrou's *Le Véritable Saint Genest* was performed at the Hôtel de Bourgogne in Paris. Val-de-Grâce exemplifies novelties and liberties, such as twisted and irregularly-spaced columns, which baroque architects introduced by adapting artistic forms from the Greeks and applying them to Christian churches. Although "les colonnes torses" were criticized greatly, Marcel Reymond comments that trees rarely grow straight and round like a column and are often wrapped in ivy. Beauty, tradition, and examples in nature support the use of twisted columns. In the seventeenth century, architects designed the antique colonnade as a portico in front of the church. Rather than designate the same amount of space between each of the columns, they widened the space between the central columns, thus marking the main entrance and inviting the spectator/participant to enter.[6]

As dramatic evidence of the baroque style in Val-de-Grâce, framing the altar, the monumental baldachin with six twisted columns delineates a stage for the enactment of the divine ritual and directs the spectator/participant's attention to the magnificent cupola. This dome is decorated with a fresco depicting heaven in which Pierre Mignard painted two hundred figures, each one three times life-size. The increased space between the columns in front of the altar encourages the spectators' eyes to converge in that space and leads the observers to marvel at the elaborate staging and to participate in the re-enactment of their salvation.

Pierre Charpentrat explains that in the seventeenth century "l'homme dans une ville, devant une façade de palais, dans une nef d'église devient avant tout spectateur".[7] In the design of the baldachin the spectator sees that in a dizzying movement the columns spiral upward as the curves glide one into another until the movement is stopped momentarily by six pedestals supporting lifelike angels. Once again the eye is enticed to continue looking up along the arches emerging from behind the angels and forming an airy, light, openwork dome which crowns the six columns. While the arches of the openwork dome repeat the curved lines of the columns, the designer changes the lines by enlarging them; consequently, he creates new vibrancy and life. With some of their hands gesturing toward the heavens, the tall angels reinforce the vertical directionality of the baldachin, introduce the celestial realm into the structure itself, and lead the eye to the decorative spike topping the crown. Finally, the spike points to Mignard's fresco in the dome. By highlighting the altar and the fresco, light, radiating from the sky through the windows in the dome, accentuates paradise and reinforces the influence of the heavens on the world.

The architect François Mansart applied the baroque concept of art as persuasion to Val-de-Grâce. In order to encourage the spectator to convert to Christianity or to deepen his faith, Mansart appeals to man's senses and emotions to arouse his passion. The design of the church suggests upward movement, theatricality, and illusion: the twisted columns, the winged angels, the illusionism in the dome, and the repetition of curves gracefully slipping into different sizes and forms. Spontaneous change is evident in the free-flowing transformation of curves and lines as they repeat, enlarge, contract, and shift form. Mansart blurs the distinction between the real world and the supernatural and creates a co-extensive space intermingling the two realms. While watching the celebration of the sacrifice of the Mass, the spectator/ participant is moved by the surrounding visual feast designed to draw the observer into the communion of the faithful by awakening his passion and aspirations for eternal glory with God.

"LA GLOIRE DU VAL-DE-GRÂCE"

In Molière's poem "La Gloire du Val-de-Grâce" (1669), "gloire" refers to Pierre Mignard's baroque fresco in the dome of the church. The design of the church and baldachin highlights this representation of the divine persons in God, the angels, and the saints. In addition to glorifying Louis XIV in this poem, Molière praises the fresco for its invention, diversity, movement, chiaroscuro, and its ability to dazzle and influence the spectator. The church itself stands as a perpetual reminder of the glory of Louis XIV. However, since death is every person's destiny, even the common man moved to participate in the drama of salvation represented in Val-de-Grâce can realize glory in the heaven depicted in Mignard's fresco.

By introducing a traveler/spectator into the poem and situating the church in Paris, Molière anchors his description in real life and provides a role model for the reader of the poem. John Martin writes of this "baroque will to demolish the boundary separating the work of art from real life".[8] Molière paints a picture of the grandeur and majesty that strike the viewer's senses and, by extension, the senses of the poem's reader.

Although the visitor has a number of objects to view rising up against the Paris skyline, Molière contends that the "temple majestueux" attracts the "premiers regards" of the "voyageur surpris".

> Digne fruit de vingt ans de travaux somptueux,
> Auguste bâtiment, temple majestueux,
> Dont le dôme superbe, élevé dans la nue,
> Pare du grand Paris la magnifique vue,
> Et, parmi tant d'objets semés de toutes parts,
> Du voyageur surpris prend les premiers regards,
> Fais briller à jamais, dans ta noble richesse,
> La splendeur du saint voeu d'une grande princesse,
> Et porte un témoignage à la postérité
> De sa magnificence et de sa piété
>   (1–10).[9]

"Auguste", "temple", "saint voeu", "le dôme superbe, élevé dans la nue", and "piété" emphasize the spiritual identity of this place. In addition, the creation of Val-de-Grâce was the result of a reciprocal communication between the earthly and spiritual realms. Since Anne of Austria, at the age of thirty-seven, was married for twenty-two years and did not have any children, she promised God to have a magnificent church constructed in return for a child. After the birth of Louis XIV, she kept her vow. Therefore, the church itself stands as an example of communication, participation, and interaction between the world and heaven.

For Molière and for the baroque artist, the spectator's response to sense experience is paramount. After describing the imposing church against the panoramic Paris seventeenth-century cityscape, Molière moves the ever-present spectator/reader immediately to the interior of the church and insists that his "esprit est surpris" and "son oeil est enchanté" by Mignard's "éclatant morceau de savante peinture" (26, 15). Mignard's "génie" created a fresco "Comme un ample théâtre heureusement fournie"

(20). In this theatrical representation of heaven and its inhabitants, the painter, through the strokes of his brush, makes "à nos yeux vivre des choses mortes" (32) and gives birth to "les merveilles" (28). The illusion astonishes the spectator. At the altar below, especially during the Consecration when the priest elevates the Host and the Chalice, the drama of the sacrifice of the Mass points to man's reward, heaven as displayed in Mignard's fresco. The spectacle arouses and intensifies the viewer's love for God and his desire to participate in the celestial realm.

Although the poet praises Mignard's fresco as an "école ouverte" (44) dictating the importance of "l'invention, le dessin, le coloris" (47)[10] in the artistic process, Molière also describes the painter's passion, the display of the passions of the figures in the painting, and the spectator's passion in response to the marvelous display.

Passion stimulates Mignard to create the magnificent fresco. Molière associates creative passion with the divine: "Dis-nous quel feu divin, dans tes fécondes veilles,/ De tes expressions enfante les merveilles" (27–28). The *Dictionnaire de la langue française classique* defines "feu" as "passion, amour; inspiration poétique, surnaturelle, ardeur enthousiaste."[11] The *Dictionnaire des Symboles* adds to this interpretation and confirms Molière's association of fire with the divine: "La signification surnaturelle du feu s'étend des âmes errantes . . . jusqu'à l'Esprit divin."[12] The "feu divin" denotes artistic inspiration but, at the same time, incorporates the artist's passion, his love, his feeling for the subject matter, God and heaven, made visible in the masterpiece. The fresco forms a continuum with the architecture of the church itself, and both work in harmony to make visible the creator's "feu divin" in order to stir the emotions of the spectator. Through this example Mignard teaches artists "de fuir un discord apparent/ Du lieu que l'on nous donne et du sujet qu'on prend/ Et de ne point placer dans un tombeau des fêtes/ Le ciel contre nos pieds, et l'enfer sur nos têtes" (69–72).

In addition to displaying his own inspiration and passion, Mignard consciously exhibits the passions of the angels and saints and expects the viewer, represented by "l'oeil", to note each of these passions. Molière points out:

> Il nous montre à quel air, dans quelles actions,
> Se distinguent à l'oeil toutes les passions,
> Les mouvements du coeur, peints d'une adresse extrême,
> Par des gestes puisés dans la passion même,

> Bien marqués pour parler, appuyés, forts et nets,
> Imitant en vigueur les gestes des muets,
> Qui veulent réparer la voix que la nature
> Leur a voulu nier, ainsi qu'à la peinture
> (145–152).

Similar to the gestures of "les muets" who wish to compensate for the voice they lack, the exterior appearance of the figures and the gestures in the artistic depiction illustrate the passions vividly; they speak in place of the words that cannot be spoken by the images. In effect, the exterior appearance and gesture are utilized "pour parler". Roger de Piles in *Cours de Peinture* states that "La véritable peinture est donc celle qui nous appelle . . . par la force de l'effet qu'elle produit . . . comme si elle avait quelque chose à nous dire".[13] Because the painting speaks by displaying its passions, the implication is that a spectator will respond to that communication. In Mignard's fresco, since the focus is God in His diversity, manifested by the three persons, Father, Son, and Holy Spirit, the surrounding figures embody their rapturous love for God and their happiness in experiencing eternal life.

European baroque art exemplifies and stresses the importance of the viewer's involvement in the artist's creation. For example, in his masterpiece of the baroque expression of passion, "The Ecstasy of Saint Teresa" (1645–52), Bernini, using the rhetoric of gesture to highlight the saint's love for God, portrays Saint Teresa in a "collapsed attitude" with "her mouth open as if moaning" and "a passionate expression on her face", while her garments, in "turbulent agitation", also reflect her state of "bodily and spiritual transport".[14] Bernini's baroque interpretation of gestural rhetoric focuses on Saint Teresa's instantaneous and spontaneous passionate response to the intervention of the supernatural. In his poem "La Gloire du Val-de-Grâce", Molière credits Mignard with this emotional visual representation of passion shown in the angels' and saints' response to God's presence. Their visible response is designed to persuade the spectator to desire to share in their rapture.

Chédozeau describes the Catholicism of the baroque period as "inattingible par le raisonnement discursif . . . mais toujours présent au coeur humble et aimant du plus modest fidèle . . . on ne peut en parler que par toute une littérature du détour, de l'image et de l' affect."[15] Molière aptly captures the emotions and passion of the spectator responding to Mignard's representation of heaven:

> Qu'il vous est cher d'avoir sans cesse devant vous
> Ce tableau de l'objet de vos voeux les plus doux,
> D'y nourrir par vos yeux les précieuses flammes,
> Dont si fidèlement brûlent vos belles âmes
> D'y sentir redoubler l'ardeur de vos désirs
> D'y donner à toute heure un encens de soupirs,
> Et d'embrasser du coeur une image si belle
> Des célestes beautés de la gloire éternelle,
> Beautés qui dans leurs fers tiennent vos libertés,
> Et vous font mépriser toutes autres beautés
> (217–226).

The predominant image illustrating the spectators' intense passion consists of beautiful souls burning in "les précieuses flammes". Flames are a symbol of purification, illumination, spiritual love, and transcendence.[16] The sight of heaven not only nourishes and sustains the viewer's passion but also augments its intensity and causes the spectator to reveal his passion physically through his sighs. The emotional response is rooted in his desire to become like the depicted saints and to participate in their joy.[17]

What differentiates the emotional response of the spectator in classical aesthetics from the emotional response of the viewer in baroque aesthetics? In classical aesthetics the representation of passions elicits laughter, terror, and pity from the spectator. These viewers, however, remain exterior to the action. Chédozeau, speaking of spectator response to drama, describes this "intériorisation classique" by distinguishing it from the "intériorisation baroque":

> Plus intellectuelle et plus renfermée au spectacle de passions qui ne s'exprimeront que rarement par l'action . . . elle est plus proprement spectaculaire en ce qu'elle maintient, par le rire, ou par la terreur et la pitié, une distance souvent ironique excluant par principe la forte volonté d'assimilation vécue que semble impliquer l'intériorisation des dramaturges baroques.[18]

Baroque creation promotes action on the part of the spectator and encourages the spectator himself to witness "les mystères profonds" (42) and to experience metamorphosis through a lived assimilation. The impact of the image of "la gloire éternelle" is so powerful that it takes away his "libertés", and he is forced to despise "toutes autres beautés". As a result of his intensifying desire, the spectator identifies with the saints portrayed in the fresco or in a baroque drama such as *Le Véritable Saint Genest* and assimilates their passion with the intention of joining them and participating in eternal happiness in heaven.

The fresco located in the dome of Val-de-Grâce is the culmination of the architectural design which draws the spectator into the church and engages the spectator's gaze in an upward spiraling movement pointing to the representation of heaven. The real space of the church occupied by the spectator merges with the illusionistic space of the fresco. The painting itself reinforces the feeling of blending, movement, and interaction between the real world and the supernatural realm through the presence of people who have become saints, God the Son who became Man, and a globe of the world. The fresco functions as a model of passion, movement, and change.

Molière's poem praises the artist Mignard's talents: his creation of passions (197),[19] his arousal of the spectator's passion, and his distribution of shadow and light (163, 197). Illuminated by the natural light emanating from the heavens through the windows directly below, the fresco focuses on the central figures: God the Father, God the Son, and God the Holy Spirit. Saints float on clouds in ecstatic contemplation of the divine mystery. The observers, by identifying themselves with these saints, taste their mystical rapture and are released from earthly bonds. The passions of the artist, the portrayed figures, and the observers converge in this space.

LE VÉRITABLE SAINT GENEST

Jean Rotrou's play *Le Véritable Saint Genest* (1645) not only encourages the spectator to aspire to eternal glory by appealing to his senses, but also portrays the pagan Roman actor Genest's conversion and martyrdom as a specific model of transformation to emulate. During the process of performing the role of Adrian in "*The Martyrdom of Adrian*" for the pagan Roman court in a play-within-a play structure, Genest succumbs to sense experience and supernatural intervention and assimilates the passion of the character he plays. He becomes an example of the ultimate baroque metamorphosis: conversion to Christianity.

For the spectator/participant viewing Val-de-Grâce, the design of the church and Mignard's fresco, according to Molière's poem, "La Gloire du Val-de-Grâce", lead man to desire communion with God, the angels, and the saints in heaven. In *Le Véritable Saint Genest*, the actor's performance on stage gives birth to his love for God and his spontaneous conversion. When he addresses the actor playing Anthyme by his real name, Lentule, during the performance, Genest attempts to disclose his passion and conversion. He proclaims:

> Ah! Lentule! en l'ardeur dont mon âme est pressée,
> Il faut lever le masque et t'ouvrir ma pensée;
> Le Dieu que j'ai haï m'inspire son amour;
> Adrian a parlé, Genest parle à son tour!
> Ce n'est plus Adrian, c'est Genest qui respire
> La grâce du baptême et l'honneur du martyre
> (IV, 5, 1243–48).[20]

To become a role model, Genest must display his instantaneous intuition, passion, and conversion.

Rotrou prepares the Roman viewers of "*Le Martyre d'Adrian*" and the spectators of the entire play for Genest's surprising metamorphosis by focusing on "le ciel" and establishing the stage as a sacred place. In order to astonish the spectators, to motivate them to assimilate his passion and persuade them to strive for eternal glory with God, Genest provides a visual and auditory demonstration of the process of his conversion and martyrdom.

Consistent with baroque religious architecture and frescos highlighting the influence of the heavens in the real world, Genest insists that the scenery and staging incorporate the celestial realm through the presence of light, openings, and supernatural manifestations. While speaking to the stage designer in preparation for the performance, Genest as actor and director of his troupe demands that the designer incorporate effective light to draw attention to the heavens:

> Et surtout en la toile où vous peignez vos cieux
> Faire un jour naturel, au jugement des yeux;
> Au lieu que la couleur m'en semble un peu meurtrie
> (II, 1, 323–25).

The scenic backdrop alludes to the presence of the celestial realm beyond the stage.[21]

Bertolt Brecht in *Brecht on Theatre* explains foregrounding and describes the attention focused on "le ciel". Brecht speaks of "turning the object of which one is to be made aware . . . from something ordinary, familiar . . . into something peculiar, striking, and unexpected."[22] Explicit stage directions in Act II, Scene 2 indicate "Le ciel s'ouvre avec des flammes"; the flames symbolize illumination, spiritual love, the Holy Spirit, and transcendence. This image is reinforced in Act IV. Flames descend from heaven and an angel appears to baptize Genest. He describes the supernatural manifestation:

> Un ministre céleste avec une eau sacrée
> Pour laver mes forfaits fend la voûte azurée,
> Sa clarté m'environne, et l'air de toutes parts
> Résonne de concerts et brille à mes regards,
> Descends, céleste acteur; tu m'attends tu m'appelles.
> Attends, mon zèle ardent me fournira des ailes
> (IV, 5, 1251–56).

Enveloped in the celestial light and his emotion stirred by the heavenly apparition and music, Genest encourages the angel to descend. In his spontaneous response, Genest reveals his "zèle ardent". The words "ardent zeal" imply not only an intense and burning passion but also a display of vigorous activity in its support; for Genest, this means the revelation of his conversion, his attempt to convert others, and his martyrdom. However, at the moment, his intense passion provides him with wings to transport him to the celestial realm.

For Genest, the stage becomes a sacred place; it is on stage that the supernatural intervenes and communication occurs. The presence of flames, a symbol of illumination and the Holy Spirit, and the angel identify the stage as a sacred place. Mircea Eliade in *The Sacred and the Profane* states: "the theophany that occurs in a place consecrates it by the very fact that it makes it open above – that is, in communication with heaven, the paradoxical point of passage from one mode of being to another."[23] After the appearance of the angel, the stage directions indicate that Genest goes up two or three stairs and goes behind the "tapisserie". Christine Buci-Glucksmann associates stairways with the infinite: "L'imagination baroque, saisie par le démon de la théatralité, se déploie dans le vertige des escaliers qui, échappant à leur fonction utilitaire, ouvrent directement sur l'infini."[24] Genest's symbolic upward movement and disappearance represent his spiritual ascension to the Infinite.

Communication, initiated by Genest and directed to God, marks his return to the stage. The dramatist Rotrou reinforces the interaction between the two realms in the stage direction, "Genest, regardant le ciel, le chapeau à la main." In his address Genest emphasizes the progression of his intense passion from conversion to a desire for martyrdom. Referring to his baptism by the angel, Genest says:

> Suprême Majesté, qui jette dans les âmes
> Avec deux gouttes d'eau de si sensibles flammes,
> Achève tes bontés, représente avec moi
> Les saints progrès des coeurs convertis à ta Foi!
> Faisons voir dans l'amour dont le feu nous consomme,
> Toi le pouvoir d'un Dieu, moi le devoir d'un homme;
> Toi l'accueil d'un vainqueur sensible au repentir,
> Et moi, Seigneur, la force et l'ardeur d'un martyr
> (IV, 7, 1275-82).

The last word of his declaration, "martyr", focuses on his newly-formed goal, martyrdom, the means to immediate and infinite joy and glory in heaven.

In conformity with the architect's intent to persuade the spectator in Val-de-Grâce and Molière's recognition of the need to arouse and intensify the spectator's passions when viewing painting, Rotrou paints a joyous picture of the celestial realm to awaken the viewer's desire for the "laurier", a symbol of immortality and glory.

> Va donc, heureux ami, va présenter ta tête
> Moins au coup qui t'attend qu'au laurier qu'on t'apprête;
> Va de tes Saints propos éclore les effets,
> De tous les choeurs des Cieux va remplir les souhaits;
> Et vous, Hôtes du Ciel, saintes légions d'Anges,
> Qui du nom trois fois saint célébrez les louanges,
> Sans interruption de vos sacrés concerts,
> A son aveuglement tenez les Cieux ouverts
> (IV, 5, 1223-30).

The heavens are opened to erase man's blindness, his existence in a state of darkness. Adrian/Genest and the observers following his path are encouraged to move from darkness to enlightenment and participate in the sacred mystery.

According to Christine Buci-Glucksmann, "le théâtre baroque est théâtre de la Passion" which exhibits itself "comme désir et testament".[25] In this context, Genest's desire reveals itself in his infinite love for

God, his yearning for eternal glory with Him. Genest's testament, his legacy, is the model of conversion and martyrdom he leaves behind for the spectators to emulate. Chédozeau explains that the baroque of persuasion utilizes *exempla* which promote "une participation proche de la fusion . . . du spectateur avec . . . le saint dont la vie est representée."[26] Genest expects his metamorphosis from a pagan actor to a Christian martyr to serve as a model. In a moving appeal to the multiple spectators, the Roman spectators on stage, the seventeenth-century French spectators, and the spectators of all time, Genest pleads:

> Mourons donc, la cause y convie
> . . .
> Quand se dépouiller de la vie
> Est travailler pour l'aquérir
> (V, I, 1461–64).

Encouraging all spectators to assimilate his passion, Genest, in his state of ecstasy, discloses that suffering for God in martyrdom is "doux" because one anticipates the final reward in heaven "Où la couronne nous attend" (V, l, 1462, 1470).

In conclusion, through the use of illusionism Mansart's church Val-de-Grâce, incorporating Mignard's fresco of heaven, Molière's poem "La Gloire du Val-de-Grâce", and Jean Rotrou's *Le Véritable Saint Genest*, create spectacular and theatrical visions of heaven to astonish the beholder and to awaken the spectators' and readers' inner passion. The spectators, enticed by their senses, believe in the reality of the angels, saints, and God the Father, the Son, and the Holy Spirit. The purpose of illusionism is to astonish and to persuade. These baroque creative artists intend to assist the viewers to shift their desire from the material and transitory things of the world to a higher reality, eternal life in heaven. Andrea Pozzo, who in 1693 published his treatise on perspective for architects and painters, advises: "Therefore, Reader, my advice is that you cheerfully begin your Work with a resolution to draw all the lines thereof to that true Point, the Glory of God."[27] For the baroque creative artist whose intention is to persuade, at any given moment the spectator has the potential to change as exemplified in Rotrou's *Le Véritable Saint Genest*. The spectators see before their eyes the actor Genest who ignores reason and succumbs to passion and sense experience. The pagan Genest spontaneously converts and transforms himself into the Christian martyr Saint Genest; he becomes a role model for the spectators of any time who wish to attain eternal salvation with God in heaven.

Western Michigan University

NOTES

[1] Wilfried Floeck, *Esthétique de la diversité: Pour une histoire du baroque littéraire en France*, trans. Gilles Floret (Paris: Papers on French Seventeenth Century Literature, 1989), pp. 136–37.
[2] Floeck, p. 56.
[3] E. Littré, "Merveilleux", *Dictionnaire de la lanque française* (Paris: Hachette, 1875), p. 528.
[4] Bernard Chédozeau, *Le Baroque* (Paris: Nathan, 1989), p. 107.
[5] Philippe Minguet, *France Baroque* (Paris: Hazen, 1988), p. 52.
[6] Marcel Reymond, "De Michel-Ange à Tiépolo" in *France Baroque*, P. Minguet (Paris: Hazen, 1988), p. 385.
[7] Minguet, p. 18.
[8] John R. Martin, *Baroque* (New York: Harper, 1977), p. 161.
[9] Molière, "La Gloire du Val-de-Grâce", *Oeuvres Complètes* (Paris: Seuil, 1962), pp. 665–68. All further references to this edition will be included in parentheses in the text.
[10] See Bernard Teyssèdre, *Roger de Piles et les débats sur le coloris au siècle de Louis XIV* (Paris: Bibliothèque des Arts, 1957), pp. 92–120 for a commentary on Molière's poem "La Gloire du Val-de-Grâce" and the conflict between the Academy and Roger de Piles, who supported baroque aesthetics by contending that color, light, and shading are as important as drawing in a painting.
[11] J. Dubois and R. Lagane, *Dictionnaire de la langue française classique* (Paris: Librairie Classique Eugène Belin, 1960), p. 229.
[12] Jean Chevalier and A. Gheerbrant, *Dictionnaire des Symboles* (Paris: Éditions Jupiter, 1982), p. 435.
[13] Roger de Piles, *Cours de Peinture par principes* (Paris, 1708), p. 4.
[14] Martin, pp. 103–04.
[15] Chédozeau, pp. 187–88.
[16] Chevalier and Gheerbrant, p. 445.
[17] Louis Jouvet, an actor who frequently performed Molière's plays, comments that "Molière, qu'on a étiqueté l'homme de la raison, est l'homme qui a le mieux senti et le mieux compris ce que c'était que le déraisonnable, et son théâtre, qui paraît le triomphe de la raison aux yeux de ses commentateurs, est surtout, en vérité, le royaume de cette merveilleuse déraison"; cited in Francine Mallet, *Molière* (Paris: Grasset, 1986), p. 290.
[18] Chédozeau, p. 107.
[19] J. Martin in *Baroque*, p. 83 states that in Italy and France baroque "multi-figured composition" was the best medium for displaying "the passions of the soul".
[20] Jean Rotrou, "*Le Véritable Saint Genest*", *Théâtre du XVIIe Siècle*, ed. Jacques Schérer (Paris: Gallimard, 1975), p. 986. All further references to this edition will be included in parentheses in the text.

[21] Cynthia Ruoff, "*Le Véritable Saint Genest*: From Text to Performance", *Analecta Husserliana*, Vol. XXXII, ed. Marlies Kronegger (Dordrecht: Kluwer, 1990), p. 217.
[22] Cited in Ruoff, p. 218.
[23] Mircea Eliade, *The Sacred and the Profane*, trans. Willard Trask (New York: Harcourt, 1959), p. 26.
[24] Christine Buci-Glucksmann, "Le Grand Théâtre du Monde", *Magazine littéraire* June 1992: 57.
[25] Buci-Glucksmann, p. 57.
[26] Chédozeau, p. 71.
[27] Andrea Pozzo, "To the Reader", *Rules and Examples of Perspective Proper for Painters and Architects*, 1707.

RAYMOND J. WILSON III

"ET IN ARCADIA EGO" IN JOHN FOWLES'S *A MAGGOT*: POSTMODERN UTOPIA

Early in John Fowles's *A Maggot* (1985), a novel set in the eighteenth century, a character asks another what a person should do if that person had "pierced the secrets of the world to come" and found out that "this corrupt and cruel world should one day live in eternal peace and plenty"; should the prophet reveal his secret of future utopia? Alternately, suppose the seer knew that "the predestinate future of this world is full of fire and plague, of civil commotion, of endless calamity" (pp. 19–20); should the possessor of this knowledge tell other people of the discovery? The speaker thus evokes utopian peace and plenty while juxtaposing them to the idea of death; this prelude to an enigmatic novel suggests the "Et in Arcadia Ego" motif in art.

The words "Et in Arcadia Ego" mean literally "And in Arcadia I", a translation which does not immediately reveal the expression's meaning. Even knowing that Arcadia is a lost Eden-like utopia of the Greeks and Romans does not add much in the way of understanding. Erwin Panofsky explains that Latin permits omission of the verb "to-be" and that the "et" can be translated loosely – making for an interesting translation: "Even in Arcadia I am". The artistic context identifies the speaker: Death. The meaning is that death is everywhere, even in Arcadia.

The first "Et in Arcadia Ego" painting was by Giovani Guercino between 1621 and 1623.[1] A large skull rests on a pedestal on which is carved the inscription "Et in Arcadia Ego". The painting is an allegory in which the personified Death delivers a message: death comes even to people who are happy and who live in the midst of plenty – not just to the poor and miserable.

Nicolas Poussin painted two "Et in Arcadia Ego" works. He completed the first one presumably around 1630. It is called "Et in Arcadia Ego". The pedestal has been replaced by a sarcophagus on which the words have been inscribed. However, a small skull resting on top preserves the allegorical dimension as does the presence of a river god who is pouring something out of a jug, presumably the plenty which makes Arcadia a utopia. This is the form in which the motif often appears in literature.[2] In the painting, the shepherds can be interpreted as having just discovered the sarcophagus and to be interestedly exploring it.

Poussin's second "Arcadian Shepherds" picture, finished in 1635 or 1636, makes a transition. In this painting, the allegorical dimension has been transformed. There is no skull and no river god. The words "Et in Arcadia Ego" on the sarcophagus appear to be a message from the person interned within it. The words cry out to be translated "I, too, once lived in Arcadia"; allegorically, they would be interpreted as follows: "I, who am now dead, was once, like you, alive and happy". However, Panofsky demonstrates that this is not a translation permitted by Latin grammar; he points out instances when people educated in Latin misremembered the expression when they were referring to the meaning ostensibly proposed by Poussin's second painting on this motif; authors from Balzac to Dorothy Sayers misremembered the motif as "*Et ego in Arcadia*", a form which permits "Et" to connect with "ego" rather than with "Arcadia" ("Tradition", p. 307).[3] Some even remembered it as "Et tu in Arcadia vixisti", which unambiguously means "I, too, was born [or lived] in Arcadia" (Panofsky, "Tradition", p. 296). In this painting, the figures are contemplative and sad; this painting is always said to be a much greater one than Poussin's first try. Louis Marin's interpretation adds another dimension.

Marin comments that the landscape in Poussin's second Arcadian-Shepherds painting is a "desert", almost identical to the landscape in Poussin's *The Israelites Gathering the Manna*, which is meant to show the Israelites facing possible starvation in the Sinai (p. 29). Why has the un-Arcadian landscape not been noticed? Marin suggests that Poussin's title, including the word "Arcadia", imposes the surrounding narrative from outside the picture; therefore, knowledge of the utopian implications of "Arcadia" can prevent a person from seeing what Poussin has painted. Because a person knows that poets created Arcadia as a utopia, flowing with natural plenty, a person simply *cannot see* the desert that Poussin actually painted: "The written name and its memory", says Marin, "diverts the landscape of the desert into one of the delights of nature at its origin" (p. 29) – i.e. presumed instruction on what to see distorts the painting. The title predisposes a person for seeing a certain outcome. Once we see the desert landscape, we realize one source of the power of Poussin's depiction. If the lost comrade lived in a utopia which we are denied, the sadness is much greater. We do not live in utopia but in a present that is a desert in comparison to Arcadia, and a desert that is continually churned with crisis. The crisis dimension of our present brings me to the relationship between utopia and tradition which Paul Ricoeur explores.

"The entire present is in crisis", says Paul Ricoeur in the third volume of *Time and Narrative*, "when expectancy takes refuge in utopia and tradition congeals into a dead residue" (Vol. III p. 235). Richard Kearney, analyzing this aspect of Ricoeur's *Time and Narrative*, says that "the historical language of tradition is by its very nature subject to ideological distortion"; one solution, proposed by Jürgen Habermas, is an appeal "to an ahistorical ideal of undistorted communication." "The danger here", says Kearney, is that "this criterion of legitimacy may be deferred to an indefinitely utopian future without any grounds or precedents in history" (Kearney, "Between" p. 61). The "growing discrepancy", continues Kearney's analysis of Ricoeur, "between utopia and tradition lies at the root of the crisis of modernity" (Kearney, "Between" p. 63). Ricoeur himself claims that "ideology as a symbolic confirmation of the past, and utopia as a symbolic opening towards the future, are complementary; if cut off from each other, they can lead to forms of political pathology" (Kearney interview, p. 30). Here lies the opportunity and necessity for that form of narrative which surrounds myth. Guided by a critical hermeneutics, myth – embedded in narrative – can mediate between the ideology and utopia.

I propose a reading of *A Maggot*, John Fowles's second novel set in a previous century, as a meeting of myth and history within fiction. And I propose, as a source of a critical hermeneutics, the polymorphic awareness which a reader can develop from Don Ihde's procedure for sorting multiple perceptions in his book *Experimental Phenomenology*. Ihde proposes a strategy for seeing: the hermeneutic (or story) strategy. Ihde's hermeneutic strategy can be adapted analogously to explain aspects which mystify a unilateral, linear reading. We can understand the novel by placing *A Maggot* in a version of the "Et in Arcadia Ego" tradition: the story of the immense material prosperity of the twentieth century juxtaposed with its propensity for war. We need first to understand a little about Fowles's *A Maggot*.

The enigmatic opening of *A Maggot*, mentioned earlier, with its contrast between the dream of peace and the nightmare of war, is not surprising to readers of John Fowles's earlier novels. Fowles often delays a confident reading of his works; with *A Maggot*, however, he provokes the frustration through a character's story-telling rather than through her silence – as, for example, in *The French Lieutenant's Woman*. In Chapter Thirteen of this novel, Fowles said that he wished he could follow his protagonist, Sarah, into the recesses of her room and interrogate her to discover the truth. He repressed the urge to shake her, to intimidate the facts from her, explaining that he could not do so – or do the authorial equivalent of simply invading her mind – because he must give his characters their freedom from him in order "to be free myself" (pp. 97, 82).[4] He explained how the character's freedom constitutes the reader's sense of her reality.

In *A Maggot*, Fowles does interrogate his main female character, Rebecca, twice, but her stories, told in these inquisitions, leave her interrogators as far from a confident understanding as Sarah's silence had left readers in her novel. Instead, Rebecca's narrations create her own new narrative identity, and perhaps establishes the reader's belief in her reality. Ricoeur points out that we become "the *narrator* and the hero *of our own story*, without actually becoming the *author of our own life*". In fiction, says Ricoeur, "it is the author who is disguised as the narrator and who wears the mask of the various characters and, among all of these, the mask of the dominant narrative voice that tells the story we read". Ricoeur makes his point: "We can become our own narrator, in imitation of these narrative voices, without being able to become the author. This", says Ricoeur, "is the great difference between life and fiction" (Ricoeur, "Life" p. 32).

Although functionally, Rebecca seeks freedom by telling stories, her ultimate achievement is to construct a new narrative identity not totally cut off from her traditions but connected to her by a dynamic interplay between tradition and utopia. Like Scheherazade, Rebecca has the problem of saving her life, and she uses Scheherazade's narrative solution. Unlike Scheherazade, who wished to bind the Sultan to her so closely that he could not do without her, Rebecca seeks to free herself from the powerful men who try to control her. She wants to tell a story that will provoke them to send her away, to give her freedom.

Rebecca comes into the position of storyteller because, when she is taken into a cave, Fowles does not tell the reader what happens there. Rebecca tells several versions of what happened in the cave. Her first tale of witchcraft and devil worship drives away a simple-minded former soldier. The second version, of being taken into a machine that she calls "the maggot" convinces a more sophisticated lawyer, an agent of a duke, to free her from possible hanging. The scene she describes suggests space travelers or time travelers to the reader, although, of course, the lawyer can make no sense of it. Rebecca describes the utopian city she sees:

> Exceeding beautiful, like none upon this earth that I have seen or heard speak of. All built of white and gold, and everywhere was parks and plaisances, fair streets and malls, gardens and green orchards, streams and fish ponds. 'Twas more rich-peopled countryside than city. And over all, there was peace . . . This land did worship cleanliness of spirit . . . [The inhabitants were] of many nations. Some white, some olive or yellow, some brown, others black as night. (pp. 367-368)

Coming in answer to an authoritarian interrogation, Rebecca's utopian narrative functions in a way that Paul Ricoeur has noted. Utopias, Ricoeur points out, "reveal the unstated surplus value attaching to authority and unmask the pretension inherent in all systems of legitimation" ("Imagination", p. 19). Tied to her utopian significance is her ability to give multiple interpretation to the same event. And this is where Don Ihde's system contributes to our understanding.

In his first line-drawing, Don Ihde illustrates multiple interpretation with a drawing which, according to Ihde, viewers can see as a hallway or topless pyramid (p. 70). Ihde employs a version of the familiar figure/ground line drawing. "Imagining", says Ricoeur, "is, to use Wittgenstein's expression in the *Philosophical Investigations*, 'seeing as . . .'" ("Imagination", p. 8). Utopia is the "seeing as" on the whole discourse level, while metaphor is the "seeing as" on the level of individual sentences. Don Ihde in *Experimental Phenomenology* explores the strategies of "seeing as". Additionally, since Fowles says in the Prologue to the novel that *A Maggot* began as an attempt to invent the story of a single obsessive visual image, the Ihde approach might be heuristically fruitful (p. i). Rebecca's storytelling is analogous to an aspect of hermeneutic phenomenology explained by Ihde. Ihde discusses how words from an interpreter can make the reader see the line drawing alternately as a hallway or a topless pyramid; Ihde says:

> The use of story devices and (metaphorical) naming I shall call a *hermeneutic* strategy. In a hermeneutic strategy, stories and names are used . . . The story creates a condition that immediately sediments the perceptual possibility. In untheoretical contexts, this has long been used to let someone see something. Story tellers, myth makers, novelists, artists and poets have all used similar means to let something be seen. Plato, at the rise of classical philosophy, often paired a myth or fable with argument or dialectic. Within the context set by the story, experience takes shape. (p. 88)[5]

The hermeneutic strategy suggests how Rebecca's stories might function within the text, even while their content remains a mystery. In *A Maggot*, content confuses the reader in the form of multiple images of event. These images parallel the multi-stable phenomena described by Ihde: various listeners in the novel interpret what Rebecca saw according to their state of knowledge. Like the Ihde story which enables a person to see a line drawing as a three-dimensional hallway, Rebecca first tells a tale of magic and witchcraft to free herself from David Jones, a superstitious oaf. Telling the story frees her because she fits it to his reality, "sediments" it – to use Ihde's phrase – with magical thinking.

Her second tale adds complexity. In it she tells of seeing what the reader interprets as a television screen on a strange vehicle which she calls "a maggot". This second version of the story allows the event to resolve themselves into a second picture, just as Ihde's second story allows the same line drawing to resolve itself, in a sudden "gestalt-event", into a topless pyramid (p. 88). Mr Ayscough, the second interrogator, a lawyer for the duke, believes that his client's son has cleverly deceived her. Metaphorically speaking, Ayscough has seen a topless pyramid, but the reader knows that neither Ayscough nor the reader has made true sense of Rebecca's utopian story. What has happened in her confrontation with authority is parallel to what Ricoeur sees as the function of all utopias:

Is it not because a credibility gap exists in all systems of legitimation, all authority, that a place for utopia exists also? In other words, is it not the function of utopia to expose the credibility gap wherein all systems of authority exceed . . . both our confidence in them and our belief in their legitimacy? (*Lectures*, p. 17)

The best the reader can do is to avoid the *naïveté* of prematurely committing to a single interpretation. Mr Ayscough considers himself immensely more sophisticated than the soldier, and the reader would like to think her- or himself that much more sophisticated than Ayscough, because the next understanding is available only to a modern reader, a reading that further relates to Ihde's analysis of drawings.

Ihde points out that by mentally constructing a head for the figure, which Ihde supplies with broken lines, the viewer can see the figure as "a headless robot" (p. 75). Thus the line drawing is not limited to being alternately a hallway and a topless pyramid. With imaginative manipulation, it can be something radically different from either. This multiplicity has an analogue in language interpretation. The words "Et in Arcadia Ego" mean almost nothing in a simple translation: "And in Arcadia I". One art-historical context (the Guercino and Poussin's first painting) suggests a meaning: "You are happy now, but do not forget that you will someday die". But Poussin's second painting provides a context that changes the meaning: "We invariably suffer, but we are sometimes reminded of a lost, archetypal Arcadia (Eden?) where people were happy". Postmodern fiction invites, possibly provokes, and at times necessitates a similarly adventurous reading strategy.

Fowles's postmodernism especially exploits this potential for multiple readings of the same verbal text. In *A Maggot*, Fowles's text provokes the suspicion of either space travelers or time travelers. But the reader must know how to construct imaginary additions to the picture in the text, analogous to the broken lines that make up the imagined head of that headless robot in Ihde's line drawing. In the context of *Experimental Phenomenology, naïveté* would be analogous to "literal-mindedness", which insists that a thing is a thing – and only one thing (i.e., either a hallway, *or* a pyramid, *or* a robot). Sophistication in perception comes from "polymorphic-mindedness", which Ihde calls an "ascent in level", because "the ability to see both aspects is evidently superior to being able to see only one" (p. 72). Reading postmodern fiction requires such a flexible mind frame.

This open tendency contradicts the suggestion that postmodernism has an anti-humanistic subtext, or even an anti-rationalistic one. Such accusations develop because postmodern fiction appears to suggest that the human mind cannot comprehend reality, which can lead to pacifism toward the world. But multiple interpretations of the same event need not be judged negatively. By first focusing on function within the seeing process, Ihde's phenomenology provides a method for containing and dealing with multiple meanings. Perhaps we can make a tentative definition of postmodern fiction: fiction that requires the reader to experience a series of new gestalts.

Both metaphoric "seeing as" and utopian "seeing as", according to Ricoeur, hold "meaning suspended" in a "neutralized atmosphere". Both create "a free play of possibilities in a state of uninvolvement with respect to the world of perception or action". In this state, says Ricoeur, "we try out new ideas, new values, new ways of being in the world" ("Imagination", pp. 8-9). I would argue that because postmodern fiction, seen through the analogy of Ihde's diagrams, performs a similar suspension of meaning, then such fiction would be likely to have a similar productive, innovative effect provided we can return to the realm of the practical.

In the case of Fowles's *A Maggot*, the return to the realm of the practical comes in the "death" side of the "Et in Arcadia Ego" motif. Rebecca describes a sudden change on "a window" which the contemporary reader recognizes as a television screen; the screen shows a utopia of Arcadian peace and beauty transforming into ugly war and carnage. A child runs from a burning house; and Rebecca watches the child burn to death. With sufficient imaginative additions to what the lawyer could have seen, the reader can assume that Rebecca may be seeing a stylized version of future history with this episode representing the Dresden fire raid and Hiroshima erupting amid the wealth of the twentieth century, a version of death in Arcadia. The mythic/utopian television scene in *A Maggot* suggests that the story of how shepherds in Arcadia discover an allegorized figure of death – or, in later versions, a tomb – serves as an apt model for the twentieth century's combination of material prosperity with death on an unprecedented scale.

Rebecca's response to this death-in-Arcadia motif is significant: her subsequent actions form an image of active removal from the forces which drive civilization toward the fate she saw on the screen in "the maggot". She makes a non-sexual marriage and thus removes herself from relationships built on sexuality and reproductivity, and she simultaneously rejects the amassing of material wealth as the goal of human life. "Utopia", says Paul Ricoeur, "is the mode in which we radically rethink what family, consumption, government, religion, and so on are. From 'nowhere' springs the most formidable questioning of what is" ("Imagination", p. 19). The "Et in Arcadia Ego" motif synthesizes these features.

Rebecca secures her physical safety and gains an increase in freedom by narrating a utopian story to an authority figure. In his epilogue, Fowles moves from this individual level to the societal by telling the reader that Rebecca is the mother of Ann Lee, founder of the American Shakers, a utopian society that rejected not only violence and personal property but even sexuality. This move (from individual to social) parallels one made by Paul Ricoeur from individual imagination to the "Social Imaginary" ("Imagination", pp. 15–22). For Ricoeur as well as for Fowles, utopia bridges the gap in the realm of imagination between individual and society. That "power is the central question of every utopia is confirmed", says Ricoeur, "by the different attempts to 'realize' utopia". Ricoeur means the "microsocieties, whether passing or permanent, ranging from monastery to kibbutz or hippy commune" ("Imagination" p. 19). Although the Shakers passed from the scene, they may have left their mark; and in any case, Fowles uses them as an illustrative case of escape from the sexual/authoritative forces which, by creating identities for individuals, deny them real freedom. Utopian societies which attempt to create the society of "nowhere" within the "here and now" may seem eccentric, even subject to "schizophrenia", says Ricoeur, "But who knows whether this or that errant mode of existence is not a prophecy concerning man to come?" ("Imagination", p. 22).

Although Fowles employs traditional reading instructions in *A Maggot*, following these instructions leads merely to the meta-narrative of freedom which does not fully explain the novel.[6] In such a case, or when the author supplies no thematic reading instructions, the work has openness and resistance to normalization – traits that characterize postmodernism. Even so, reading may proceed intelligibly, using the polymorphic awareness provided by Ihde's hermeneutic strategy.

The postmodern novel still exists within strict limits. A novel that can only be read polymorphically will be difficult to comprehend, and this novel's initial reading community will be a fragment of the culture. A polymorphic reading strategy also implies that the readings which the strategy produces cannot approach universal consensus because any one such reading leaves open the path to other readings – just as a narrative that influences how we see a certain figure in the line drawing cannot make that figure the only possible way to see.[7]

Within these limitations, we can turn to Ihde's "second strategy" which he calls, "a *transcendental*" or "thematic" strategy (p. 89). This strategy relies on giving instructions on how to see, such as "focus upon the vertex and then push the lines either forward or back, either toward infinity or to your nose" (p. 87). To give such instructions, one must step outside the figure and metaphorically stand above it. This is analogous to what happens when a writer creates a utopia, a "nowhere" from which it is possible to see additional possibilities in the here and now. "From this 'no place' ", says Ricoeur, "an exterior glance is cast on our reality, which suddenly looks strange, nothing more being taken for granted". This "development of new, alternative perspectives", Ricoeur says, "defines utopia's most basic function" (*Lectures*, p. 16). More basic yet, Ricoeur says that utopia may define humanity:

> The utopian fantasy is that of an ideal speech act, an ideal communicative situation, the notion of communication without boundary and without constraint. It may be that this ideal constitutes our very notion of humankind. We speak of humanity not only as a species but as in fact a task, since humanity is given nowhere. The utopian element may be the notion of humanity that we are directed toward and that we increasingly attempt to bring to life. (*Lectures*, p. 253)

Perhaps, tradition supplies the stories for the hermeneutic strategy while utopia supplies the outside viewing-point needed for a transcendental strategy. Rebecca's stories give her personal freedom while Ann's utopian microsociety is a step out of history to "nowhere". Together, reinforced by the duality in Fowles's title – "a maggot" being the worm of corruption and also a light-hearted ballad – they show Fowles's *A Maggot* as an attempt to explain Western history in terms of the symbolism of Death in Arcadia – that is, Death in Utopia. In a phenomenological perspective, postmodern fiction serves a function similar to that which Paul Ricoeur sees for utopia. Postmodern fiction exploits the possibility of multiple-meaning readings of texts to "step out" – provide an external point from which our culture can be viewed. In combining a post-modern structure of multivalent meaning with a utopian vision, Fowles's *A Maggot* contributes to the hope for finding a rational way through the maze of our uncertainty.

Loras College

NOTES

[1] Dates for paintings are from Panofsky.
[2] Panofsky says that "in Evelyn Waugh's *Brideshead Revisited* the narrator, while a sophisticated undergraduate [and student of art theory] at Oxford, adorns his rooms at college with a 'human skull lately purchased from the School of Medicine which, resting on a bowl of roses, formed at the moment the chief decoration of my table. It bore the motto *Et in Arcadia Ego* inscribed on its forehead'" (p. 311). Another example can be found in W. H. Auden's poem entitled "Et in Arcadia Ego" (Auden, p. 544).
[3] Panofsky had applied the motif to Poussin and Watteau in a 1936 article ("Transience", pp. 223–254).
[4] In the parenthetical page references to this work, the first number refers to the hardback edition and the second to the paperback edition.
[5] Ihde works with simple visual examples; however, current scientific insight suggests the validity of an analogy from his insights to more complex conceptual situations.

Robert Shaw, one of the originators of new break-throughs in the deep structure of apparent chaos, is quoted in *Chaos: Making a New Science*: "You don't see something until you have the right metaphor to let you perceive it" (Gleick, p. 262). Shaw echoes a point that Thomas Kuhn made two decades earlier. Speaking of the "elementary prototypes" for "revolutionary transformations", Kuhn uses the analogy of the line drawing: "What were ducks in the scientist's world before the revolution are rabbits afterwards. The man who first saw the exterior of the box from above later sees its interior from below", and scientists "must learn to see a new Gestalt". What anyone sees, Kuhn claims, "depends both upon what he looks at and also upon what his previous visual-conceptual experience has taught him to see" (pp. 111–113). What Ihde adds to Kuhn's insight is a systematic method for guiding oneself to the new Gestalt, which includes recognizing the value of reversible Gestalts. Ihde's method, by analogy, permits a new Gestalt for interpreting *A Maggot* and postmodern fiction generally.

[6] Modern and pre-modern authors often provide "thematic instructions" on how to see/read; and by doing so, an author may simply give the reader what Fowles forces the reader to construct. In delivering how-to-read instructions, an author chooses from several techniques: through a direct authorial voice, a reliable narrator, or another character. Even when the author does not supply an overt set of instructions, she or he can suggest instructions in easily inferred implications of the work.

[7] Reading according to the narrative of "Et in Arcadia Ego", we see the interplay of tradition and utopia in a process that can free a person even from the impersonal force by which history constrains the individual's identity. Fowles says, "there's a tiny modicum of free will if you keep yourself very open", but he insists "that tiny fragment where there's a doubt is vital". "All my novels", he says, "are about how you achieve that possible – possibly nonexistent – freedom." For Fowles, the problem of gaining freedom is the "problem of seeing yourself" (interview by Ramon K. Singh, p. 185). The narrative strategy reveals that Fowles still pursues his fragment in *A Maggot*, but he now depicts the problem as that of "seeing", as that of narrating one's own story without being allowed to be the author of one's own life, and in doing so in a way that both saves one's life and frees one from the hold of ideology. This narrative "seeing one's self" is a possible prelude to breaking out of the sexual/social identity pattern which has generated the wealthiest and bloodiest century in recorded human history. It occurs in the narrative mediation between tradition and utopia.

REFERENCES

Auden, W. H. *Collected Poems*. Ed. Edward Mendelson. New York: Random House, 1976.
Fowles, John. "An Encounter with John Fowles". Interview with Raman K. Singh, *Journal of Modern Literature* 8 (1980–81): 181–202.
Fowles, John. *The French Lieutenant's Woman*. Boston: Little, Brown and Co., 1969. Rpt. New York: Signet, 1970.
Fowles, John. *A Maggot*. Boston: Little, Brown and Co., 1985.
Gleick, James. *Chaos: Making a New Science*. New York: Viking Penguin, 1987.
Ihde, Don. *Experimental Phenomenology: An Introduction*. New York: G. P. Putnam's Sons, 1977.
Kearney, Richard. "Between Tradition and Utopia: The Hermeneutical Problem of Myth".

On Paul Ricoeur: Narrative and Interpretation, ed. David Wood. Routledge: London, 1991.

Kuhn, Thomas S. *The Structure of Scientific Revolutions*, second edition, enlarged. Chicago: University of Chicago Press, 1970.

Marin, Louis. "To Destroy Painting". Trans. Larry Crawford. *Enclitic* 3, ii (Fall 1979): 3–38. The text is an excerpt of three chapters from *Détruire la peinture*, Louis Marin. Paris: Galilée, 1977.

Panofsky, Erwin. "*Et in Arcadia Ego*: On the Conception of Transience in Poussin and Watteau" (1936). Rpt. *Philosophy and History: Essays Presented to Ernst Cassirer*, ed. Raymond Klibansky and H. J. Paton. New York: Harper and Row, 1963, pp. 223–254.

Panofsky, Erwin. "*Et in Arcadia Ego*: Poussin and the Elegiac Tradition". *Meaning in the Visual Arts: Papers in and on Art History*. Garden City, N.Y.: Doubleday, 1955, pp. 295–320.

Ricoeur, Paul. "The Creativity of Language: an Interview". *Dialogues with Contemporary Continental Thinkers*, ed. Richard Kearney. Manchester: Manchester University Press, 1984, pp. 29–30.

Ricoeur, Paul. "Imagination in Discourse and Action". *Analecta Husserliana* **VII** (1978), ed. Anna-Teresa Tymieniecka: 3–22.

Ricoeur, Paul. Lectures on Ideology and Utopia, ed. George H. Taylor. New York: Columbia University Press, 1986.

Ricoeur, Paul. "Life in Search of Narrative". *On Paul Ricoeur: Narrative and Interpretation*, ed. David Wood. Routledge: London, 1991.

Ricoeur, Paul. *Time and Narrative*, trans. Kathleen McLaughlin and David Pellauer. Chicago: University of Chicago Press, 1984–88.

INDEX OF NAMES

−A−

Aaron 345
Abbey, E. 336
Abraham 143, 152
Abraham, N. 142
Abrams, M. H. 337
Adam 81–83, 85, 86, 111, 228, 340, 341
Albanese, C. 327, 335, 336
Alberti, L. B. 302, 311
Alexander III 222
Alleau, C. 294, 295
Anaxamander 216
Anderson, M. D. 233
André, J. 153
Anne of Austria 356
St. Anselm of Canterbury 208
Antiochus 345
Apter, E. 268
Arendt, H. 164, 167
Aristotle 35, 37, 41, 42, 43, 166–68, 203, 212, 302
Arndt, J. 333, 336
Arnold, B. 153
Atkinson, G. 226, 230
Auden, W. H. 32, 376
St. Augustine 43, 49, 135, 142, 177, 194, 195, 206, 211, 237, 243, 332, 335
Autenrieth, G. A. 219

−B−

Bachelard, G. 73, 74, 79, 268, 326
Bagrow, L. 350
Balzac, H. de 290, 368
Barth, K. 329
St. Bartholomew 314
St. Basil 244, 245
Bateson, G. 50, 57
Baudelaire, C. 251, 274, 288, 289, 292, 295

Baudri of Dol 342, 350
Bazille, F. 267
Beatrice 291
Beatus of Liebana 340, 348
Beaupuy, M. 246
Becherucci, L. 310, 316
Beckett, S. 49–57, 66
Beise, A. 230
Bembo, P. 302, 310
Bénézech, M. 142
Bérard, P. 267
Bercovitch, S. 336
Berger, H. 37, 42
Bernhard, T. 89, 92–99
Bernini, G. L. 358
Berry, T. 329, 336
Berry, W. 326
Betthausen, P. 338
Bevington, D. 232, 237, 238
Bia 305
Bianchi, M. D. 118
Biese, A. 335, 336
Bigg, C. 211
Billington, R. A. 327, 336
Binder, H. 98
Black Elk 324
Blanc, C. 266
Blau, H. 51, 57
Boccaccio, G. 27, 34
Boime, A. 294, 295
Bone, R. A. 158
Bosch, H. 330
Boswell, J. 335
Botticelli 41, 299
Bourgeois, M. 142
Bourguignon, A. 142
Bourgeault, C. 237, 238
Bowie, M. 60
Bowles, S. 113

INDEX OF NAMES

Bradford, W. 334
Brecht, B. 361
St. Brendan 222
Breslauer, B. H. 348
St. Bridget of Sweden 345
Bronzino, A. 297–317
Brown, J. 324
Brown, P. 332, 336, 332
Brown, R. E. 206
Browning, R. 326
Brueggemann, W. 329, 330, 331, 336
Buci-Glucksmann, C. 362, 363, 366
Bunyan, J. 334
Burckhardt, J. 299
Burke, E. 335
Burne-Jones, E. C. 243
Burnett, A. 61, 62, 67
Burton-Bradley, G. 143

–C–

Campbell, J. 327
Campbell, T. P. 237, 238
Carson, R. 336
Carus, C. G. 290
Castiglione, B. 36, 42, 302
Catanzaro, M. F. 57
Cavafy, C. 327
Cellini, B. 302, 306
Cervantes, M. de 29
Cézanne, Mme. 288
Cézanne, H. 276, 283
Cézanne, L.-A. 276
Cézanne, M. 288, 295
Cézanne, P. 32, 271–296
Cézanne, P. *fils* 276
Chandler, R. 81
Chappuis, A. 293
Charles V 345
Charles VI 344, 345
Charonton, E. 279, 280
Charpentrat, P. 354
Chaucer, G. 330
Chavez, A. 337
Chédozeau, B. 353, 358, 359, 364–66
Cheney, D. 43
Chevalier, J. 132, 365

Chocquet, V. 277
Church, F. 335
Ciardi, J. 296
Claudel, P. 132
Claudian 224
Clemenceau, G. 267, 268
Clement X. 139, 140
Clendenning, J. 145
Cole, P. 342, 343, 348, 350
Cole, T. 335
Columbus, C. 225–27, 327, 332
Comte, A. 281
Condivi, A. 300
Conrad, J. 85
Constable, J. 335
Constantine 340
Cooper, J. C. 296
Coopland, G. W. 350–52
Courtine, J.-J. 316
Coutagne, D. 294
Couture, T. 294
Cowan, J. 321, 336
Cunliffe, J. R. 219, 220
Curtius, E. R. 25

–D–

Daigrepont, R. M. 158
d'Ailly, P. 225
Damisch, H. 316
Dante 23, 27, 274, 290–92, 296, 302, 309, 327
da Sangallo, F. 302
Davidson, C. 232, 234, 235, 238
da Vinci, L. 198, 302, 308, 315
Day, J. 329, 336
de Andrade, O. 136, 142
Degas, E. 290
DeJean, J. 59
Delaney, W. 83, 86
Deleuze, G. 66
del Sarto, A. 308
de Marval-McNair, N. 207
de'Rossi, B. 299
Derrida, J. 32, 142
Descartes, R. 27, 32, 42
Díaz, N. V. 266

INDEX OF NAMES 381

Dickenson, E. 101–118
Diderot, D. 34
Diels, H. 220
Dijkstra, B. 294
Dillard, A. 336
Di Scanno, T. 132
Doll, M. 57
Donne, J. 28
Doob, L. 325, 336
Doria, A. 309
Dorival, B. 273, 293
Dragonetti, R. 33
Dryden, J. 29
Du Bartas, G. De S. 353
Dubois, J. 365
Dufrenne, M. 133
Dupré, J. 266
Durand, G. 64
Durand-Ruel, P. 267

–E–

Eckhart, J. 333
Edwards, J. 334
Eichner, H. 286, 295
Eissfeldt, O. 158
Elder, M. 268
Eleanor of Toledo 309
Eliade, M. 133, 339, 350, 362, 366
Eliot, T. S. 27, 132, 171
Elizabeth I 36
Elman, R. 329, 336
Ely, B. 294
Emiliani, A. 310, 316
Emmons, J. W. 267
Emrich, W. 97, 99
Engell, J. 249
Etchegaray, B. 142
Eusebius 340
Eve 83, 111, 228, 304
Eykman, C. 99

–F–

Fairchild, 335
Falk, J. H. 328
Fantin-Latour, H. 290
Fauris de Saint-Vincens, M. 294, 295

Feest, C. F. 337
Fellion, G. 142
Fergusson, F. 295
Ferrater Mora, J. 212
Fetz, G. A. 99
Février, P.-A. 294
Ficino, M. 43
Fitzgerald, F. S. 71, 146, 147
Flanigan, C. C. 237, 238
Flaubert, G. 274
Floeck, W. 365
Forge, A. 268
Foster, E. 158
Fowler, A. 43
Fowles, J. 367–378
Fox, M. 329, 331, 332, 336
Fragonard, J.-H. 267
St. Francis of Assisi 332
Frank, G. 230
Franklin, R. W. 118
French, D. R. 339, 350
Friar, K. 337
Friedman, J. 342, 350
Friedrich, C. D. 335
Frost, R. 326
Fulcher of Chartres 342

–G–

Gadamer, H.-G. 235
Ganz, P. F. 98
Garber, K. 34
Garcia Bacca, J. D. 208
Carcía-Gómez, J. 206, 207, 209
Garcia-Zambrano, A. 328, 336
Gauguin, P. 255
Gauricus, P. 307
Geffroy, G. 262, 268
Geist, S. 283, 284, 295
Gheerbrant, A. 132, 365
Ghiberti, L. 331
Giacometti, A. 56
Giamatti, A. B. 229
M. Gilbert 275
Gill, S. D. 322–24, 336
Gilson, E. 211
Gimpel, R. 268, 269

INDEX OF NAMES

Girardon, F. 64
Gleick, J. 377
Godmer, G. 316
Goethe, J. W. v. 274, 286, 287, 292, 295
Gordon, R. 268
Gossouin 223
Gray, M. 66
St. Gregory the Great 332
St. Gregory of Nyssa 331, 340
Gretlund, J. N. 83, 86
Guercino, G. 367, 373
Guibert of Nogent 343, 345, 350
Guillemain, A. 352
Guillemot, M. 268
Guillén, J. 132
Gurevich, A. I. 222, 229

–H–

Habermas, J. 369
Hadrian 340
Hale, J. R. 229
Hampson, M. L. 118
Hanning, R. W. 236, 238
Hardison, O. B. 233
Haroche, C. 316
Harrington, A. 352
Hartmann, H. 322, 337
Hawthorne, N. 85, 334
Hegel, G. W. F. 136
Heidegger, M. 32, 42, 82, 91, 99, 137, 138, 142, 164, 165, 174–185, 203, 205–210, 212, 213, 216–220
Heine, H. 326, 337
Hélein-Koss, S. 268
St. Helena 340
Henel, H. 91, 98, 99
Henry of Albano 343
Henry the Navigator 222
Henry, A. 63
Heraclitus 209, 216–19
Herbert, R. L. 266
Herod 237
Herrera, R. A. 209
Hesiod 135, 142, 169, 326
Hesse, H. 31
St. Hildegard of Bingen 332

Hillerman, T. 323, 335, 337
Hiss, T. 337
Hodler, F. 290
Hoffman, Matilda 158
Hoffman, Melchior 333
Hölderlin, F. 137, 138, 142, 173, 174, 176, 178, 180–83, 194, 205, 207, 208, 219
Homer 25, 33, 213–220, 224, 326, 327
Honour, H. 335, 337
Hoog, M. 293
Hopkins, G. M. 326
Horace 224
Hoschedé, A. 256–58, 268
Hough, G. 43
Hrabanus Maurus 345
Hudson, H. 146
Hull, R. F. C. 57
Hultkrantz, A. 322, 324, 337
Humbert of Romans 346, 347
Husserl, E. 42, 43, 82, 86
Hussey, C. 337

–I–

Ihde, D. 369, 371–373, 375–377
Innocent III 332, 343
Iorga, N. 351
Irving, W. 145–160
Isaac 143
Isaacson, J. 267
Ishmael 152

–J–

Jakobson, R. 142
Jaye, M. C. 338
Jeffers, R. 336
Jenkins, R. 62, 66, 67
St. Jerome 332, 340
Jesus Christ 82, 86, 102, 111, 113–116, 140, 141, 228, 330, 340–45, 347–49
Jeutter, R. 99
Job 199, 200
St. John the Baptist 330
St. John of the Cross 332, 337
Johnson, C. B. 158
Johnson, S. 335

INDEX OF NAMES 383

Johnson, T. H. 117, 118
Joinville, J. de 222
Jones, M. 82, 86
Jorgenson, J. 351
Jouvet, L. 365
Judas Maccabee 351
Julian of Norwich 332
Jung, C. 57, 72, 79
Jürgensen, M. 99

–K–
Kadushin, M. 208
Kafka, F. 32, 89–92, 94–99
Kahrl, S. 233
Kaiser, R. 324, 337
Kant, I. 335
Kaplan, E. K. 295
Aunt Katie 112
Kazantzakis, N. 327
Kearney, R. 369, 377
Kelly, J. F. 142
Kervyn de Lettenhove, H. 351, 352
Kiefer, C. 278, 293
Kittel, G. 208
Klein, R. 304, 316
Kolodny, A. 327, 337
Kolve, V. A. 233
Kramer, V. 87
Kranz, W. 220
Krumrine, M. L. 293
Kselman, T. 280, 294
Kuhn, T. 377

–L–
Lacan, J. 142
Lagane, R. 365
Langlois, C. V. 229
Lattimore, R. 214, 220
Lawson, L. 87
Leach, M. 158
Le Clézio, J. M. G. 121–133
Lee, A. 374
Leibniz, G. W. 32
Leopold, A. 336
Levinas, E. 117
Lewis, M. T. 295, 296

Liszt, F. 288
Littré, E. 280, 294, 365
Livingstone, D. 46
Longfellow, H. W. 326
Longsworth, R. 233
Lopez, B. 336
Loti, P. 255
Lotto, L. 297, 299, 316
Louis IX 222
Louis XIV 354–56
Lyman, T. 267

–M–
Maccabees 345
MacCorquodale, C. 316
Mack, G. 294
Maguelone 282
Mails, T. E. 133
Majumdar, S. R. 47
Malet, G. 345
Mandowsky, E. 316
Manet, E. 266
Mansart, F. 355, 364
Manuel Komnenos 222
Marcel, G. 83, 86
Marco Polo 222
Marin, L. 368
Maritain, J. 212
Maritain, R. 212
Marius, G. 277, 278, 294
Marks, E. 59
Marshall, A. 278, 294, 295
Martin, J. R. 356, 365
Martin-Vignes, N. 294
Marx, L. 327, 334, 337
Virgin Mary 274, 279–283, 286–89, 291, 292, 294, 347
Mather, C. 150, 329, 334
Mattathias 345
Matthews, W. 324
Mauch, G. B. 99
Maundeville, J. 222
Mauner, G. 293, 295
Mauriac, N. 60, 66
McCully, R. S. 142
McKenzie, J. L. 158

Medici family 312
Medici, C. de 308, 310
Melkley, G. v. 25
Menzel, A. 335
Merleau-Ponty, M. 133
Mézières, P. de 339–352
Michelangelo 300, 302–304, 307, 312–14
Michelet, J. 274, 284, 295
Mignard, P. 354–58, 360, 364
Millais, J. E. 243
Miller, P. 337
Millet, J.-F. 266
Milton, J. 168, 225, 230
Minguet, P. 354, 365
Mohammed 344
Molière 353–360, 363, 365
Moltmann, J. 330, 337
Monet, Camille 253–56
Monet, Claude 251–269
Montaigne, M. de 39, 43, 136
Monteux, 28
Morantz, E. 67
Moreland, S. 333, 337
Morrison, S. E. 230
Moses 345
Motolinia 333, 337
Muir, J. 335
Mukhopadhyay, P. K. 47
Muller, M. 63, 66
Mumford, L. 328, 337
Murdoch, I. 205

–N–

Naomi 191, 192
Nasgaard, R. 296
Nash, R. 324, 325, 327, 328, 331, 333–5, 337
Navarrette, F. de 225
Needham, G. 267
Nelson, A. 233
St. Nicholas 146
Norcross, L. 102
Norcross family 103, 104, 112
Novak, B. 335, 337
Nunes, B. 142

–O–

Odoni, A. 299, 300
Olmsted, F. K. 335
Optiz, H. 28
Origen 332
Orpah 191
Ortega y Gasset, J. 209
Ovid 25, 59, 61, 67, 224, 313
Owst, G. R. 233

–P–

Panofsky, E. 316, 367, 368, 376, 378
Parmenides 216
Percy, W. 81–87
Petrarch, F. 27, 31, 34, 302, 309, 335
Pharaoh 346
Phelan, J. L. 333, 337
Philo of Alexandria 331
Philostratus 302
Phineas 345
Picasso, P. 32, 292
Pierre I 345
Pierre de Provence 282
Piles, R. de 358, 365
Pincus-Witten, R. 291, 296
Pino, P. 306
Pius IX 280
Plato 24, 33, 34, 36, 41, 168, 185, 188, 206, 209, 210, 243, 302, 309, 316, 371
Pliny the Elder 302
Plotinus 38, 41
Plutarch 277, 293
Pontormo, J. da 302
Pope, A. 29
Pope-Hennessy, J. 297, 299, 316
Porro, G. 227
Poulet, G. 132
Poussin, N. 367, 368, 373, 376
Pozzo, A. 364, 366
Prest, J. 230
Pritchard, J. 329, 337
Propertius 31
Proust, M. 59–68
Ptolemy 340
Pucci, P. 219, 220

# INDEX OF NAMES

Puvis de Chavannes, P.-C. 265
Pythagoras 174

–R–
Rabelais, F. 221, 229
Racine, J. 273, 293
Raleigh, W. 332
Raphael 308
Raphael, M. 273, 293
Regaldo, N. 349
Reichard, G. A. 324, 337
Renoir, P.-A. 64, 267
Rewald, J. 293, 295
Reymond, M. 354, 365
Reynolds, G. 335, 337
Ricard, R. 333, 338
Richard II 344, 345
Ricoeur, P. 369–371, 373–76, 378
Rilke, R. M. 132, 173–212
Ringe, D. A. 158
Riopelle, C. 64
Ripa, C. 297, 298, 316
Robert of Rheims 342, 350
Roberts, D. 99
Roger-Marx, C. 269
Rosen, E. 53, 57
Rossellino, A. 304
Rossellino, B. 304
Rossetti, C. 243
Rossetti, D. G. 243
Rothko, M. 33
Rotrou, J. 354, 360–365
Rousseau, T. 266
Rubens, P. P. 353
Rubin-Dorsky, J. 158
Runge, O. 335
Ruoff, C. 366
Rutebeuf 228
Ruth 191, 192, 199, 200
Ruysbroeck, J. van 333

–S–
Sacks, S. 142
Saladin 346
Salz, S. 267
Santmire, P. H. 329–332, 338

Sappho 59, 61–64
Sargent-Baur, B. N. 344, 350, 351
Sartre, J. P. 209
Sayers, D. 368
Schapiro, M. 287, 293, 295
Scheper, G. L. 331–35, 338
Schiller, G. 350
Schutz, A. 209
Schwabe, C. 291, 292
Scott, W. 297, 294
Seattle 323, 324
Segal, C. 67
Seifert, J. 326, 337
Sewall, R. 105, 118
Lord Shaftesbury 335
Shakespeare, W. 28, 141
Shattuck, R. 66, 267
Shaw, R. 376
Sheingorn, P. 232, 235–38
Sidney, P. 40, 43
Sieberth, R. 137, 142
Siguret, F. 316
Angelus Silesius 333
Singh, R. K. 377
Smith, J. Z. 339, 349
Smohalla 323
Sneyd, H. 153
Snyder, G. 326, 336
Socrates 24, 25
Sokel, W. 90, 97–99
Solari, E. 279
Solari, P. 279
Solovyev, V. 173, 180, 185, 193
Southern, R. 233
Spenser, E. 33, 34, 35–44
Splitter, R. 62
Standing Bear 328
Stanner, W. E. H. 322, 338
Steiner, G. 60, 63, 65, 205
Sterling, C. 280, 294
Stevenson, R. L. 255
Stone, L. 326, 338
Straßburg, G. v. 25–27, 34
Streidter, J. 142
Stuckey, C. E. 268, 269
Susannah 304

INDEX OF NAMES

–T–

Tagore, D. 45, 46
Tagore, R. 45–47, 133
Tasso, G. B. del 302
Tauler, J. 333
Tennyson, A. 244, 327
St. Teresa of Avila 332, 338, 358
Teyssèdre, B. 365
Thierry, A. 279, 294
St. Thomas Aquinas 83, 197, 203, 211, 212, 332
Thomas, D. 326
Thomson, J. 145, 156, 335
Thoreau, H. D. 335, 338
Thoss, D. 33
Titian 299, 308
Tornabuoni, L. 299
Torok, M. 142
Tribolo 302
Tu Fu 324
Turner, F. 327, 328, 331, 332, 334, 337, 338
Turner, F. J. 327
Turner, J. M. 335
Tydeman, W. 233
Tyler, J. 158
Tymieniecka, A-T. 20, 23, 132, 206, 268

–U–

Urban II 342–45, 348

–V–

Van de Leeuw, G. 337
Vanden Burgh, R. L. 142
Van Dyck, J. A. 295
Van Liere, E. 268, 293
Válery, P. 93
Varchi, B. 302, 303, 306, 308, 310, 312, 313
Vasari, G. 300, 302, 305, 306, 311
Velz, J. 233, 234, 238
Venturi, L. 293
Verrocchio, A. del 307
St. Victor 278, 293
St. Victurien 293

Villeger, J. 142
Virgil 25, 224, 276, 326
Vitry, J. de 343, 350
Voltaire 32

–W–

Waddell, H. 332, 338
Wagner, R. 274, 287–89, 292, 295
Waley, A. 324, 338
Walker, P. 295
Wang Wei 324, 338
Watenhall, J. 293
Watson, B. 67
Watteau, J.-A. 253, 267, 376
Waugh, E. 376
Weigand, H. J. 90, 98
Weinburg, F. 67
Wells, G. N. 284, 295
Wesley, J. 334, 338
Westermann, C. 330, 338
Wharton, J. 335
Wharton, T. 335
Whitman, W. 326, 327
Wickham, G. 233
Wigglesworth, M. 334
Wildenstein, D. 267–69
Williams, A. 43
Williams, G. 333, 338
Williams, R. 334
Williamson, J. B. 350
Wind, E. 43
Winthrop, J. 334
Wittgenstein, L. 371
Wordsworth, J. 338
Wordsworth, W. 243–249, 326

–Y–

Yeats, W. B. 326
Yerkes, A. 293
Yi-Fu Tuan 321, 322, 324, 338
Yves de Paris 353

–Z–

Zamyatin, Y. 136
Zola, E. 273–76, 281, 283, 284, 292–96

Analecta Husserliana

29. Tymieniecka, A-T. (ed.), *Man's Self-Interpretation-in-Existence.* Phenomenology and Philosophy of Life. – Introducing the Spanish Perspective. 1990
ISBN 0-7923-0324-5
30. Rudnick, H. H. (ed.), *Ingardeniana II.* New Studies in the Philosophy of Roman Ingarden. With a New International Ingarden Bibliography. 1990
ISBN 0-7923-0627-9
31. Tymieniecka, A-T. (ed.), *The Moral Sense and Its Foundational Significance: Self, Person, Historicity, Community.* Phenomenological Praxeology and Psychiatry. 1990
ISBN 0-7923-0678-3
32. Kronegger, M. (ed.), *Phenomenology and Aesthetics.* Approaches to Comparative Literature and Other Arts. Homages to A-T. Tymieniecka. 1991
ISBN 0-7923-0738-0
33. Tymieniecka, A-T. (ed.), *Ingardeniana III.* Roman Ingarden's Aesthetics in a New Key and the Independent Approaches of Others: The Performing Arts, the Fine Arts, and Literature. 1991
Sequel to Volumes 4 and 30 ISBN 0-7923-1014-4
34. Tymieniecka, A-T. (ed.), *The Turning Points of the New Phenomenological Era.* Husserl Research – Drawing upon the Full Extent of His Development. 1991
ISBN 0-7923-1134-5
35. Tymieniecka, A-T. (ed.), *Husserlian Phenomenology in a New Key.* Intersubjectivity, Ethos, the Societal Sphere, Human Encounter, Pathos. 1991
ISBN 0-7923-1146-9
36. Tymieniecka, A-T. (ed.), *Husserl's Legacy in Phenomenological Philosophies.* New Approaches to Reason, Language, Hermeneutics, the Human Condition. 1991
ISBN 0-7923-1178-7
37. Tymieniecka, A-T. (ed.), *New Queries in Aesthetics and Metaphysics.* Time, Historicity, Art, Culture, Metaphysics, the Transnatural. 1991
ISBN 0-7923-1195-7
38. Tymieniecka, A-T. (ed.), *The Elemental Dialectic of Light and Darkness.* The Passions of the Soul in the Onto-Poiesis of Life. 1992 ISBN 0-7923-1601-0
39. Tymieniecka, A-T. (ed.), *Reason, Life, Culture, Part I.* Phenomenology in the Baltics. 1993
ISBN 0-7923-1902-8
40. Tymieniecka, A-T. (ed.), *Manifestations of Reason: Life, Historicity, Culture.* Reason, Life, Culture, Part II. Phenomenology in the Adriatic Countries. 1993
ISBN 0-7923-2215-0
41. Tymieniecka, A-T. (ed.), *Allegory Revisited.* Ideals of Mankind. 1994
ISBN 0-7923-2312-2

Analecta Husserliana

42. Kronegger, M. and Tymieniecka, A-T. (eds.), *Allegory Old and New*. In Literature, the Fine Arts, Music and Theatre, and Its Continuity in Culture. 1994   ISBN 0-7923-2348-3
43. Tymieniecka, A-T. (ed.): *From the Sacred to the Divine*. A New Phenomenological Approach. 1994   ISBN 0-7923-2690-3
44. Tymieniecka, A-T. (ed.): *The Elemental Passion for Place in the Ontopoiesis of Life*. Passions of the Soul in the *Imaginatio Creatrix*. 1995
      ISBN 0-7923-2749-7
45. Zhai, Z.: *The Radical Choice and Moral Theory*. Through Communicative Argumentation to Phenomenological Subjectivity. 1994   ISBN 0-7923-2891-4
46. Tymieniecka, A-T. (ed.): *The Logic of the Living Present*. Experience, Ordering, Onto-Poiesis of Culture. 1995   ISBN 0-7923-2930-9

Kluwer Academic Publishers – Dordrecht / Boston / London